THINKING LITERATURE ACROSS CONTINENTS

RANJAN GHOSH · J. HILLIS MILLER

THINKING
LITERATURE
ACROSS
CONTINENTS

Duke University Press · Durham and London · 2016

© 2016 Duke University Press
All rights reserved
Printed in the United States of America on
acid-free paper ∞
Typeset in Chaparral Pro by Westchester Publishing
Services

Library of Congress Cataloging-in-Publication Data
Names: Ghosh, Ranjan, author. | Miller, J. Hillis
(Joseph Hillis), [date] author.
Title: Thinking literature across continents / Ranjan
Ghosh, J. Hillis Miller.
Description: Durham : Duke University Press, 2016. |
Includes bibliographical references and index.
Identifiers: LCCN 2016024761 (print) |
LCCN 2016025625 (ebook)
ISBN 9780822361541 (hardcover : alk. paper)
ISBN 9780822362449 (pbk. : alk. paper)
ISBN 9780822373698 (e-book)
Subjects: LCSH: Literature—Cross-cultural studies. |
Literature—Study and teaching—Cross-cultural
studies. | Culture in literature. | Literature and
transnationalism. | Literature—Philosophy.
Classification: LCC PN61 .G46 2016 (print) |
LCC PN61 (ebook) | DDC 809—dc23
LC record available at https://lccn.loc.gov/2016024761

Cover art: Kate Castelli, *The Known Universe* (detail), 2013.
Woodblock on nineteenth-century book cover.
Courtesy of the artist.

CONTENTS

J. HILLIS MILLER

PREFACE

As its title says, this book juxtaposes views of literature by two scholars who live and work on different continents. Ranjan Ghosh teaches English at the University of North Bengal, while J. Hillis Miller is an emeritus professor of Comparative Literature and English at the University of California, Irvine.

Our book, after an introduction by each author, is made up of ten interwoven chapters, paired in sequence, one by each of us on five topics: (1) What Literature Is and Why It Still Matters Today; (2) Poetry as a Literary Form; (3) The Problems of World Literature; (4) Teaching Literature; (5) Ethics and Literature. Though each of us was free to write an essay of any sort on each of these five topics, each chapter also includes dialogical comments by its author on the matching essay by the other author. The explicit dialogical aspect of this book is crucial. It is a book that results from several years of vigorous interaction on our topics, across continents.

The two authors by no means, however, straightforwardly represent India or the United States. For one thing, literary study, literary theory, and the teaching of literature are immensely diverse in each country. Each of us speaks conscientiously for himself, represents himself, not the country or university where he teaches. One of the strengths of this book will be to introduce Western readers who may know little about it to the Sanskrit, Hindi, and Bengali concept of literature as Sahitya. Nevertheless, many of Ghosh's citations and references come from Western theories of literature. His theory is the result of what he calls an (in)fusion from many sources. Many of Ghosh's examples of literature are also Western. Miller's commitments in literary study and teaching to rhetorical reading and to the use of speech-act theory are by no means universally accepted in the West. In the United States, any position on these issues is likely to be strongly contested. Assumptions about literary study and the ways it matters are centers of much debate these days in the United States, as in the West generally.

Our book, we hope, contributes to that debate not only by juxtaposing essays on our five topics, but by making explicit through the dialogical insertions the ways we differ from one another about what literature is, why it matters, and how it should be written about or taught. I have certainly learned immensely from Ranjan Ghosh's parts of this book.

RANJAN GHOSH

ACKNOWLEDGMENTS

This book has been a long journey for me, my thoughts and reflections on literature for the last five years. I thank Miller for reading every single chapter in detail and commenting on each one of them. Indeed, we read each other's chapters very closely, building an intense, collaborative, thinking project. I stay beholden to the anonymous readers of the manuscript for their insightful suggestions, leading to an immense improvement on what is now the final draft. Also, our editors at Duke, Courtney Berger and Sandra Korn, commented on the manuscript with their characteristic insight and critical intelligence. Berger, our commissioning editor, deserves a special mention for her warm enthusiasm for this rather unconventional project, and the outstanding cooperation and confidence that she showed during the long course (indeed worked across different continents!) that the book took to reach where it is now.

Chapter 1 is a reworked version of "Literature: The 'Mattering' and the Matter" in *SubStance* 131, no. 42.2 (2013): 33–47. A shorter version of chapter 5 was published as "Intra-active Transculturality," in *Modern Language Notes* 130 (December 2015): 1198–1220. A portion of chapter 7 was published as "Reading and Experiencing a Play Transculturally" in *Comparative Drama* 46, no. 3 (fall 2012): 259–81. Chapter 9 is a reworked version of my earlier work, "Aesthetics of Hunger," in *Symploke* 19, nos. 1–2 (2012): 143–57.

ACKNOWLEDGMENTS

I gratefully acknowledge all those who have helped me in the preparation of my part of this book, especially, of course, my coauthor in the project, Ranjan Ghosh, as well as those students and faculty in various places around the world who have listened to earlier versions of material in this book and have asked helpful questions and made helpful comments that have aided me in revision and reorientation. I thank also all those at Duke University Press who have been so efficient and generous.

Several sections of my part of this book have already appeared in early forms in journals or books, or were given as lectures, and have recently been collected in *An Innocent Abroad: Lectures in China*. All these segments have been elaborately revised and reoriented for this book to become part of my international dialogue with Ranjan Ghosh about various aspects of reading, writing about, and teaching literature today. I have also revised them to fit my current convictions about literature.

An earlier version of some parts of chapter 2 has appeared in chapter 15 in *An Innocent Abroad: Lectures in China*. The first version of the essay was a lecture titled "National Literatures in the Context of World Literature Today," presented first at Tsinghua University and again at Peking University during a visit to Beijing, September 10–12, 2012. In a different and longer form, the lecture was published as "Literature Matters Today," in *Does Literature Matter?* , a special issue of *SubStance*, edited by Ranjan Ghosh, *SubStance* 42, no. 2 (2013), 12–32. I am grateful to Professor Ghosh for agreeing to a translation of my essay into Chinese, and to the essay's adaptation and revision for this book. A translation into Chinese, by Xialin Ding, of the first half of "Literature Matters Today" appeared in Beijing University's *Guo wai wen xue* (Foreign literature) 2 (2013): 3–8.

An earlier version of some parts of chapter 6 has appeared in chapter 12 of *An Innocent Abroad: Lectures in China*. The earliest version of those parts of this chapter was a lecture presented at the Fifth Sino-American Symposium on Comparative Literature, held August 11–15, 2010, at Shanghai Jiao Tong University, where Wang Ning, Chen Jing, and Sheng Anfeng extended many courtesies to me during my visit. At the time of this symposium, I had already expressed my concerns about so-called world literature, not only in a lecture presented in 2003 at Tsinghua University, Beijing, and again at Suzhou University (see chapter 7 of *An Innocent Abroad*) but also in a second lecture, presented first at Tsinghua University in 2003 and again in 2004 at Zhengzhou University (see chapter 8 of *An Innocent Abroad*). For chapter 12 of *An Innocent Abroad*, I used an augmented version of my Shanghai Jiao Tong symposium lecture. The additions are my responses to an admirable paper given at the symposium by Thomas Beebee. The augmented version appeared as "Challenges to World Literature" in the bilingual Chinese-English journal published by Shanghai International Studies University, *Comparative Literature in China* 4 (2010): 1–9. The following year, a revision of the augmented text was published as "Globalization and World Literature" in *Comparative Literature: Toward a (Re)construction of World Literature*, a special issue of *Neohelicon* edited by Ning Wang, *Neohelicon* 38, no. 2 (2011): 251–65. This special issue of *Neohelicon* gathered papers from the 2010 symposium held in Shanghai. I am grateful to Shanghai International Studies University, *Comparative Literature in China*, to Wang Ning, to Peter Hajdu, editor of *Neohelicon*, and to Akadémiai Kiadó Zrt. for permission to use in revised and altered form material from this essay in *Thinking across Continents*.

An earlier version of some parts of chapter 8 has appeared in chapter 13 of *An Innocent Abroad*. The lecture that became chapter 13 of that book was presented in September 2010 at the International Conference on Literature, Reading, and Research, held in Guangzhou (once called Canton) at the Guangdong University of Foreign Studies. Guangdong is the name of the province. I chose in my lecture to take Yeats's poem "The Cold Heaven" as a paradigmatic example of the difficulties involved in deciding whether we should read or teach literature now. The poem also exemplifies the difficulties of explaining such a text to students, at home and globally. It comes from Yeats's volume of 1916, *Responsibilities*. The text of the lecture was published in revised form in a wonderful book of essays edited by Paul Socken, *The Edge of the Precipice: Why Read Literature in the Digital Age?*, and in another first-rate book edited by Jakob Lothe and Jeremy Hawthorn, *Narrative Ethics*.

I am grateful to Northwestern University Press for allowing me to reuse this material in revised and changed form. I am also grateful to Ranjan

Ghosh, Wang Ning, Paul Socken, Jakob Lothe, and Jeremy Hawthorn for instigating me to write the first versions of this material and for overseeing the publication of these preliminary versions.

The section of chapter 10 on Anthony Trollope's *Framley Parsonage* was originally instigated by an invitation several years ago from Ortwin de Graef and Frederik Van Dam, of the University of Leuven, Belgium, to present a plenary paper at a conference there in September 2015, to honor the two hundredth anniversary of Trollope's birth. Since I was unable to come in person, I offered to present a paper by video. The video was made at my home in Deer Isle, Maine, in the summer of 2015, with part of it my oral presentation of sections of my paper on *Framley Parsonage*. That presentation is a segment of a documentary of my current life on Deer Isle. The video was presented September 19, 2015, at the University of Leuven's Trollope Bicentennial Conference. The section on Trollope's *Framley Parsonage* in chapter 10 of this book is a fuller version of my remarks on that novel in the video. What I said has been much revised and reoriented to fit the topic of the ethics of literature and my dialogue with Ghosh. I am grateful to Ortwin de Graef and Frederik Van Dam for turning my attention back to Trollope.

RANJAN GHOSH

INTRODUCTION

Thinking across Continents

I love India, but my India is an idea and not a geographical expression. Therefore I am not a patriot—I shall forever seek my *compatriots* all over the world.
—Rabindranath Tagore

So long as the seeing is something to see, it is not the real one; only when the seeing is no-seeing—that is, when the seeing is not a specific act of seeing into a definitely circumscribed state of consciousness—is it the "seeing into one's self-nature." Paradoxically stated, when seeing is no-seeing there is real seeing; when hearing is no-hearing there is real hearing.
—Daisetz Teitaro Suzuki

Turning outside to inside over and over, turning the inside out: what he is waiting for is not there—visibly; that which is not, neither the outside nor the inside.
—Michel Deguy, "Catachreses"

In the context of Jean-Luc Nancy's "Euryopa: Le regard au loin," a short and baffling text written in 1994, Rudolphe Gasché explains how Nancy raises the philosophical question of Europe by investigating the question of the world, sense, finitude, and horizon—a pregnant and operative clutch of terms that our book prefers to settle with by *thinking across continents*. Gasché explains:

> Nancy's starting point is the admittedly questionable etymological meaning of Europe, *Euryopa*—originally an epithet of Zeus, meaning, either *wide-eyed*, or *far-sounding* (i.e. *thundering*). *Der Kleine Pauly* renders it as "far-sounding and looking far into the distance" and goes on to mention another possible but equally questionable etymology, to which Nancy also has recourse, namely the semitic pre-Greek *ereb*, obscurity. According to this origin, the name "Europe," to cite Nancy, "would mean: the one who looks in the distance (or, as well, the one whose voice is farsounding)." But Nancy brings to bear the other possible etymology

of the word, thus determining *Euryopa*'s glance as a "look far into the obscurity, into its own obscurity."[1]

If Europe, as an idea, is looking into the distance, where the world is realized by being world-wide, it is also a way of looking that problematizes finitude and infinity in our understanding of the world. Looking into obscurity and into one's obscurity is holding a position as the world, where infinite means "the infinity of finitude, of the infinitely finite." Martta Heikkilä points out that under such notions of finitude "there is no idea that goes beyond the world by giving it any end, reason, or ground. A world is a space for the infinite of truth and existence: a world free of a horizon. The world is made up beings that are infinitely exposed to existence as a nonessence. Thus they are singular or finite beings that make up the finite and horizonless world, a world which is infinitely finite, hence infinite."[2] This makes me think about Asia, the continent, the world, which I am writing from in a slightly different way. We don't have a consensus on the origin of the word *Asia*. It could have been derived from Ἀσία first attributed to Herodotus (about 440 BC), where we locate a reference to Anatolia, or the Persian empire. Perhaps more authentically, it emerges from Akkadian ("to go out, to rise") with a borrowed allegiance to the Semitic root *Asu*, which is a reference to the rising sun. Asia then becomes the land of sunrise. But presently it is not what it used to be: it has drifted away as a geographical mass, got a new name, footprints of new cultures, marks and remarks of new thoughts and ideological formations. Also, with light, Asia becomes a land or a space that gets light first and loses light first. It first gets noticed and then allows others to get noticed by withdrawing from prominence. Losing light is not losing sight but about sighting others and sighting oneself. Losing light, then, is not darkness but no light, not possession but a sharing with others, a light that comes to it only to be distributed to others. Again the light that it loses to its others comes to it as its light and also the light of others. That light dissolves and sublates itself. So the figure of Asia is always behind the figure, the idea that hides to project, retraces to reaffirm. Asia demarcates itself from its self (light and no light, blind spots?) and also self-demarcation (it is the host to a light and then dispossessed to become, in the process, both the guest and the host). Like the light that goes away and returns upon itself, Asia always has an Asia before itself. Sounding Nancyean, I would like to argue that when there is light Asia sees itself. When light disappears, Asia thinks, seeing changes to thought and discovering the power of invisibility. A reality first (light there is) and then a possibility, which is both self-demarcation and demarcation from others. Asia, for me, thus, continuously doubles itself.

So our book, *Thinking across Continents*, speaks of no finite Asia or Europe or America—self-contained, harmonically hermetic. This finitude, falling back on Nancy, "does not mean that we are noninfinite—like small insignificant beings within a grand, universal, and continuous being—but it means that we are infinitely finite, finitely exposed to our existence as a nonessence, infinitely exposed to the 'otherness' of our own being."[3] We are caught in the across, not simply going from one end to another (from Asia to America) but *an cros*, in a crossed position (Anglo-French origin of across, literally "on cross"), subjected infinitely to finite spots of meditative singularities. We restore and rejuvenate our across and cross positions through dialogue (*regard*, lending to others, two minds in conversation and a host of thoughts across times and traditions). Our dialogues have evinced our presentness in a culture and tradition of thought and have also given "birth to presence" where we have begun without beginning and ended without having a beginning and an end that we can claim are just ours. This is because we have thought about literature within a world and yet did not forget about its potential to go world-wide. Our positions and transpositions belong to us and to the other.

I approached the book as a deep victim of trans-habit. *Trans*, as a prefix, means "across, beyond, to go beyond," from the Latin *trans-*, from the prepositional *trans* "across, over, beyond," probably originally the present participle of the verb *trare-*, meaning "to cross."[4] This crossing, going *across*, and staying perpetually crossed is what motivates and characterizes my doing of literature. Brought up in a family of academics in which my father taught physics and my mother taught history, I submitted to the stirring liminality of getting curious about disciplines such as quantum mechanics, Indian and Western philosophy, evolution, and the ramifications of Indian history. Our library shelves housed Richard Feynman and Albert Einstein, flanked by Satyajit Ray, Sarvepalli Radhakrishnan, Victor Turner, Mircea Eliade, J. S. Mill, and Vincent Smith. My early life amid a wide variety of knowledge regimes, macerated by training in Hindustani classical music and the Bengal school of painting, augmented the fecund frequencies that refused to stay confined to a border but became interference (*-ference* in the sense of "carry over, ferry across").[5] Deeper investments in literature in later years, then, could not have come without the crossaffiliation—my affair of *ference*—revealed in joyriding philosophy, history, political and social theory, comparative aesthetics and religion, cultural theory and criticism. I stood jauntily entranced. This book, then, comes with its own logic of manifestation ignited through an already embedded deposition and disposition, my across factor.

My transposition is built around what I have called the (in)fusion approach, a philosophy of seeing, a hermeneutic desire, that diffracts to interact. Reflecting on the (in)fusion approach, John W. P. Phillips succinctly argues that the sense of "*fusion* (melting, liquefying by heat, and joining by, or as if by, melting), the *infusion* (the pouring of liquid over any substance in order to extract its active qualities) and the Latin (*fundere, fusum*) which can be either to pour (the warm water over the herbal mixture) or to melt (the wax before sealing a letter)" create the operative and dynamic spaces that perhaps "allow us to sidestep the normal institutional barriers"; the (in)fusion approach, both as method and nonmethod, inspires us "to consider what it might mean for a scholar to be steeped in the minute intricacies of an idiom, patiently picking through its margins, and at the same time allowing this work to melt the boundaries of the idiom itself so that other idioms all of a sudden are effectively in play."[6] Staying "crossed," rather acrossed, is what I would like to correspond with the "exteriority within phenomena" that diffractively brings continents together, builds knowledge houses whose relational windows, as Karen Barad argues, are perpetually open and inviting.[7] It is the space outside that works within, as not in its exteriority but as "folded in," enfolded, unfolded, refolded. But going across is not staying crossed in the perpetual whir and whirl: it develops an archive of thinking, a stratum of knowledge, creases and strategies of understanding without losing touch with the force of the across—Deleuze's "new cartographer."[8] Being across breeds the pleasure of being "out of place," a toss amid our "heretical geographies."[9]

(In)fusion, then, can be considered an orientation, a kind of investigative spirit that respects knowledge regimes, the boundaries of tradition, the sacrality of paradigms, but also dares to infringe on them. The infringement is diffractive like an earthworm, as Karen Barad has illustrated resonantly: "Earthworms revel in . . . helping to make compost or otherwise being busy at work and at play: turning the soil over and over—ingesting and excreting it, tunneling through it, burrowing, all means of aerating the soil, allowing oxygen in, opening it up and breathing new life into it."[10] Tunneling through a concept and then transposing it through the gamut of culture and time is what (in)fusion does, much to its productive joy. It assumes a cross-epistemic and transcultural entanglement in a concept or an idea making it "behave" with a difference and some travelling momentum. (In)fusion has a deep tendency to go across, crisscross, find the crossed point of delicate intersections to enable an epistemological experience gain a vein of life. All my chapters in the book, thus, walk across thoughts, between ideas from a variety of cultures and traditions, making for an experience of literature that is diffractive, mostly, out of time, in the whirl of the "now"—the now that Barad argues "is not an infinitesimal slice but an infinitely rich condensed node in a changing field diffracted across space-time in its ongoing iterative repatterning."[11] My (in)fusion-now is folded into "événement" and the now, in Deleuzian terms, becomes the "prehensions of prehensions," where "echoes, reflections, traces, perspectives, thresholds and folds" prehend and operate as conditions of possibility.[12] However, (in)fusion, through its powers and strategies of melting and smelting, need not be misjudged as a debilitating carnivalesque. The zone of trans maps the effects of difference between communities of thought and paradigms of ideas without being oblivious of the difference, the specificities, the peculiarities that each thought through its own cultural parentage carries with it.

The trans-moment or trans-now is about enacting a communication—difficult and debatable—between apparently incompatible paradigms of thought and concepts. This conflict as communication is not easy to experience and execute because one has to be sure that difference comes through as "differencing," made manifest through intra-activity, an entanglement which preexists our investigation into the forms and modes of difference. My emphatic point is that cultures of thought are intra-active, deeply meshed across different backgrounds, cultures of inheritance, and positionalities. (In)fusion-now is a way, a provocation, to look into the potency of such entanglement (a manifest demonstration of this critical spirit runs through chapter 3).

But (in)fusion-now generously concedes a kind of immanence whose workings might develop both deconstructive and diffractive potential. I revise my earlier entrenched position to link (in)fusion with interdisciplinarity, for I can see the immanence of this approach, its inventive and yet viscous and involved workings within and outside the discipline and in deference to the cardinal principles that disciplinary paradigms love to protect and have remained possessive about.[13] It is not always mediatory, brokering disciplinary dialogues: rather, it is committed to a subtle decrusting of sedimented thinking through conviction of the deep, intra-active, and involved transmediatory existence of literature and concepts and theories by which we try to make sense of literature. This is the power of the across, clearing spaces and promoting and acknowledging forms of appearing and appearances or emergences. It announces events as ruptures, which Elizabeth Grosz calls "nicks": ruptures into our systems of thinking to figure out an issue and explore what possibilities a concept or an idea can be put to, inciting within limits a force of asystematicity.[14] The untimely and the unaverage is what (in)fusion-now aspires for, an "open-ended cohesion, temporary modes of ordering, slowing, filtering."[15] (In)fusion-now creates frames that are its conditions of understanding and motors of the across.

Infusion-trans-now is the refusal to see our intellectual doing as simply "keeping up with literature," as one of our "constantly shrinking fields," and believing that "steady progress is being achieved simply because, as the field gets smaller, the objects left in it look larger."[16] Our readings of literature usually come with footnotes: sites carefully cited to provide the institutionalized performatics of knowledge and its address. If literature has gone across borders, we are obligated to account for such movements through a method or a rule and enshrine such moves within a tradition and pattern that should sacerdotalize an inheritance. Not that I am belligerently opposed to such institutional keys that unlock our readings of literature. I am not disrespectful either of the specificities that culture and tradition are highlighted with. But like Michel Serres, relishing a kind of nonanxiety of adversarial modes of knowledge formation (the hard as against the soft, as Serres argues in *Five Senses*) where frames, and hence borders, determine our sense of the world and world-meaning, I plunge into literature, most often without footnotes (endnotes, however, materialize to evince how my spirit of the across, staying footloose, has stayed afoot through the book!). Thinking literature saves itself from the "end of thought" by not merely avoiding footnotes but by not feeling their necessity. J. Hillis Miller and I thought across in ways that are varied and made allowance for literature to speak back to us; we dialogized on the literary, and eventually found ourselves on either side of the fence without forgetting that "something there is that does not love a wall."[17] We experienced the footnoted locality of our continent and again forgot what we were "walling in" and "walling out." Experience, excursus, energy were our software of literature. Literature, I admit, exists without us.

We remember, with Serres, that a "cartload of bricks isn't a house."[18] Working out a reading of literature is also about mapping one's worldview, abilities toward world-making. Serres shows us how we are "as little sure of the one as of the multiple."[19] Somewhere, going across is also about believing in monadologies and letting them fall away through our ever mounting investigations. The (in)fusion-trans-now thesis throws us into the space where a unitary knowledge of cultures and traditions of thought, the collectivity and indivisibility of knowing and the understanding of life and literature, are under question. There is the confidence and commitment to drop anchors across systems and orientations but not always with a rounded certitude in operations that would make the *across* a well-tested medium, a calculus to understand literature and literary thought. The now, as I have demonstrated in chapter 5, has both defined and undefined boundaries, something I have argued as the phenomenon of the "taking-place," where the globality and locality of doing literature become a process that is viscous, "a lake under the mist," in the words of Serres: "The sea, a white plain, background noise, the murmur of a crowd, time. I have no idea, or am only dimly aware, where its individual sites may be, I've no notion of its points, very little idea of its bearings. I have only the feeblest conception of its internal interactions, the lengthiness and entanglement of its connections and relations, only the vaguest idea of its environment. It invades the space or it fades out, takes a place, either gives it up or creates it, by its essentially unpredictable movement."[20]

I am happy to see the now as having Serres's parasite: the noise, the perturbations, the disorder in a system of exchange.[21] The now builds a turbulence that intercepts literature with an energy, new contracts, contacts, and topologies. Literature stays healthy through such violence. My reading of "Daffodils," in chapter 5, of "Birches," in chapter 1, of *Endgame* in chapter 7, and of "The Scholar Gipsy," in chapter 9, are all in some ways a parasitic imbalance in exchanges, the imperfect balance sheet in the operation of the now but not as emergences of simple disorder but rigorous disorder. The parasitic now also has the character of Deleuze's "series," which is not simply the mechanism of resemblance and analogy but "multi-serial in nature," an *agencement* (as the process of "laying out") and a structure for connections and dislocations.[22] (In)fusion-now is in the character of a judgment that is not overpowering but a force, a "non-organic vitality" that works across thought-traditions, becoming combative among a variety of forces and leading to a "new ensemble."[23] It sponsors a growth of thinking and movement that produces a milieu (meaning an experience, middle, and medium, in the French sense of the word). It is across, without beginning or end, "but always a middle *(milieu)* from which it grows and which it overspills."[24] The infusion-now is the *rumeur* (murmur) of assemblages, of affection across subjects and sources.[25] Literature builds its affective accumulation in making potent investments in the now.

What does this now map? It is multiplicitous and both strategic and imaginary, complex and curious. I am greatly tempted to see this mapping as akin to the "psycho-geographic" formations that the situationist theorist Guy Debord theorized from his walks across Paris. The thrust with Debord, as it is with my now, is about aspiring to hit detours, dare the destandardization of connections, and aim configurations through seeming aimlessness—the *dérive*, a drift of a meaningful flâneur, an experimental momentum. The now-as-derive seeks to find communication in interruption, making dialogues possible across formally settled incompatibles. The now is naked but not without its own threads of chance, "redolent passageways, shocking landscapes, superimposing routes and spaces onto each other." Now as "new cities" is our provocation to "*détournement* to monkey-wrench accepted behaviour, to create light, to *disalienate*."[26] So I have tried to meet literature half way: a sort of gathering-up of thoughts, concepts, parameters from various ends of culture and tradition into a poetics of relationality.

Remapped Asia, both as the epistemic site I am writing from and as an atopos, becomes the "being with" and is the continent that believes in the "taking-place" where light, no light, relight come together not in continuity (as it might appear) but works through contiguity. So my Asia (my *sahitya-darshana*, philosophy of literature) exists predominantly as an ensemble, as in-betweenness, a fractal, an otherwise than being. The doing of literature has its center as a relation, most often, an inoperative relation working through reticulated and articulated singularities. My Asia exceeds itself to form another Asia, an other Asia; awareness of Asia is also about an awareness of being "out of Asia," being with non-Asia, being without my Asia-logos. I invest my relation with Asia and non-Asia in the *across*, which is not about taking Asia beyond the local into the arms of the global (the non-Asia, America, or Europe). Asia is out in the world, at large, has always been the world, has stayed world-wide (immanentism).[27] It is my sahitya in the book. Thinking literature begins in destroying literature, an experience of the impossible through excess, singularity, and eccentricity. My thinking across continents, then, is decartographized: geography becoming a vision, a topology, a thought in process. In across as desire, I have lost my home (*aAsia*) but have surely found a world, my *sahit* with continents, forms of a worldling, found my finitude without horizons. *Sahit* is my *across*, "a crossover in attributes of another origin," that thought the book to life, conceived literature as *compatriot*.[28]

INTRODUCTION CONTINUED

The Idiosyncrasy of the Literary Text

Before I begin my introduction proper, let me say how much I have learned from Ranjan Ghosh's part of this book, for example, his introductory essay above. His goal is much different from my own. He wants, if I understand him correctly, to develop, more or less, a unified, universal, and transnational theory of literature. He will then potentially use that theory to account for literary works of all sorts. This happens, in different chapters by him in this book, for Wordsworth's "Daffodils" and Frost's "Birches." He calls his theory and methodology of studying literature "(in)fusion." That word names the amalgamation of the elements that go into it, as tea is an infusion of tea leaves in boiling water. Though many of Ghosh's impressively learned and diverse citations in support of his (in)fusion theory come from Hindi or Sanskrit sources, many are from Western sources, as in his citations from Jean-Luc Nancy or Gilles Deleuze in his part of our introduction or in the abundant etymological notations there, as for the word *Asia*. Ghosh's work in this book, both in his introduction and in his chapters, is an impressive example of "thinking (across) continents," to borrow his name for what he does.

My own procedures in literary study are quite different from Ranjan Ghosh's, as my introductory remarks here demonstrate. I most often start from a literary work or some text, including, but not exclusively, theoretical and philosophical ones. My goal is to account inductively, as best I can, for what some text says and how it says it. Those differences between us generate the dialogical aspects of this book, in our comments along the way about one another's chapters.

I Am Not a Deconstructionist

I am not a deconstructionist. Let me repeat that once more: I am not a deconstructionist. Why do I begin this part of my introduction to this book with this sentence? To clear the ground to start with, so there will be no misunderstanding. I say I am not a deconstructionist for two related reasons: because my work does not fit the widely accepted misunderstandings by academics and by the media of the work of Jacques Derrida (who coined the term *deconstruction* as a critique of Heidegger's term *Destruktion*), or the work of Paul de Man, or my own work, such as it is, and because I have discovered, to my sorrow, that the erroneous understanding of deconstruction, promulgated by the mass media and by many academics, as I have said, is almost impossible to correct, however carefully, patiently, and circumstantially, with many citations, you explain its wrongness. The word in its mistaken understanding is now used in all sorts of areas to name not destroying something totally but taking it apart, as in "first we deconstructed the building." The problem begins when this meaning of the word is applied to a procedure of interpretation.

The almost universally believed, mistaken conception of so-called deconstruction as a reading method is a spectacular example of a deeply rooted ideological distortion. As Marx (in *The German Ideology*), Louis Althusser (in "Ideology and Ideological State Apparatuses"), and Paul de Man (in "The Resistance to Theory") have in slightly different ways asserted, just being circumstantially and persuasively shown that you are mystified by an ideological mistake by no means cures you of your mystification.[1] Climate-change deniers go right on denying humanly caused climate change in the face of rising waters, fires, floods, droughts, and unprecedented storms.

I have a lot to say in my essays in this book about the uses of rhetorical reading to unmask ideological distortions. Therefore, I need not anticipate those demonstrations in this introduction. Let me stress again here, however, that I do not claim in this book or elsewhere that this unmasking will cure those under the spell of an ideological mistake. The mistake about deconstruction as a reading procedure is a splendid example of this. I give two examples out of innumerable possible ones in both the media and in academic writing.

A recent short essay in *Scientific American* by Michael Shermer is entitled "Scientia Humanitatis," with a subtitle as follows: "Reason, empiricism and skepticism are not virtues of science alone."[2] Here is a scan of the essay as it appeared in the print version of *Scientific American*:

This essay is one in an ongoing series by Shermer identified, as you can see, at the top left-hand corner of the page as "Skeptic by Michael Shermer; Viewing the world with a rational eye." Shermer's one-page, two-column essay praises a recent book by Rens Bod.[3] Bod advocates a return

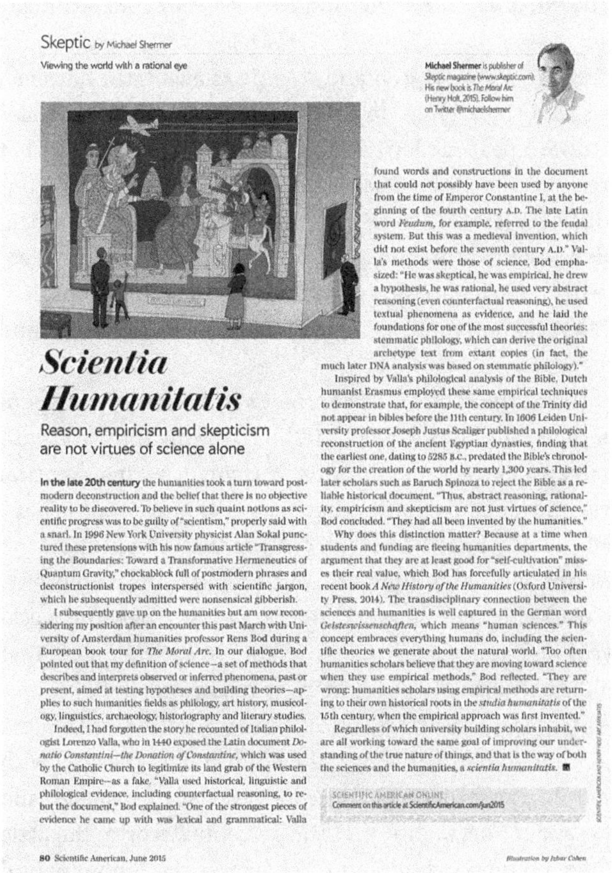

Skeptic by Michael Shermer

Viewing the world with a rational eye

Michael Shermer is publisher of *Skeptic* magazine (www.skeptic.com). His new book is *The Moral Arc* (Henry Holt, 2015). Follow him on Twitter @michaelshermer

Scientia Humanitatis

Reason, empiricism and skepticism are not virtues of science alone

In the late 20th century the humanities took a turn toward postmodern deconstruction and the belief that there is no objective reality to be discovered. To believe in such quaint notions as scientific progress was to be guilty of "scientism," properly said with a snarl. In 1996 New York University physicist Alan Sokal punctured these pretensions with his now famous article "Transgressing the Boundaries: Toward a Transformative Hermeneutics of Quantum Gravity," chockablock full of postmodern phrases and deconstructionist tropes interspersed with scientific jargon, which he subsequently admitted were nonsensical gibberish.

I subsequently gave up on the humanities but am now reconsidering my position after an encounter this past March with University of Amsterdam humanities professor Rens Bod during a European book tour for *The Moral Arc*. In our dialogue, Bod pointed out that my definition of science—a set of methods that describes and interprets observed or inferred phenomena, past or present, aimed at testing hypotheses and building theories—applies to such humanities fields as philology, art history, musicology, linguistics, archaeology, historiography and literary studies.

Indeed, I had forgotten the story he recounted of Italian philologist Lorenzo Valla, who in 1440 exposed the Latin document *Donatio Constantini—the Donation of Constantine*, which was used by the Catholic Church to legitimize its land grab of the Western Roman Empire—as a fake. "Valla used historical, linguistic and philological evidence, including counterfactual reasoning, to rebut the document," Bod explained. "One of the strongest pieces of evidence he came up with was lexical and grammatical: Valla found words and constructions in the document that could not possibly have been used by anyone from the time of Emperor Constantine I, at the beginning of the fourth century A.D. The late Latin word *Feudum*, for example, referred to the feudal system. But this was a medieval invention, which did not exist before the seventh century A.D." Valla's methods were those of science, Bod emphasized: "He was skeptical, he was empirical, he drew a hypothesis, he was rational, he used very abstract reasoning (even counterfactual reasoning), he used textual phenomena as evidence, and he laid the foundations for one of the most successful theories: stemmatic philology, which can derive the original archetype text from extant copies (in fact, the much later DNA analysis was based on stemmatic philology)."

Inspired by Valla's philological analysis of the Bible, Dutch humanist Erasmus employed these same empirical techniques to demonstrate that, for example, the concept of the Trinity did not appear in bibles before the 11th century. In 1606 Leiden University professor Joseph Justus Scaliger published a philological reconstruction of the ancient Egyptian dynasties, finding that the earliest one, dating to 5285 B.C., predated the Bible's chronology for the creation of the world by nearly 1,300 years. This led later scholars such as Baruch Spinoza to reject the Bible as a reliable historical document. "Thus, abstract reasoning, rationality, empiricism and skepticism are not just virtues of science," Bod concluded. "They had all been invented by the humanities."

Why does this distinction matter? Because at a time when students and funding are fleeing humanities departments, the argument that they are at least good for "self-cultivation" misses their real value, which Bod has forcefully articulated in his recent book *A New History of the Humanities* (Oxford University Press, 2014). The transdisciplinary connection between the sciences and humanities is well captured in the German word *Geisteswissenschaften*, which means "human sciences." This concept embraces everything humans do, including the scientific theories we generate about the natural world. "Too often humanities scholars believe that they are moving toward science when they use empirical methods," Bod reflected. "They are wrong: humanities scholars using empirical methods are returning to their own historical roots in the *studia humanitatis* of the 15th century, when the empirical approach was first invented."

Regardless of which university building scholars inhabit, we are all working toward the same goal of improving our understanding of the true nature of things, and that is the way of both the sciences and the humanities, a *scientia humanitatis*. ■

SCIENTIFIC AMERICAN ONLINE
Comment on this article at ScientificAmerican.com/jun2015

80 Scientific American, June 2015

Illustration by Izhar Cohen

Figure I.1 A scan of the essay *Scientia Humanitatis* as it appeared in *Scientific American*, June 2015.

to empirical methods in the humanities, for example, the use of lexical and grammatical methods to date documents, as Lorenzo Valla did in 1440 to show that the famous *Donation of Constantine* was a fake and could not have been written in the fourth century A.D. because it uses Latin words and constructions not around in the fourth century A.D. I'm all for the use of such methods. They are indispensable. They have their limits, however, as in the quite correct omission of rhetoric, in the sense both of the knowledge of persuasion and the knowledge of figurative language, from Shermer's phrase "lexical and grammatical." These words name two members, if you take *lexical* as involving logical argumentation, of the basic medieval *trivium*, grammar, logic, and rhetoric, but conspicuously leave out rhetoric.

Before beginning his praise of Bod and *scientia humanitatis*, however, Shermer opens his essay by saying: "In the late 20th century the humanities took a turn toward post-modern deconstruction and the belief that there is no objective reality to be discovered. To believe in such quaint notions as scientific progress was to be guilty of 'scientism,' properly said with a snarl." This is a blatantly ignorant, robotic repetition of an ideological mistake, with no evidence of skepticism about received opinion. I'll bet, however, that no one could convince Shermer he is ignorant and wrong.

Let me look a little at the rhetoric of Shermer's byline, title, and opening sentences. Shermer calls himself a skeptic, but "viewing the world with a rational eye" is not at all the same thing as "viewing it with a skeptical eye." A rational eye presumably knows what reason is and says, "What I see is a hummingbird. Any rational person can see that." A skeptical eye would say, "That looks like a hummingbird, but I could be mistaken. Perhaps my eyes are deceiving me." In any case, the phrase "view the world with a rational eye" is a figure of speech. It is a figure so commonplace that its figurative quality likely passes most readers by unnoticed. But of course it is not the eye that is reasonable or skeptical, but rather the mind behind that eye, or perhaps one should rather say "the brain behind the eye," with its training, its neurological structures, its memories, its language set, and its presuppositions about how to interpret the perceptual world. The little bird is behaving like a hummingbird and is feeding at the hummingbird feeder, and therefore it is most likely actually a hummingbird. Seeing that it is or is not a hummingbird is not at all the same as reading in a rhetorical way, that is, with attention to the implication of the figurative language used to assert the results of perception, such as the words "viewing the world with a rational eye." My use of the cliché "my eyes could be deceiving me," by the way, is another figure, this time a personification of the eyes as like a deceitful person.

Between those series-title words in small type in the upper left-hand corner of the page and the title proper ("Scientia Humanitatis") comes an illustration of a nuclear family (father, mother, and small son) looking in a museum at a large and at first inscrutable, medieval-looking painting. As the title under the painting in the museum (*Donatio Constantini*) and as Shermer's essay later indicates, it is a (changed) painting of the forged *Donation of Constantine*, "by which," says Wikipedia, "the emperor Con-

Figure I.2 "Sylvester I and Constantine," by unknown medieval artist in Rome.

stantine the Great supposedly transferred authority over Rome and the western part of the Roman Empire to the Pope."[4] Sure enough, Shermer or the artist who devised the illustration in *Scientific American*, Izhar Cohen, most likely also used Wikipedia, since the *Scientific American* page reproduces, with significant amusing changes, the same painting as the one in the Wikipedia entry. Here is the original painting:

This is a thirteenth-century fresco in Santi Quattro Coronati, Rome, of Sylvester and Constantine, showing the purported donation. In the version cleverly presented as part of Shermer's essay the theme of anachronism detected by Valla's rational analysis of lexical and grammatical features of the *Donation of Constantine* is brilliantly represented by the airplane flying overhead that is being looked at (unless my eyes deceive me) through a telescope by one of the men on the horse. The art editors of *Scientific American* or Izhar Cohen himself probably designed the picture. As Paul de Man says, we must learn "to *read* pictures" rather than "to *imagine* meaning," in this case by comparing the original fresco and the satirical parody of it.[5]

I have not yet done with my reading of the opening of Shermer's essay, however. To call it with a Latin name, *Scientia Humanitatis*, is a slightly pretentious way to claim to be a learned person, as is Shermer's use later in his essay of the grand German word for the human sciences,

Geisteswissenschaften. The words tell the reader Shermer is in the know, so to speak. A good deal of rhetoric, both in the sense of persuasive language and in the sense of figurative language, characterizes Shermer's first two sentences: "In the late 20th century the humanities took a turn toward post-modern deconstruction and the belief that there is no objective reality to be discovered. To believe in such quaint notions as scientific progress was to be guilty of 'scientism,' properly said with a snarl." The first sentence turns on the metaphor "took a turn," with its embedded notions of history as some kind of straight-line journey which in this case took a wrong turn. The ominous "his condition took a turn for the worse" is also echoed. No one is blamed for this bad turn. It just happened. The humanities took a turn. Suddenly people just believed "that there is no objective reality to be discovered." Nor is any evidence given from any scholar who represents this bad turn. Nor is anything said about the historical conditions that might have been a context for this bad turn. The sentence just hangs there in the air, uttered without evidence but with bland, apodictic certainty. The implication is that everyone knows this happened and that something so universally accepted as true no longer needs any proof or explanation. The bad turn happened, and everybody knows it. The second sentence is a bit more openly polemical. It mimes the absurdity of postmodern deconstructionists by saying they hold that belief in scientific progress is a "quaint notion," perhaps as quaint as believing walking under a ladder brings bad luck. Shermer's formulation imagines someone's dismissing scientism as, in a powerful personification, a nasty person's speaking "with a snarl." The next sentence brings in the famous Alan Sokal nonsense parody, published in a major humanities journal, "chockablock full of postmodern phrases and deconstructionist tropes interspersed with scientific jargon." The implication is that postmodernists and so-called deconstructionists all write that way. I discuss below the way the publication recently of immense numbers of fake and nonsensical scientific papers could be used, falsely, to discredit science generally. Sokal's paper is the only one I know of that parodies deconstruction, whereas the number of fake scientific papers is enormous.

So-called deconstruction never says there is no objective reality to be discovered, nor that science does not progress. The scholars Shermer attacks would hold, however, that science progresses to a considerable degree precisely through correcting earlier mistakes about "objective reality." Shermer could hardly disagree with that. Shermer gives no evidence whatsoever that he has ever read a word by Derrida, or de Man, or even me. He is relying, it appears, only on second-hand mistaken accounts in the media or on distorted academic accounts.

Shermer goes on to say, "I subsequently gave up on the humanities." This is as stupid and ignorant as if I were to say, "I gave up on science when I heard about the uncertainty principle, Gödel's incompleteness or 'undecidability' theorems, physicists' inability to identify what dark matter and dark energy are, and all those fake scientific papers published in reputable scientific journals."[6] Everyone would think, correctly, I was an idiot if I were to give up on science for those reasons.

Shermer's error about deconstruction is a good example of a blithely believed ideological mistake repeated as a universally acknowledged fact needing no empirical evidence. Such mistakes are more or less impossible to root out, as Marx, Althusser, and de Man, among many others, assert. It is therefore, I conclude, best for me not to use the word *deconstruction* at all to name something I do, but to name it "rhetorical reading."

I have just, dear reader, given an example of such a reading in my brief investigation of the rhetoric of Michael Shermer's *Scientia Humanitatis*.

Another example of the resistance to the unmasking of ideological mistakes comes from China. *Ideology*, by the way, has, I long ago discovered on my first visit to China, in 1988, a quite different valence in China from what it has in the West. For us, the word names a prejudiced mistake, as in my usage in this introduction. For the Chinese, *ideology* tends to mean something good the authorities must persuade you to believe. That is, in my judgment, by the way, a profoundly un-Marxist use of the word. The Chinese appear, to echo Paul de Man's phrasing, to be "very poor readers of Marx's *German* Ideology." I have visited China many times and have given over thirty lectures at conferences there, though I still consider myself an innocent when I am in China. I remain someone who is never quite sure what is going on, to a considerable degree because I do not know Chinese. Many of my essays and books, however, have been translated into Chinese and published in China. I have often been interviewed in China, have had a number of dissertations written there on my work, and keep close contact with many Chinese colleagues. For the most part, my work seems to have been correctly read and well understood in China. I greatly value that.

Nevertheless, a recent interchange of e-mail letters indicates that a quite highly placed Chinese academic holds stubbornly to something like Shermer's ideological mistake. "In the mentality of Chinese scholars," asserts my Chinese correspondent, "deconstruction is a powerful trend of thoughts which rejects reason, doubting about truth and trying to subvert order. Its manifestation in literary criticism is denying all the previous criticism, advocating decentralization and anti-essentialism, and deconstructing the fixed meaning, structure and language of a given text, or to use your own words, it's 'something that could be separated into fragments or parts, suggesting the image of a child's dismantling his father's watch into parts that cannot be reassembled.'" My Chinese correspondent does not mention which or how many Chinese scholars share this mentality. This is Shermer's mentality too, spelled out in much more detail in my email from China. As anyone knows who has read with care any work by Derrida or de Man, this is at every point a caricature of so-called deconstruction. In particular, that passage about a child's dismantling his father's watch is used to make me say the exact opposite of what I actually said, so powerful in this case is the force of ideological (in the Marxist sense) misconceptions.

Here are the two sentences in their entirety in my original text: "The word 'deconstruction' suggests that such criticism is an activity turning something unified back to detached fragments or parts. It suggests the image of a child taking apart his father's watch, reducing it back to useless parts, beyond any reconstitution."[7] The passage, when returned to its context in my essay, by no means says deconstruction really is like a child's taking his father's watch apart, in an act of rebellion against the father, or against a paternalistic tradition. It says, on the contrary, that the word *deconstruction* misleadingly and falsely suggests such an image. The sentence is ironically contrary to fact. When I tried to explain this to my Chinese correspondent, he replied, in the translation another scholar supplied, since he does not know English, just as I, to my shame, don't know Chinese: "On receiving your letter, I re-examined your original sentence in its context and found that if the sentence was read by itself separately, there could be misunderstanding. After this sentence, you immediately explain that deconstruction is for construction. [Not really quite what I said. I said the two prefixes *de* and *con* must both be taken into account when parsing the word.] This once again proves that our dialogue will promote a more accurate understanding of your academic positions." He doesn't say that there is misunderstanding, but that there could be misunderstanding. Nor does he by any means say that the "mentality of Chinese scholars" is an ideological mistake, similar to the one American scholars such as Michael Shermer make.

I therefore conclude that it is best not to use the word at all any more, since it has such a distorted meaning in the mentality of even highly educated people in both China and the West. As a result I say, "I am not a deconstructionist." Whether or not Chinese textbooks, as my correspondent says, actually have so-called deconstruction so categorically wrong could only be ascertained by looking at them, which my ignorance prevents me from doing. Nor do I know why it is that so many of my Chinese academic acquaintances seem to have escaped being bewildered by such mistakes about deconstruction. Nor do I know what the relation is between what the "Chinese mentality" is said to believe about deconstruction and the Chinese campaign by Minister of Education Yuan Guiren, enunciated on January 29, 2015, and reported on January 30, 2015, in Western media, to ban in China all university textbooks that promote "Western values." Is their parody of so-called deconstruction taken by them as a Western value? These possible connections would be well worth investigation by someone who is more learned than I in matters Chinese, not to speak of having the indispensable knowledge of the Chinese language.

He who would make a pun would pick a pocket, as the proverbial saying goes. It is now attributed to John Dennis. Now that I have, I hope, cleared the air a little about so-called deconstruction, though I am not dumb enough to assume that I have cleared the fog completely, I turn to a brief introductory account of my presuppositions in the chapters by me in this book.

As opposed to Ghosh's apparent desire, if I read him right, to affirm a universal system of literary theory and then turn to read actual literary works, my deeply rooted procedure is to go the other way, that is, from specific literary works through their detailed reading to whatever tentative generalizations I can make on that basis about literature in general. The generalizations are only as good as is the empirical evidence acquired from trying to read individual works. Citations from others' theories are only useful to me as ways of helping me formulate what I have found in whatever particular work I am trying to read.

My fascination with literature began when I was five years old and taught myself to read so I could read Lewis Carroll's *Alice in Wonderland* for myself, rather than having to depend on my mother to read it to me. Two things absorbed me about the Alice books: first, their ability to transport me into an imaginary world, as if I had gone down a rabbit hole or through a looking-glass. Even the most "realistic" novel, such as any one of Anthony Trollope's novels, does that. It is a basic feature of any literary work, for example of Johann David Wyss's *The Swiss Family Robinson*, which absorbed me in the same way as *Alice in Wonderland*, though a few years later on in my childhood. Second, the wonderful puns and wordplay in the Alice books, which I found, and still find, hilarious. The puns in *Alice* were my introduction to the figurative dimension of language in one of its most powerful forms.[8] Many other kinds of wordplay besides the pun are represented in the Alice books, but all in one way or another depend on figurative displacements. The rhetorical reading I have practiced as an adult stems directly from what I learned about language from Lewis Carroll. Growing up, for Alice, means learning to understand that a single word or word sound may have wildly different meanings. Both of these features of Alice's experience with language are named by her with the word *curious*. What she experiences is said to be "curiouser and curiouser!"[9] That word is Alice's version of what I have called the "strangeness" of literature.

I give just one example. Alice has been listening to the mouse's tale, but she imagines it as having the shape of the mouse's tail. The book shows graphically what the mouse says as curving back and forth down the page like a tail.

"Mine is a long and sad tale!" said the Mouse, turning to Alice and sighing.

"It *is* a long tail, certainly," said Alice, looking down with wonder at the Mouse's tail; "but why do you call it sad?" And she kept on puzzling about it while the Mouse was speaking, so that her idea of the tale was something like this:

"You are not attending!" said the Mouse to Alice, severely. "What are you thinking of?"

"I beg your pardon," said Alice very humbly: "You had got to the fifth bend, I think?"

"I had *not!*" cried the Mouse, sharply and very angrily.

"A knot!" said Alice, always ready to make herself useful, and looking anxiously about her. "Oh, do let me help to undo it!"

"I shall do nothing of the sort," said the Mouse, getting up and walking away. " "You insult me by talking such nonsense!"

"I didn't mean it!" pleaded poor Alice. "But you're so easily offended, you know!"

The Mouse only growled in reply.[10]

In my considered judgment, anyone who does not find this extremely funny as well as disquieting does not have much talent for literature. I learned also from such passages, without at all being able to articulate

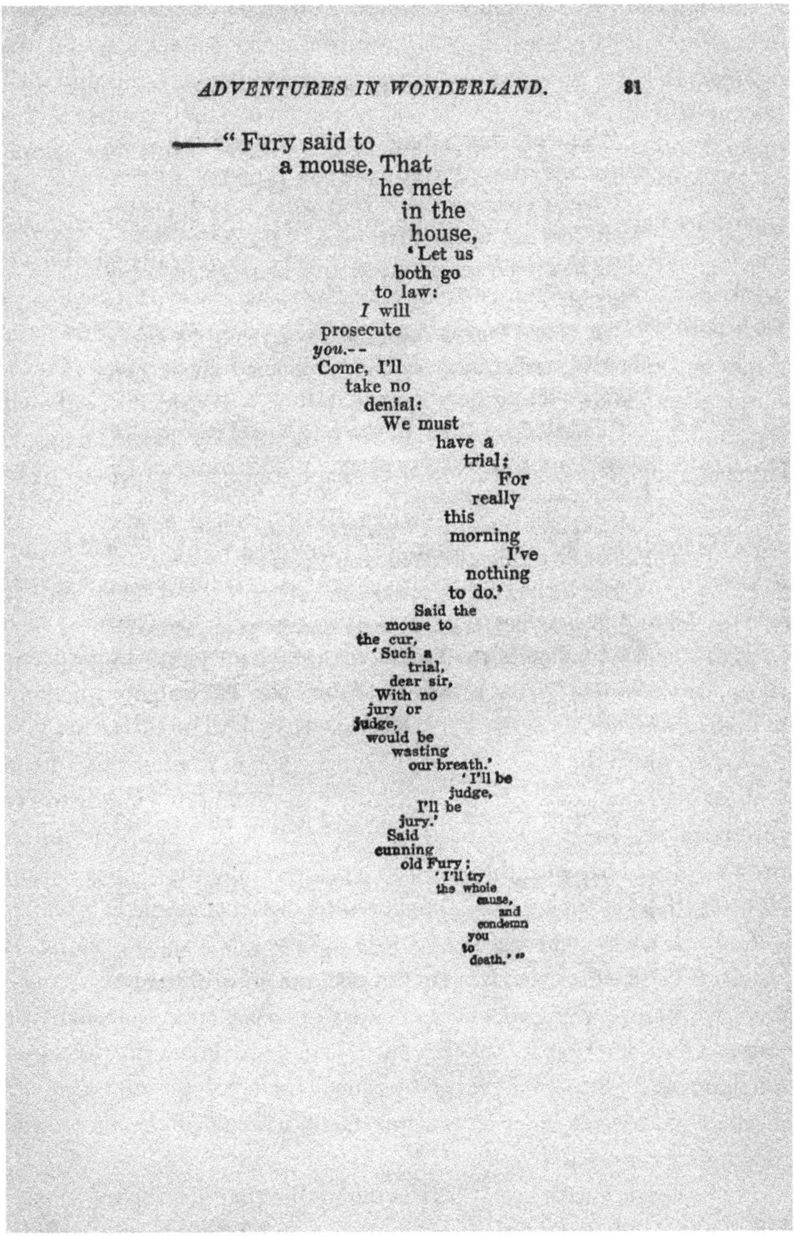

——" Fury said to
        a mouse, That
                he met
                    in the
                        house,
                        ' Let us
                        both go
                        to law:
                    I will
                prosecute
            you.--
        Come, I'll
            take no
                denial:
                    We must
                            have a
                                trial:
                                    For
                                    really
                                this
                                morning
                                        I've
                                    nothing
                                to do.'
                        Said the
                        mouse to
            the cur,
                ' Such a
                        trial,
                    dear sir,
                    With no
                jury or
            judge,
                would be
                    wasting
                        our breath.'
                                ' I'll be
                                    judge,
                            I'll be
                        jury.'
                        Said
                cunning
                    old Fury;
                            ' I'll try
                            the whole
                                cause,
                                    and
                                    condemn
                                you
                        to
                            death.' "

Figure I.3 A scan from *Alice's Adventures in Wonderland.*

what I had learned, how important irony, that trope that is not a trope, is in literature. The irony arises in this case, as is usual in literature, from the discrepancies among what the characters know and understand, and what the narrator, the author, and the reader may understand. Readers in this case can see that Alice is not yet grown up enough to understand word-play, but the mouse is no better. He is only made more and more angry by what Alice says, while Alice does not understand the linguistic mistakes she has made, just as I surely missed some when I first read the Alice books. Alice can only plead, "I didn't mean it," when she offends the mouse, in anticipation of Stanley Cavell's *Must We Mean What We Say?* That issue comes up explicitly later in *Alice in Wonderland* and may be Cavell's source for his formulation.[11] Only the narrator, author, and reader, in different ways and degrees, can be presumed to "understand irony" (if we can indeed speak of understanding it, a dangerous assumption), and to get the joke.

I resist the temptation to turn aside and continue my reading of the Alice books. I give, however, two more examples of wordplay that are not exactly puns but examples of the tropes buried in ordinary language that lead to absurdities if taken literally, like Shermer's "took a turn." In one, from *Through the Looking-Glass*, Alice finds herself in a shop run by a knitting sheep, who asks her, "What is it you want to buy?" Alice answers politely, in perfectly idiomatic English, "I should like to look all round me first, if I might," to which the Sheep replies, "You may look in front of you, and on both sides, if you like, . . . but you can't look *all* round you—unless you've got eyes at the back of your head." On the next page, Alice finds herself rowing a little boat with the Sheep as passenger. The sheep cries repeat-edly, "Feather! Feather!" and "You'll be catching a crab directly." Neither Alice nor I, when I first read the Alice books, knew that "feathering" is the name (a catachresis, in fact, since it does not substitute for some more literal word) for turning your oars sideways when you take them out of the water so they don't catch the wind. She also does not know, nor did I, that "catching a crab" is the name for getting your oar stuck in the water through digging it too deeply (another catachresis). But I could go on and on, and must resist temptation.

My experience with literature has taught me that literary works (and philosophical or theoretical works, too) are each sui generis, unlike all the others. Each therefore demands its own procedure of being read and ac-counted for. Moreover, each reading of a given work by a given reader will differ from all the others, as will different readings at different times by the same reader. As Heraclitus said, "You can't step twice into the same river, for other waters are continually flowing in." The pleasure, intellectual excitement, and benefit of reading literary works, really reading them, comes from these perpetual differences. These differences mean, among other things, that a given reader can always return to read once more a given work with the expectation of new pleasure, new intellectual excitement, and new benefit. My decades of literary study are, in short, empirical and inductive, not deductive from general presuppositions. I do take for granted that literary works are made of language, including figurative language, so that investigating a literary work is always an investigation of linguistic constructions. Language is the matter to be empirically investigated, not consciousness, or history, or society, or nature, or intersubjectivity, although these may be referred to in the language of this or that literary text.

The consequence of these assumptions, or, rather, of my ingrained experiences of trying to account for literary works, is that each of my five chapters is centered on the attempt to read some specific work, including in one case a philosophical or theoretical work: Tennyson's "Tears, Idle Tears," for chapter 2; Wallace Stevens's "The Motive for Metaphor," for chapter 4; Nietzsche's *Die Geburt der Tragödie aus dem Geiste der Musik* (The birth of tragedy), for chapter 6; Yeats's "The Cold Heaven," in chapter 8; and Anthony Trollope's *Framley Parsonage*, for chapter 10. These readings are not meant to support theoretical propositions I have initially put forward in a given chapter. They are what the chapters are centrally about, that is, the attempt to read this or that work, with a given topic in mind in each chapter. Chapter 2 focuses on why literature matters. Chapter 4 is about the lyric. Chapter 6 centers on the problems of world literature. Chapter 8 investigates the justification of literary study in today's world. Chapter 10 is about the ethical dimensions of literature. The works I read, one in each chapter, are chosen as exemplary from among the many works that I admire. Several chapters are fairly elaborate revisions of previous essays I have published or will publish. Others are newly written for this book. These are part of my current investigation of what actually happens when I read a poem or a novel. I claim that what happens is stranger than one might think. It is different for every reader or even different for different readings by the same reader. I have put my chapters explicitly in dialogue with Ranjan Ghosh's matching chapters and have made them fit better my current convictions about the topics of the five sections. My part of this book is a fairly elaborate rethinking of my positions on these topics.

A good bit of each of my chapters, however, is made up of contextual assertions that try to establish the circumstances within which literature is read, taught, and written about in the West today. These contexts somewhat dismayingly suggest that literary study faces some obstacles today, to say the least. I now identify the most conspicuous ones as a conclusion of this brief introduction. Each is in one place or another, or in several places, discussed in more detail in my chapters, especially in chapter 8. My claim is that the rhetorical reading I advocate and try to practice will help us at least to understand what is happening to us and what is making literary study more and more marginal for most people: The overwhelming threat of catastrophic climate change, along with its widespread denial by many people, threatens us, even now. The epochal shift from a print culture to a digital culture looms, as does the marginalization of the humanities in our universities as they are transformed more and more into trade schools teaching primarily STEM subjects (science, technology, engineering, and mathematics) to prepare students for work in a technologized, digitized, and commoditized society. An almost unheard of discrepancy in the wealth and income of the rich and poor accelerates dangerously, as between the 0.01 percent or 0.001 percent and the rest of us. The result is that elections, in the United States at least, are more and more bought by the rich, to a considerable degree through the manipulation of the mass media that are a result of new teletechnologies, as is the ubiquitous advertising that keeps us in thrall to commodity fetishism. And we are beset by globalization (brought about by new teletechnologies, such as the Internet), with a paradoxical increase in isolationisms and commercial as well as military conflicts among nations.

Reading, teaching, and writing about literary works today must be carried on, if at all, in these not entirely cheerful contexts. Most people these days, in the United States at least, let's face it, spend much time using iPhones, Facebook, or Twitter, watching Fox News, or playing video games, not reading Trollope's *Framley Parsonage* or Tennyson's poetry. That is the case even though Trollope's novel and Tennyson's poetry, like so much of the rest of old-fashioned print literature, are easily available in free Guttenberg e-text form to be read on any laptop, iPad, or iPhone with an Internet connection.

As Tom Cohen has demonstrated in a brilliant essay, "material inscription," in the de Manian sense, plays a crucial role in all five of my contextual situations, as well as in all the literary texts I try to read.[12] Just what is material inscription in the de Manian sense? Here is the crucial formulation at the end of de Man's "Hypogram and Inscription: Michael Riffaterre's Poetics of Reading." De Man's target is Riffaterre's reading of a short poem by Victor Hugo:

> Every detail as well as every general proposition in the text [Hugo's poem] is fantastic except for the assertion that it is *écrit*, written. That it was supposed to be written, like Swift's love poem to Stella, as words upon a window pane, is one more cliché to add to those Riffaterre has already collected. But that, like Hegel's text from the *Phenomenology*, it was written cannot be denied. The materiality (as distinct from the phenomenology) that is thus revealed, the unseen "cristal" whose existence becomes a certain *there* and a certain *then* which can become a *here* and a *now* in the reading "now" taking place, is not the materiality of the mind or of time or of the carillon [a topic in Hugo's poem]—none of which exists, except in the figure of prosopopeia—but the materiality of an inscription. Description [de Man means the naming of the things, events, and actions, such as the carillon, in Hugo's poem], it appears, was a device to conceal inscription. Inscription is neither a figure, nor a sign, nor a cognition, nor a desire, nor a hypogram, nor a matrix, yet no theory of poetry can achieve consistency if, like Riffaterre's, it responds to its [inscription's] powers only by a figural evasion which, in this case, takes the subtly effective form of evading the figural.[13]

Investigation of what happens to the materiality of inscription in the new digital media is approached indirectly here and there in my chapters of this book, but I claim, with Cohen, that the materiality of inscription, in various forms, operates as much in climate change, in the financial world, in the new media, in politics, and in globalization, as in printed poetry or fiction. Though in the citation I have just made de Man mostly tells the reader all the things the materiality of inscription is not, the figure of the invisible glass on which a poem might be scratched gives the reader a glimpse of why it is that the materiality of inscription is "unseen," nonphenomenal. In de Man's figure, borrowed from Hugo, we cannot see the materiality of the glass because the mind attends not to the invisible "cristal" but to what is scratched on it, something phenomenally visible and instantly read as interpretable language. It is a case of description's concealing the materiality of inscription. The reader must remember, however, that de Man's figure of the words upon the windowpane is another "figural evasion." By no means is it a direct confrontation of the materiality of inscription. That materiality is not phenomenally visible. It cannot be confronted (another prosopopeia).

I must end here by encouraging you to read carefully de Man's "Hypogram and Inscription" and his "Anthropomorphism and the Lyric," the first in *The Resistance to Theory*, the second in *The Rhetoric of Romanticism*.[14] I also encourage you to read Cohen's wonderful essay, mentioned above. That essay is, among many other things, a long gloss or riff on de Manian materiality of inscription, as it might help us to understand where we are now, "in the twilight of the anthropocene idols."

PART I

The Matter and Mattering of Literature

MAKING SAHITYA MATTER

The most ingenious way of becoming foolish is by a system.
—Third Earl of Shaftesbury

No biases are more insidious than those leading to the neglect of things everyone knows about in principle.
—Stephen Jay Gould

Rabindranath Tagore (1860–1941), the Indian poet-thinker, describes a delightful experience on the river Padma:

> It was a beautiful evening in autumn. The sun had just set: the silence of the sky was full to the brim with ineffable peace and beauty. The vast expanse of water was without a ripple, mirroring all the changing shades of the sunset glow. Miles and miles of a desolate sandbank lay like a huge amphibious reptile of some antediluvian age, with its scales glistening in shining colours. As our boat was silently gliding by the precipitous river-bank, riddled with the nest-holes of a colony of birds, suddenly a big fish leapt up to the surface of the water and then disappeared, displaying on its vanishing figure all the colours of the evening sky. It drew aside for a moment the many-coloured screen behind which there was a silent world full of the joy of life. It came up from the depth of its mysterious dwelling with a beautiful dancing motion and added its own music to the silent symphony of the dying day. I felt as if I had a friendly greeting from an alien world in its own language, and it touched my heart with a flash of gladness. Then suddenly the man at the helm exclaimed with a distinct note of regret, "Ah, what a big fish!" It at once brought before his vision the picture of the fish caught and made ready for his supper. He could only look at the fish through his desire, and thus missed the whole truth.[1]

The poet was disappointed to see this disconnect with nature. For the helmsman, greed and utility eclipsed a glimpse of the other world. What is this other world? Which world had the poet seen that the boatman had missed?

An incident related to one of Chuang-tzu's (an important Chinese philosopher who lived around the fourth century BC) revealing walks echoes Tagore's experience.

> Chuang-tzu was walking on a mountain, when he saw a large tree with huge branches and luxuriant foliage. A wood-cutter was resting by its side, but he would not touch it. When he was asked about the reason, he said it was good for nothing. Then Chuang-tzu said: "This tree, because of its uselessness, is able to complete its natural term of existence." Having left the mountain, Chuang-tzu lodged in the house of his friend. The friend was glad and ordered his waiting lad to kill a goose and boil it. The lad said: "One of our geese can cackle, and the other cannot; which of them shall I kill?" The host said: "Kill the one that cannot cackle." Next day, his disciple asked Chuang-tzu , saying: "Yesterday we saw the mountain tree that can complete its natural term of existence because of its uselessness. Now for the same reason, our host's goose died. Which of these positions would you, master, prefer to be in?" Chuang-tzu laughed and said: "I would prefer to be in a position which is between the useful and the useless. This seems to be the right position, but is really not so. Therefore, it would not put me beyond trouble."[2]

There is a uselessness that is celebrated in both the events. The boatman found the fish useless because it could not be caught right then, and the fish could not complete its natural term of existence because it was useful as food. What then do we say of a world that resides in the liminality of the useful and the useless? What does it mean to say, like Chuang-tzu, that succeeding in the useless comes to be of greatest use? This takes us beyond the acquisitive and the rational (events) to choose *sahit* (connection and communication) with the useless leaping of the fish, the fading beauty of the setting sun on the river, the value of the useless goose, and the nonutility of the luxuriant tree for the woodcutter. These can be termed as nonevents that combine, as I shall argue in the course of this chapter, with events to produce the sacred of sahitya.

In Sanskrit, *sahitya* is derived from the word *sahita*, "united together." V. Raghavan argues:

> The concept of Sahitya had a grammatical origin. It became a poetic concept even as early as Rajasekhara [an eminent Sanskrit dramatist,

poet, critic]; as far as we can see at present, the *Kavyamimamsa* [880–920 CE] is the earliest work to mention the name Sahitya and *Sahitya-vidya* as meaning Poetry and Poetics. Even after Rajasekhara, grammatical associations were clinging to the term up to Bhoja's time. Kuntaka [950–1050, Sanskrit poetician and literary theorist], about the time of Bhoja himself, was responsible for divesting Sahitya of grammatical associations and for defining it as a great quality of the relation between *Sabda* [word] and *Artha* [meaning] in Poetry. Sometime afterwards, Ruyyaka or Mankhuka wrote a work called *Sahitya-mimamsa*, which was the first work on Poetics to have the name Sahitya. Afterwards, Sahitya became more common and we have the notable example of the *Sahitya-darpana* of Visvanatha [a famous Sanskrit poet, scholar, rhetorician writing between 1378 and 1434].[3]

The word *sahitya* retains its Sanskrit origin but is now commonly understood as literature encompassing poetry, plays, poetics, and other forms of creative writing. Although *sahita* means "united together," this does not point to fusion or intermelding but connection (the across-momentum), a kind of being-with. By *sacred* I mean a mystery and a meaning, a substance and a secret. I have used the word *sacred* in a sense that is completely different from what we commonly understand (holy, consecrated, pertaining to or connected to religion). The sacred of sahitya is the substance that stays withheld, a kind of withdrawal from its readers, a febrile anxiety to see itself exhausted at the hands of its readers. What kind of sahit does sahitya create? How does this sahit matter in helping sahitya matter meaningfully? With what matters does sahitya concern itself, to help us understand its mattering? Do the complexities of sahit confer upon sahitya the status of being sacred? Is sahit the troubling feature that has never deserted the attempt to understand sahitya? Is there a way of completing the natural process of sahitya, just as Chuang-tzu's tree was allowed its full lifespan because it was useless?

Sahitya and the Sacred

Paul Hernadi rightly observes that there inevitably has to be a vigorous dissensus over "whether or not the question 'what is literature?' should be answered. Given the multiplicity of ways literature has been intended, produced, transmitted, stored, and mentally processed since prehistoric times, it is hardly surprising that no definition commands widespread acceptance."[4] Lacking a fixed definition, and hence a constant, the Dao of literature, I would contend, is puzzling. To borrow figures from the Chinese text *Tao Te Ching* (a Chinese text ascribed to Laozi, an ancient Chinese philosopher and poet usually dated to around the sixth century BC and reckoned a contemporary of Confucius), sahitya can be described to turn within itself to emerge and prance backward to establish a solid ground for moving forward. The Dao, or the sacred, is amenable to being named, identified, and discoursed about (*daokedo*), but that naming exists in a creative opposition to being considered unnamable, ineffable, and infinite (*changdao*). This begets both a resistance (guarding the secret) and a surrender (exposed to or making allowance for meaning) in sahitya, as it submits to the realities of human understanding and also to our troubling anxiety about the incomprehensibility of experiences. Here are a few lines from *Tao Te Ching*. It must be pointed out that this Chinese text does not talk about what literature should be. But frameworked within my understanding of across poetics of reading, where varied sources come into making unlikely and yet productive correspondences, my arguments here appropriate (in)fusionally a few concepts from this Chinese text to make a different sense of sahitya.

> The way that can be spoken of
> Is not the constant way;
> The name that can be named
> Is not the constant name.
> The nameless was the beginning of heaven and earth;
> The named was the mother of the myriad creatures.
> Hence always rid yourself of desires in order to observe its secrets;
> But always allow yourself to have desires in order to observe its
>   manifestations.
> These two are the same
> But diverge in name as they issue forth.
> Being the same they are called mysteries,
> Mystery upon mystery—
> The gateway of the manifold secrets.[5]

The way of sahitya results in two kinds of desires: one makes sahitya express itself in forms, images, and thoughts, and the other is the desire to stay unnamed and avoid making itself a desire machine of theoretical formulations. These two forms of desire are not incompatible and divergent but dialectical. Sahitya cannot be an experience in explorative desires alone—the fierce urge to investigate what it really means, establishing the institution of sahitya as something that is constant. But sahitya's sacredness is its power to avoid being named always; it is a desire that sahitya has about keeping up with its regenerative abilities. These are the mysteries: the meaning generated through desires (the assigned, the assertive, and the ascribed, the Chinese *you*) and the meaning sans desires (the surprise and seduction, "follow a way that cannot be walked," the *wu*, which has no somethingness, no conscious design or prejudice): "Mystery upon mystery—/ The gateway of the manifold secrets." I choose to implicate the nonaction of sahitya (this is another dimension of sahitya's sacredness), where

> Something and Nothing (*you* and *wu*) produce each other;
> The difficult and the easy complement each other;
> The long and the short off-set each other;
> The high and the low incline towards each other;
> Note and sound harmonize with each other;
> Before and after follow each other.

Therefore the sage keeps to the deed that consists in taking nonaction and practices "the teaching that uses no words."[6]

Sahitya is deeply invested in words and yet speaks and teaches beyond words. The sacredness of sahitya holds and projects "manifold secrets" that involve what language can represent (events), the failure of language, the rationalization of meaning and representation (events), and spaces that do not listen to the strictures of language, formulation, and theorization (the nonevents). It is beholden to a variety of sahit, to what we understand and benefit from, to what refuses our categories of understanding and, consequently, contributes to the development of a different aesthetic of meaning and affect.

The sacredness of sahitya creates the ability to fraternize intimately (the desire to network, sahit) with—and to extend boundaries to include—whatever it engages. In fact, the pleasure and puzzlement that Miller points out in the next chapter are owed, in my opinion, to the imaginary that literature is able to generate and inhere within. Tennyson's "Tears, Idle Tears" bears out the dialectical dimension of sahitya's sacredness. Miller experiences the poem both in its constancy and inconstancy of meaning. The sacredness of the poem becomes on one hand the power (the hermeneutical strength) that enables Miller to make sense of the poem, and on the other hand it generates a secret (the levels that the poem did not allow Miller to touch and experience) that makes him undertake several visits to garner more meaningful experiences. Miller, in my reading, has grown a different kind of sahit with the poem.

The sahit comes to matter differently when Miller tries to demonstrate our experiences of literature through the intricate exchanges between man and machine. Tennyson's poem read on a Kindle, or imagine Tagore's typing his poems on an iPad, cannot just qualify as an exciting event. It is predominantly about changing the dynamics of experiencing literature by encountering it through a different material medium. Caught in such "prestidigitalization" when something speaks—"some impersonal inner voice"—to Miller through the medium, we encounter an excess. This is what I see as the surplus that literature in its complicated matrices, with a newfound medium, is able to deliver to us. This is another level of mystery, somewhat spiritualist and spooky, that makes literature transmit telepathically. Miller's idea of prestidigitalization, the "migration of the literarity" to digital media, sees new modes of finding sahit between the reader, his body, his mind, his understanding, and his emotions. There is, thus, an excess that things bring to our understanding of literature: the materiality of matter that is how the *dravya* (things) contribute to the *visaya* (the subject of sahitya), about which I have spoken at length in my discussion of ethics of sahitya in chapter 9.

Rabindranath Tagore observes that "man daily extends in literature the field of what is dear to him, that is, the field of his clear realisation. Literature is the realm of his unresisted, strange and vast play (*lila*)."[7] The *lila* (it can also be interpreted as a pervasive kinetic energy, an unpredictability that makes something happen with surprise and excess) of sahitya is its norm, the quintessential paradigm to achieve its natural process, whereas hermetic entrapments of meaning resemble, metaphorically, the woodcutter's chopping a useful tree and the goose's being served for dinner. For Tagore, when art focuses on nature, it is a humanized nature whose relationship with man is touched by human emotions that constitute its content. For him, sahitya has never gone beyond man. Yet the nonprivate self, the surplus in man (Kant's "supersensible substratum" and Schiller's *ästhetische Zugabe*, the aesthetic supplement) is the source of creation.[8] The deepening of world consciousness is coterminous with self-consciousness. Sahitya owes its origin and texturing to a connection between the artist's self and the Greater Being or the Great Further. (These are Tagore's words for the Infinite self; Infinite is not God or divinity. Rather, it is a spirit of creation that exists beyond the realm of our creaturely and material needs.) This is a process that is more invested in becoming (a sense of the not-yet) than knowing. Metaphorically speaking, it is not the fish that leaped out of the water, but the greater world beyond the fish, which is always alluringly yet to be.

Sahitya is about knowing man, the world, and knowing beyond man and the world. In sahitya, man is engaged in the "work of knowing himself," and "the truth of his knowing rests on his actual realisation and not on the verity of any objective fact."[9] The poetic truth is truer than factual truth; the poet's imagination is truer than Ayodhya, as Tagore notes in his poem "Balmiki." (Ayodhya is the birthplace of Lord Rama in the Hindu epic *Ramayana* and a small town in the state of Uttar Pradesh, in India; here it becomes an aesthetic imaginary beyond the geography of the place.) To know about the rose is one thing, and to feel something about it is another. In one case, we have a truth-value, in another the issue is taste-value. The truth about the rose comprises both these values: "We must not merely know it, and then put it aside, but we must feel it because by feeling it, we feel ourselves."[10] Tagore argues that rocks and crystals are "complete definitely in what they are and keep a kind of dumb dignity in their stolidly limited realism. But human beings are teased by their creative ideal, and if divested of it, they are turned into a rock or crystal like being. In fact, God has decorated the peacock in a wide range of quaint colours. He has not done so to man; rather, has installed a bowl of colour inside him and said, 'you have to deck yourself in your own hues.' He has said, 'I have put everything in you, but with all those ingredients you have made yourself strong, beautiful and wonderful. I shall not prepare it for you.'"[11] Sahitya is the manifestation of those ingredients inside man. Consequent upon its creation, sahitya builds its own sacredness, its own bowl of colors, which starts to color the mind of the readers. Readers are often successful in identifying the colors of sahitya but, with the bowl of color inside it, sahitya can deliver a new set of colors, resulting in fresh experiences for the readers.[12]

Pointing to an inner power of creativity, the force that is less visible or rationalizable, Tagore writes in "The Wakening of Shiva":

By the force that drives my feelings, roses open;
By the impulse of ecstatic discovery that opens new leaves,
I hurl forth my songs.[13]

The sacredness of the songs lies in the force that does not merely help us to see the roses and the leaves, but makes us a part of their opening. This likewise makes us a part of both the natural process of the fish, and its termination as envisioned by the boatman. Poetic reality embodies a vision that encompasses matter and spirit, being and nonbeing. This vision is due to a superabundance that is free from Platonic doubt and able to perform beyond "the claims of necessity, the thrift of usefulness."[14] For Tagore, utility is just a state of dark heat. The excess of pure utility is like white heat that is expressive. The excess feeds the disclosive power of art and translates into *ananda*, "the power of feeling delight"[15] in sahitya. So *ananda* is experienced in submitting to an Infinite, revealing that "aspect of our personality which overflows in excess of all our creaturely needs and [is] exhausted by all pressures of practical living. It is this excess in which man is most truly revealed."[16] The Infinite is love. It is the unnameable and a power. Our finite self connects with it to generate more meaning and keep up its liveliness. The presence of the Infinite implicates the incompleteness of the finite ways of existence. The sense of incompleteness does not change the reality of life to a great extent, but the reality of poetic truth and truth in art keep changing their form and expression. Creativity becomes a continual reconstruction of the artist's personality—the "encroachment of man's personality has no limit."[17] So the conflict and conflation with the Infinite result in the giving, which, as Tagore notes, is a process that "can be classified and generalized by science" but is itself "not the gift."[18] Sahitya's sacredness shows the significance of the giving (the named, the useful) and also the importance of not being overpowered by the gift. This is another invitation to the useless.

Sahitya is our *sadhana* to unbind ourselves (*sadhana* is about accomplishing something through a meditative commitment; the word is used here not in the religious sense but in a performative sense that approximates the combined effect of *abhyasa*, practice through reflection and observation, and *kriya*, action). Tagore writes: "What then is revealed through literature? It is our wealth, our plenitude, that part of our being which overflows in excess of our actual needs, which has not been exhausted in the process of practical life. In such excess is humanity truly expressed. That man hungers is true, but that he is brave is still more. The superman, the ideal toward which man is progressing, is being evolved by his literature, and such permanent ideal is being accumulated therein as a guide for each succeeding generation."[19] On most occasions, the excess emerging from the useless goes untapped, resulting in sahitya's being understood as an "artificial product" (in Tagore's words) incarcerated within certain codes and modes. Consequently, sahitya is limited to becoming a tree that the woodcutter always finds useful or a fish that the boatman would always enjoy eating. Tagore observes that "art and literature belong to that revolutionary region of freedom where need is reduced to unimportance, the material is shown to be unsubstantial, and the ideal alone is revealed as the truth; there all burdens are lightened, all things are made man's very own."[20] Indeed, the value of uselessness prevents sahitya from performing as a moral teacher. Sahitya cannot just take up the "job of school masters."[21] Tagore notes: "What I have to remark is, that it does not amount to the whole truth to say that the Good pleases because of what it does for us. That which is really good is both useful and beautiful, that is to say, it has a mysterious attraction for us over and above that of such purposes of ours as it may serve. The moralist declares its value from the ethical standpoint, the poet seeks to make manifest its unutterable beauty."[22] The sacredness of sahitya produces the unutterable quotient that exists outside the parameters of pragmatism and didacticism.

The struggle to connect with the Infinite, the bountiful other world that the fish reveals in a glimpse, is endowed with a surplus of imagination that Tagore considers love. This love is transformative and enabling, exhausting and fulfilling. Therein lies an extinction and an exfoliation, a loss "which leads to greater gain." It "turns the emptiness of renunciation into fulfilment by his own fullness" and upholds the complexities invested in "what is in us and what is beyond us; between what is in the moment and what is ever to come." Loving, as joy, becomes the means of loving more, of finding "abounding joy" and ways of enhancing love. This love has a rhythm that does not encourage the knowledge of a rose by merely learning about the constitutive chemistry of its petals; rather, it espouses the rose as *maya*, an image, an experience that is not confined to what we merely see and materially experience, whose "finality has the touch of the infinite."[23] For Tagore, the rhythm, the finding of proportion in apparent irrelevancies, is a kind of manifestation of surplus. This rhythm in literature is like the "stars which in their seeming stillness are never still, like a motionless flame that is nothing but movement."[24]

Sahitya has survived by expressing itself and also by continually guarding and extinguishing itself. This guarding attests to a continuity, the *lila* about which I have spoken extensively in chapter 5. However, sahitya does not exhaust itself to a point where love of the Infinite ends. The Infinite transcribes the everyday, wherein repetition (say, watching the sun rise every day) is not without infinite possibilities. Tagore observes that forms must always move and change and that "they must necessarily die to reveal the deathless."[25] What is the deathless in literature, then? Isn't this what Miller expresses when he writes about the endless approach to the unapproachable imaginary? Do we exhaust our uses of sahitya to reveal the useless, a category that leads us to interact with the Infinite? The fish has to be useless to the boatman to become deathless in its interface with the Infinite. The tree has to die in the woodcutter's view in order to emerge in its deathlessness.

The surplus, or the deathless, in sahitya comes close to being expressed in an idea of the early Chinese painter and art theorist Gu Kaizhi (346–407) concerning the "blank eye pupil." Ming Dong Gu explains that long before Gu Kaizhi's time, the eye was viewed in the Chinese tradition as "the window to a person's inner spirit."[26] According to a legend, Gu Kaizhi left the pupils of a portrait unpainted for years, so that he might have ample time to contemplate how to paint them. This notion of the eye as the element that transmits the spiritual essence of the represented person or animal has persisted in Chinese aesthetic thought. In the sixth century, Emperor Wu, of the Liang dynasty, erected many Buddhist temples. A famous artist painted four dragons on the wall of Anle Temple, in Jinling, but left their pupils unpainted. When queried, he responded that if he had painted the pupils, the dragons would have flown away. Under pressure, he later added pupils to two of the four dragons. Almost immediately a violent storm struck the wall. The two dragons with pupils flew away, while the other two remained. Thereafter the expression "to bring the painted dragon to life by adding the pupils" came to refer to the finishing touch that brings a work of art to life.[27] Sahitya can at times be left with an eye painted without pupils. If painting the dragon's pupils made it fly, this demonstrates how sahitya's sacredness lies in securing an eye without pupils. It invites us to make sense of waste, which is the other name for excess. The blank eye of sahitya is its mystery, the restless sacredness in both the *daokedo* (the finite) and *changdao* (infinite).

Sahitya's Mattering

Understanding the sacred brings me closer to the *Su P'u*, the Uncarved Block (*p'u*, or *pu*, literally translated, means "uncut wood"). Wai-Lim Yip argues:

> When Lao-tzu said, "Tao, told, is not the constant Tao. Name, named, is not the Constant Name" and proposed to return to the Su P'u (Uncarved Block) or the "Great Undivided Institution" he intended to implode the

so-called kingly Tao, the heavenly Tao, as well as the naming system of the feudalistic ideology of the Chou Dynasty, so that memories of the repressed, exiled, and alienated natural self could be fully reawakened. The Taoist project, from the point of view of the naming system, is a negating, abandoning, and even an escapist act; but from the point of view of "no naming" (that is, before the territorialisation of power) and that of the Uncarved Block, it helps to break the myth of the reductive and distortive naming activities, affirm the concrete total world that is free from and unrestricted by concepts, and move toward reclaiming the natural self as well as Nature as it is. Thus we can say that the Taoist project is a counterdiscourse to the territorialisation of power, an act to disarm the tyranny of language; it is not, as most superficial readers believe, a passive philosophy.[28]

Uncarved wood, in its totality, unrestricted by pregiven concepts or sanctioned structures of use, comes with all possibilities. Each piece territorializes, rather, canonizes a certain advantage or a use. The apparent passivity of the Uncarved Block conceals radiant and vibrant possibilities of creation made possible through negating and abandoning. While negating creates the possibility of sahitya to name the nameless (profanization) and make naming a continuous game, abandoning, holding the noun *abandon* within it, foregrounds acts that lack inhibition and restraint. This keeps the naming game alive. Arthur Danto observes that "to treat the work of art as Leonardo treated his spotted wall as an occasion for critical invention which knows no limit" is not to say that literature is about perennial unmasking or unveiling.[29] But efforts to unwrap sahitya concern both meaning that we create out of literature, and the meaning that literature imperceptively creates in us. Sahitya's use is not merely what readers subjectively create, not the blasé acceptance of "Yes-Yuh," like Zarathustra's ass. Sahit is inscribed in a kinesis, in a consciousness of something waiting to appear and waiting to be found.

It is in the intricacies of coming together that the sacredness of sahitya lies. Sahit performs itself in ways that remind us of what Jacques Rancière calls the paradox of the mute pebbles. In speaking of the new democracy of literature that blossomed in the nineteenth century, Rancière writes:

Literature is this new regime of writing in which the writer is anybody and the reader anybody. This is why its sentences are "mute pebbles." They are mute in the sense that they had been uttered long ago by Plato when he contrasted the wandering of the orphan letter to the living logos, planted by a master as a seed in the soul of a disciple, where it could grow and live. The "mute letter" was the letter that went its way, without a father to guide it. It was the letter that spoke to anybody, without knowing to whom it had to speak, and to whom it had not. The "mute" letter was a letter that spoke too much and endowed anyone at all with the power of speaking.[30]

Rancière's "democratic disorder of literariness" is closely connected with the "uncanny."[31] Mute pebbles are the uncanny that haunt literature to speak across time periods and cultures. Experiences of literature become ways of appreciating the fraught relations between literary influences, literary history, and a transcultural poetics of reading. The disorder speaks through reiteration, repression, and the reanimation of meaning. These are separate processes that make literature speak beyond the already spoken, clearing spaces across different contexts, backgrounds, eras, and cultural specificities. Literary texts, then, are both part of a historical, literary continuum and a disorder that lives and flourishes outside it. They acknowledge their moment of composition, their background and time-sense, but cannot forget that they have a life outside these coordinates.

In "What Does Poetry Communicate?" a reading of Herrick's "Corrina's Going A-Maying," Cleanth Brooks writes: "I think our initial question, 'What does the poem communicate?' is badly asked. It is not that the poem communicates nothing. Precisely the contrary. The poem communicates so much and communicates it so richly and with such delicate qualifications that the thing communicated is mauled and distorted if we attempt to convey it by any vehicle less subtle than that of the poem itself."[32] Sahitya becomes the frissive point of exhaustion and subtlety. Tagore sees the leaping fish and the fish becomes a desiring machine. But this desire is not about trying to exhaust and maul the fish but is a sahit with everything that exists beyond its species-state. The lumber that the woodcutter chops out is meant for use and profit. But to leave the living tree to fulfill its cycle is to find communion with the mystery of its other side, the love of the Infinite. The tree found useless by the woodcutter can also be a useful site for nesting birds, blooming flowers, a tangled kite, a possible lightning strike, the shadows of clouds, or a climbing boy. Of what use are these for the woodcutter? The woodcutter's indifference makes the tree manifest with a difference. The birch trees in Robert Frost's "Birches" are not meant and willed for firewood, nor desired to be used to make fences and furniture. They exist for swinging, a carefree and useless activity. But this swinging inheres in a power that effectuates a variety of sahit. So a string of questions disturbs the poem from within: What is the "truth" and "love" in the poem? What is this going and coming back? How can earth be the right place for love? What does it mean to keep one's poise and yet be a swinger of birches? How can one learn that learning is about not launching out too soon? What does it mean to ask, "Am I free to be poetical?"

Frost's "Birches" and Uselessness

Early editions of Robert Frost's "Birches" included this question, set apart by parentheses like an ironic aside: ("Am I free to be poetical?") It followed line twenty-two, introducing the transition from the factual account of ice storms to the evocation of his boyhood swinging. The poet chose to delete it from subsequent editions of the poem.

> I was going to say when Truth broke in
> With all her matter-of-fact about the ice-storm
> (Am I free to be poetical?)
> [. . .]
> So was I once myself a swinger of birches.
> And so I dream of going back to be.
> It's when I'm weary of considerations,
> And life is too much like a pathless wood
> Where your face burns and tickles with the cobwebs
> Broken across it, and one eye is weeping
> From a twig's having lashed across it open.
> I'd like to get away from earth awhile
> And then come back to it and begin over.
> May no fate willfully misunderstand me
> And half grant what I wish and snatch me away
> Not to return. Earth's the right place for love:
> I don't know where it's likely to go better.
> I'd like to go by climbing a birch tree,
> And climb black branches up a snow-white trunk
> Toward heaven, till the tree could bear no more,
> But dipped its top and set me down again.
> That would be good both going and coming back.
> One could do worse than be a swinger of birches.[33]

The birches swing into play what is seen and what is seen as, which is the Heideggerian way of trying to see the poem as a faceoff between undifferentiated contemplation and a differentiated experience. "Birches" addresses a system of thought and is also a contemplation that cannot be compartmentalized conceptually. It speaks of an act of conceptualizing or an act of perception that is useless, an experience without understandable direction. Such moments of uselessness, in fact, precede grounding in history. We cannot ignore the experience that precedes historical exegesis and our surrender to taxonomic frames of reality and existence. The poem also has a strategy of clear expression to boost its place within the canons of readerly acceptance. Sahitya's sacredness does not always reside in blocks, however; rather, it is in the continuity and discontinuity ("going and coming back") of the natural process of meaning. Hence the lines "Earth's the right place for love" and "(Am I free to be poetical?)" can be seen to have moved out of the contextual immediacy of the poem, to have moved beyond any kind of block of understanding (in both senses of the word). Frost anxiously questions the wholesome efficacy of being poetical. The word *free* suggests that freedom can lead to an exciting and intense activity of the poetic mind, expressing thereby the struggle between life and art. Freedom here is also about self-interrogation; the anxiety to be poetically free is vexatiously related to Earth (the "right" place for love), to a faith in life as represented by Earth, and to a desire to be poetical that goes beyond Earth. The query that hangs over the freedom to be poetical leads us to the ambiguity of the poetic mind in its ways of creation.

Frost's creative mind is like the boy whose movements are simultaneously creative, destructive, and deformative. Creation comes with caution, care, and cheer. So how much daring can the boy afford? The birches under the swinging impact of the boy are a part of the transmutative everyday. They participate in the ideal of rebeginning, coming back and beginning again, a combination of pragmatism and metaphysics. The boy is both a captive of the birches and a swinger who seeks liberation from them. The sacredness of the birches is in the swinging that only the boy can effect. He tries to conquer the alienation that the birches in their reality bring, their stiffness and the snow crust. At the beginning of the poem, the boy interacts with the birches as a human would traditionally meet a nonhuman, a tree. But we see a change as the poem progresses. The boy becomes the poet and the trees are transformed into art. This transformation resembles the way Stephen Dedalus, in *A Portrait of the Artist as a Young Man*, describes a transition: "Out of the sluggish matter of the earth a new soaring impalpable imperishable being emerges."[34] Swinging renews the apparently unchanging earth as much as it revisions the stiff and stern heaven—"alchemistically enhanced."[35] This is not *conjunctio oppositorum* but is about questioning the eternal good of flying away from earth, as well as the goodness of staying rooted to it, the problematic of subjecting imagination to truth. Is swinging an achievement in wholeness or does it have the undertow of skepticism? Does the boy, through the urge to be poetical, become part of a romantic ideal, or is he a skeptic who struggles to occupy fixed positions? Life, as a pathless wood, is a skepticism that does not expire in disappointment but expresses the dialectical merit of being matter of fact and at the same time being poetical. The swinging suggests a skepticism about receiving life at the level of the plain, the ordinary.[36] The birches resist being ordinary and soar out of the sluggish matter of the earth into a new being, becoming poetical.

The birches and swinging bid certain thoughts into existence. The boy "whose only play was what he found himself" combines what has been with what awaits to be. He engages nearness by being afar; the swinging gives him more spaces to explore the now and the after and then return with a certain openness. In fact, the swinging confuses the point of origin and telos, in that it becomes a continuity. This continuity does not allow anyone to understand the swinging in the form of a narrative that has an exclusive point of origin, followed by the next point of progress, before a series of points leads to the end. With poetic creativity understood as a continuity, the boy-poet meaningfully makes the connection among the poetical, earth, place, and love. The boy "learned all there was / To learn about not launching out too soon" and swings in communication (nearness, proximity to meaning) and muteness (afar, the unnamed and indeterminateness of meaning) in uncertain ways of being and acting that I would call, in mock solemnity, the metapolitics of swinging. Coming close is not always about coming near. The sacredness of literature regulates its closeness and nearness with readers and reception.

The birches, in their transformation into art, offer moments of revealed truth that the boy communicates through the nearness he creates in swinging. This enables the birches to speak.[37] The swinging enables the birches to break their silence because the boy, through his imagination and craft, attends to their silence. In the process, he learns from the birches the art and the pleasure of becoming poetical. Annie Dillard notes that "we have drained the light from the boughs in the sacred grove and snuffed it in the high places and along the banks of sacred streams. We as a people have moved from pantheism to pan-atheism. Silence is not our heritage but our destiny; we live where we want to live."[38] The birches, like Tagore's fish and the tree the woodcutter chose to ignore, achieve, on the contrary, the status of the deathless. They have sublated into new spheres of meaning.

The analysis I have provided does not come anywhere close to the canonical codes of understanding the poem. Settled and structured forms of understanding (the useful) include the autobiographical, like, say, Frost's own childhood experiences with swinging on birches, a popular game for children in rural areas of New England during his time, and his own children were enthusiastic about it (see daughter Lesley's journal). The established understanding also includes the thematic, like the notion of "borders" (one can trace this in many of his other poems, such as "After Apple Picking"), where the trees serve to provide the link between earth or humanity and the sky or divine. The stylistic is also widely agreed and structured: as when the poem is read through what Frost calls the "sound of sense." The psychoanalytic is settled in the dominant sexual connotations of the poem. The philosophical is understood in the dialectic (we may term this as "swinging") between youthful innocence (the imagination to reach beyond Earth) and adult responsibilities (the truth being that Earth is the right place for love), the worries over aging and loss pitted against a carefree youth—the "going and coming back." But do such paradigms of reading exhaust the poem of all it can deliver? Would my reading have helped Frost to come closer to his intended meaning in the poem? Does it give the reader easy access to the center of the poem, making her enjoyment memorable? The answers are not encouragingly positive. However, these negatives, the points of extinguishment, bring us to the use of the useless and render the encouragements to configure the completion of its natural process.

The Mattering and the Matter

The swinger of birches fabulizes, arriving at truths that make us undergo a kind of self-forgetfulness, what Hans-Georg Gadamer calls "being outside oneself." This state is a prelude to connecting "wholly with something else." The self-forgetfulness that sahitya produces in us is a state in which the reality of our understanding comes into question, since, as Gadamer points out, "what we experience in a work of art and what invites our attention is how true it is—that is, to what extent one knows and recognizes something and oneself."[39] Sahitya creates the perceiver's space, where the ordinary breaks into an aesthetic that revises our understanding of the ordinary. Perhaps sahitya does not make things happen all the time. Most often it leaves things at the point of happening, on the edge of possible multiple happenings. Experiences emerging out of such happenings are, on most occasions, beyond our actual realizations of life experiences. "It [literature] creates after the finite," as Laurent Dubreuil notes, "in order to signify in spite of all. For our joy."[40]

Heidegger considers poetry the "most innocent of occupations," language the most dangerous of possessions, and the foundation of being poetic.[41] I am tempted to replace *poetry* with sahitya. Arguably, sahitya's sacredness is poetic. It affirms its own existence and upholds an intimacy in which the writer, the text, and the reader grow in a relationship of possession, communication, and contradiction. There is a contradiction in what the reader wants from sahitya and what she gets in the end, making for a conversation involving both the outside (stylistics, imagery, words, figures of speech, background, biography, etc.) and the inside (silence, waste, and uselessness) of sahitya. The profanization of the sacred is what makes sahitya continue with its meaning and worth and yet preserve its own enticement, a deep intimacy with language, resulting in what Heidegger calls "opening." Heidegger writes: "Without this relation an argument too is absolutely impossible. But the one and the same can only be manifest in the light of something perpetual and permanent. Yet permanence and perpetuity only appear when what persists and is present begins to shine. But that happens in the moment when time opens and extends. After man has placed himself in the presence of something perpetual, then only can he expose himself to the changeable, to that which comes and goes; for only the persistent is changeable."[42]

The sacred is perpetual and, on occasion, is the apolitical in literary experiences. The sacred evokes the before and after of literature. "Literature each time says," as Dubreuil argues, "all literature again; so, it is never 'the same.'"[43] Caught in the across, "Birches" is surely presence and opening, corroborating Heidegger's observation: "Poetry rouses the appearance of the unreal and of dream in the face of the palpable and clamorous reality, in which we believe ourselves at home. And yet in just the reverse manner, what the poet says and undertakes to be, is the real."[44] "Birches" has this unreal yet near-tangible reality to it. It exemplifies how poetry creates a reality that we struggle to control, a fulfillment that in reality has always eluded us. It embodies a kind of mute writing that Rancière says "would no longer be the silent language engraved in the flesh of material things." Rather, the birches have the "radical muteness of things."[45] They express not only meaning and will but nonsense too, an indifference to our clock-work life lived in partitions of the sensible, the visible, and the sayable.

Too much thought has perhaps been expended on what sahitya is capable of doing. Not enough leeway is allowed for sahitya to be left, as it is hanging in the sacredness of its existence, in the swinging between the event and the nonevent. The Zen way of life, qualifying the nonevent, would say, "The moon is reflected deep inside the lake but the water shows no sign of penetration."[46] We continue to brush up against and miss the sacred, the event that is a nonevent. Although the frisking fish exists both as a material and an aesthetic object, it can also open a mode of experience where these identities collapse into each other. The fish can be perceived beyond both these approaches, which is its closeness to the Infinite. It is at this point that Frost's query, "Now am I free to be poetical?" can be answered in the affirmative.

LITERATURE MATTERS TODAY

Ranjan Ghosh and I have agreed to add within our paired essays comments by each of us on the other's essay of a given pair. This initial pair (chapters 1 and 2) consists of somewhat programmatic statements by each of us about the nature and function of literature as we see it. Ghosh's essay is challenging in a number of ways. I have read it repeatedly in order to get the hang of it as best I can. I have learned much from it, for example, about Sanskrit or Hindu literary theory and also about Rabindranath Tagore. I also have a new understanding of Ranjan Ghosh's own theory of literature. Of these three things I had been only partially informed. Now some further light has dawned.

I begin this chapter by stressing, as I have in the preface, that neither of us speak for a whole culture, Ghosh for Indian culture, I for U.S. culture. Both those cultures are immensely diverse. Many different conceptions of literature abound in each. Simona Sawney, for example, in *The Modernity of Sanskrit*, has argued for the heterogeneity both of modern Indian literature in Hindu and of the Sanskrit tradition that has so deeply influenced it.[1] My conception of literature is only one among the many different ones that are salient in the United States today. To some of my compatriots, perhaps to many, my position may seem idiosyncratic. Ghosh and I speak for ourselves, though each is a representative, on the one hand, of one Indian way to define literature, or, on the other hand, of one U.S. way.

Nevertheless, something of cultural or national difference may lie behind the way the two essays are strikingly different in their conceptions of what literature is and why it matters. Their stylistic and methodological procedures also differ. I shall insert some dialogical observations about these two forms of difference here and there in my chapter. In spite of these differences, however, an unexpected consonance between our two views of literature ultimately emerges. It was unexpected by me, at least.

Why and How Literature Matters to Me

Matters! This is an odd word when used as a verb. Of course we know what it means. The verbal form of *matter* means "count for something," "have import," "have effects in the real world," "be worth taking seriously." Using the word as a noun, however, someone might speak of "literature matters," meaning the whole realm that involves literature. The newsletter of the Maine chapter of the Appalachian Mountain Club is called *Wilderness Matters*, punning on the word as a noun and as a verb. We might say, analogously, "Literature Matters," as my title does. In medieval Europe, learned people spoke of "the matter of Rome," "the matter of Arthur," "the matter of Greece," meaning the whole set of stories that lay behind Aeneas's story, the Arthurian romances, or Odysseus's, Achilles's, and Oedipus's stories. The verb *matter* resonates with the noun *matter*. The latter means sheer, unorganized physical substance. Aristotle opposed unformed matter to form. This suggests that if something matters its import is not abstract. What matters is not purely verbal, spiritual, or formal. It has concrete effects on materiality, in the form perhaps of human bodies and their behavior. Does literature matter in that sense today?

It matters quite a bit, however, what we mean by "literature" when we ask whether literature matters today. I am assuming that *literature* means printed books that contain what most people ordinarily think of these days as literature, that is, poems, plays, and novels. Just what is literary about poems, plays, and novels is another matter, to which I shall return. I shall also have something to say in other chapters about the migration of the literary to new digital media. I call this magic transformation prestidigitalization.

It is often taken for granted that what most matters about literature, if it matters at all, is the accuracy with which it reflects the real world or functions as a guide to conduct for readers living in that world. The mimetic paradigm, two and a half millennia old, going back to the Greeks, in its multitude of permutations, has had, and still has, great power, at least in the Western world. A little reflection, however, will show that this paradigm is extremely problematic. It is easily contested or easily made more complicated, as I shall later on briefly show.

The reader will also recognize that adding *today* to *literature matters* is a move that matters. Literature's import differs in different times, places, and societies. My interest is in the question of whether literature matters now, today, here in the United States of America (since I know that best). I am also interested in the global here and now, within which all we human beings, Americans and the rest, more and more live from moment to moment today. I note from the outset that the multitude of books and essays, such as this book, on whether or not literature matters any longer would not be necessary if the mattering of literature today were not in doubt. All who love literature are collectively anxious today about whether literature matters. No such books and essays would likely have seemed necessary in Victorian England, for example, my original field of specialization. To literate Victorians, both middle class and upper class, the assumption that literature mattered quite a lot was so much taken for granted as almost never to be a matter for interrogation.

Literate and *literature* have the same root, meaning written letters. You are literate if you can make sense of written letters. You are then "lettered." Literature is made of letters, marks made on paper by some writing technology or other. The primary technology was printing presses, in the epoch from the seventeenth century to the present. That was the period of what we Westerners generally mean by *literature*. Most Victorian readers took it for granted that printed literature, especially in the form of novels, reflected back to them the everyday social world they lived in. Novels, moreover, taught them how to behave in courtship and marriage, as well as in many other regions of everyday life. That way of assuming that literature matters may explain the continued power, even today, of the mimetic, realist paradigm.

Literature, however, was also the chief way Victorians could enjoy the pleasures of entering into an imaginary world invented for them by someone more gifted than they in manipulating language. Those pleasures were often seen as guilty and dangerous, especially for young women, but also for young men. Think of Catherine Morland, the heroine of Jane Austen's *Northanger Abbey*, or of Conrad's Lord Jim. Flaubert's Emma Bovary is the paradigmatic example of fictional characters corrupted by reading literature.

These two assumptions about why literature matters were in tension in Victorian culture and in European culture generally. That tension defined the social role literate Victorians, of the middle class and the upper class, assumed literature to have. Think of it! The Victorians had no film, no radio, no television, no video games, no DVDs, no Internet, no iPhoto, no Kindles, no iPads, no smartphones, no Facebook. Such technological impoverishment! They had only printed books, newspapers, and magazines to satisfy their needs both for reflective mimesis and for enjoying the imaginary.

The reader will note already how different, both in style and in concept, this chapter is from Ranjan Ghosh's "Making Sahitya Matter." On the one hand, my chapter is relatively cool, rational, and objective, with only a pervasive evanescent scent of irony to distinguish it from some forms of standard academic discourse in the United States. My instinct is to begin with somewhat ironic comments on the complexity of everyday words in English, such as *matter*. This, like irony in general, is a way of being both inside and outside at once. Ghosh, on the other hand, does not refrain from writing poetically, nor from appropriating the poetic writing of others, for example, passages from Tagore and Chuang-tzu, as the best way to communicate what he wants to say. His references to a Hindu or Sanskrit concept of poetry is buttressed by reference to Chinese analogues. By "writing poetically," I mean appropriating the language modes of his examples for his own discourse. He assumes that explaining literature can only be done to some degree poetically, or, to use one of his words, by "fabulizing" it. I would be more likely to use the term *parable* (as in the parables of Jesus in the New Testament of the Christian Bible) or the term *catachresis* (the Greek name for a word that is not literal but does not substitute for any literal word, such as "leg of a table" or "face of a mountain"). But a fable, too, speaks by indirection about something that cannot be spoken of directly. Ghosh uses Tagore's stories of the fish and Chuang-tzu's story of the tree and two geese and Frost's poem "Birches" (the last in an extended discussion) as parabolic, catachrestic, or fabulist exemplifications of what literature does. For Ghosh, literature indirectly names, through its sacredness, the unnamable other world that orients literature.

Ghosh also frequently uses poetic or alogical linguistic devices like paradox or the simultaneous affirmation of opposites. The implication is that *sahitya* is not open to exposition in strictly logical language only. The sacred, as Ghosh argues, is both about the meaning that sahitya's utility generates and the meaning that emerges beyond its utility. On the one hand, Ghosh gives much allegiance to the Sanskrit concept of literature as sahitya, even though he gives Western formulations equal allegiance. The term *sahitya* is formed from the word *sahit*, "union." It names union with the Dao (the sacred), that is, with the hidden world that literature expresses indirectly. I, on the other hand, would hesitate to use the word *sacred* to characterize secular literature, that is, printed novels, poems, and plays in Western languages. In my tradition, that is, broadly speaking, in the Western tradition, the only texts that are widely assumed to be sacred are the Bible, both the Hebrew Bible and the Christian Bible, and the Koran.

Secular texts, for example Dante's *La Divina Comedia* and many others, may be religious through and through, or register religious experience, but they do not have the sacred authority the West ascribes to the Bible. Ghosh uses the word *sacred* in a way quite different from my habitual usage. In a lucid note to me, Ghosh explains just what he means by *sacred*: "I am using the word 'sacred' to mean a part of literature which is 'untouched,' something that does not give easy access to its readers. This has nothing to do with 'divine' or sacramental authority. Sacred is the secret power of literature to generate more meaning when conventional understanding of literature becomes aporetic."

I shall now dare to speak briefly about why literature has mattered to me. Here is another important difference between my position and Ghosh's. Ghosh makes many references to Western texts (Heidegger, Gadamer, Rancière, etc.) that are in resonance with Sanskrit sahitya. His bottom line is the assumption that the Sanskrit concept of poetry is just one version of a worldwide theory of literature, perennially true, that has much diversity and complexity. This theory is not limited in time, culture, or language. I, on the contrary, claim that my theory of literature's nature and uses has validity only for me, even though others (I hope) may agree with me.

In spite of my many years of studying literature, teaching it, and writing about it, I remain to this day puzzled by literary works. I remember the poem that exemplified my puzzlement and still does so. This is a short poem by Tennyson, one of the songs in *The Princess*, called "Tears, Idle Tears." It is a wonderful poem. I read this poem when I was still majoring in physics as an undergraduate at Oberlin College and found it an exceedingly strange use of language. In my science courses, I was taught to say the truth straightforwardly, to explain anomalies, and to use language in as uncomplicated a way as possible. Tennyson seemed to me to do no such things. The poem begins:

> Tears, idle tears, I know not what they mean,
> Tears from the depth of some divine despair
> Rise in the heart, and gather to the eyes,
> In looking on the happy Autumn-fields,
> And thinking of the days that are no more.[2]

I asked myself, what in the world does this mean? What does Tennyson mean by calling his tears idle? In what sense are these tears idle? Why did he write, "I know not what they mean?" I did not know what they mean, either. The poem is very beautiful. There is no doubt about that, but so what? And "tears from the depth of some divine despair?" What does "divine despair" mean? It might mean despair of some god. What god? Gods are not supposed to despair. What is this god in despair about? Why are the autumn fields happy? I thought they were just inhuman matter. In short, I had dozens of questions about just these few lines. It seems to me that simply to read the poem out loud to students, as teachers often used to do, and to say how beautiful it is, is not enough. Yes, I agree. It is beautiful. But what does it mean? I think we are justified in demanding a high degree of explicability from literary works and in demanding that our teachers help students in this hermeneutic work.

Why, I continued to wonder, should it matter to me whether I read and understand this poem or not? I wanted to figure out answers to these questions, to account for the poem in the way astrophysicists account for data from outer space. Decades after my shift from physics to literature, I wrote an essay trying, belatedly, to answer those questions I had about "Tears, Idle Tears."[3] What was wrongheaded about my original project took me some years to discover. I am still discovering, that is, still trying to come to terms with what de Man identifies as the irreconcilability of hermeneutics and poetics, meaning and the way meaning is expressed.[4] I shall discuss what de Man says in chapter 4. A shorthand description of my mistake would be to say that data from the stars and the linguistic matter that makes up poems require fundamentally different methodologies of "accounting for." I have spent my whole life trying to account for various presumptively literary works. That is my vocation: reading, teaching, lecturing, and writing about print literature. Literature matters a great deal to me.

My citations from literature, as opposed to Ghosh's, for example, my quotation from "Tears, Idle Tears," are used to exemplify my puzzlement about just what literary works in the Western tradition mean, say, or are meant to do to their readers. Ghosh's citations are meant to exemplify the way literature's sacredness is mostly inscribed in the unnamed and the unstructured. I am more interested than Ghosh is in making rhetorical, formal, or stylistic analyses of literary works. I am more willing than he is to consider positively literature's contribution to empirical knowledge about the social world and its role in the formation of ethical norms, whereas he stresses the sacredness of literature's "uselessness" in the everyday world of getting enough to eat or keeping warm in cold weather. I am also much more concerned than he is with the medium of poetry, in particular the epochal change going on right now throughout the world from print culture to digital culture, from printed books to computers, Kindles, and iPads. Ghosh says nothing about this in his chapter 1. For Ghosh, in his chapter 1 at least, literature as sahitya apparently remains literature, when expressed in whatever medium. For him, to recall H. Marshall McLuhan's famous formulation, the medium is *not* the message. The message is in the words in whatever medium.

Well, how much does literature matter in the world in general today? It is easy to see that literature, in the sense of printed poems, plays, and novels, is mattering less and less. We are in the long, drawn-out twilight of the epoch of print literature, an epoch that began less than four centuries ago and could end without bringing about the death of civilization. Though, of course, literary works are still widely read all over the world, in different degrees in different places, literature matters less and less to many people, including highly educated ones. Recent statistical studies have shown that fewer and fewer young people read books of any sort for pleasure. The double role of allowing the pleasures of entering imaginary worlds and of learning about the real world and how to behave in it are more and more shifting to new technological devices of telecommunication: films, video games, television shows, popular music, Facebook, and so on. I include television news broadcasts as forms of the imaginary. They have almost as much interpolated advertising as news. Advertising is another form of the imaginary. The ability or the need to create imaginary worlds out of words on printed pages is less and less an important part of most people's lives. Probably people are becoming less adept at doing it. Why go to all the bother to read that extremely difficult novel, Henry James's *The Golden Bowl*, for example, when you can so much more easily watch the splendid BBC television version?

The new telecommunications devices have made a fantastically rapid change worldwide in human culture. Literature, too, has been radically and irreversibly changed. Downloading and reading on a computer screen, or on a Kindle, or on an iPad, George Eliot's *Middlemarch* or any of the hundreds of thousands of other literary texts now floating in cyberspace is in obvious ways, and in more subtle ways, too, greatly different from reading a literary work in a printed book. This is partly because the digital version is searchable and can be cut and pasted, partly because its material base, its matter, its *subjectile*, as Derrida calls it, is so different.[5] A digital text has a radically different surrounding context. That new context is all the unimaginable heterogeneity of cyberspace as against the neat rows of alphabetized books in a library. Each context has a different form of portability and a different location, or nonlocation. The nonspace of cyberspace accessed by those ghostly letters on a computer screen is strikingly different from a printed book in a private or public library. A printed book is a solid object you can hold in your hands, not evanescent letters on an electronic screen.

The process of inventing literary works has also been radically changed. The underlying matter of literature, its material base, has been revolutionized. For most poets or novelists, no more writing successive drafts by hand on paper with a pen or pencil, then laboriously typing and retyping the text to get a final draft ready to be typeset. This typesetting happened at first, during the early print epoch, letter by letter. Subsequently it was done by linotype, with successive proofs to be read and marked by hand. These were set and then reset again when the second proofs had been checked. That was still the case when I began my scholarly work.

The composition of literary works on the computer has changed all that. The ease of revision of a computer file means that a new literary text is never really finished. It can always be further revised, as I am revising this essay at this moment (5:56 PM, April 16, 2016), and have revised it repeatedly in the past several years. The successive drafts of computer files are, for the most part, lost forever. That puts a whole scholarly industry out of business: the study of early drafts of a given text. This new form of literature exists from the beginning in a quasi-disembodied form, as zeros and ones on a hard drive or in some cloud memory. Though the file may ultimately take print form, that printing is now done flawlessly from a computer file. That file often exists as a PDF. More and more, literary works come out simultaneously in print form and as e-texts. People who read literature at all anymore often choose to read it on line, in another form of the prestidigitalization of literature.

As I said in a book title, *The Medium Is the Maker: Browning, Freud, Derrida and the New Telepathic Technologies*,[6] the mode of materialization of a given literary work fundamentally determines its meaning and its performative force. The matter of literature matters. The new computer medium makes literature radically different from its old self, different, that is, down to its roots, which is what *radical* etymologically means. *Medium* must be taken here in the sense both of a new material base and of a seemingly, but of course not actually, somewhat spooky, spiritualist, mediumistic, telepathic means of transmission. Something speaks to me through the medium, for example, from the computer screen, but by an entirely explicable technological process. Ranjan Ghosh is much less concerned than

I am with the effect of the medium on meaning. At least he writes little about it. For him, just as "the Sacredness of Literature" is perennially valid as a concept of what literature is and what it does, so it does not seem to matter in what medium a given work is encountered. Frost's "Birches" remains Frost's "Birches," whether we read it in printed book or on an iPad, in a digitized version. That is a plausible assumption, but I am arguing otherwise. For me, the medium is an important determinant of meaning.

Strangely enough, one thinks with one's fingers when writing. I am not a creative writer, just someone who writes about, and roundabout, literature, in endless circumlocution. Nevertheless, I have gone through the difficulty of changing from inventing words with a pen in my hand, as I used to do, to inventing them with my fingers on a computer keyboard, as I do habitually now. The latter is happening right now, with the words that are at this moment flowing through my fingers from who knows where in my nervous system, onto the keyboard and then magically appearing on my computer screen. Some impersonal inner voice seems to speak them as they are keyed in. They come into being by an inventive bodily process that is more discovering than deliberately making up, to recall the bifurcated meaning of invention.

Derrida long ago identified literature, in our modern Western sense, with the several centuries of print culture and its attendant technologies, with the appearance of modern democracies and modern capitalism, and with the concomitant rise of a literate middle class granted nominal (I stress nominal) freedom to say and write anything in a literary work and not be held accountable for it.[7] An author could always say, for example, of the narrator of a novel or of the speaker of a lyric poem she or he has written, "That is not me speaking but an imaginary person created out of words." Derrida also long ago prophetically foresaw, in a notable passage in the "Envois" section of *La carte postale: De Socrate à Freud et au-delà*, that computer technology would bring literature, along with a number of important other cultural institutions, to an end. One of Derrida's imaginary postcard writers asserts: "An entire epoch of so-called [*ladite*] literature, if not all of it, cannot survive a certain technological regime of telecommunications (in this respect the political regime is secondary). Neither can philosophy, or psychoanalysis. Or love letters."[8] I use this passage as the epigraph for my chapter 8 in this book and discuss it further there. The technological regime, for Derrida, overpowers any political regime, as we can see in the transformations in North Africa of repressive regimes. These transformations have been made possible, to a considerable degree, by mobile phones. Derrida elsewhere writes in "Envois" about how psychoanalysis, as a quasi-science and as a social institution, would have been radically different if Freud and his associates had been able to communicate by e-mail rather than having to depend on the postal system and the telephone.[9] The same thing can be said of literature. Suppose Shakespeare or Fielding, Wordsworth or Dickens, had been able to compose on the computer and self-publish an e-text version on a personal website or on Facebook! The mind boggles at the thought!

The signs that Derrida was right, that is, the signs of a gradual vanishing of print literature as a cultural force, are everywhere visible, in different degrees and in different ways in each country. I discuss these in some detail in my chapter 8. We do not have time, today, it might well be argued, to worry about whether literature any longer matters. Who cares? How can we justify taking time to care about something so trivial, something that matters so little, when we have such big problems?

I have elsewhere argued for an anachronistic reading of older literary works. I mean by *anachronistic* a reading of literature in the context of our situation today, not by way of some attempt to put oneself back inside the mind-frame of a Renaissance man or woman in order to read Shakespeare, or of a middle-class Victorian to read Dickens or George Eliot.[10] The concept of a uniform period mindset, as in *The Victorian Frame of Mind*, or *The Elizabethan World Picture*, is in any case extremely problematic.[11] Victorian and Elizabethan frames of mind, the evidence shows, were quite heterogeneous. Even if a uniform period mindset existed, why would identifying oneself with it be an attractive thing to try to do, except for literary historians, those putatively impersonal and objective scholars? Why pretend we are still Victorians or Elizabethans? The answer, I suppose, is that it will make us better readers of *Middlemarch* or of Tennyson's *The Princess*, but literary works create their appropriate frames of mind in their readers, a different one for each text, however much explanatory historical footnotes may help. In place of the virtues claimed for the so-called historical imagination, I argue in some detail in chapter 8 that literature matters most for us if it is read for today, and read rhetorically, to some degree as training in ways to spot lies, ideological distortions, and hidden political agendas such as surround us on all sides in the media these days.

I give here one example: NBC evening news, on television in the United States, ends almost every day with another "Making a Difference" segment. These are typically moving human-interest stories about how some person, family, or group is helping neighbors. One typical segment told the story of a family in Texas that is sending $2,000 a month to a family in Alabama in which the breadwinners have lost their jobs and have had their mortgage foreclosed. They were about to lose their home because they could not make the monthly mortgage payments. The father is also being aided in his job search. Who would not admire the charity, the human sympathy, of that family in Texas? The hidden political message, however, drummed in implicitly day after day by ever new versions of such stories, is that we do not need to have higher taxes on rich people and large corporations, better education, regulation of banks, other financial institutions, and credit card companies, and stimulus spending by the Federal government to create jobs, universal health care, control of carbon dioxide emissions, and so on. We do not need these because charitable families in Texas or elsewhere will always save the needy. It is an attractive fantasy.

Teaching people how to read rhetorically those old poems, plays, and novels could make studying literature concentrated training in reading the media. By *rhetorically* I mean teaching literature by way of a distinction between hermeneutics and poetics, what is meant and the way that meaning is expressed. I borrow these terms from Paul de Man, who borrows them from Walter Benjamin and from the *Hermeneutik und Poetik* series of conferences and conference books from the University of Konstanz.[12] De Man claims, correctly, that hermeneutics and poetics are incompatible.

Of course this incompatibility can also be taught by way of items in the new media, for example, by explaining the hidden message in the way the spokespersons in television commercials for oil, gas, and coal are consistently briskly attractive women, or minorities, or bearded intellectuals, not the more or less ruthless and greedy white men who actually run Chevron, Halliburton, the fracking companies, and the rest. Many of the best and most exemplary rhetorical readings, however, are of literary works, or of philosophical and theoretical texts, for example, readings by de Man and Derrida. Literary works, moreover, offer more concentrated and complex examples.

Teaching students how to read in the light of the distinction between poetics and hermeneutics is a way literature can still be brought to matter. This way of teaching students how to read literature is, alas, unlikely to become a widespread program. It is a Utopian dream. This dream may become reality in isolated cases, but most teachers of literature are not taught to teach in that way. Literature, as I have said, is in any case taught less and less in any way at all, at least in the United States. To many people here, literature does not matter.

Now it might be argued that the satisfaction of human beings' insatiable desire for the literary, for the imaginary, that is, for a certain figurative or fictive use of words or other signs, has simply migrated to other media, for example, to films, including animated films, or to video games, or even to punning newspaper headlines, or to television advertising. "A certain figurative or fictive use of words or other signs" is an extremely problematic definition of the literary, by the way, warranting extensive commentary. Derrida is right, I believe, to assert, in his interview with Derek Attridge in *Acts of Literature*, that "there is no text which is literary *in itself.* Literarity is not a natural essence, an intrinsic property of the text. It is the correlative of an intentional relation to the text, an intentional relation which integrates in itself, as a component or an intentional layer, the more or less implicit consciousness of rules which are conventional or institutional—social, in any case."[13] *Intentional*, here, is a Husserlian or phenomenological word naming the orientation of consciousness toward something or other. Newspaper headlines and television ads are often conspicuously witty and imaginative. If Derrida is right, we might well be justified in intending them as manifestations of literarity, that is, taking them as literature. A television commercial often takes the viewer or listener instantly into a conspicuously wacky or slapstick imaginary world, as in the one that shows a little dog rushing back and forth trying to find a safe place to hide a bone. This is an analogue, it turns out, for human beings' search for a safe place to put their money. It is an ad for an investment firm.

Such ads employ an extremely sophisticated set of conventions. They often use animations and other advanced cinematic devices. Most such commercials, by the way, have a large component of outright lies or at least of ideological distortions, as in my example of NBC's "Making a Difference" series, or in the many ads on behalf of oil, gas, and "clean" coal companies. Lies are a potent form of the imaginary. If Shakespeare were resurrected today, he might be creating video games or advertising spots, not writing plays. The digital world is where the big money is.

This migration of literarity is certainly happening, but this movement happens at the expense of literature in the traditional sense. Printed literature is, in the West, gradually becoming a thing of the past.

Let me now get serious and ask again why literature (in the old-fashioned sense of printed poems, plays, and novels) ought still to matter even in these dire times. In order to be more specific, to get closer to the actual matter of literature, let me give a series of citations from the openings of several works, all in English (with one exception) that I claim are literature. Most people worldwide would probably agree that my citations are examples of what is commonly meant by *literature*. I take openings because they strikingly reveal the way each work shows itself to be different, unique, even within the oeuvre of a given author. The opening of each work instantly takes the reader into a distinctive imaginary world cut off from the real world, though a transformation of it. Entering such a world is what I mean by the "pleasures of the imaginary." And an intense pleasure it is! That pleasure is a good in itself. I postpone, for a moment, explaining what I mean by "the imaginary," a phrase so far taken too much for granted in this chapter. In order to illustrate one of my points, I shall call down all my opening lines from cyberspace, downloading each by way of an almost instantaneous Google search:

> *Elsinore. A platform before the castle.*
> FRANCISCO at his post. Enter to him BERNARDO
>
> BERNARDO: Who's there?
> FRANCISCO: Nay, answer me: stand, and unfold yourself.
> BERNARDO: Long live the king!
> FRANCISCO: Bernardo?
> BERNARDO: He.
> FRANCISCO: You come most carefully upon your hour.
> BERNARDO: 'Tis now struck twelve; get thee to bed, Francisco.
> FRANCISCO: For this relief much thanks: 'tis bitter cold,
>   And I am sick at heart.
>
> —Shakespeare, *Hamlet*[14]

> OF MANS FIRST DISOBEDIENCE, AND THE FRUIT
> Of that Forbidden Tree, whose mortal tast
> Brought Death into the World, and all our woe,
> With loss of EDEN, till one greater Man
> Restore us, and regain the blissful Seat,
> Sing Heav'nly Muse
>
> —John Milton, *Paradise Lost*[15]

> IT is a truth universally acknowledged, that a single man in possession of a good fortune must be in want of a wife.
>
> —Jane Austen, *Pride and Prejudice*[16]

> A slumber did my spirit seal;
> I had no human fears:

She seemed a thing that could not feel
The touch of earthly years.

—William Wordsworth, "A Slumber Did My Sprit Seal"[17]

Tears, idle tears, I know not what they mean,
Tears from the depth of some divine despair

—Alfred Lord Tennyson, "Tears, Idle Tears"[18]

Call me Ishmael. Some years ago—never mind how long precisely—having little or no money in my purse, and nothing particular to interest me on shore, I thought I would sail about a little and see the watery part of the world.

—Herman Melville, *Moby-Dick*[19]

"I can never bring myself to believe it, John," said Mary Walker,
the pretty daughter of Mr. George Walker, attorney of Silverbridge.
Walker and Winthrop was the name of the firm, and they were
respectable people, who did all the solicitors' business that had
to be done in that part of Barsetshire on behalf of the Crown, were
employed on the local business of the Duke of Omnium who is great in
those parts, and altogether held their heads up high, as provincial
lawyers often do. They,—the Walkers,—lived in a great brick
house in the middle of the town, gave dinners, to which the county
gentlemen not unfrequently condescended to come, and in a mild way
led the fashion in Silverbridge. "I can never bring myself to believe
it, John," said Miss Walker.
"You'll have to bring yourself to believe it," said John, without
taking his eyes from his book.
"A clergyman,—and such a clergyman too!"

—Anthony Trollope, *The Last Chronicle of Barset*[20]

Suddenly I saw the cold and rook-delighting heaven
That seemed as though ice burned and was but the more ice . . .

—W. B. Yeats, "The Cold Heaven"[21]

Longtemps, je me suis couché de bonne heure. Parfois, à peine ma bougie éteinte, mes yeux se fermaient si vite que je n'avais pas le temps de me dire: "Je m'endors."

—Marcel Proust, *À la recherche du temps perdu*[22]

In Hydaspia, by Howzen
Lived a lady, Lady Lowzen,
For whom what is was other things.
—Wallace Stevens, "Oak Leaves Are Hands"[23]

Well, there is literature for you, the real right thing! I could extend the list indefinitely, in a litany of remembered literary pleasures. Do those pleasures matter? What makes reading them pleasurable? Is it a guilty pleasure? I stress seven features my examples share:

*Each is markedly different from all the others. Each is unique, incommensurable with the others, even though each in one way or another uses perfectly ordinary words that name things and actions familiar in the real world. Those words are, nevertheless, here transformed. They are appropriated to name imaginary worlds that have no referential correlates in the real world. You can meet Lady Lowzen and visit Howzen only in Stevens's poem, even though "by Howzen" is a play on the German or Pennsylvania Dutch phrase *bei Hausen*, meaning "next door." The imaginary is next door to the real. All the informative, realist specificity of *The Last Chronicle of Barset*'s masterly opening lines is a sham, and readers know it is a sham. No Walker family and no apparently felonious Rev. Josiah Crawley exist anywhere but in the pages of the novel, or, rather, in the imaginary realm to which those words on the page give the reader access.

*Each citation provides entrance into a distinctive imaginary world by the magic "open sesame!" of a few inaugural words. These words work like Alice's passing through the big mirror into the looking-glass world at the beginning of Carroll's *Through the Looking-Glass, and What Alice Found There*.

*This entry into the imaginary happens "suddenly," to borrow Yeats' word. It happens in an instant, in a decisive break with whatever may have preceded the reading of these particular words, for example, the reading of a previous example. It is a plunge in medias res, but into strange and alien things, like finding oneself suddenly in a foreign country.

*Each opening passage, in one way or another, conspicuously uses figurative transfers or plays on words, though not in any predictable or uniform way.

*The effect on the reader, on me as reader, at least, is to create an almost irresistible compulsion to go on reading in order to find out what happens next. These inaugural instants are each, in one way or another, enigmatic, puzzling, partly because leaping into the middle of things seems in each case to presuppose all sorts of things the reader does not yet know, for example, the name of the presumably felonious clergyman, Josiah Crawley, in the opening of Trollope's *Last Chronicle*. You want to go on reading to find those things out, to orient yourself. Each example, moreover, is, in a different way in each case, clearly the beginning of some kind of narrative, a story. Human beings, we know, love stories.

*Though the reader knows perfectly well, or thinks he or she knows, that each fictive realm is created by the language that tells of it, nevertheless, it seems, in my experience at least, but only seems, that each realm has been there all along. It seems to have been waiting somewhere to be entered and described with the open sesame of so-called literary language. Invention, as making up, seems, fallaciously, to be invention as discovering, as the antithetical Latin word, *inventio*, can also mean.

*Each inaugural passage, though, in a different way in each case, even Shakespeare's *Hamlet,* by way of its stage directions, creates the illusion of a speaking or writing voice, a storyteller. Nevertheless, even when, as in many of my examples, that voice speaks explicitly as an "I" the narrative voice is characterized by a certain strange impersonality. This speaking or writing enunciator is like that strange voice that speaks within me, to a considerable degree out of my control, the words I am writing down at this moment. The words come from who knows where and are spoken within me by who knows what impersonal linguistic power. I take responsibility for them, but they are not me speaking, any more than the real person Herman Melville speaks or writes, "Call me Ishmael."

Maurice Blanchot, in a notable essay, called this strangely alien voice, a voice already coming from a fictive or imaginary world, "La voix narrative (le 'il,' le neutre)" (The narrative voice, the "he," the neutral).[24] I shall return later in this chapter to a more extended discussion of Blanchot's theories of narrative. Blanchot is, in my judgment, one of the greatest literary critics and theorists of the twentieth century. His work has had a considerable influence over the years on my own conceptions of literary theory and of literary criticism. Hegel, Émile Benveniste, Paul de Man, and, most recently, John Namjun Kim have in different ways brought into the open the abyssal ambiguity, duplicity, or, better, "ironic undecidability," of the words for the ego in different Western languages. This especially so when they are used in openly literary texts, as in so many of my examples.[25] One conspicuous example is Yeats's "Suddenly I saw." The "I" who speaks in a literary text seems at first to be a person, a self, perhaps the self of the author, but reveals itself to be at the same time an empty placeholder ("eine leere Flasche") for anybody, in the end for nobody but an impersonal power of literary speech, Blanchot's "neutral."

To develop this line of thought adequately would take another long essay, but I break the line now by citing the two wonderfully vertiginous passages de Man cites and comments on from Hegel's *Enzyklopädie der philosophischen Wissenschaften* in "Sign and Symbol in Hegel's *Aesthetics*": "So kann ich nicht sagen was ich nur meinen," which de Man translates as meaning, among other things, "I cannot say what I make mine," "I cannot say what I think," and "I cannot say I." I add: "So I cannot say what I only (or simply) mean." The other passage from Hegel de Man calls a "quite astonishing sentence," as indeed it is: "Ebenso, wenn ich sage: 'Ich,' meine ich mich als diesen alle anderen Ausschließenden: aber was ich sage, Ich, ist eben einen jeder" ('When I say "I," I *mean* myself as *this* I to the exclusion of all others; but what I say, I, is precisely anyone; any I, as that which excludes all others from itself').[26] The great Hegel, master of pure reason, has here stumbled into the abyss that lies beneath the innocent word *I*, as well as into the way repeated phonemes call attention to themselves as pure sound: "Wenn ich sage: 'Ich,' meine ich mich."

It is a universal feature of so-called literary texts, or of any piece of language taken as literature, intended as literature, read as literature, different from one another as they all are, that in them the *I* of the author is transformed into an impersonal, anonymous, neutral, neutered power of language, an empty flask. An everyday and seemingly innocent example of this transformation is the familiar omniscient, or, better, telepathic, narrator of canonical English novels.[27] Among my examples, the narrators of Austen's *Pride and Prejudice* and of Trollope's *The Last Chronicle of Barset* illustrate this. Trollope's *Framley Parsonage*, discussed in chapter 10 here, is another example. The anonymity and undecidability of such language is evident in the pervasive irony of fictional narrative voices. "Was ich sage, Ich, ist eben jeder." ("What I say, I, is precisely anyone.")

Of just what kind of matter are the imaginary worlds entered by this strange literary use of language made? Why does crossing a border and entering them matter? I have so far used the words *fictive* and *imaginary* interchangeably. Most people, even literary theorists from Aristotle on, assume that a fictive text takes words from the everyday real world and uses them to name, by imitation (mimesis), a virtual reality that has no referential counterpart, even though real persons, places, and events may often be transposed into the fictive.

Matters are not quite so simple, however. Just here, work by two unlikely theoretical bedfellows, Maurice Blanchot and Wolfgang Iser, will help my formulations. I have in mind Blanchot's *Les deux versions de l'imaginaire* (Two versions of the imaginary) and his "Le chant des Sirènes" (The Song of the Sirens").[28] For Iser, I shall focus on a late work, *Das Fiktive und das Imaginäre* (*The Fictive and the Imaginary*).[29] Both Blanchot and Iser, in different ways, but in ways that are in unexpected resonance, propose a triad rather than a doublet of just two terms, *real* and *fictive*. Iser names the elements of this triad: the real, the fictive, and the imaginary. What Iser says in the preface and in the first chapter, "Fictionalizing Acts," of *The Fictive and the Imaginary* is complex. It is at a high level of abstraction. It may, however, be summarized as follows: Iser contests the long tradition, with its many permutations going back to Aristotelian mimesis, defining the fictive more or less exclusively in terms of its oppositional or dialectical relation to the real. Iser asserts that a third term, "the imaginary," must be invoked. The imaginary, he says, "is basically a featureless and inactive potential" in human beings for dreams, "fantasies, projections, daydreams, and other reveries," as well as for activating fictions. The imaginary is, in a phrase not translated into the English version, "*diffus, formlos, unfixiert und ohne Objektreferenz*": diffuse, formless, unfixed, and without objective reference.[30] Iser's imaginary must not be thought of as in any way a transcendent entity, a divine realm of potential forms. Iser's thinking is resolutely areligious, anti-idealist. In spite of Ghosh's somewhat unusual use of the word "sacred," what Iser says is, somewhat unexpectedly, not altogether different, at least according to my understanding, from Ghosh's definition of "the Sacred of Literature." For Iser, the imaginary is an exclusively human potential. Ghosh insists that his sacred of literature is not religious in the usual sense. In a note to me, Ghosh explains this clearly: "For me 'sacred' is the unique imaginary that literature keeps close to its heart. We read literature, interpret it, make sense of it and yet there is something to which literature does not allow easy access.

This is the 'sacred' which keeps our interest in literature alive and endows literature with the power to attract us forever. So every time you read Tennyson's poem the text 'puzzles' you; this puzzlement comes from what I call the 'sacred' of the poem. The poem always leaves something behind for you every time to seek to 'resolve' your puzzlement. The 'sacred' of the poem is its 'comeback power'!"

Nor are the real, the fictive, or the imaginary thought of by Iser as purely linguistic entities. Though he recognizes that literary texts, as embodiments of the fictive, are made of words, and though he talks a lot about "semantics," Iser appears to have a prejudice against language-based literary theories. He says firmly and categorically: "Wer Sprache verstehen will, mehr als nur Sprache verstehen muß" ("Whoever wants to understand language must understand more than just language").[31] That sounds plausible enough, but it tends to lead Iser to downplay the constitutive role of language in generating fictions. He says, for example: "Daraus ergibt sich die für jeden fiktionalen Text notwendige Selektion aus den vorhandenen Umweltsystemen, seien diese sozio-kultureller Natur oder solche der Literatur selbst" ("Every literary text inevitably contains a selection from a variety of social, historical, cultural, and literary systems that exist as referential fields outside the text").[32] The literary text, however, it is easy to see, does not contain items from those systems as such. It uses, rather, the names for them, as Iser's phrases *literary systems* and *referential fields* do, after all, imply.

Iser, in the German original cited above, calls these referential fields the *Umweltsystemen*, a word not easily translated into English. "Contextual systems" misses the force of *Umwelt* as "surrounding world." "Surrounding-world-systems" is a more literal translation of *Umweltsystemen*, but is not good English. The fictive set of borrowings from the surrounding world systems, however, does not simply provide new critical perspectives on the real, though Iser allows for the importance of that function of literature. Literature brackets and outstrips reality by using elements from it to give form to the formless imaginary. That is its chief function. "Reality, then, may be reproduced in a fictional text, but it is there in order to be outstripped, as is indicated by its being bracketed."[33] The essential function of the fictive "as if" is to give quasimateriality to the diffuseness of the imaginary: "Our subsequent journey to new horizons translates the imaginary into an experience—an experience that is shaped by the degree of determinacy given to the imaginary by the fictional 'as-if.'"[34] The literary text, as defined by Iser with another quasitechnical term, is "the pragmatization of the imaginary."[35] The matrix of the literary text is not the real and it is not fictive language. It is rather "the multiplicitous availability of the imaginary."[36] In giving pragmatic embodiment to the formless imaginary, the fictive outstrips language. Here is another example of Iser's suspicion of language-based theories: "Thus the cardinal points of the text defy verbalization," says Iser in the final sentences of "Fictionalizing Acts," "and it is only through these open structures within the linguistic patterning of the text that the imaginary can manifest its presence. From this fact we can deduce one last achievement of the fictive in the fictional text: It brings about the presence of the imaginary by transgressing language itself. In outstripping what conditions it, the imaginary reveals itself as the generative matrix of the text [*als den Ermöglichungsgrund des Textes*]."[37] *Generative matrix*, as a name for the imaginary, must be read with the full force of the obstetric image in *matrix* as "mothering source." I have given a little of the original German for my citations from Iser because the English translations, accurate though they are, do not give the distinctive idiomatic flavor of Iser's German terms.

This all makes perfect sense. It is a magnificently persuasive and original theory of the imaginary, one that, so far as I know, has no close parallels either in work by other scholars today or in the long Western tradition of wrestling to define the fictive as-if. It does, however, resonate to a considerable degree with Ghosh's transcultural and transcontinental (in)fusionist approach to literature. I stress "to a considerable degree" because both Iser and Ghosh have distinctive ways of expressing what they want to say. Iser's "imaginary" and Blanchot's "image" (discussed below) are not quite the same as Ghosh's "sacredness," but all three do resonate.

Just what human good is achieved by the fictive? Why do human beings need fictions? Iser's answer is unequivocal. Though the fictive may give us new critical perspectives on the real, and though it may also be a pleasure in itself, its most important function is to expand the number of "pragmatizations" of that basic human "plasticity" Iser calls "the imaginary." That human beings are essentially to be defined by their plasticity is Iser's fundamental anthropological assumption. "If the plasticity of human nature allows," he avers in his preface, "through its multiple culture-bound patternings, limitless human self-cultivation, literature becomes a panorama of what is possible, because it is not hedged in by either the limitations or the considerations that determine the institutionalized organizations within which human life otherwise takes its course."[38] Fulfilling as many as possible of the limitless ways to be human is a good in itself. Using fictionalizing acts as a means of giving form to the formless plasticity of the imaginary is the best way to do that.

This gives one answer to the question of whether literature matters. We should read literature now and at any other time because doing so is the best form of limitless human self-cultivation. How should we read literature? By opening ourselves to the imaginary worlds literary works make available. For Iser, the chief value of literature, the reason literature matters, is the pleasure of the fictive as a pragmatization of the imaginary. It has its source (its generative matrix) in the imaginary, but enjoying it and being influenced by its perspectives on the real can become additional ends in themselves. Iser investigates a signal example of this in the second chapter of *The Fictive and the Imaginary*: the European Renaissance pastoral, as both social critique and a pleasure to read.

The closest thing that I know in Western literary theory of the twentieth century to Iser's idea of the imaginary is Maurice Blanchot's concept of the imaginary in the essays I have mentioned, and in many other of his essays, too. A full reading of Blanchot's idea of the imaginary would take many pages, no doubt a long book. I limit myself to brief and somewhat oversimplifying remarks. In place of Iser's more or less unproblematic word *fictive*, as a name for the nature of literary language, Blanchot puts a subtle theory of "the image." This is his name for the essence of the imaginary as embodied in literary language. For Blanchot, the imaginary is made of images or glimpsed through images. Speaking, for example, in a characteristic torrent of paradoxes, of Proust's breakthrough when two sensations coincided in a time out of time that made it possible for him to become a writer at last, Blanchot says: "Yes, at this time, everything becomes image, and the essence of the image is to be entirely outside, without intimacy, and yet more inaccessible and more mysterious than the innermost thought; without signification, but summoning the profundity of every possible meaning; unrevealed and yet manifest, having that presence-absence that constitutes the attraction and the fascination of the Sirens."[39]

As opposed to Iser's cheerful celebration of fictive pragmatizations of the imaginary as benignly fulfilling limitless human plasticity, Blanchot's imaginary is a dangerous vanishing point within which one might be swallowed up and disappear. This danger is figured in the threat to Ulysses of the Sirens' song. Blanchot tends to indentify the imaginary with death or with an often-repeated motif in his work: the endless process of dying.[40] The imaginary also exists as *le récit* [the narrative], as opposed to the evasions of the novel. Blanchot's examples in the essays I have cited are Ulysses in his approach toward, or refusal to approach, the real song behind the Sirens' infinitely luring song, Proust's Marcel in his search for lost time, and Ahab's pursuit of the white whale in *Moby-Dick*. Here I let Blanchot, now a voice from the grave, speak, mostly in English translation, for himself, or itself:

> The narrative begins where the novel does not go but still leads us by its refusals and its rich negligence. The narrative is heroically and pretentiously the narrative of one single episode, that of Ulysses' meeting and the insufficient and magnetic song of the Sirens. . . . Narrative is not the relating of an event but this event itself, the approach of this event, the place where it is called on to unfold, an event still to come, by the magnetic power of which the narrative itself can hope to come true. . . . Narrative is the movement toward a point—one that is not only unknown, ignored, and foreign, but such that it seems, even before and outside of this movement, to have no kind of reality; yet one that is so imperious that it is from this point alone that the narrative draws its attraction, in such a way that it cannot even "begin" before having reached it; but it is only the narrative and the unforeseeable movement of the narrative that provide the space where the point becomes real, powerful, and alluring.[41]

The reader will note how Blanchot's point, like Iser's imaginary, is not entirely unlike Ghosh's sacredness of literature. One might add as further examples of *récit* (narrative) given by Blanchot the ambiguous ending of Proust's great novel and Ahab's climactic death-dealing reencounter with Moby-Dick in Melville's masterwork. You will see how close Blanchot is to Iser, and yet how far away from one another they are in tone and valence. What is for Blanchot a somewhat sinister attraction to a vanishing point that he identifies with death is for Iser a happy materialization of limitless human plasticity. For both, however, a third realm, the imaginary, must be added to the real and to the fictive transposition of that real. For both, the true function of literature is to put the reader in relation either to Iser's imaginary as a "potential" that is "formless and diffuse, unfixed, and without objective reference," "featureless and inactive," or in relation to Blanchot's unknown, obscure, foreign, dangerous point from which the récit begins.

Both Blanchot and Iser, however, allow, in spite of their differences, for two other ways in which literature matters. First, literature gives the reader critical perspectives on the real (including the most urgent political and social realities: dangerous income inequality, prolonged global recession and catastrophic climate change today, for example). Literature does this by means of transposing the real into the fictive. Second, literature gives an irreplaceable pleasure in itself, a pleasure Blanchot identifies with the novel: "With the novel, the preliminary voyage is foregrounded, that which carries Ulysses to the point of encounter. This voyage is an entirely human story; it concerns the time of men, it is linked to the passions of men, it actually takes place, and it is rich enough and varied enough to absorb all the strength and all the attention of the narrators."[42] The wonderful specificity of Homer's *Odyssey* is Blanchot's example here. I might well have cited its opening invocation myself except that it was hardly a printed book in its original form. Today all but a few lucky people, moreover, know the *Odyssey* only in modern printed translations. The epic invocations at the beginnings of the *Odyssey* and of *Paradise Lost* are striking examples of the way another voice is experienced as speaking through the author in literary texts. So here is one more open sesame. Homer begins the *Odyssey*, in Robert Fitzgerald's translation, with these words: "Sing in me, Muse, and through me tell the story/of that man skilled in all ways of contending."[43] The *Odyssey* is not Homer speaking. It is the Muse speaking through him, ventriloquizing him, making him its medium.

I am greatly attracted by Iser's and Blanchot's forceful articulation of their triads, though with awareness of their not-quite-perfect congruence, and with some lingering anxiety about affirming something so far outside everyday assumptions, even by teachers of literature, not to speak of journalists, about why literature might matter today. I have expressed my resistance to Ghosh's use of the term *sacred* to characterize literature, since my own usage of the word is so different. I have recognized, however, somewhat to my surprise, that Iser and Blanchot, neither greatly influenced by Hindu thought about *sahitya*, so far as I know, affirm something not entirely unlike Ghosh's transcultural concept of literature. *Sacred* is a word for secular literature that neither Iser nor Blanchot nor I would use. What they say is nevertheless undeniably in resonance with what Ghosh says. I leave the reader of our two chapters to work out the larger implications of this resonance.

I have stressed in this essay, as does Ghosh, the sheer pleasures of reading literature, along with present dangers to the survival of printed literature. Literature matters because it serves three essential human functions: social critique, the pleasure of the text, and a materialization of the imaginary or an endless approach to the unapproachable imaginary.

Though human civilization would not come to an end if literature in the old-fashioned sense of printed books were to vanish in an age of prestidigitalization, much would be lost that video games, films, television, popular songs, and Facebook can hardly replace. That is so even though these new media are also, in their own ways, alternative forms conjoining in their dispersal the real, the fictive, and the imaginary.

PART II

Poem and Poetry

THE STORY OF A POEM

You have imposed the rules of your logic upon us; lying in poetry supersedes truthfulness.

—al-Buhturi

Why don't you study The Book of Poetry? Poetry can serve to inspire (*xing*), to reflect (*guan*), to communicate (*qun*) and to admonish (*yuan*).

—Confucius to his disciples

There is a scene from a film whose director I cannot remember, a boy is chasing his girl friend in a cab, racing alongside the train where the girl sits. Her hair blowing in the wind, and then the cab has a puncture. The boy gets out, closes the cab door and starts running. And he outruns the train, running straight into the horizon, while the train chugs along behind. The speed of his need was faster than any speed the train could ever hope to achieve! That's where it (the scene) becomes poetry.

—Joy Goswami

The Story Begins

The story begins on a note of anxiety, not particularly on a crest, for one cannot deny the career of the poem as having hit an undulation in our times, when speed is the cult of living and uptight alertness is preferred over sensitivity. Christopher Clausen points out that poetry "is widely distrusted for two contradictory reasons: it is at once too simple in its language to be very important, and too difficult in its figurative qualities to be understood."[1] Riding the cyber revolution, we now have increased accessibility to major poetic writings, accessed through poetry archives that have, consequently, improved the visibility of poetry in the public space. Dana Gioia observes that "although conventional wisdom portrays the rise of electronic media and the relative decline of print as a disaster for all kinds of literature, this situation is largely beneficial for poetry. It has not created a polarized choice between spoken and printed information. Both media coexist in their many often-overlapping forms. What the new technology has done is slightly readjust the contemporary sensibility in favor of sound and orality."[2] I concur with Gioia about the possibility that electronic media has generated far greater nonspecialist encounters with poetry, both in and out of the academy. Gioia finds "an opportunity of recentering the art on an aesthetic that combines the pleasures of oral media and richness of print culture, that draws from tradition without being limited by the past, that embraces form and narrative without rejecting the experimental heritage of Modernism, and that recognizes the necessary interdependence of high and popular culture."[3] Despite a life in the new aesthetic, a fresh tradition of reading and experiencing poetry, I am not very ecstatic about the future of serious meditative poetry in the Indian subcontinent. A good poem is a serious art, complex and compelling. Patience and taste for a good poem are at a premium, but the consternation over its complete extinction does not look a reality yet.

Clausen notes that technical innovation and consequent spaces of recreation and experimentation have hit our concept of literary generation hard where "each poetic cell" is "jealously isolated from every other cell," giving "birth to new cells through mitosis."[4] I don't agree with the thought that there is a dramatic decline of interest in poetry but surely pitch myself with the lugubrious note that underpins the collective disinterest for serious poetry and the hollowing out of a sensibility and fine patience that poetry has always demanded from its readers and has needed for its own survival. The possible ambit of the audience for poetry has extended, but the committed poetry-reading community has shrunk. Poetic sentiment has been struggling to find its real home. Its generic importance has conspicuously downsized.

Poetry in the Indian subcontinent is largely confined to departments of literature and other regional language publications. It has somewhere lost its touch with our soul, with our readerly curiosity and habitation. It shows a kind of disconnect with the life that people ordinarily live, because what is poetry today is mostly elitist, self-indulging, subculturish, and cryptic to the general reading public. Poetry readership is sharply divided among the curious and cerebral institutional minority as against a sneering and restless majority. People have no time to join readings, appreciate the rare occasions when such functions are organized. A poem demands a separate kind of thought, a different rhythm of thinking, a distinct strain of sensibility and perseverance with language. Is a poem beautiful only because it is commonly understood and generally intelligible?

Poetry does not receive its due share of institutionalized love during the years when it ought to: students in high school in India read a poem as effectively as reading Alexander's invasions in India or Newton's laws of falling bodies. A poem is preponderantly treated as a mechanism to be understood, committed to memory, and competently ventilated through examination modules. Undergraduate courses in Indian colleges make poetry a segregated domain within literature departments. A poem, most students think, is either too easy (for instance, William Blake's "The Lamb") or so disturbingly challenging (like T. S. Eliot's "The Waste Land") that reading becomes routine and no longer fun. Most of us lost the fun with poems quite early in our lives.

The problem that I find in most good poetry written today is the imbalance between world consciousness—be it cultural, political, or social—and a peculiar penchant to be idiosyncratic and convoluted. This has generated a disconnect with the common understanding of poetry, washing it away from the common currency of reading into a world where most readers balk at the threshold. The Indian part of the poem's story is mostly about struggling to join the two ends, the diversity of the content in the largest democracy of the world and the overly private and entangled form in which a poem is created. Subject and expression often do not harmonize, resulting in most poems being written without readers. A poem is not for the poet alone but is surely an art that enriches in sharing, vitalizes in communication, sustains in readerly revisits. Not that all poetry written in the subcontinent is soft in the center and is mere expression of a poetic affect. Good poetry has become rare and bad poetry in its profusion and permeability has made poetic experience avoidable; it has prevented the formation of a sensible readership. A poem cannot be read with literacy alone. A poem needs education, a cultivation of a different kind of mind and taste. Regretfully, the nation that can take pride in Kalidasa, Rabindranath Tagore, Jibanananda Das, Agha Sahid Ali, A. K. Ramanujan, Jayanta Mahapatra, and many others—the list can be long and illustrious—has more readers than ever before but has lost the taste of *living* with a poem.

So poetry is produced at the expense of a poem. Writing a poem is not like writing a dissertation accented on a specific discourse. A poem has its laws and also a life in lawlessness. Are publishers looking for poems written in a particular way? Is publishing poetry close to being a predestined project? I wonder how much of public and private funding, writers in residence programs, creative writing fellowships, exist for the poets in India today. Apart from a couple of private universities and Jadavpur University, there is no creative writing faculty: no professional appointments in literature departments will consider the candidate's profile in creative writing because, unfortunately, an essay published in a middle segment academic journal will always be privileged over writings published in magazines like *Granta*. Unlike the American poetry scene, the issue of reading poetry in India is spread and operated across regional languages—a country which has a huge population of *bhasakabita* (language poets, i.e., poets who do not have polylingual presence). Regional languages can sometimes preclude poems from leaping over fences of culture and communities. I am not talking in the sense of globalizing a poem. But the anxiety of nativism, at times, may prove inhibitive by way of a certain ideological embargo. Consequently, the reading of poetry becomes a part of a subculture, a minority act, restricted and sectarian. English-language poets have their visibility but a restricted readership because poets read poets and so do scholars, forming a select and specialized community. A poem has more means to reach the public now but attention to poetry has not altered significantly.

Dana Gioia notes that "for most newspapers and magazines, poetry has become a literary commodity intended less to be read than to be noted with approval. Most editors run poems and poetry reviews the way a prosperous Montana rancher might keep a few buffalo around—not to eat the endangered creatures but to display them for tradition's sake."[5] Poems are for poets, friends of the poets, for a minority claiming sensitivity to poetry: a great poem rarely speaks to the common man. Perhaps educated readership is also shying away from poetry, because, strangely, patience with poems is a casualty before the cult of speed in our age. Why do not people try to rethink what a poem has to say? If a computer has its own language, if a book manuscript has its own negotiations with a style sheet for a camera-ready copy, by what logic should a poem dumb its expressive powers down to a level where getting the readers' attention becomes more its responsibility than the commitment of its readers? But I refuse to admit that all poetry has become irrelevant; perhaps, the decline is more in the neglect that the mainstream metes out to poetry. The story of the novel is more attractive today than the story of the poem.

Edwin Muir, in *The Estate of Poetry*, looks into the role of the poets to make their poems less obscure, espouse great themes and have them treated clearly. But clearness in a poem is a different kind of clearing; a poem is not a documentation of experience, not necessarily a discursive treatment of a subject. Its alethic and disclosive power can be reasons for its excellence and subsequent alienation. Muir warns that "there remains the temptation for poets to turn inward into poetry, to lock themselves into a hygienic prison where they speak only to one another, and to the critic."[6] But does not a poem also generate its own relish through inwardness? Wendell Berry's observations are too apposite to ignore:

> We would be ungrateful and stupid to turn our backs on the work of inward-turned poets. That work contains much of value that we need to cherish and learn from. It is only necessary to understand that that work has flourished upon, and has fostered, a grievous division between life and work, as have virtually all the other specialized disciplines of our time, and that that division has made it possible for work to turn upon and exploit and destroy life. There is in reality no such choice as Yeats's "Perfection of the life, or of the work." The decision to sacrifice either one for the sake of the other becomes ultimately the fatal disease of both. The division implied by this proposed choice is destructive because it is based upon a misconception of the relation between work and life. The perfections of work rise out of, and commune with and in turn inform, the perfections of life—as Yeats himself knew and as other poems of his testify. The use of life to perfect work is an evil of the specialized intellect. It makes of the most humane of disciplines an exploitive industry.[7]

Poetry, then, is "an empty basket: you put your life into it and make something out of that."[8] The poet's feeling the world makes the poem worldly, that is, closer in themes to the taste and preferences of its readers. When poetry was a tribal business and an integral part of religious ceremonies (poetry festivals were funded, fostered, and feted) the poem had more people to acknowledge its stories and its existence was far more intensely materialized. Living with a poem was a soothing option, a recreational alternative to existential encounters. However, caught in the "pranks and easements of technology," the poem no longer disturbs: indeed, its disturbance is scarcely given its worthy dues. But in our times, we need a poem because technology has, unfortunately, touched our body but never much our emotions, the inner recesses of our thinking, the epiphany of our daily wear and tear. Mary Oliver has her fingers exactly on the nerves I am alluding to: "We need those orderings of thought, those flare-ups of imagination, those sounds of the body and its feelings, proclaiming our sameness, calling the tribal soul together. The man out there, cutting the grass, is more astute than we give him credit for. He knows that the poem must transcend its particular origin and become a poem about his life. He goes on, cutting the straight rows, apparently not listening. But when the poem is his, he will fall headlong into it and be refreshed and begin listening for more."[9] The transcendence, the plunge, the dream, the transmutation, and the listening aestheticize a poem's calling. It is a story or stories that might make the common audience shrivel but that should not in any way discourage us from the retelling. The tale told in the following pages is not a repeat of what got told in the past: the story unfolds, grows, and stops but only to carve another beginning.

Act I

A poem is never lost. Finding a poem permanently is difficult, too. Shrinking readership and dwindling publishing interests influence but cannot configure the essential story of the poem. A poem is no hermetic possession of a culture and nation alone. *Rasa*-experience can let the story of the poem overflow traditions, thoughts, and theories to make sense of its exemplarity.[10] What follows is my experience and understanding of a story told dialogically, across cultures and traditions whose dimensions are varied and vibrant, delicate and disturbing. How can the story of a poem be made to unfold so that reading poetry is not determinatively judged with the economy and commerce of production, with the collaborative indispensability of a career with the printing press, and the visibility granted by an acknowledging multitude?

Lu Ji writes:

At the beginning of the process of writing,
The poet closes himself to sight and sound,
Deeply he contemplates, widely he enquires in spirit;
His spirit roams in the eight directions,
His mind traverses a distance of thousands of ancient yards.
When the opportune moment to write arrives,
The poet's feelings gradually dawn to increasing clarity,
And objects become clear and present themselves to him
in a stable order.[11]

Here begins the story, a very complicated, delectable, and fine-spun story of inspiration, skill, and mystery, touching unusual elegance and depth.

When Jibanananda Das (1899–1954), one of the most prominent modern Bengali poets in the post-Tagorean era, writes, "All are not poets: only a few are," in his *Kobitar katha* (The story of a poem) the exemplarity of a poem's coming into being is boldly vindicated.[12] I would add to that by saying that all of us cannot be readers of poetry; some are and it is because of such readers that poetry has survived. A great poem is not for all. (Sylvia Plath writes: "Surely the great use of poetry is its pleasure—not its influence as religious and political propaganda. . . . I am not worried that poems reach relatively few people. As it is, they go surprisingly far—among strangers, around the world, even.)[13] A great poet speaks to all but is not understood by everyone. Das points out that a poem is more than an inspiration, certainly more than a divine inspiration. A poem is not just about writing poetry. People who think that a poem can be best written after one has educated herself in the native traditions and in the past and present of his or her poetic culture are destined to be on a wrong path. A poem is a moment, a flicker of the candle light against a world in fragments and disarray, a pause where the experience of it gradually moistens the heart and wells up in the head. Any desertion of this experience forbids the birth of a poem; it does not forbid the writing of poetry, though. It initiates the debates and arguments that poetry can bring through its deeply encompassive association with the world. A poem cannot always be discouraged from engaging with the circumambient world of politics, ideologies, thoughts on culture, religion, and society. Many great poems have constituted themselves through such investments. However, Das believes in a method where the poet cannot begin with a conscious submission to congeries of thoughts and discourses, a decisive devotion to established patterns of thinking; even if the poet does begin with conscious submission, it is the radiance of imagination that redeems such prefabricated, thoughtful drive. Allegiance to such strains of thought must hide the dominant beauty of a poem like blood corpuscles, veins, and arteries. A poem can unveil the problems and issues of life, but the unveiling is not conducted as if by a social scientist but in beauty, through satisfactions of the desires of imagination. Eliseo Vivas notes that "what the poem says or means is the world it reveals or discloses in and through itself, a new world, whose features, prior to the act of poetic revelation, were concealed from us and whose radiance and even identity will again be concealed from us the moment our intransitive attention lapses and we return to the world of affairs and of things in which we normally live."[14] This is the *kavya rasa* (the *rasa* generally associated with poetry) that is to be distinguished from the emotive experiences generated out of mere studious encounters with culture, science, and history.

Visvanatha, in *Sahityadarpana* (one of the most important treatises in Sanskrit poetic theory, written in the late fourteenth century) considers poetry the soul, a kind of ordered, harmonious organism that can be understood through the congruence and consonance of parts to the whole and also through the whole itself. Poetic composition is both a process and a project for closer (functional) examination that eventualizes in the production of *rasa*. Bharata, in *Nāṭya Śāstra*, written during the period between 200 BCE and 200 CE, in classical India, points out that without *rasa* there is no *artha* (meaning). A poem without *rasa* is unthinkable. Visvanatha considers the existence of *rasa* equivalent to the experience of *rasa*; a poem builds its own taste much the way it is appreciated by a "man of taste" with his learning, experience, and understanding of *jibon* (life) and sahitya. *Rasa* ensures that the poem has a life in its readers. Understanding *rasa* is synonymous with the understanding of a poem. Visvanatha identifies certain features for *rasa*: heightening of *sattva* (truth, goodness), its self-revelatory power, its ability to produce joy, thought, and wonder. *Rasa*, thus, inculcates a kind of intelligibility, the poetic intelligibility. Honeywell argues that "in terms of the distinction between potentiality and actuality, the parts of a poetic composition fall into a hierarchy. The sentences, in both their representational capacity and their stylistic forms, are necessary conditions for the representation of conditions, consequents, and transitory feelings; these three parts are necessary conditions for the representation of a dominant emotion; and the dominant emotion, in turn, is the necessary condition for the experience of *rasa*. It is as the ultimate member of this hierarchy that rasa is said to exist as the actualization of the full potentiality of the poetic composition."[15] *Rasa* is indivisible and contributes to the unification of the poetic experience. But it is a unity that is difficult to analyze because *rasa* is considered indivisible. Parts of a poem, Visvanatha argues, are analyzable where each part contributes to the experience of the whole. But the whole is a *rasa* experience that exceeds analyzability and yet makes for the organization of the poem, its principle of order and orientation. *Artha* (meaning), as Bharata has argued, is deeply housed in *rasa*, which then functions as a poetic necessity. A great poem, as Ramaranjan Mukherjee points out, will have five elements: *rasa*, *dhvani* (suggestion, resonance), *aucitya* (propriety), *vakrata* (poetic deviance), and aesthetic unity.[16] Mukherjee works this out through a reading of Keats's "Ode on a Grecian Urn," demonstrating how the *adbhuta* (marvelous) leads to *vibhava* (development of a particular state of mind), then to *anubhava* (direct perception or cognition), and finally to the experience of the quietistic (*santarasa*). Working through profound suggestiveness, the poem, in the end, provides an aesthetic relish in *santarasa* (the calm, the poise), an equanimity provided through the coming together of beauty and truth. The whole poem, Mukherjee points out, "has emerged as a single aesthetic entity and when the appreciative reader gets absorbed in the Ode he neither remains conscious of the division of the poem into parts nor of the exact distinction between the explicit and the implicit."[17] So poetic meaning is a compound experience that cannot always remain open to the common minds. The immediate meaning is not enough to make the ultimate sense of a poem. This *rasadi* (the *rasa* mode) is integrally connected with *kavi-vyapara* (creative workings of the poet's mind).

To what *kavyarasa* are Lu Ji (261–303), Tao Qian (365–427), and Liu Xie (465–522), the major poets and thinkers on poetics in Chinese literature, referring to when they try to figure the way meaning, words, expression, and emotion are bound together in a poem? Lu Ji describes poetic inspiration but fails to understand "the causes of its ebb and flow."[18] Tao Qian, echoing Zhuang Zi's paradox, believes that "great eloquence does not speak." Liu Xie struggles to clarify the harmony between *yi* (idea) and *si* (intuitive thought). In these Chinese writers, *kavyarasa* is generated out of the paradoxical nature of poetry. Playing on the polysemy of the word *jin*, which can mean "fully express," or "depleted," or "finish," Jiang Kui (1155–1221, *Baishi Daoren shishuo*, the white-stone Daoist's discourse on poetry) indicates that "if one can fully put into effect (*jin*) his discourse on poetry, one will be able to write poetry, but if one thinks that this discourse has exhausted (*jin*) all the secrets of poetry, one will not be a true poet."[19] This reminds me of how Confucius, in his reference to *Shi jing* (The book of poetry), looks into the four aspects of poetry: *xing* (to inspire), *guan* (to reflect), *qun* (to communicate), and *yuan* (to admonish). Wang Fuzhi's commentary is appreciatively cogent: "What is inspiring (*xing*) can be reflected (*guan*), thus making *xing* more profound; what is reflected (*guan*) can be inspiring (*xing*), thus making guan more manifest; what is communicated (*qun*) leads to admonition (*yuan*), thus making *yuan* more unforgettable; what is admonished (*yuan*) leads to communication (*qun*), thus making *qun* more sincere and authentic. . . . There arises a natural flow of emotions and feelings. The poet expresses his thought or message with consistency whereas the reader undergoes an individual experience of diversity due to his own emotions or mood."[20] Perhaps a poem invites us to read after it has been understood. Yang Wanli (1127–1206) writes:

> "Now, what is poetry about? [You may say] "Esteem its words; that is all." But I say, "One who is good at poetry gets rid of the meaning." "If so, then, having got rid of the words and the meaning, where would poetry exist?" I say, "Having got rid of the words and the meaning, then poetry has somewhere to exist." "If so, then, where does poetry really exist?" I say, "Have you ever tasted candy and tea? Who is not fond of candy? At first it is sweet, but in the end it turns sour. As for tea, people complain of its bitterness, but before its bitterness is over, one is overcome by its sweetness. Poetry is also like this; that is all."[21]

A poem ends and ends in a nonending, too, an exhaustion of words and an inexhaustibility of meaning. Yan Yu (1195–1245) believes in the construction of a poem, but the act of piecing it together into a singular whole might not always be possible. A poem can be "like sound in the air, color in appearance, the moon in water, or an image in the mirror; the words have an end, but the meaning is inexhaustible."[22] So a poem is "impure," as Charles Simic astutely notes: a poem "is an attempt at self-recovery, self-recognition, self-remembering, the marvel of being again. That this happens at times, happens in poems in many different and contradictory ways, is as great a mystery as the mystery of being itself and cause for serious thought." I agree with Simic that a poem can, sometimes, be smarter than the poet.[23]

Act II

A poem immured to its cultural conditions of emergence is an act of unacceptable reductionism. It is more than the culture that it springs from; rather, it is a culture by itself. Brett Bourbon argues that poems are "odd, funny kinds of things—and that is both their danger and their promise and a further reason for the dependence of our interpretations on our judgments about the kind of thing a poem is."[24] A poem is not like a chair. Bourbon notes, "When we want to cast poems or art as like chairs or suchlike objects, we ascribe functions to art, including the function of having no function. Such functions are stipulations. There is no nontendentious way to establish a link between the posited function and the thing the poem is."[25] So a poem is a source for worry, the unflappable worry of trying to make use of it in much the same way a chair is used and pinned down to a particular function. A chair has a logic, a science of constructedness, a pattern of comprehension and completeness; a poem performs its best when it surpasses the logic of everyday use and effectiveness. Language is what becomes the vehicle of poetic thought and it is language again that aggravates the worry over a poem's failure to produce a chairlike completeness and efficacy. Bourbon's observation that "poems are radically dependent on ideas of poetry and that they do not constitute a particular kind of thing" is quite interesting.[26] He argues that we eat the cake but we do not eat the concept; but, analogously, when we eat poems we also eat the concept of a poem. He argues: "It is not just that a particular poem is dependent on the concept of a poem in a particularly intimate way but that poems are funny kinds of things that are always concepts of poems and never just poems. Hence there is always an idea of poetry as such being expressed in a particular poem—and if we deny that, we turn the idea of poetry into something else—like the idea of culture or desire or of mind or of language."[27] Perhaps my exegesis on Wordsworth's "Daffodils" in chapter 5 of this book is a challenging rejoinder to a poem's overcoming of the superintending power of the idea of poetry, Romantic poetry in particular. A poem makes its own place, makes itself out of place, is found, is lost, is discovered, is nothing, is ignored. It scarcely has the logic of a novel and a play.

Kavyarasa can have its own logic; it is, on one hand, drawn from the full-bodied, structured, and familiar world and yet is not only facts. Charles Pierce considers any thought that ascribes what is not fact as poetry as "nonsense." A poem is not just a fact alone.[28] *Kavyarasa* emerges out of the poem's ability to "repair to the material of experience," as Santayana argues, "seizing hold of the reality of sensation and fancy beneath the surface of conventional ideas, and then out of that living but indefinite material to build new structures, richer, finer, fitter to the primary tendencies of our nature, truer to the ultimate possibilities of the soul."[29] So the poem is a poem in its analyzability (I would argue, as the facts or the logic of a poem), within the summation of understanding that individual parts provide and yet how it is a "poem beyond a poem" in its surplus. William Poteat writes:

> What we have to say, then, is that the poem in one sense is "about" the poem in another sense; that as having analyzable parts it is about an unanalyzable totality; and that no behavioural test—linguistic or otherwise—can be used to determine that the poem as being about itself has been grasped. Or we may put it thus: the poem in itself as a totality is an aesthetic object, and, if anyone asks to be told what this is, nothing can be said except that it is that to which the poem in its analyzable parts

refers; it is the plus which is more than the analyzable parts and about which nothing else can be said, other than that there is something which the poem is "about" concerning which nothing can be said.[30]

The "plus" is what, most often, makes a poem. The plus is a poem, too. Poetry often builds its own knowledge, a consciousness of itself, without being aware of an activity outside itself. It is a world to itself, commits a deep faith in "worlding" and has its own mysteries—its own unique ways to awaken to itself, the poetic state; but, it also is not merely mysterious and enigmatic. Inwardness is not just poetic knowledge. Maritain writes beautifully:

> It is surely true that one can be a poet without producing—without having yet produced—any work of art; but if one is a poet, he is virtually turned toward operation: it is essential to poetry to be in the line of operation just as the tree is in the line of the fruit. But in becoming self-conscious, or aware of itself, poetry releases itself in some measure from the work to be done. For knowing itself means turning back upon itself, upon its inner sources. Thus poetry enters into conflict with art, though by nature poetry is bound to follow the way of art. Whereas art requires an intellectual shaping according to a creative idea, poetry, under such circumstances, asks to remain passive, to listen, to descend to the roots of being, to the unknown which no idea can circumscribe.[31]

This is the "in-drawing magic" of the poem that Abbe Bremond qualifies as the call "to a quietude, where we have nothing more to do than be carried, but actively, by one greater and better than we are. Prose, a lively and leaping phosphorescence which pulls us away from ourselves. Poetry, a reminder of the inward."[32] There is something strongly "inward" about a poem. A poem does not forget its own independence to come into being: eating the poem (experiencing and feeling the poem) but not the concept of poetry. If a poem has its conflict with art and again manifests its subservience to art, one must know how a poem practices the art of going beyond art—the poem going beyond a poem.

A brief note on Muhammad Mandur's *shi'rmahmtis* (whispered poetry) can be interesting here. Mandur, a foremost thinker in Arabic literary criticism, saw *ulfa* (intimacy) as the serious demerit of contemporary Egyptian literature. Literature, primarily poetry, has to be "sincere." Whispered poetry is difficult to describe: a difficulty which is its charm, begetting a melody that is not ordinary rhythm and also delicate sentiments which suggestive language evokes. It is a compound experience and not something that legitimizes the overloading of ideological content. Semah explains that Mandur did not consider poetry "a collection of plain statements but a mixture of suggestive images; in it music is equally, if not more, effective in capturing the reader's mind." Contributing to the tradition of New poetry, Mandur speaks of the importance of delicate emotions and vivid perceptions in poetry and how that needs to be reflected with subtlety through poetic expression. New poetry, "by virtue of its genuineness achieves the quality of whispered secrets," a quality that is "distinct from rhetoric and jingling verse."[33] Semah points out further that "poetry was no longer a kind of oratorical composition to be declaimed at public ceremonies, for which the old form might still be suitable. It was now intended to be read and 'whispered'; in many cases it became a kind of confidential dialogue between human beings. The new musical scheme was the most appropriate for this dialogue which, far from resorting to rhetoric, contented itself with 'whispering truth' (sidqhdmis)."[34] But poetic experience is not wholly conceptualizable: it is not about grasping the foundations of experience. A poem is a flow and not pronouncedly a code whose essences and experiences are never realized noisily through the "tin-opener" theory of interpretation that peers into the poem with investigative triumph.[35] Maritain argues that "poetry dislikes noise" and insightfully warns that "if you try to make use of poetic knowledge for knowing, it vanishes in your hands."[36]

A poem is both a plan and a chance, Frost's momentary stay against confusion, achieved through clarification and "lucky events."[37] It is directed and is directional. Indeed, I share Stevens's not-too-confident assertion that "perhaps there is no such thing as free will in poetry."[38] Chance and choice hang together—fairness of will and the strangeness of impulse. The figure that a poem makes is both about a poet's being a "poetic mechanism" and the poem's having an autonomic growth, in the sense that "it is what [the poet] wanted it to be without knowing before it was written what [he] wanted it to be, even though [he] knew before it was written what [he] wanted to do."[39] Writing a poem, Stevens notes, is like reading the page of a large book where the poem, with its resonant and rhythmic steps, builds like an "an unwritten rhetoric that is always changing and to which the poet must always be turning."[40] While writing a poem, the poet knows "the pleasure of powers that create a truth that cannot be arrived at by the reason alone."[41] The conscious and the unconscious, known and the unknown, meet in a chiaroscuro. So a poem is an "integration" of two states of experience, which, however, is mostly fortuitous: "It is not always easy to say whether one is thinking or feeling or doing both at the same time." A poem has its own "taking place," a power that the mind lends the poem and the power that it draws out of us without our being conscious about it. Stevens delicately argues that "it is curious how a subject once chosen grows like a beanstalk until it seems as if there had never been anything else in the world."[42] But experience, as I have tried to argue, has to connect with language; rather, "style" and the subject are peculiarly ligatured. Language needs to be ambitious to accommodate and carry over experiences, resulting in more *dhvani* (resonances, obliquity). Ingenuity of language makes a better story out of the poem. Every word has a beginning in the story of a poem and every word does not end with a beginning. Beginning continues every time a poem settles in to grow. The vocabulary of the poem is seldom preformed.

Miller's adroit demonstration of the motive of metaphor through an engaging discussion of Stevens's "The Motive for Metaphor" happily motivates me here to see what metaphor and its transcontinental cousins *rupaka* (metaphor) and *bi* (to compare) in Sanskrit and Chinese poetics do in the story of a poem. Miller rolls his rhetorical reading into top gear to produce several interesting spaces in meaning and poetic experience and leaves me to wonder whether metaphor could be considered one of the ways of looking at the philosophy and aesthetics of across (exhilarations of exchanges), which is my predominant motif in the book. Metaphor in poetry carries the vector of transference (in the Aristotelian sense of the term) and indirectness that does not meet with much enthusiasm from thinkers like Thomas Hobbes and John Locke. Metaphor, indeed, is much more than a rhetorical device (book 3 of Aristotle's *Rhetoric* and chapters 21–25 in his *Poetics* tell us this). Metaphorization is an art—an intuitive poetic ingenuity—that generates an efficacious contiguity of apparently disconnected things or thoughts ("unapprehended relations of things," as Shelley points out in *A Defence of Poetry*), resulting in pleasure, wonder, and charm.[43] Miller, I would like to believe, must be in agreement with me over the "inherent tension" that metaphor holds and in being considered, often, as poetry itself. Metaphor changes, through shock and unusual rapprochement, the way we look at a poem, its world, and the world we inhabit. The poem, then, is like constructing an "interminable building" reared by the "observation of affinities / In objects where no brotherhood exists / To passive minds."[44] Persian literary criticism sees *istiʿāra* (metaphor) as eloquently pregnant; metaphor states with signification and potency and often exists as a puzzle waiting to be unveiled before the discerning eye. Seyed-Gohrab points out that "Persian rhetorical manuals concentrate on various categories of metaphors. Metaphors usually underlie other rhetorical figures, and the other figures are commonly used to enhance a metaphor. One of the most common terms for metaphor is *isti'āra*, meaning literally 'to borrow.' The term is often regarded in rhetorical manuals as a subcategory of *majāz* and stands in contrast to literal (*haqīqī*) meaning. Metaphor is also discussed in philosophical and religious manuals, with somewhat different definitions in the various disciplines. Authors define the term in relation to other adjacent terms such as simile (*tashbīh*), exemplification (*tamthīl*) or rhetorical ornament (*badī'*)."[45] Ideas of affinities and resemblance (borrowing as a critical act) get us closer to *yi* in Chinese, which means "to attach or cling to." The Confucian scholar Kong Yingda (574–648) points out: "To cling means to cling to analogies. If one wants to learn poetry, one must first cling to and rely on extensive analogies. If one does not study extensive analogies, one cannot master poetry, for poetry is analogies."[46] Michelle Yeh shows us how the word *bi* also functions to demonstrate the complexities of comparison and analogy: "*Bi* as the trope of analogy or metaphor in the poetic tradition is derived from a number of sources, all of which suggest affinity and complementarity. Compared with Western metaphor, there is an essential difference in their etymological import. Whereas metaphor literally means 'to carry (*pherein*) over (*meta*),' thus underlining the movement of transference from the vehicle to the tenor, from the signifier to the signified, *bi* emphasizes affinity or intimacy (*yi*) and even sameness (matching)."[47]

Understanding *bi* and the dynamics of metaphor gets us trans(in)fusionally across to *rupaka* in Sanskrit poetics. Miller's strong and subtle understanding of motive in and for metaphor in Stevens draws me closer to Frost's critical obsession with metaphor, or *rupaka*. Frost considers metaphor not as a simple and static pairing-off correspondence but as a way to establish *abheda-pradhana* (non difference dominant). Kapil Kapoor points out that metaphor established *abheda* "non difference" between two different entities and "teachers of poetics prefer to use the concept of *abheda*, identity, to describe the effect of the metaphor." And so when the *bheda*, difference, is removed from a simile, we are in the world of metaphor that is creative and vital and endowed with critical amplitude.[48] Frost's principle of correspondence in metaphor finds a parallel in the way Visvanatha in *Sahityadarpana* perceives the critical unfolding of rupaka, as a way of discriminating meaning from the language that contains it.[49] Let us try to understand this point by an instance from "Birches" again.

> He always kept his poise
> To the top branches, climbing carefully
> With the same pains you use to fill a cup
> Up to the brim, and even above the brim. (35–38)

The obviousness of the comparison underlines the pain, restraint, care, and poise that combine to lend the proper spirit to art. The metaphor of the cup's filling up to the brim without being threatened by a spillover forms the very essence of Frost's poetic art. This apparently simple but superbly delicate metaphor addresses the notions of Frost's dual answerabilities to society and individual energy, pointing to the urgency of maintaining poise. His conscious art lies in understanding the brim and how measuring up to it can be disguised as spontaneity. This metaphor, also, has the quality of letting us know that there is an aesthetic buildup, a careful attitude to art (*careful* being one of Frost's favorite words) and also a step that is careless. Frost's art strives to perfection through a careful design that is not made meretriciously obvious but is adroitly guised in its expressive depth and amplitude, word-idea integration, and the synchronicity of meter and feeling. Frost's metaphorization is akin to Rudrata's (a ninth-century Kashmiri poet and literary theorist) idea of *pushtartha*, the maturity in meaning and ideation. It is not mere *anumana* (inference) through intellection but an investment in possibilities that probe the inherent relations among images, words, and ideas; this results in new formations, figures. Frost's insistence on the proper poetical education by metaphor approximates an aesthetic creativity that hinges on *upamaprapancha*—the construct (with a strong creative bias) of similitude, an important organizing principle in Sanskrit poetics. Yet, such aesthetic creativity hinging on *upamaprapancha* is neither a self-determinate progress nor a jumping grasshopper "whose day's work gets him nowhere."[50] One can easily note that the metaphor has neither a predisposed march in its meaningful expansion nor a directionless consequence; rather, in its inherent richness of networking relations (what we can term *sambandha*, deep correspondence) we discover an organizing principle whose function depends on thought formations and poetic knowledge. Effective figural expression is bound to have a wider reach as it contributes through discipline and direction to the concretization of feeling.[51]

So metaphor is *meta-phora*, literally meaning "between motion," initiating a kind of change (*phora*), a translocation of meaning, a momentum for the across. The emphasis, through readerly intervention and linguistic potency and prowess, on the poem's ability to see one thing, something, another thing, and another thing as coming together in radiant exhilarations can bear extraordinary consequences where words can lose their "painful definiteness," words can have their career "without meaning," and words get "murmured over and over, in continuing suspiration" (in the words of Miller). I am tempted to join voices with Miller by arguing that metaphor provokes roads not taken, which shrink from "the weight of primary noon, / The A B C of being," for there is something that stands beneath and holds the poem up. Miller perceptively observes that "if the poet can bring metaphors to bear can he hope to escape." This makes the category of the "X," mentioned in the poem's final line, mysterious—an amazing cohabitation of affect through the use of words such as *vital* and *fatal*. A poem has its own allegiance to truths that it cannot shrink from. But a poem is also built through shrinking from the "weight of primary noon."[52] The trans character of metaphor is interesting to understand poetry: metaphor, *rupaka*, *yi* and *isti'āra* exist as resemblance. Stevens writes in "Three Academic Pieces": "As the mere satisfying of a desire, it is pleasurable. But poetry if it did nothing but satisfy a desire would not rise above the level of many lesser things. Its singularity is that in the act of satisfying the desire for resemblance it touches the sense of reality, it enhances the sense of reality, heightens it, intensifies it. If resemblance is described as a partial similarity between two dissimilar things, it complements and reinforces that which the two dissimilar things have in common."[53] This holds an intimate, figurative, rhetoric, productive, and transportative dimension. A poem would know how to find the "organism" among things.

A poem's truth is a distinct form of knowing, a belief in situatedness, a tradition, as Gadamer would argue. Embeddedness in tradition is not response to neutrality, but a response to values, "fore-meanings," or prejudices.[54] Gadamer's restitution of prejudice is not relativism but invitations to horizon meanings across cultures and historical situations. A poem, for me, cannot overcome its prejudices, that is, the prejudgments, the logical-linguistic space for understanding both itself and its limitations. It answers questions and questions itself within an aesthetic that recognizes both the virtues of the poem and what the poem does to us. A good poem always outbounds its premises, its formalist aesthetic thresholds, the poem going beyond the poem. So a poem does not have an "alienated consciousness" and is competently enabling in its connection with both itself and its outside. It is disclosive and also makes us see again what we always saw and have been seeing—a delicate mix of aesthetics and ethics, of art and life, the reordering game between the past and present. A poem's morality is in the "other," in building a community, staying in communities and in generating a taste. It, to appropriate Gadamer again, is like celebrating a festival where intention brings all under the common sky, although perspectives and positions can be different. A poem is the common ground, the site of celebration, the rendezvous of the ordinary and extraordinary. It has an order that is strangely elusive. This results in its becoming dispensable, a nonserious art consigned to be read when one has temporal abundance and vacuous leisure.

Act III

William Matchett rightly observes that "a poem may include arguments, however, or may even end with an overtly didactic summary, as long as such arguments or summaries are not destructive of the form of the experience. Nevertheless, to abstract the idea from the experience—which is the poem and to call that abstraction the 'meaning,' is to deny the poem's very significance. Not the abstract idea but a complex and vital experience—the poem—is the meaning. The poem is its own meaning; there is no paraphrase for it."[55] What precision can language produce in communicating poetic experience? A poem cannot have the purity of mathematics, where language communicates facts with precision and definitude. The imprecision in language, the resonance, the bee in the bottle, owes to a poem's investments in communicating "human experience" that cannot always be defined with scientific rigor. Matchett observes pertinently that a "human being is the continuing fact of his own consciousness. This is his point of contact with the world, a world which can come to him, from moment to moment and at any given moment, only through his awareness of it. Even his own thoughts, memories, and dreams can impinge only as experiences if he is to 'have' them. His life consists in his continuing perception, in the unremitting flow of complex experiences—inter-related sensations, thoughts, and feelings—with his sense of self at the center of this flow. Science can explain many aspects of perception, and of things perceived, but it cannot deal with the primary human fact of experience itself."[56] A poem and its relationship with language, then, is invested in nicety, suggestion, and discrimination.

A poet can work with words as objects but the poem is not something that forms out of a particular arrangement of material objects. A poem surpasses the "material" to become not merely ineffable but an event that cannot be logically burnt out. Words change and just don't stay words as material objects—undispersed and immovable. Working into a poem they frame their own narratives, stories in sounds and images. Poems are set in motion, unremitting and persistent. Words will be repeated. Structures (meter and rhyme, for instance) will be repeated, too. But repetition is a way of undoing the word, the image, the thought, the affect, and the materiality of expression. This undoing is the real doing of a poem.

The whole question of the poetic is inscribed in "play." The Wittgensteinian silence over poetic language, the creative refigurations of the language-games, does not discount a kind of acknowledgement of the rough ground of the ordinary and living language (as revealed through a closer reading of *Philosophical Investigations*). Unlike Wittgenstein, who struggled to move out of the rule-boundedness of language, Gadamer is more sensitive to the empowerments that the language of poetry may have—the everyday language and how that *forms* into the language of poetry. Everyday language, as Gadamer notes, "points to something behind itself and disappears behind it."[57] But how does the "small change" of everyday language change into the "gold coins" of the language of poetry?[58] Words have intention and are expected to be intentional but intention is never always truth serving (in the sense in which the truth of words is trustworthy) or meaning efficient. It can also be participation in the creation of a different level of answerabilities (language standing before us), unintended acts of speaking, and problematical investigations of "intentions." Gadamer sees "eminent sense of the word," the sense that retrieves the word from being lost into the materiality of use.[59] Words disappear but gold-like reveal a corporeality that is eminent, a coming to life that becomes an event in poem-encountering. This makes us consider the "fusion of horizons" at a new level of understanding. The language of poetry builds in dialogue; it is performative and cannot merely be a propositional submission to truth-functionality. It draws on a kind of livingness, forms of life and riddles that words create in trying to express life and conditions. There is no denying Gadamer that a text also has to return to speech, the contexts of speaking, the address and establishment of the written word. But how do we deny play? A poem plays with rules and the arbitrariness of rules, a strange, regulative beauty that is socially derived, drawn up on internal kinesis, and built through a logic that is not always restrictive. It is a truth, a story, that tells many tales playfully, through games, often superseding the consciousness of the individual. So a poem is not how the individual plays with it but a play itself, a playfulness that involves reason and the reason to outplay reason.[60]

This playfulness is the *dhvani* (suggestion) on which a poem builds itself. Suggestiveness brings out the full strength of language. A poem is the "connect" with experiences that we sundered ourselves from, the experiences that our daily grind deadened us to. So a poem is like a stained glass, arresting "attention in its own intricacies, [confusing] it in its own glories, and is even at times allowed to darken and puzzle in the hope of casting over us a supernatural spell."[61] This reminds me of how Octavio Paz reconsiders this connection with words and the experiences of the world around us. Words need our passions, senses, eagerness, and curiosities to be born and stay alive. They examine the world, the poet, and the poem itself. Words connect with the circumambient world, with our sensations, our thoughts, and desires, and in the process seize the poem, too. Comparing Paz with André Breton, Ricardo Gullón observes that "the language of passion and the passion of language are on good terms with one another, that they are the recto and verso page of the same attitude. Moreover, language is where song happens. There is no song without words, even though a song can be diminished to a susurration or concealed in a number."[62] This faith in words circumscribes the Spanish poet Jorge Guillén's vision of poetry, where the language of poetry does not discount any word in advance because any expression, as Guillén points out in *Lenguaje y poesia*, "can give shape to the phrase."[63] It has a democratic approach to words but implicates a closer examination of words than what we usually do in prose. The relationship between language and experience is vexed and opinions are divided over the acceptance of the insufficiency of language and unrepresentability of experiences. I would like to see both, the insufficiency of language and the reparative and restorative ability of the poet's craft, as constituent paradigms in the making of a poem. What Gérard Genette calls "secondary Cratylism" brings home the dialectic of the arbitrariness of linguistic signs and the poet's commitment to redeem them through care, concern, and convergence.[64] The language of poetry is inscribed in this tension and, through *dhvani* and *vakrokti* (oblique expression), continually prepares to remunerate, rather, refurbish language's inbuilt deficits and constraints.

Dhvani is an important segment in the story of the poem, in the unfolding story of resonant poeming. *Dhvani* is the unsaid meaning, the suggestiveness of the poem, its unique strength and charm. Anandavardhana in his *Dhanyaloka* would consider the indirectness of meaning as the poet's greatest art. I would interpret this as the kind of indirect listening that a poem generates. Anandavardhana was the "first Indian critic to state that a *rasa* cannot be directly expressed" and *rasa* and suggestive poetry are integrally connected.[65] He believed that only those "figures of speech which are in conformity to *rasa* are capable of imparting suggestivity to the sense."[66] Rasa and suggestion can work together to produce three kinds of poetry: *Dhvanikavya* (the highest form of poetry, where *dhvani* and *rasa* are intertwined to produce the best of poetic effect), *Gunibhutavyangyakavya* ("it is that kind of poetry in which *rasa* is suggested, but it is made subservient to the striking features of the primary sense. Here the suggested sense contributes to the primary sense by enhancing its beauty."), and *Citrakavya* (the lowest class of poetry, where the emphasis is on the "varieties of expression" and where *rasa* is thinly felt).[67] A poem is an emotion of a thought (in the words of Frost) and both a *rasa* of a *dhvani* and *dhvani* of a *rasa*.

Dhvani can be seen to have a corresponding approval in Chinese poetics, where *Anshi* (suggestion) comes with surplus and meaning that invariably surpasses words. There is, indeed, a text beyond the text, brought about through *yan wai zhi yi* (meanings beyond the expressed words), *xian wai zhi yin* (the sound of the string), *xiangwai zhi xiang* (images beyond the image), *weiwai zhi zhi* (flavors beyond the flavor), and *hanxu* (subtle reserve).[68] Wang Fuzhi expresses the importance of suggestiveness over descriptiveness: "Where the spirit of the ink shoots out, it reaches the extremities of the four directions without being exhausted. Where there are no words, the meaning is everywhere."[69] A good poem finds what Liu Xie calls the *yin* (the concealed, the rich implications beyond the text). The *yin* in the story of the poem lends *vaicitrya*. It is a diversity that draws its life from what Kuntaka advocates as *vakrokti*. *Vakratva*, or *Vakra-bhava*, creates a striking expression (*ukti-vaicitrya*) that makes the poetic experience extraordinary and exciting. It is here that the poet exhibits his skill (*kavi-kausala*) and acts of imagination (*kavi-vyapara*). Kuntaka argues that a special kind of *vakya-vakrata* (obliquity of expression) must combine the *svabhava* (character) of an object, whether *sahaja* (natural) or *aharya* (worked up), and this "forms the legitimate theme for heightened expression," allowing it as "one of the elements of the simpler *Sukumara-marga* (delicate style)."[70] *Vakrokti*, as poetic deviance, is not completely what Dandin calls *atisayokti* (hyperbole) because that narrows the scope of the concept. It transgresses the ordinary and induces strikingness that lends charm to a poem.

Sethna observes, "Poetry shot through and through with mystery by a movement of intense rhythmical feeling which weaves a word-pattern whose drift eludes the thinker in us: this is Housman's conception of 'pure poetry.' But he does not say that poets should aim at nothing except such a word-pattern. What he emphasizes is that any poetic word-pattern is poetry by an element that, however, mixed with thought, is really independent of it and can be best considered a stir of emotion. To touch us and move us is the function of poetry."[71] A good poem moves us, makes claims on patience, keeps us embraced in a thought, allowing a certain experience to build in words and ideas to have a tenure of their own. Reading poetry is not rushing the subway of thought to catch the train of meaning. It is education in toleration for thoughts that baffle, is sustainment in complicated bends of thinking and metaphorical trajectories—"drunken song" (in the words of Frost) with a happy-sad blend. Dylan Thomas notes that "a good poem is a contribution to reality. The world is never the same once a poem has been added to it. A good poem helps to change the shape and significance of the universe, helps to extend everyone's knowledge of himself and the world around him."[72] Caught amid different takeoff points in life, experiencing a poem is both an ordinary and extraordinary act, as the Indian poet-philosopher-mystic Sri Aurobindo affirms. For him, the planes of consciousness and poetic inspiration are connected: his overhead note in poetry mentions the Higher Mind, the Illumined Mind, the Intuitive Mind, and the Overmind, which considers sight as the essential poetic gift, the inner seeing and sense, a vein of comfort touching points of life-truths, values, fun, and play.[73] The story of the poem adds to the stories of our lives, our worlds, our own understanding of who and what we are. However,

If, in writing poetry, you insist it must be *this* poem
Then certainly you are not one who understands poetry.[74]

A poem poems. The story begins.

WESTERN THEORIES OF POETRY

Reading Wallace Stevens's "The Motive for Metaphor"

I begin with some dialogical comments on Ranjan Ghosh's chapter 3, "The Story of a Poem." I agree with what he says at the beginning about the effect of current changes on writing, reading, and teaching poetry. He emphasizes, as I do, social, political, and technological changes, especially ubiquitous digitalization.

Ghosh's chapter, moreover, is, among other things, a learned and lucid introduction to Sanskrit, Chinese, and Arabic theories of poetry. Most Westerners know little about these. Ghosh's chapter is especially original in the way it mixes his accounts of Eastern theoretical terminology about poetry with many citations from diverse Western sources. The implication, as in Ghosh's other chapters for this book, is that a comprehensive set of transcontinental ideas about poetry exists, though that set is complex and diverse. Ghosh tends to assume that a poem may be reasonable but gives the reader access to something beyond reason.

I have learned especially from Ghosh's chapter about the ancient Sanskrit concept of *rasa*. Rasa is to a considerable degree the key or sovereign term in Ghosh's account of Eastern theories of poetry. Ghosh's chapter develops a subtle, complex, and capacious theory of poetry. His chapter makes use of conceptual and figurative assertions from many traditions, including diverse ones in the West, about what poetry is and what it is good for. A good example is the passages, often depending on figures of speech, about poetry and writing poetry that Ghosh cites from Wallace Stevens's letters and prose works. He does not, however, in his chapter investigate whether or not Stevens's poetry fits what Stevens says about poetry. That strikes me as an important question. Ghosh, happily, leaves it to me to try to do that in what follows in this chapter.

I have a quasi scientific commitment to beginning with the evidence. The evidence in this case is a short text that most people would agree is a poem. I want to clear my mind as much as possible (it is not really possible, of course) of presuppositions about what poetry is and does. I want to try to identify as exactly as I can what actually happens when I read Stevens's short poem "The Motive for Metaphor."

My primary interest in teaching and writing about literature has always been accounting for specific literary texts by reading them for myself. I want to identify what they really say, how they say it, and how that matters to me. Theory, for me, is ancillary to reading poems. Theory is a handmaiden, not a queen who is a sovereign end in herself. Theory, for me, comes inductively, after reading, not before. In this I agree with Aristotle. Aristotle's *Poetics*, after all, the founding text in Western literary theory, is essentially a reading of Sophocles's *Oedipus the King*. Aristotle wants to develop an abstract terminology to account for the salient features of that play in its context of other Athenian tragedies and their social uses.

I have, in my chapter 10 for this book, identified, under the aegis of questions about "the authority of literature," the main theories of poetry in the West. What is most striking about these theories is their diversity and their rootedness in changing historical contexts. My goal in this chapter is not to explore these theories. It would take a book to do this adequately, and then some. I just want to account for what happens to me when I read a single poem by Stevens.

I do not know at this point just where my exploration of Stevens's "The Motive for Metaphor" will lead me. If I knew already where I am going with my reading of this poem, it would not be worth the bother of going there. In its own modest way, my account of Stevens's poem will exemplify what Stevens himself says, in a passage Ghosh cites from Stevens's *Opus Posthumous*, about his own experience of writing a poem: "It is what I wanted it to be without knowing before it was written what I wanted it to be, even though I knew before it was written what I wanted to do."[1]

What I want to do is to account for what happens in my mind, feelings, and body when I try to come to terms with Stevens's "The Motive for Metaphor." My claim is that this is much stranger than one might assume. It is not something that can be summarized as "making logical sense of the poem." Here is the poem in its entirety. It is the second poem in Stevens's *Transport to Summer* (1947).[2] How do I know for sure it is a poem? For various reasons. It appears in a book by Wallace Stevens entitled *The Collected Poems*. It fits the usual conventions in the West for the way a poem, especially a modernist poem, should look on the page. It is printed in lines, the first words of which are capitalized. The lines do not go to the right margin. It is printed in five four-line stanzas separated by blank lines. The printed lines more or less (not always) alternate five beat lines with four beat ones, though rhyme is not used. Most literary scholars in the West would agree that it is a poem. One might guess from the absence of rhyme that it is a modernist poem. It would seem perverse to say that it is not a poem. I emphasize this because assuming it is a poem brings in all sorts of conventional expectations about the text's form and meaning, as well as the question of the relation between hermeneutics and stylistics that operates when you try to understand it:

THE MOTIVE FOR METAPHOR

You like it under the trees in autumn,
Because everything is half dead.
The wind moves like a cripple among the leaves
And repeats words without meaning.
In the same way, you were happy in spring,
With the half colors of quarter-things,
The slightly brighter sky, the melting clouds,
The single bird, the obscure moon—
The obscure moon lighting an obscure world
Of things that would never be quite expressed,
Where you yourself were never quite yourself
And did not want nor have to be,
Desiring the exhilarations of changes:
The motive for metaphor, shrinking from
The weight of primary noon,
The A B C of being.
The ruddy temper, the hammer
Of red and blue, the hard sound—
Steel against intimation—the sharp flash,
The vital, arrogant, fatal, dominant X.[3]

Why have I chosen this poem? I have done so somewhat arbitrarily, but primarily because it is, like only three other poems by Stevens, not only overtly about metaphor but also has the word *metaphor* in its title. Many or even most people would agree that metaphor and other related figures of speech are essential to the way poetry works. Aristotle in the *Poetics*, after all, said, in his inaugural wisdom, "By far the greatest thing is the use of metaphor. That alone cannot be learnt; it is the token of genius. For the right use of metaphor means an eye for resemblances."[4] Moreover, the power of metaphor is one of the big topics in Stevens's prose works, gathered in *The Necessary Angel* and in *Opus Posthumous*.[5] These works are full of provocative formulations about metaphor. An example is one of the *Adagia* (a wonderful collection of adages about poetry) that says, "Metaphor creates a new reality from which the original appears to be unreal."[6] If I were to try to account for all Stevens affirms about metaphor in his prose works, or even just about what he says about the motive for metaphor, I might never be done with doing that, so subtle, abundant, and contradictory is what Stevens says. I might never be able to turn to "The Motive for Metaphor." So I set all that aside, as I will do later with Aristotle, Benjamin, de Man, and Derrida.

Well, what actually happens in my mind, feelings, and body when I (you) read the poem? Let me confess at once that it is impossible for me to read the poem without theoretical presuppositions, however tacit, just as it impossible for me to read it without the implicit awareness of all I remember (quite a lot) about Stevens's life and work, about other criticism of his work, and about the many previous essays I have written about Stevens's poetry. I have not just stumbled on a copy of the poem among autumn leaves, an ignorance the American New Critics tended to assume was the best starting point for reading a poem. An example is Cleanth Brooks and Robert Penn Warren in *Understanding Poetry*.[7] Many of the students who used *Understanding Poetry* in courses were in just that situation of fairly complete ignorance.

Just to put my terminological cards on the table at once, let me say that I have had much in mind recently the distinction Paul de Man, following Walter Benjamin, makes between hermeneutics and poetics or stylistics. Rhetorical reading or stylistics or poetics (de Man uses all three terms) is attention to the way the tropological dimension of any discourse interferes with its statement of a clear, logical meaning. That is one reason I was attracted to Stevens's "The Motive for Metaphor." It seems to be about that issue. Benjamin, and de Man after him, claims that poetics (*die Art des Meinens*, the way meanings are expressed) interferes with hermeneutics (*das Gemeinte*, what is meant).

Here is what de Man says, in a wonderfully ironic passage in "Conclusions: Walter Benjamin's 'The Task of the Translator,'" about this interference:

When you do hermeneutics, you are concerned with the meaning of the work; when you do poetics, you are concerned with the stylistics or with the description of the way in which a work means. The question is whether these two are complementary, whether you can cover the full work by doing hermeneutics and poetics at the same time. The experience of trying to do this shows that it is not the case. When one tries to achieve this complementarity, the poetics always drops out, and what one always does is hermeneutics. One is so attracted by problems of meaning that it is impossible to do hermeneutics and poetics at the same time. From the moment you start to get involved with problems of meaning, as I unfortunately tend to do, forget about the poetics. The two are not complementary, the two may be mutually exclusive in a certain way, and that is part of the problem which Benjamin states, a purely linguistic problem.[8]

The play of pronouns here (one, you, I) implies that I cannot avoid repeating, for example, in this essay, the betrayal de Man names and with rueful irony confesses to performing. I do hermeneutics at the expense of poetics, as when I try, more or less in spite of myself, to identify what Stevens says in this poem, even though I say I just want to report what happens in my mind and imagination when I read the poem. The latter is something quite different from hermeneutics. Asking what Stevens really says implies that what he says can be clearly identified and paraphrased, that such clarity is not fatally interfered with by the way Stevens says it.

Theory is resistance to reading, as de Man argues in his extremely complex essay entitled "The Resistance to Theory," though he does not say so in so many words.[9] Theory is resistance to reading, apparently because theory pretends to foresee clearly the results of reading (demystification of aberrational acts of taking metaphors literally), whereas reading itself is unpredictable. You never know beforehand just what you are going to find in a given text. Each genuine reading is, consequently, sui generis. It is not reducible to the application of a formula that knows what it is going to find. I claim, therefore, that the distinction between hermeneutics and stylistics raises questions rather than programming answers.

When you read "The Motive for Metaphor," you may first note that the title tells you that the theme of the poem, its hermeneutical meaning, is identification of the motive for metaphor. The poem is about the question of what motivates the poet or any other person to use the evasions of metaphor to avoid thinking of the "A B C of being," whatever that is. You may also note that *motive* and *metaphor* alliterate. This suggests some obscure connection between the words, perhaps by way of the fact that *motive* can also mean "motif," which a metaphor might be, especially if it or similar metaphors recur in a text.

I then note that *you* is the first word of the poem. Stevens does not say, "I like it under the trees in autumn." He says, "you like it under the trees." The *you* works in two ways at once. The poet is clearly addressing himself, self-reflectively, dividing himself into two persons: the one who likes it under the trees in autumn and the one who reflects on what that liking means. At the same time the poet is addressing the reader as "you" and inviting me, him, or her, to put himself or herself in the place of some you who likes it under the trees in autumn.

I doubt whether when you read "The Motive for Metaphor" initially you are likely to stop with the title or worry about that *you*. When I first read the poem, I went right past all that and began creating in my mind three imaginary scenes, one after the other. The first is an autumn scene. The second is a spring scene. The third is a strange scene of pounding with a hammer on some object glowing with heat from a forge and making a big spark fly. The creation of these three imaginary scenes on the basis of the words on the page is spontaneous and irresistible. I may know that the autumn and spring scenes in poem are in aid of conveying a theoretical concept, that is, what Stevens claims is the motive for metaphor, but that does not stop me. The motive for metaphor Stevens finds is quite different, by the way, from Aristotle's praise of the gifted poet for having an eye for resemblances. For Aristotle, metaphor helps the poet make the reader see something more vividly. For Stevens, metaphor helps the poet avoid seeing what is there to see. The scenes that arise spontaneously in my mind when I read the poem exceed any conceptual use *you* can make of them. Those scenes are also, I would claim, different for every reader, and never quite the same twice for the same reader.

I have said the interior scenes in my mind and feelings are imaginary. I mean by that not that it is wrong when you read the poem to think of Wallace Stevens himself, walking in the autumn woods near Hartford, Connecticut, or out for a nighttime moonlight stroll in the spring. I mean rather that nothing is said about that in the words of the poem. The parallel is much more with the vivid mental images I have of the characters and their surroundings when I read a novel. The words of a novel create a purely imaginary world. Once more these are different for every reader, and they are based on relatively limited verbal evidence. I have, for example, vivid mental images of Lucy Robarts and Lord Lufton in Anthony Trollope's *Framley Parsonage* (discussed in chapter 10 of this book). I would know Lucy if I saw her (by her match with my imaginary picture of her). Trollope's words, however, are not by any means as specific as my mental image of Lucy or my feelings of admiration and affection for her. She exists only in the imaginary world the novel's words create when I read them. In the same way, I create my mental images, my feelings for them, and my subliminal muscular movements of walking in Stevens's autumn and spring scenes, as well as the feeling in my arm of hammering when I read his forge scene, from my knowledge of New England autumns and springs, and from my memories of the sparks flying at my grandfather Critzer's farm forge in Virginia when I visited there as a child. There is no use telling me these are irrelevant associations. My mind, feelings, and my sympathetic muscular reactions are too strong to be negated by that common-sense advice. *Spontaneous* is the key word here. Don't blame me. I cannot help it.

If you look a little harder at the words on the page, however, some big problems begin to arise. Just what is the status of those three scenes? Are they ends in themselves? That is, are they what the poem is "really about?" Does the poem intend primarily to call up in the reader ("you") some version of those scenes? Is everything else in the words merely ancillary to that? Or are these scenes in some way figurative expressions of something else, perhaps examples of metaphorical transformations? Perhaps they do what they say, as speech acts, as performative utterances that resist the weight of primary noon. The poem, after all, is the second item in a book of poems Stevens called *Transport to Summer*. *Transport* is a more or less literal translation of the Greek word *metaphor*, which means "carry over." Is the poem an example of the way the poems in *Transport to Summer* intend to carry the reader, performatively, from spring to summer, transport her there?

As any adept reader of Stevens knows, however, the names of the seasons, for Stevens, each had a complex symbolic or figurative meaning. Autumn and spring were for him times of transition or change, while winter and summer were times of fixed states. Winter was, for Stevens, the time of seemingly endless cold, as in "The Snow Man," one of his most famous and often-anthologized poems.[10] Summer was, for him, a poise at warm, high noon, as in the wonderful "Credences of Summer."[11] "The Motive for Metaphor" exemplifies that coding in the figurative meanings of autumn, spring, and summer that the poem asserts. Both autumn and spring, transitional seasons on the way to winter and summer, respectively, exemplify the "exhilarations of changes." Enjoying those changes through language is the motive for metaphor. My three imaginary scenes, so spontaneously vivid in my mind, feelings, and body, turn out by no means to be what the poem is literally about. They are figurative examples of what metaphors do.

At this point I am (you are) beginning to see that neither Aristotle's definition of metaphor ("an eye for resemblances"), nor Benjamin's or de Man's clear theoretical distinction between hermeneutics and stylistics are of much use. They are theoretical formulations to be tossed out when the actual work of reading "The Motive for Metaphor" begins.

Aristotle apparently means that the metaphorical term or, as I. A. Richards put it, in a mixed metaphor, the "vehicle," helps us see what he called the "tenor," or literal meaning, more vividly. The vehicle and the tenor resemble one another. Aristotle's example is "the ship plows the waves." A ship is like a plow. A plow is like a ship. Not insignificantly, this example of a metaphor is a means of transport, a ship. The example turns back on itself to do what it says. You see the ship more clearly in your mind's eye when you say it plows the waves.

That does not really work, however, in "The Motive for Metaphor," for example, with Stevens's ostentatious and grotesque simile: "The wind moves like a cripple among the leaves." I can see in my mind's eye a cripple moving among the autumn leaves all right, but it is a big stretch to say that resembles the autumn wind's way of moving. It is as much a startling dissemblance as a resemblance. I suppose the comparison is based on Stevens's assertion in the line before that he likes it under the trees in autumn "because everything is half dead." You could say a cripple is half dead. In any case, "like a cripple" is not much like Aristotle's more conventional metaphor, based on resemblance: "The ship plows the waves." Stevens's "like a cripple" also, it happens, is a personification or prosopopoeia, which Aristotle's plow is not, except covertly, insofar as a plow implies a plowman. Stevens explicitly personifies the autumn wind as "like a cripple" struggling through the leaves. Ghosh's dialogical intervention about the tradition of theories about metaphor in various cultures is, by the way, much more in tune with Aristotle's "eye for resemblances" than with Stevens's idea of metaphor as evasion.

Moreover, when I try to apply the distinction drawn by Benjamin and de Man to "The Motive for Metaphor" I find it does not really work as a theoretical tool any better than Aristotle's definition of metaphor. I discover I cannot easily distinguish hermeneutics from stylistics in what I must say about the poem. Are those scenes that arise so powerfully in my mind's eye hermeneutical meanings or stylistic devices? I think any decision about that would be arbitrary and unfounded. Is "like a cripple" a simile for the literal meaning of the way the wind moves in autumn woods, or is that scene not already a figure? Is "like a cripple," therefore, a metaphor (or rather simile) of a metaphor? Stevens says in one of the *Adagia*, "There is no such thing as the metaphor of a metaphor. . . . When I say that man is a god it is very easy to see that if I also say that a god is something else, god has become reality."[12] The first metaphor becomes the literal, of which the second locution is a metaphorical resemblance or transport. Stevens's choice of an example, by the way, is surprising and by no means innocent. It implies that metaphor is always grounded in some theological scheme.

Moreover, what happens to me is the reverse of what de Man says happens to him. He tries to do stylistics and ends up deplorably doing hermeneutics. I try to do hermeneutics, that is, to account straightforwardly for the meaning of "The Motive for Metaphor," but I almost instantly end up getting snarled in stylistics, for example, in trying to establish the linguistic status of "like a cripple," or the linguistic status of those three scenes that rise up in my imagination when I read the poem.

As you can see, I am just getting more and more entangled when I try to use my two theoretical formulations, the one from Aristotle and the one from de Man. I had best jettison them both, along with all that Stevens says elsewhere about metaphor, and go back to reading "The Motive for Metaphor" as best I can on my own, without their help.

Let me then turn back once more to "The Motive for Metaphor" to try to see what it really says. The first thing I note when I do this is that the grammatical armature of the poem is not descriptive or referential (e.g., "everything is half dead. / The wind moves like a cripple among the leaves"), but a series of subjective assertions, each followed by one of the scenes I have mentioned. Each turns on a word that names your feelings, your intimate emotions: "like," "happy," "desiring." "You like it under the trees in autumn." "In the same way, you were happy in spring." "Desiring the exhilarations of changes." These locutions explain the motive for metaphor. The motive is pleasure in feelings of liking, happiness, or desire.

As the poem says, the motive for metaphor is to escape from "the weight of primary noon." Autumn and spring figure such an escape, and you therefore like them, or they make you happy, as the poem says. They are the location of things that are neither this nor that, but both at once, in transport or transition. You like the fall because "everything is half dead," neither fully alive, nor fully dead. You were happy in spring because it is the time of "the half colors of quarter-things." Such things are not quite one color or another color, and not quite one fully developed thing, in diminishing portions: half colors, quarter things.

This exhilarating escape to things that are not quite anything definite is expressed in the wonderful description of a spring evening as the dusky place of things that are not quite one thing or another thing, and that are in constant, exhilarating change. This constant changing is expressed by present participles ("melting," "lighting"): "The slightly brighter sky, the melting clouds, / The single bird, the obscure moon— / The obscure moon lighting an obscure world."

It was a big mistake on my part to leap to those vivid, imaginary images of the three scenes as somehow primary, that is, as what the poem is about. That this was a mistake is indicated in part by the way each of the segments naming them ends in a reference to language. The wind that moves among the leaves like a cripple "repeats words without meaning." Such locutions are something you like because though the sounds are words, they are words without the painful definiteness of words that have a fixed meaning. When are words not words? When they are words without meaning and when they are murmured over and over, in a continuing suspiration.

The phrase *words without meaning* recalls Walter Benjamin's "pure language." Such expressions exist between, below, above, or outside all languages, in the form of sounds or meaningless marks. "In this pure language," writes Benjamin, "which no longer means or expresses anything, but is, as expressionless and creative Word, that which is meant in all languages—all information, all sense, and all intention finally encounter a stratum in which they are destined to be extinguished."[13] The scene lighted by the obscure moon in an obscure world is a "world / Of things that would never be quite expressed." These things are neither expressed nor not expressed. This obscure world (in the sense that a text may be obscure, hard to read, such as "The Motive for Metaphor") means that when you enter it you can escape being a fixed self. This is a scene "where you yourself were never quite yourself / And did not want nor have to be."

Please note that these assertions about the languages of autumn and spring are not hermeneutical meanings but figures of speech, manifestations of stylistics or poetics. Autumn winds, for example, in reality, don't repeat any words at all, not even words without meaning. They only do so figuratively, by a poetic metaphor. "The Motive for Metaphor" is a tissue of metaphors from one end to the other, with nowhere a literal meaning that you can hermeneutically identify, except to say that the whole poem explains what the motive for metaphor is. That explanation can only be done, it turns out, in metaphor.

A tissue of metaphors without literal referents is a series of catachreses, that is, displaced locutions for things that have no literal name, as in "leg of a chair," or "face of a mountain." A catachresis is neither literal nor figurative. It is not literal, because that stick of wood that holds a chair up is not really a leg. It is not figurative, because the word *leg* does not substitute for some literal word. "Leg of a chair" is what you call it. Aristotle, in his wisdom about figurative language, already called attention to such strange locutions and to the way they put in question the neat distinction between literal and figurative words.[14] The word *catachresis* in Greek means "forced or abusive transfer," "against usage." Many catachreses are personifications, as in *leg*, *face*, or, indeed, as in "like a cripple among the leaves," among my examples.

Stevens calls the referent of the metaphors that make up his poem, in the last word of all, X. X is the sign in mathematics for an unknown and as yet unspecifiable number that can be identified by solving the equation. I think Stevens's equation cannot be solved. The X remains unknown except as a "sharp flash," an evanescent glimpse.

That brings me at last to an attempt to account for the last two stanzas of "The Motive for Metaphor." These are the most obscure and difficult lines by far. I shall dare to try to read them. The grammar of these lines in their context of the whole poem is clear enough. The poem says you like autumn and spring because you desire "the exhilarations of changes" that occur in those seasons, both in the outside world and in your subjectivity, including in your selfhood itself. You desire these ongoing changes because you are constantly, through time, "shrinking from / The weight of primary noon, / The A B C of being." Metaphors aid in that shrinking. That is the motive for inventing them, not, for example, the search for resemblances that Aristotle saw as the motive for metaphor.

The difficulties with reading those last two stanzas begin when you try to explain to yourself or to others two things: the exact meaning of its various phrases and the exact relation among the cascade of phrases and words that are given in that grammatical relation called apposition, that is, in a list bound together by commas as ligatures: "The weight of primary noon, / The A B C of being, / The ruddy temper, the hammer / Of red and blue, the hard sound— / Steel against intimation—the sharp flash, / The vital, arrogant, fatal, dominant X." That sequence is really weird. It is by no means to be accounted for by my correct but somewhat desperately reductive attempt to read it as a scene of hammering on an anvil at a forge. The reader will note that there are two appositive lists, the primary one and then a secondary one within that first one made up of a series of adjectives modifying X.

The problem with appositive lists is that it is difficult, if not impossible, to decide whether each item is another way to say the same thing or whether they progress or digress in some way or another. Each may say something different from all the others. Only by looking at the semantic meanings of each can we hope to work toward an answer. It might be safest to assume that Stevens uses so many words in apposition because no single word is adequate.

What the "weight of primary noon" is can be guessed. Stevens often makes a parallel, in a kind of code language, between the round of the seasons and the times of a twenty-four-hour day. It is not an accident that Stevens's spring scene takes place under an "obscure moon," neither the pitch dark of midnight, nor the broad daylight of noon, but in between, as the clouds melt. Midsummer is primary noon, that is, a moment when everything inside and outside the self freezes for a moment. The solar context of the phrase I cite below, from "Credences of Summer" ("without evasion by a single metaphor"), confirms that reading. At primary noon, everything is just what it is. Stevens's you in this poem (though not in "Credences of Summer") finds that fixity an intolerable weight. He will do anything to escape it. He believes metaphors will provide that escape in "the exhilarations of changes."

What then is "the A B C of being," the next item in the appositive series? Is it just another way to say "the weight of primary noon?" Well, yes, but not quite. *Being* is a loaded word in Stevens. This could easily be demonstrated by many citations from his work. Roughly speaking, *being* has an Aristotelian or Heideggerian overtone in Stevens's work. These authorities affirm two quite different meanings for *being*, by the way. *Being* means, for Stevens, I dare to assert, not just what is, "things as they are," "without evasion by a single metaphor," but also the invisible ground or rock beneath.[15] This ground is the substance of things, not only in the sense of their isness, their existence, but also in the etymological sense of what stands beneath them and holds them up (their sub-stance).

That seems to explain *being*, but why "A B C?" B echoes *being* all right, so the phrase has an internal alliteration, but so what? An A B C is, of course, the common name for the basic alphabet of English. It is often used metaphorically to name the rudimentary knowledge you have of a given topic: "I know my A B C's about that!" As for Heidegger, so for Stevens in a slightly different way, being is inextricably entangled with language. The references to language in this poem attest to that ("words without meaning," "things that would never be quite expressed"). Primary noon is a time when being is reduced to absolutely literal locutions, without possible evasion by a single metaphor. The spaces between the first letters of the alphabet, as Stevens gives them, invite the reader to think of a finite and exhaustive appositive series going all the way to Z: "Being is A, is B, is C, . . . is Z." Only if the poet can bring metaphors to bear can he hope to escape "the weight of primary noon" even by way of the evasions of metaphor employing "The A B C of being."

Tom Cohen, in a recent e-mail to me, has brilliantly suggested a possible relation between the metaphors for being and that fatal X. Cohen writes: "Rumination: Does the 'abc of being' forestall the latter [being] by the seriality and inescapability of the former [A B C]—leading to an X that wants to get out of the bind (x marks the spot), but is itself a letter, and a Chi at that." Cohen here suggests that the inescapable seriality of metaphors for being forbids ever reaching being itself, only more metaphors for it. The letters of the alphabet, intoned in sequence, as we were taught to do in grade school, finally reaches the letter X. It is a letter, all right, but differs from other letters in being a traditional catachresis, not a metaphor, for being itself. As Cohen says, "X marks the spot." X is chi, both a Greek letter (uppercase X, lowercase χ) and Ch'i or *qi* (氣), "energy force" in Chinese culture. Though Stevens may or may not have known about Chinese Ch'i, his X certainly names being as a pervasive energy that is present in everything, for example, the autumn wind in the fallen leaves, as well as being outside everything as its dominating master. As Cohen also says in a subsequent e-mail, X is an example of the blank materiality of inscription, in the de Manian sense of that phrase. "Inscription," writes Cohen, "harasses tropes, like a fox scattering the hens."

The final stanza is the hardest of all to explicate hermeneutically. I claim it is a series of items that would be present when someone strikes a glowing piece of metal with a hammer in a forge. These items are in apposition not in the sense of being different words for the same thing, but in the sense of being a progressive series. You pound with a hammer the glowing metal in order to temper it, that is, to make it harder by changing the way its molecules are ordered. You turn iron into steel by adding carbon and other ingredients. That, to some degree, explains "ruddy" (that is, red hot) and "temper." An obscure play on *temper* as "feelings" is also present.

The hammer is "of red and blue" not just because it is glowing hot from striking the piece of metal it is tempering, but also because the words "red" and "blue" are part of Stevens's private color code. "Red" is for reality, things as they are, and "blue" is Stevens's name for "imagination." Imagination, for him, changes things as they are into other things, as opposed to the fixity of being's X. These changes happen primarily by means of metaphors, in the extended sense of figures generally, seeing what is, the weight of primary noon, as a potentially endless series of other things, from A to Z. You see the wind in the autumn leaves as a cripple. In a typical evasion, Stevens does not say "steel" against "iron," but "steel against intimation." Intimation is, I take it, a name for the glowing metal that is being tempered by a steel hammer. The metal being forged (evocative word in the light of the language theme in the poem) is full of intimation of the other molecular forms it might become when it is tempered. Red and blue are the twin poles of Stevens's constant oscillation in his poetry. That oscillation brings about the exhilaration of changes. The clash of steel against intimation brings a "sharp flash" like the spark that flies when the forger's hammer strikes the metal glowing from the forge that is being tempered by that blow.

The sharp flash of that spark is then called "the vital, arrogant, fatal, dominant X." The flash is a momentary glimpse of being, generated by the blow of imagination and reality against intimation. That final series of words in apposition ("vital, arrogant, fatal, dominant") names in personifying catachreses what has no proper name, what is just a nameless unknown X, that is, being. The sound of X is like the brief explosion of a sharp flash when the glowing hammer hits the glowing metal. *Steel* is Stevens's name here either for the metal being forged or for the hammer. The spark from the glowing metal being tempered is called intimation because it intimates the other things it can become: "steel against intimation."[16]

It would seem that the poem ends with an example of the triumph of metaphor over the weight of primary noon. The ending is not quite so simple, however. A metaphor substitutes a figurative name for something that has a proper name, as when we say the ship plows the waves. A catachresis confesses in its enunciation its powerlessness to give adequate language for what it gestures toward. Moreover, Stevens conspicuously grants sovereign power to the X of being by naming it in a series of personifications. These call the X of being some sovereign, no-doubt masculine, vital, arrogant, fatal, and dominant person. A personification is more properly called a prosopopoeia. The word means, etymologically, "to give a name, a face, or a voice to something that has none of these." The poem ends with a striking submission of the you to the irresistible power of something, an X, that cannot be touched by the evasions of metaphor. It is bigger than "you," much bigger. Nevertheless, the X can be alluded to in extravagant metaphors or, rather, personifications.

"The Motive for Metaphor" is therefore, in the end, a poem not about the triumphant power of metaphor but about the failure of metaphor to evade primary noon. This, however, can only be said in that peculiar figure called catachresis.

I have read Stevens's "The Motive for Metaphor" as best I can, with help from Tom Cohen. I have also found, pace de Man, that I cannot do hermeneutics in writing about this poem without doing poetics or stylistics in extravagant ways at the same time. As I might have known, my reading turned out to be more complicated than I expected it would be. I also meant it when I said I did not really know where my reading was going to lead. I especially did not foresee that turn at the end in which the weight of primary noon wins out, after all, over the powers of metaphor. Nevertheless that winning out is expressed in that strange species of metaphor that is not a metaphor, catachresis. My reading confirms the hypothesis that that you never know just where a reading is going to lead you until you do the reading. It confirms also my further hypothesis that all the theoretical knowledge in the world is of little help in the actual business of reading a given poem in its uniqueness and in its resistance to oversimplifying theoretical presuppositions.

PART III

Literature and the World

MORE THAN GLOBAL

The intellect acquires critical acumen by familiarity with different traditions. How much does one really understand by merely following one's own reasoning only?
—**Bhartrihari**

The wide world, extensive as it is, is only an expanded fatherland, and will, if looked at correctly, be able to give us no more than what our home soil can endow us with also. What pleases the crowd spreads itself over a limitless field, and, as we already see, meets approval in all countries and regions. The serious and the intellectual meet with less success, but those who are devoted to higher and more productive things will learn to know each other more quickly and more intimately.
—**Goethe**

Do not so much as imagine that I will show you the way to a world literature. Each of us must make his way forward according to his own means and abilities. All I have wanted to say is that just as the world is not merely the sum of your ploughed field, plus my ploughed field, plus his ploughed field—because to know the world that way is only to know it with a yokel-like parochialism—similarly world literature is not merely the sum of your writings, plus my writings, plus his writings. We generally see literature in this limited, provincial manner. To free oneself of that regional narrowness and to resolve to see the universal being in world literature, to *apprehend such totality* in every writer's work, and to see its interconnectedness with every man's attempt at self-expression—that is the objective we need to pledge ourselves to.
—**Rabindranath Tagore**

If literature is truly sacred in the sense that I have tried to explain in chapter 1, then it is crucial to read each literary work more or less in detachment from its local roots in a specific author and locale, as well as in detachment from its place in so-called world literature. The work's sacredness, that is, its complex relation to an imaginary realm, is what is most important about it, more important than its local and global affiliations.

Literature is nowadays often said to be at once global and local. This, by extension, also means that, after all, there is nothing either local or global about literature. Djelal Kadir's sensible proposal to associate the lexis "world" with "no particular or necessarily predictable referent" means that the development of world-literature programs is neither logical nor inevitable:

> This discovery makes it unavoidable for us to have to explain the phenomenon we are referring to as the predicate object or as the predicative process of our worlding actions—which world, at what time, in what location, through which language, and with what intentions. World, in other words, can never be taken as a given since it is invariably the constructed outcome of our particular performative interventions. And, by extension, the literature it conditions becomes a particular literature whose specificity is a derivative of the instance of the phenomenon "world" we define as predicative referent of our action in the verb to world.[1]

The acts of "worlding" are deeply performative and transfigurative. Such acts (in)fusionize; that is, they fold the "inside" of our experiences (by which I mean one's own local contexts, the specificity of native tradition, the train of inheritance of a thought in a particular culture and knowledge system) into the "outside" (the epistemic and cultural contexts of different traditions and knowledge worlds). The revelations of the inside and the outside do not come together in a two-way course in which either the local reaches for the global or the global tries to find connection with the local. Although we cannot ignore the strict divisions between the inside (we may for clearer understanding call it local) and the outside (global), the acts of worlding demonstrate that connections, the scale enlargements, are not built in a unitotal pattern. Worlding promotes "planetary time," which Wai Chee Dimock argues is "supranational time" that "goes backward (a recursive loop in the past), and it goes forward (a projective arc into the future)." Dimock points to a

> jurisdictional order whose boundaries, while not always supranational, are nonetheless not dictated in advance by the chronology and territory of the nation-state. As a set of temporal and spatial coordinates, the nation is not only too brief, too narrow, but also too predictable in its behavior, its sovereignty uppermost, its borders defended with force if necessary. It is a prefabricated box. Any literature crammed into

it is bound to appear more standardized than it is: smaller, tamer, duller, conforming rather than surprising. The randomness of literary action—its unexpected readership, unexpected web of allegiance—can be traced only when that box is momentarily suspended, only when the nation-state is recognized as a necessary but insufficient analytic domain, ceding its primacy upon scale enlargement.[2]

This promises a "more," the unexpected web of meaning, which I have termed the "more than global." On the surface, the local and the global have their usual separateness and rupture; but, in what I argue is more than global, such ruptures often become a kind of provocation to question the promise and latency of a dialogue between the two. Diffractive refigurings produce the more than global phenomenon that acknowledges how globality becomes the "enclosure in the undifferentiated sphere of a unitotality" and is suppressive, as Jean-Luc Nancy points out, of "all world-forming of the world."[3] Literature cuts "together-apart" leaving the local-global in new temporalities—"spacetimematterings."[4] Doing literature is "entangled intra-relating," which is, as Karen Barad explains, "not to say that emergence happens once and for all, as an event or as a process that takes place according to some external measure of space and of time, but rather that time and space, like matter and meaning, come into existence, are iteratively reconfigured through each intra-action, thereby making it impossible to differentiate in any absolute sense between creation and renewal, beginning and returning, continuity and discontinuity, here and there, past and future."[5]

So the more than global is inscribed in what I call "intra-active transculturality," which is not about going beyond the global or reducing the local to a form of representation or meaning-formation. It is the destruction of an expressive and organic "totality" but is also a way of providing a sense of a totality, a world-wide-forming totality, whose access is not always in accessibility.[6] The more than global is radical immanence, not a choice but an event.

Worlding formed through intra-active transculturality inheres in a complicated reading of *monde* (world). Jean-Paul Martinon observes:

There is indeed a strange parallel between globalization and what Nancy calls "world-forming" (*mondialisation*). This parallel shows that neither comes full circle, both exceed each other, thus never allowing for sense (world-forming) to make *absolute* sense or for non-sense (globalization) to end in either a *parousia* of (scientific) meaning, or total annihilation.

In this way, there is no escaping this impossibility to recycle properly because creation is what goes radically beyond the logic of production (and therefore recycling), and, yet, the possibility of this production never leaves the horizon of creation. The two always go together while always exceeding themselves. This is not a circular thought; it is the facticity of thought itself, that is to say, it is the facticity of the world itself. In this way, there is no pure creation or world-formation as such. There is an exposure or opening that both creates *and* for good or bad also produces.[7]

The more than global, much in the spirit of monde, the problematic involving the contrastive acts of production and creation and making sense of *horizein* or *horos* as bound or landmark, staves off the ascendancy of "homo-hegemonization" to reveal sense and contradiction among multiple points of articulation. In world-wide-ization, in processes of worlding, connections through intra-action and autoimmunization are built mostly through reflective, interpretive judgments. Commenting on Derrida's "Globalization, Peace, and Cosmopolitanism," Victor Li rightly observes:

The importance of establishing *mondialisation*'s Euro-Christian provenance is that it enables a deconstructive genealogical examination of globalization together with its ethico-politico-juridical concepts of national sovereignty and territory, cosmopolitanism, human rights, and international law. . . . Such a genealogical deconstruction would establish globalization not as a neutral, objective process, but as *mondialisation*, or, even better, as *mondialatinization*, a worldwide-ization emanating from a Christian Europe. Thus, since globalization is really *mondialisation* or *mondialatinization*, we have to concede that it is, as Derrida bluntly notes, "Europeanization." But just as *mondialisation*'s European genealogy elliptically interrupts globalization's universal encompassment or encirclement of the earth, so too *mondialisation* as the Europeanization of the world suffers its own elliptical interruption in the form of an autoimmunitary process. In other words, we are witnessing, Derrida tells us, a "double movement": "globalization [mondialisation] of Europeaness and contestation of Eurocentrism.[8]

Intra-active transculturality, revealed through the more than global, eventalizes sense more than the mere reclaiming of Europeanness, which is symbolic of creating and producing horizons. The critical habitation of

Wordsworth's "Daffodils" within some parameters of Sanskrit poetics, as exemplified in the next section of this chapter, is not a contestation of Eurocentrism, an act that becomes another polarized, Eurocentric way of seeing procedures of knowledge formation, but a form of world-wide-ization. The more than global is not a project to dehistoricize and deterritorialize Eurocentric filiations, because in its intra-active embeddings the approach worlds and unworlds its always already inscribed rootings and routings. We don't globalize (horizoned, hence, landmarked in globularity and sphericality) but stay globalized and presentified with the ap*prehension* of *totality* in its world-wide-ness.

The more than global, then, is not "after global" and, thus, does not necessarily demand an exegesis of what happened to literature in its postnational constellations. So to consider the more than global as merely resulting in world literature is to undercut my arguments. It is a taking place that forms and norms its own ways of address. This address, as Nancy notes, is a kind of thinking that "addresses itself to 'me' and to 'us' at the same time; that is, thinking addresses itself to the world, to history, to people, to things: to 'us.'"[9] The more than global is our "curious 'being-with one-another' [*être-les-uns-avec-les-autres*], toward our addressing one-another."[10] How can meaning be generated beyond the "me" and invested in the "us"? How can the me (local) find its meaning not in the other (global) but in us? This implies that meaning is not just in the local or the global or after global or before local but exists in an immanent and continued circulation that is more than global. Nancy observes: "If one can put it like this, there is no other meaning than the meaning of circulation. But this circulation goes in all directions at once, in all the directions of all the space-times [*les espace-temps*] opened by presence to presence: all things, all beings, all entities, everything past and future, alive, dead, inanimate, stones, plants, nails, gods—and 'humans,' that is, those who expose sharing and circulation as such by saying 'we,' by *saying we to themselves* in all possible senses of that expression, and by saying we for the totality of all being."[11] The more than global is obligated to make sense of this circulation as a singular, plural entanglement. The singularity of the more than global makes us realize that "every one is just as singular as every other one, and consequently substitutable. Communication both singularizes them and divides them out; what is commensurable is their incommensurability."[12] The more than global worlds through what Nancy argues is the coextensivity of understanding, where the acts of grasping and escaping are coenactments.

More Now

Zhang Longxi points out that "once we recognize the diversity and heterogeneity of the Other, as we do of the self, cross-cultural understanding can be seen as part of our effort at understanding in general, of our endless dialogue with others, with ourselves, and with the world at large."[13] However, cross-cultural understanding is not merely about reaching out for the other through dialogic interplay among cultures, civilizations, and concepts. It is also about judging and orienting one's peculiar nativism, cultural exclusiveness, constellative patterns of beliefs, manners, and languages in an intra-active negotiation involving "unpeace," the *excès sensible* (the profusion and fusion of sense or sense making) that inscribes the contesting territories of power, domination, obscurity, obfuscation, and elision across time and historical periods. Unpeace is the other name for seduction, assemblage, and curiosity, the immanent power to world the already existing, yet imperceptible, establishment, the being-with that "manifests in concrete, contract, commerce and most profoundly in confiance."[14] Miller implicates this unpeace when he raises the question: How can world literature avoid being dominated by some single national academic culture? And again: How can a discipline of world literature respect the many different conceptions of literature in different times and places throughout the world? Appropriating the brilliant and resonant vocabulary of Michel Serres, I would like to see the more than global in "displacements, confusing allegiances" that do not ignore "wide pages and tenuous differentials" and,[15]

> as if chance fluctuation, unexpected storms or atmospheric disturbances, spread stochastically through the space of the high seas, suddenly led to (the formation of) a temporarily stable locality, an island where another time would come into being, a local time forgetting the past, the ordinary and the time of the journey. Remote in relation to the methodical path, these islands create order through fluctuation, a different order that could well be called exodic. You will never find these islands with a methodical approach. Exodic, exotic, ergodic, they lie outside the global equilibria of the episteme. Method minimizes constraints and cancels them out; exodus throws itself into their disorder.[16]

The inherent antagonism (unpeace) in world or comparative literature is not in view of a meeting of opposites but a sort of refusal to accept the existence of opposites. Worlding sees incommensurability with approval, a provocation to avoid the encyclopedia and endorse what Serres calls a "scalenopcedia"—not an isosceles, right-angled or equilateral triangle, but "unbalanced in parts, scalene signifies lameness, like Hephaistos, an inventor and the husband of Aphrodite, lame like several relatives of Oedipus, with sore feet, like him; scalene describes an oblique, twisting, complicated path."[17] Construction, conjoining, and conflict become a single act. Comparative literature must deeply invest in the unpeace, in the intra-action, and indulge in "leaping sideways," wandering "as free as a cloud," gazing in every direction and improvising. Serres observes that "*improvisation is a source of wonder for the eye. Think of anxiety as good fortune, self-assurance as poverty. Lose your balance, leave the beaten track, chase birds out of the hedges.*"[18] However, wandering and improvisation are not absolutely without and outside sense. In fact, cultural specificity is a part of a process where circulation and comparison consort antagonistically without ignoring certain irreducible differences that are inherent in transcultural negotiations. My more than global program of thinking indisputably acknowledges cultural specificities and exemplarities, certain unchangeable dimensions in a particular thought-tradition and system of knowledge because without such acceptance and understanding of certain specificities the whole idea of doing literature transculturally is destined to get chaotic and inconsequential. So both the specificity and the irreducible differences among cultures and traditions synergistically intensify and complicate the exchange value of a given work. This contributes to the circulation, the sense-making, of the more than global where specificities and paradigm-transcendence are intra-related, augmenting the off balance factor in literary understanding. But any critical inclusiveness is deeply opposed to hegemonies inflicted upon us by certain languages in their global circulation. Several languages spoken by large numbers of people, and, thus, blessed with a significant corpus of literature, can generate a conceptual pool to globalize an idea or a paradigm. This implies, for instance, that the hermeneutic nexus among Hindi, Chinese, Spanish, German, and English can clearly ignore Sanskrit. Being global can then become a kind of self-imprisonment within an insular local. This generates the stultifying provinciality of being global from which literary studies must seek its own modes of independence.

Comparative literature, working out of its traditional penchant for sources and inevitable comparison of cultures and times and thought, came to identify, with the publication of the American Comparative Literature Association report of 1993, a course removed from traditional Eurocentrism that was vectored to be global (Miller provides an account of the growth of comparative literature in North America in the next chapter).[19] But the question that has been debated here is whether comparative literature exists only to become comparatist in our doing and understanding of literature or any close reading of literature is removed from the domain of such practices. But has literature ever been without its peers—distant or teleomorphic? Being conscious of initiating a comparative framework is one aspect; the other aspect is the belief in literature's embedded comparative status—the entangled status, the molecularity, and what I call its intra-active transculturality. Jonathan Culler argues that "comparative literature should accept the differential possibility that the evolution of literary and cultural studies has created, as the site for the study of literature as a transnational phenomenon, did not gain many adherents, and the question of what comparative literature should be has remained as much in dispute as ever, except insofar as we agree that it is the nature of comparative literature to be the site at which the most diverse options of the humanities contend—not just a discipline in crisis but by its very nature a site of crisis."[20]

Indeed, literature, or sahitya, is a site of crisis whether one disciplinizes it as comparative or leaves it alone to manifest its own nodes and modes of comparison—a panorama and not a landscape, to follow Serres. Comparative literature is less a discipline in need of promotion and establishment than a norm and an inevitable urge (the more) to understand what literature can do and is capable of doing. Fernando Cabo Aseguinolaza rightly notes that "literature is a European concept—even Eurocentric in the most radical sense of the word—both in terms of its genealogy and in its fundamental link to the alphabetically written word and to the idea of the book. So, too, are the corpora with which it was originally associated and the basic fields towards which the first historiographic attempts, from Bacon on, were oriented."[21] Through intra-active transculturality, I intend to dilate the radius of literature's meaning-making ability, rendering an aesthetic whose generous tenancy shall include non-European writing with cognition and recognition. It is also a strategy to re-premise "Angloglobalism" arguing for an inclusion of the complexity of the European space (comparison can also be intra-European or intra-Asiatic).[22] This works against the imperialism of canonicity or ideological group behavior in literary studies that are adamantly unidirectional in trying to see the evolution and formation of literature as literary models, graphs, and maps.[23] It is about changing the measure of critique—the geo-politics and spatiality of knowledge—of literature irrespective of whether we label it as world literature or comparative literature. There is much more than is usually understood both in Gottfried Herder's concept of the globe as inscribed in incommensurable cultures and in the interdenominational capaciousness of Goethe. Goethe's *Weltliteratur* involves a critical ecumenism whose dynamics has always been far more complicated than what the matrices of the global-local divide and of the theory of epochs have allowed us to conceive. Being global is not simply a reaching out constricted by the strengths of the reigning critical methodologies; it is also a reaching in, voyaging centripetally to form more global configurations of understanding, a reconceived Weltliteratur.[24]

My arguments built on intra-active transculturality are out of rhythm with what Zhang Longxi, endorsing the popular cooptative momentum in comparative literature, affirms in *Unexpected Affinities*. Longxi does this, for instance, by way of a comparative exegesis of John Bunyan's *The Pilgrim's Progress* and the sixteenth-century Chinese *Journey to the West* (*Xi you ji*). Longxi clusters Liu Xie, John Keats, Gustave Flaubert, Heinrich Heine, A. E. Housman, Ralph Waldo Emerson, Alfred de Musset, Franz Grillparzer, and others to elucidate the Confucian notion that poetry provides an outlet for the suffering soul.[25] Here the predominant spirit tries to avoid the shock, the adventure, and risk of bringing unfamiliar patterns and paradigms of reading into serious play. Intelligent and investigative, with citation of pertinent passages, Longxi's text rides the "going global" mode. He leaves out the dystopian unease, or the unpeace that intra-active transculturality brings. He minimizes the vagaries of incommensurability, does not let critical world formations inhere in what Rosi Braidotti's calls "transposition" and, hence, reduces the potentialities of "taking place."[26] Comparative dystopic unease then invites the anxiety of conflictive exchanges, the "gradient" of comparison and difference, dismantling, most often, the enclaves of literary systems that preserve canonicity or hori*zones* of world literature.[27] The more than global, through sense-able (the ability to generate sense and also about making sense able) and sense-less (the act of not finding conventional sense all the time) unease, introduces the impurity in our reading of literature across time and cultures—an eroticism that refuses to stay exclusively immured in specificity, culture-boundedness, and conceptual autonomy. Going global has a direction, but the more than global is a possibility. This might head and veer otherwise, where difference is sens-ing. Veering (connected to the French verb *virer*, to turn or turn around, and the Latin verb *vertere*, to turn), as Nicholas Royle argues, "involves contemplating all sorts of turns, funny and otherwise."[28] He points out that veering "entails an experience or event of difference, of untapped and unpredictable energy."[29] It might go "*toward* something open," as Paul Celan writes, "inhabitable, an approachable you, perhaps, an approachable reality."[30] So the dystopian unease in comparative thinking can surely come from a transpoetical veering in which the subject is irrevocably split horizontally to announce itself with *différence*.

When we formally identify the world and the globe in the global, we miss what it means to experience the more than global. I am arguing for a recircumscription—both in the deeper inflection implied by Herodotus's *oikoumene* and home as the world. I am certainly not gesturing toward a boundless chaos. "It rather suggests," as Didier Coste observes, "that we should move away from the priority of any single origin and consider the one-and-whole both as origin and goal, and thus itself bi-centered. Comparative thinking, as it moves away from that one-and-wholeness in order to make sense, creates its own bipolarities, around which it is up to our anthropological self-consciousness to move—elliptically also in the sense of an omission, an abbreviation, an encryption and a forgetting."[31] These moves, Coste suggests, import a radical openness and a newfound familiarity among correspondences of ideas and paradigms widely separated in time, context, and culture. With this come cognitive shifts, chronomorphic transits, the unease that interpretative profits in cultural translation bring, and the conceptual inflections that result from epistemic interplays. So the worlding through intra-active transculturality is clearly not produced additively but generates itself coadunatively replete with the peculiar modes of (in)fusion, subtraction (the shrinking of meaning-premises to generate reterritorialization), and inwardness, which for me is a movement in perception and insight that reinterrogates the capaciousness, viability, and horizoning power of concepts.

The more has an undertow of joy. This is a joy that does not make us, as Rabindranath Tagore argues, "limited by the power of the intellect or the power of work," but makes us experience ourselves without any "cover or calculation in between."[32] Tagore continues:

> The son is dear not because we long for the son, but because we long for the *atma*, our true self. Property is dear not because we desire the property but because we desire the *atma*, or the self. This means that in whatever we experience ourselves *more* fully, we desire that. The son

eliminates my shortcomings; I find myself all the *more* in my son. In him, I become *more* of myself. This is why he is my dearest kin; he is a manifestation of my self outside of me. It is the truth I experience so certainly within myself that makes me experience love; that very same truth I know in my son and therefore my love for him expands. That is why to be close to someone is to know what they love. It is thus that we understand where, in this wide world, they have located themselves and how far they have spread their souls. Where my *affection* does not lie, my soul only skirts the rim of its own boundary.[33]

The more than global is an affection that leads one to experience the other outside oneself and eventually to know oneself better. The local is known better outside itself as much as the global is understood better in the more than global, which is, however, not beyond global. It is a profound desire that dwells in the joy emerging out of being local and global at the same time—the father (the global, as it were) finding himself in the son (our assumed local). This enables the son to become dear to the father. In turn, the father comes to know himself more in the affective momentum leading him to reach out to the son. This is his desire to locate himself in his son. That desire, again, is developed paradoxically, through a reaching-in, in modes of inner immigration, leading the father to find himself. So finding oneself more in others is to become more of oneself. The dharma of the more than global then is the *sambandha*, the astute listening where the father (global) and son (local) address each other in a resonant relationality. In *sambandha*, the global finds itself in the local, enabling a knowledge that helps the global to discover its globality, as when the father finds more of himself in his son. Here lies the more that produces joy when one's own truths become the truths of the world. In the words of Tagore: "The house it [I refer here to the more] inhabits is not merely a structure of bricks and mortar—it attempts to make it a home and colours it in its own hues."[34] Compared to a house, a home in its affective and aesthetic configurations is more fluid, less constricted, and knows the art of accommodativeness where the father and the son can live and learn and make more senses out of their living (*sambandha*) at different points of time. I would like to argue that the house of the local and the global built out of the bricks and mortar of ideology, principles, traditions, and cultural individualities becomes the home of the more of the global, where the local and the global, like the son and the father, exceed themselves in the joy of discovering and reaching out for each other. The flow of knowledge in such continued disequilibria is not between the local's reaching for the global and the global's reaching down to meet the local. It rather becomes a moment, a now, that is both achronic and cross-chronic. In this constructed now, the father finds himself to be more than what he is. The son realizes the amount and kind of "father" that was already there in him. So going global that is not understood within the premises of what I call the comparative dystopian unease is not global enough.

The impregnated more in the intra-active transcultural now disturbs us with a presence. Bill Ashcroft rightly argues that the presence in transcultural encounters is a

> moment of sudden awareness in which the reader engages an excess, the "beyond" of interpretation in what may be understood as a sense of cultural "otherness." When this works most successfully, the otherness is one's own. This moment may overlap and merge with the aesthetic and indeed cannot be fully separated from it, but it encompasses a radical unfamiliarity that is perhaps better understood as an encounter with the uncanny, the *umheimlich*. The strangest feature of this encounter in the transcultural text is that this uncanny space becomes, potentially, a space of negotiation.[35]

Presence is absence in process. Presence is in "to be" and what was "not to be." It undoes the presentness of meaning. It, as Nancy argues, is "not form and fundament, but the pace, the passage, the coming in which nothing is distinguished, and everything is unbound. What is born has no form, nor is it the fundament that is born. 'To be born' rather is to transform, transport, and entrance all determinations."[36] Intra-active transculturality presences, is itself a presence, which is always already there but "neither in the mode of being (substance) nor in that of there (as a presence)." It is mostly in the mode of being born where meaning is not a representative fixity (global or local) because birth "effaces itself and brings itself indefinitely back." So the birth of a literary text "is this slipping away of presence through which everything comes to presence."[37]

In intra-active transculturality, a text's taking place—presence to presence—does not necessarily need a precondition to come to power. In agential intrarelating a text builds resonance and "travelling frequencies." These frequencies, Dimock argues, are "received and amplified across time, moving farther and farther from their points of origin, causing unexpected vibrations in unexpected places. . . . Texts are emerging phenomena, activated and to some extent constituted by the passage of time, by their continual transit through new semantic networks, modifying their tonality as they proceed."[38] The resonance and presencing demonstrate how much noise a text carries inside it. A literary text, for me, is always a noise, an intricate and challenging mix of sound and frequencies. It is when we ascertain a meaning of a text that we adjust its frequencies to generate sense (consonance and clarity). But all music is fundamentally noise because the slightest of maladjustment of registers can turn music to noise. So it is noise that is an ontological reality and the music that comes out of it is only a reality manifested through fine-tuning and studious adjustment. If we consider Wordsworth's "Daffodils" as a romantic poem, we are merely adjusting the noise of the poem to a certain frequency; it is music to many and will continue to stay as a particular genre of music (romantic nature poem) to many for many years. But the event of the more than global is mostly about engaging with the noise and, hence, the poem, as we shall see in the following pages, struggles to speak in unitotality: it thickens its tonality, develops inflections, and reverberates with new pitches and rhythms. These noises are what I argue to be contradictions, the fermenting sources that a text generates intra-actively.

The more than global produces a now with multifold presents making the poem available through spacetimematterings. The now is an exposure in and to the new, where no memory of a contradiction or incommensurability comes to infringe on the domain of the not-yet formed. The freedom emerging out of the exposure has a life of its own outside the memories that all presents (with their competences and contradictions) usually bring into the crucible of the now. What I mean by this is that my reading of "Daffodils" within the now will not have any memory of how the poem was read at different points of time and space. This is achieved in a detemporalized flicker of interfusing concepts—the nowing of diverse cultural and epistemic hemispheres hitherto thought of as foreign to the poem. The more-now exists in every location of space and time. It functions in a swirling inclusiveness that is formless and characterless and yet prodigiously productive. T. R. S. Sharma claims that "there is nothing like an ageless concept, for concepts age like men, sometimes even faster. The more ancient they are, the more recent they sound, and often the most ancient concept turns out to be the most modern or post-modern or easily lends itself to a post-modern appropriation."[39] The traveling differential that such fluidity generates makes Raimundo Panikkar's "diatopical hermeneutics" an important dimension to world-ization.[40] Understanding "Daffodils" is not about putting two periods, two times, and two texts together in contrast, comparison, and correspondence. This understanding is not the result of a simple strategy of interwelding the *desivad* (nativism) with *videshibad* (Euro-Americanism). G. N. Devy has seen this strategy as the dialectical tension between *mārga* (the mainstream) and *deśî* (the local or regional).[41] The creative antagonism, revealed through the taking place of "Daffodils," to be presented in the pages that follow, is not informed by Devy's entrenched attitude about adducing nativist empowerment through the appropriation of deśî traditions and thoughts; rather, it has the presence-power of intra-active transculturality that allows the *mārga* and the deśî to intersect and flow into each other, creating a diffractive *sudesivad* (neonativism) in entangled topoi and mythos.[42]

Comparatists might leap into an attack, claiming, perhaps rightfully, the legitimacy of the coming into contact of diverse cultural paradigms in intra-active, transcultural world-formations. I don't deny their anxieties. I believe that literature's worlding is not achieved by cheering a chaos born out of the incoherent interplay of ideas. We need to accept that there are certain irreducibles in linguistic, cultural, and epistemic formations, without which literature cannot proceed in its meaning-making. This, indeed, makes for a yes-no space. But intra-active transculturality continually reorients questions that are phrased not as "why this?" but as "why not this?"

Taking Place

"Daffodils" is a simple, seemingly innocent, poem. Dorothy Wordsworth notes: "When we were in the woods beyond Gowbarrow Park we saw a few daffodils close to the water-side. We fancied that the lake had floated the seeds ashore, and that the little colony had so sprung up. But as we went along there were more and yet more; and at last, under the boughs of the trees, we saw that there was a long belt of them along the shore, about the breadth of a country turnpike road. I never saw daffodils so beautiful."[43] William Wordsworth, placing the poem in "Poems of the Imagination" (1815), observes: "The subject of these Stanzas is rather an elementary feeling and simple impression (approaching to the nature of an ocular spectrum) upon the imaginative faculty, than an *exertion* of it. The one which follows . . . is strictly a Reverie; and neither that, nor the text after it in succession, 'The Power of Music,' would have been placed here . . . except for the reason given in the foregoing note."[44] Despite its notional anchorage in elemental feeling, imagination, beauty, reverie, and seeing— the approved and authentic principles of understanding Wordsworth's poetic art—intra-active transculturality worlds the poem's taking place in a diffractive space where the poem builds an entangled habitation in certain domains of Sanskrit poetics. Spacetimematterings produce contact points that generate sense but do not reduce meaning to itself. The more than global happens through these contact points which are substantial and have their own singularities. The meaningful happening of "Daffodils" through "contacts" with some particular paradigms of Sanskrit poetics and Hindu philosophy is the co-incidence, a kind of trans-immanent event. The event of the poem and its Sanskrit territorialization are being-with—superpositions that generate correspondence through already existing disruptions and dispositions. So the simple taxonomies of a supposedly romantic poem and certain elective dimensions of Sanskrit poetics are not held in a dialectical play but stay world-wide-ized in an entangled relationality. Comparative dystopian unease spooks the poem with certain aspects of Sanskrit poetics, and is, hence, haunted and *re-turning* unannounced. The taking place is both an exposure (a world of nows to its already existing presents) and a deposition (the sedimentation of presents worlding a repository of meaning, the plurality of nows) where the text in question subtracts itself to add to its life. Subtraction is the poem's ability to withdraw from itself, its nature, its already existing music developing a nothingness that presences, from the already-always to not-yet. Comparative dystopian unease decimates the binary and makes sense of the restlessness of intrarelated correspondences beyond the brute givens. The world cannot be worlded and worlding cannot stay worlded to enable more than global formations. Urs Stäheli appropriately notes that "using discourses on the local and global, then, is a particular way of making invisible the constitutive paradox of the world—the impossibility of its unity."[45] So the world of the poem stays withdrawn enabling Sanskrit (in)fusionist modes to enliven a radical articulation of its blind spots.

The intra-active transcultural development of the poem happens through the singularity of dance and joy. The poet is united in a dance (all four stanzas of the poem mention the word *dance*). In this dance, the existential unites with the cosmogonic:

The waves beside them danced; but they
Out-did the sparkling waves in glee:
A poet could not but be gay,
In such a jocund company:
I gazed—and gazed—but little thought

What wealth the show to me had brought:
For oft, when on my couch I lie
In vacant or in pensive mood,
They flash upon that inward eye
Which is the bliss of solitude;
And then my heart with pleasure fills,
And dances with the daffodils. (lines 13–24, italics mine)

The dance is the synthesizing principle and a celebration of aesthetic delight. It is a consciousness of joy that finds a diffractive entanglement with the spirit of the *Brihadaranyaka Upanishad*, where individual creative delight is seen as part of a universal continuum of immanent and immutable joy.[46] The poet commits to a power to encompass the life, the spirit, and the truth that is undergirded by joy. The *Upanishad* tells us— *ananda rupam amritamyad vibhuti*, from the speck of dust at our feet to the stars in heaven—that all is a manifestation of truth and beauty, of joy and immortality. Joy manifests itself through the poet's submission to the daffodils and the objects orbiting around them, as it were. The poet who "could not but be gay" relishes the experience with a stable delight, a radiant joyousness of spirit (*prasada*). It is significant to observe that he moves among the objects of sense with a mind brought under his control. This control of the mind is not for a joyless ascesis but for a tranquility that generates happiness. The "bliss of solitude" accompanies a "pensive mood" and the *ananda* (joy) becomes the state of self-sufficiency. It is a repose within itself where the daffodils, as objects of poetic desire, are assimilated into the poetic being, resulting in blissful exaltation. Within the inherent *anandavada* (principle of joy) of the poem we find clear concentric lines of the expansion of the ego. From beholding the flower, the ego moves to embrace the clouds, the trees, the bay, the sparkling waves, and then transits to the inner thoughts. This inward movement effectuates a confluence of the blissful heart (inner being) with the daffodils and, finally, dilates into an all-pervasive manifestation that Rabindranath Tagore would point out as *ananda dhara bohiche bhuvane* (currents of joy are flowing across the universe). The poet and this immanent bliss are partners in being and becoming where "every event is virtually present or immanent in every other event."[47] This projects the periodic transition of the poetic ego, the *ahamkara*. Each stage of transition is subversion and submission proceeding from that stage and into the next one. The anterior reality of the ego (the consciousness that bursts into the relish of nature) is sutured to the *madhyamavastha* (the middle phase) where the poetic ego proliferates into *bhavas* (myriad sentiments) as it comes into contact with other elements of nature. The disruption in *madhyamavastha* sublates into the *uttarakoti* or *paramakashtha* (the final phase or period) that is the present now of a higher unity where the "flash upon that inward eye" is made possible. Indeed, the poem itself has a flash (the wonder and the joy) in its eruption and, also, in its experience of the harmonic, pensive point of creativity. Such flashes of experience, realization, and achievement point to what in Zen Buddhism is called the Buddha-nature, whose unity is not determinate but dynamically *sunya* (empty), not in the sense of a vacuum but in a form that is procreative. This is what I would like to interpret here as the brimming vacant mood.

The "wealth" revealed externally and eventually relished within prepares the ground for a "flash upon that inward eye." This is not a transition to the state of absolute transcendence but is the attainment of a kinship with the daffodils. It is an interface of the self with becoming. The poetic being meditatively feels the rhythm of the creation, the life pulsating around the poet, resulting in the bliss of solitude. The flash of an experience in the inner being of the poet is a dip in solitude that gets him closer to the deepest layers of the spirit in nature. The flash, "all at once," of "a host of golden daffodils" is a sudden illumination that brings Wordsworth in accord with an inward vision. This enables him to connect with a consciousness that is both aesthetic and metaphysical.

There is a projective desire in the poem that through its self-subversiveness collapses the interior and the exterior of aesthetic relish. This relish intra-actively finds its entanglement in the *tathata,* the "thus-being of things." This tathata, through a suspension of discrimination and choice, encourages a nonduality and nonconditionality of things. The poet and the circum-ambient objects are held harmonically together by the flash; they are discriminated from one another. So any choice to privilege one element over the other is suspended. The poetic self moves in points of multiple convergences toward an aesthetic evolution. In such a consummate experience with the daffodils the *rasavada* (aesthetic consciousness) and *brahmasvada* (mystical consciousness) integrate into each other, *ānandaikaghana* (bliss of unity).

Calling into question the global exemplarity of reading a poem that belongs to early nineteenth-century British literature, the discussion so far produces an access to a new operative now where relevant dimensions of Sanskrit poetics and a poem by Wordsworth are caught in manifest, more-than-global sense-formations (I-other-I). Each exceeds its own formations and provenance to find itself in the other and in more than the other, in the more. This is a greeting of the other by encountering the relevance of the other in the "I." It serves the double purpose of saving the "I" from being overwhelmed by the other. "I" means the other not merely as the "promised" (the present or presents) but also as the promising (surplus or presence). The "I" is saved by greeting the other because saving need not be considered as the rigid preservation of hermeneutic sanctity. Through submission to the other, the "I" is salvaged and its retention is made possible.[48] Under the I-other-I bind, generated through intra-active transculturality, the poem has a problematic homecoming where the homecoming is in a *sahit* with the otherness of one's being. The poem is not in the alterity of the other. The agential intra-actions trigger both this expansion of interlocking epistemes and a folding back onto itself. "I is someone else," as Arthur Rimbaud has reiterated.[49] So the dance being the I is also the other. The taking place, thus, neutralizes the hierarchy and power that self and the other construct within a local-global bind. This leaves us in the midst of the more-effect.

The more-effect can be substantially argued through an intra-active understanding of the dance. The dance of the daffodils stimulates nature and cosmically sets off the *lila*, or play of creation. The Vedantic text *Brahmasutra* affirms that Brahman's creative activity is not undertaken by any need on his part but by way of sport.[50] This *krida* (sport) is aesthetic creativity. The dance of the daffodils stimulates the *lila*, the *krida*, in the poet. The dance *of* the poet and the dance *in* the poet are aesthetic realizations in space and time, resulting in a joyous overflow of energy. This surge, a plenitude of energy, is not anarchic but *kridaniyakam* (play) that promotes a life of sensitivity, aesthetic consciousness, and commitment to a harmonic consummation. Here the *lila*, or sport, finds an aesthetic poise in the poet who surrenders to its intrinsic delight.

The delight and the bliss of solitude are manifestations of *santarasa*. This is an important emotion within the *rasa* theory signifying tranquility and also *sthayi* or the stable. The poet is close to achieving *santapraya*, the blissful serenity of liberation. However, the *santarasa* paradoxically emerges out of the participatory world (the poet's highly intense interaction with the objects around him) as *uddipanavibhava*, the enhancing stimulus. It uncannily owes its joy to the *lila* and the *alaukika-ahlada*, the transmundane pleasure. The complex dynamics of *santa* (tranquil) corresponds to the *krida*. *Santa* thereby becomes an event of sportive quiet.

The *lila*, the *ananda*, and the *santarasa* come together in *samapatti* (synergy), which is the poet's *sthitaprajna* (poise). This is the *yukta-viyuktadasa*, the bond-liberated state. The poet is *yukta* (bound) to the daffodils and to their circumambient milieu through his immediate experiences of delight and wonder. He is also *viyukta* (liberated) beyond the immediacy of experiences into a moment that becomes his very own. This produces the pensive mood and opens the inward eye. In these moments of aesthetic and sensual relish, the poet has the privilege of being himself and another. In this *yukta-viyuktadasa*, the dance with the daffodils becomes *cittavistara* (the expansion of consciousness). The poetic soul with its ingathered joy becomes *rasenatripta*—satiety in emotions. With this *cittavistara*, the waves, the breeze, the trees, the lake, and the "never-ending line" of daffodils become interwoven beings. They inter-are with all the others. The aesthetic relish—"my heart with pleasure fills"—receives the impulsion of the inner "bliss of solitude" and the poet reaches the *uttarakoti*, the final phase. In this climax, the poetic ego is liberated to the point where it enjoys at once *santarasa* and *krida*. He makes meaning out of his *yukta-viyuktadasa*. It is a kind of *rahasya mudra* (a mysterious posture). This posture is something that Tagore metaphorically finds in a bee who "must sit, steady and unwavering, on the pollen if it is to taste the honey hidden in the heart of the flower."[51] The *rahasya mudra*, the mysterious poise, whose center is afflicted with a serious disquiet, shows that the poet's succumbing to a joy is not a revel or a riot as it might seem. His joy is the result of a dialectic between *santarasa* and *kridaniyakam* that makes it indeterminate and diaphanous. It is a *lila*, an *ananda*, that de-centers itself continually to find a center (*sthitaprajna*) in flashes of experiences caught in diachronic moments of creative relish. So the present of the dance meets the present of the *lila*. The "I" and the other are caught in a pleasant perplexity—the *lila* taking place both inside and outside the poet is Wordsworth's *rasenatripta* (*rasa* consummation). This makes him find his pensive poise through a deep interiority of aesthetic experiences. The *lila* in nature builds its presence in Wordsworth, resulting in *vivarta*, or transformation of the poetic being, in which the *lila* within and without converge and resonate. The pleasure springs from the *lila* mystique and the poet strikes the *rahasya mudra*, balancing all the forces within him, the jocund clutch of forces in clouds, vales, hills, lake, trees, breeze, stars, bay. He experiences the paradox of poise in *lila*, the leisure in sport, a pause in the flow, a dynamism in the quiet integration of forces. It is the *rahasya* (mystery) of creation.

Within this more than global phenomenon, the poem has come through as a kind of Nancyean fragment that has "accidental and involuntary aspects of fragmentations." Benjamin Hutchens argues that such fragmentation in its singularity becomes "ecstatic and exploratory in nature." Nancy points out,"If the fragment is indeed a fraction, it emphasizes neither first nor foremost the fracture that produces it. At the very least, it designates the borders of the fracture as an autonomous form as much as the formlessness or deformity of the tearing."[52] The more than global enables the poem to realize the value of textual tearing, the searing of systematicity, frissiveness of fraction, and the entropic energy of world-formations. The poem, in its negotiation with a few accredited parameters of Sanskrit poetics, forms itself as a fragment-event, not a romantic poem understood in a kind of traditional interpretive fatigue and its concomitant satiety but through inscription and exscription with an undecidable energy and a collapse of sense. Within the more than global intra-active band, the poem begins always as an interruption through an immanent worldview that betrays the always already fragmentary state. Sanskrit poetics does not come as anachronic to its exposition; its incidence is invested in the areality of its power and praxis as a work of art. "Daffodils" is both a sharing of sense and a circulation of sense. Hutchens shows us that sense, for Nancy, "is its own constitutive loss. It presents itself in 'the very opening of the abandonment of sense, as the opening of the world.' The fact that there is a 'there is,' a world of existing singularities, testifies that thinking itself is the possible opening of sense. Within the exigencies of sense, nothing truly 'has' sense, but everything in the nonsense of its being reveals sense to the opening of thought."[53] A Sanskrit reading is not outside the poem because by being *entre-nous* it is *cum*, staying and making "sens-able" singularizing "while at the same time connecting these singularities."[54] In the sense-ridden, comparative, dystopian grid exposure is exposition.

Post-Posts

In his reading of Nietzsche, Miller initiates a complex negotiation between what Nietzsche calls the burden of the past and a liberating reading in the present. Nomadism can develop as productive experiences, and it happens when the silent pressures on the local to overcome its immediateness result in a reading of the local with a consciousness of the global currents of experience that are considered not just as dissonance. It is antagonism or transfigurative distress, resulting in both knowing and ignorance. This means that literature can be experienced, as Miller argues elsewhere, as catachresis and as black holes. Miller's discussion becomes an interesting invitation to dialogue on this subject of critiquing the now and the principle of the more. *Sudesivadism* is my rejoinder to the specter of barbarism that Miller critiques in Nietzsche. Nietzsche's opposition to *Weltliteratur* stems from the fear that it would lead to an overabundance of unmanageable knowledge. Miller implicates this "more than enough" in world literature and rightly considers how Nietzsche's distress over universalizing literature is paradoxically a way of exploring more meaningful experiences. Distress turns into a lively unease that leaves us in a circulation where one's own local conditions and milieu of understanding are infected by certain centrifugality. This is a healthy nomadism that does not aspire for Hegelian totality or for the impossible sovereignty in knowledge sought by George Eliot's Casaubon in *Middlemarch*. I concur with Miller on how world literature escapes what Nietzsche considers Alexandrianism by generating the more and exploring the now. It does not give us comfort but inflects the distress as a way to understand and live productively.

A few lines from Lao Zi can help us to understand the more at a different level:

Thirty spokes share a hub: where *absence* is,
there the *use* of the carriage lies.
Mix clay to make a vessel: where absence is,
there the use of the vessel lies.
Drill holes as doors and windows to make a room: where
absence is, there the use of the room lies.[55]

The more in the global is the absence—the sense withdrawn, nothing as sense—that is where the use of literature lies. The absence that lies in the vessel or in the room is the vacuum that provides form and accommodates content. Similarly, the category of the more in globalizing literature creates absences that are not vacant but are points where thinking begins to open sense. Literature's absences thus exist ahead of our occupancy and invite us to connect with the joy that Tagore has brilliantly analyzed. We may see this somewhat in the light of Buddhist emptiness. It is a pregnant *sunyata* in which the tireless plurality of nows becomes events that are intra-relating and forever coming to be. Literature's local specificities are embedded in history, context, and time. Nevertheless, they are perennially exposed to an openness of thought that is not simply about taking a text out of its home base and throwing it into the domains of different cultures in time and place. The restive openness can be qualified as a disclosive affect of totality both in the sense of its accommodativeness and immanence. Zen master Dogen's seeing of the absoluteness of the bird and the fish as being continuous with the sky and the water is analogous to our intra-active habitation in "Daffodils": "When a fish swims in water, there is no end of the water no matter how far it swims. When a bird flies in the sky, fly though it may, there is no end to the sky. However, no fish or bird has ever left water or sky since the beginning. . . . But if a bird leaves the sky, it will immediately die, and if a fish leaves the water, it will immediately die. You must understand that the water is life, and the air is life. The bird is life and the fish is life. Life is the fish and life is the bird."[56]

The poem becomes self-forgetful in a life of its own. The intra-active fluidity that conceptual figurations of *deśī* and *videsi* bring creates a sustaining life for the more than global. Literature cannot survive without the entangled more, just as the bird or the fish will die without air or water. If air and water are life, the bird and the fish are life, too. If the local and the global are life, the more than global is life, too. This attests to the totality that the life of literature cannot do without. Literature has a life of its own. It has a life in being made global, has a life in not being rendered global, never becoming global, preglobal, and in being more than global, too. The more is the life and the life is the more. Perhaps, the more makes literature disappear better, as Emerson foresaw.[57]

The intra-active enactment in negativity and presence is Nancy's "trembling," the act of being affected, staying in vibration both in visibility and in the *nihil*.[58] Comparatism unleashes a desire to connect, while the more than global is predominantly about a nothingness, the nothing being the "differential spacing for an encounter with the other—a just-between-us—from which worlds are created by sharing in the same performative modality as sovereignty and the self."[59] The more than global makes sense of the performative *we*. It is informed in the we where Nancy locates the access to sense. The poem's access to sense is the entangled event of being coimplicated within Sanskrit poetics. Hutchens explains:

> The origin of the world emanates from any contact composing a "we." Each singular self has access to the presence of the world, but it is only contiguity with other singular selves that enables it to have "access to an access." That is to say, there is a multiplicity of presences of the world within the "we," and each proximity provides a multiplicity of accesses to the presences. If each singularity is co-implicated within the world, then the originary existential state of all singularities is a sharing in

the world, not any ontological divorce from it into a state of transcendence. The "world" is not merely some extrinsic horizon of singular existence, but the coexistence that enables existences to be exposed to the circulation of sense and the presences of a world.[60]

The potency or wealth of the we decimates the sovereignty of the local and global as the two limiting points of understanding literature. The more than global (both *mundas* and *immundas*) is about making sense of the end, the end as the inauguration of creativity. Intra-active transculturality finds the "wandering labour of sense" in the poem—a sense that is not predominantly produced but out there, there itself, letting-it-be, interleaved, insinuated and interlarded. It urges us to read literature with trans-immanence freeing us from our conservatism into a conceptual warfare where a meaningful harvest is presenced out of the ruins of finitude. It is in the radical nonequivalence of worlding that literature can find its experiences of freedom.

GLOBALIZATION AND WORLD LITERATURE

And fast by hanging in a golden Chain
This pendant world, in bigness as a Starr
Of smallest magnitude close by the Moon.
Thither full fraught with mischievous revenge,
Accurst, and in a cursed hour he hies
Milton, *Paradise Lost*, bk. 2, lines 1051–55

Ranjan Ghosh's orientation and argument in his chapter 5, "More than Global," are considerably different from what I say in this chapter. I have learned much from his chapter, both about his own way of thinking and about the Sanskrit and Hindi theory of literature in the context of his transcontinental, (in)fusion theory of literature. The dialogical differences, however, emerge from differences between our two ways of reading texts, Ghosh's reading of a Western poem, Wordsworth's "Daffodils," my reading of a passage by Nietzsche. A juxtaposition of the two readings is perhaps the clearest way of seeing what is at stake in the dialogue between us.

Dialogue, by the way, can have two somewhat contradictory meanings. It can mean a Habermasian give and take of conversation that has consensus as its goal, or it can mean a two-centered (dia-logue) conversation between persons who will remain in dissensus. My interchanges with Ghosh mix these two forms of dialogue. Sometimes we come to agree. At other times we remain in disagreement.

On the one hand, Ghosh reads "Daffodils" as triumphant confirmation of Rabindranath Tagore's exhortation (in Ghosh's epigraph) that one should strive "to free oneself of that regional narrowness and resolve to see the universal being in world literature, to apprehend such totality in every writer's work, and to see its interconnectedness with every man's attempt at self-expression—that is the objective we need to pledge ourselves to."

I, on the other hand, am enough dubious about what it would mean to read a poem as an example of "world literature" that I have not even tried

Figure 6.1 Satellite photo of earth as "Blue Marble." Credit: NASA Goddard Space Flight Center. Image by Reto Stöckli (land surface, shallow water, clouds). Enhancements by Robert Simmon (ocean color, compositing, 3D globes, animation).

to do so. Instead, I have tried to read as best I can a passage from Nietzsche's *The Birth of Tragedy* in the context of Nietzsche's own life situation as a nineteenth-century professor of classical philology at the University of Basel, Switzerland. I am also much more concerned than Ghosh usually is with the specificities of technological change that have brought about what we call globalization, and its concomitant, a new form of the discipline called world literature. I am also fearful that this new discipline will simply universalize Western theories of literature, whereas Ghosh does not hesitate, though with many nuances, qualifications, and caveats, and with recognition of the local in every literary text, to universalize a "more than global," that is, to advocate a transcontinental theory and practice of poetry that is exemplified as much by Sanskrit *sahitya* as by all the

Western sources Ghosh cites. Hindi or Sanskrit theory is, for Ghosh, when combined with Western theories, as useful for reading Wordsworth's "Daffodils" as it is for reading a literary work in Sanskrit or Hindi.

My instinct, on the contrary, is to hold that a special theory should be derived in each case as much as possible from the terminology of the text at hand in the light of its specific surrounding historical, biographical, and linguistic context. Doing that, of course, is extremely difficult, if not impossible, since any readings, even the ones most submissive to the language of the text, manifest in one way or another individual commitments on the reader's part, for example, my commitment to a rhetorical reading of the tropes in a text, as opposed to Ghosh's (in)fusion theory, which tends to relate details in a poem to larger conceptual issues, such as, in his chapter 5, "worlding" or "the more than global." He discusses for twenty manuscript pages citations from a large number of Eastern and Western authors, both theorists and writers of poems and novels, before he turns to a reading of Wordsworth's "Daffodils" that develops a more than global way of reading Wordsworth's poem.

World literature, in its recently resurrected form, is indubitably a concomitant of economic and financial globalization, as well as of new, worldwide telecommunications. Marx and Engels long ago, in a famous passage in the *Communist Manifesto* (1848), prophetically said just that:

> And as in material, so also in intellectual production. The intellectual creations of individual nations become common property. National one-sidedness and narrow-mindedness become more and more impossible, and from the numerous national and local literatures there arises a world literature."[1]

We are on all sides asked by the media to think globally and are given daily new information about globalization in its current form. We have also been granted, for the first time in human history, an ability to look at the earth from outer space, that is, from outside what is happening here. Millions of people all over the world have seen one or another of the unsettling space-ship or satellite photographs. They provide a distant and detached perspective on the earth, with a vengeance. To be, or to pretend to be, wholly detached and objective is, nevertheless, perhaps diabolical. Milton imagined Satan as one of the first space travelers in literature, as in the passage from early in *Paradise Lost* I have begun by citing.[2] Satan was not exactly detached, since his goal was to bring about the fall of man, but he certainly could see the whole earth from a distance, hanging in space, as all the sons and daughters of Eve can do nowadays. We are not exactly detached and indifferent, either.

World literature's time has come (again). The current return to world literature is perhaps an inevitable concomitant of globalization, but I see some problems with it. The problems I see are quite different from Ghosh's rejection of world literature in the name of what he calls the more than global. He means by that the participation of every literary work in whatever language and from whatever local culture in what he calls the "sacredness of literature."

The present context for developing a rigorous discipline of world literature is not the same as the context in which Goethe, two centuries ago, proposed the reading of *Weltliteratur*. For one thing, the current flowering of a new academic discipline called world literature is, in the West at least, a permutation of the still relatively new discipline of comparative literature, something that did not yet exist in Goethe's day or in Marx's. Western comparative literature was determinately Eurocentric in its creation and consolidation. Some of its early champions, such as René Wellek, were from the Prague semiotic school, or from Slavic linguistics generally, or were exiles from Germany. In the United States and Europe, literary study was still firmly divided into departments of this or that language or family of languages, English, German, romance languages, classics, near Eastern languages, East Asian languages, Scandinavian languages, etc. Having a separate department for something called comparative literature met with a lot of resistance from those entrenched centers of power. I well remember that from my experience teaching in the English Department at The Johns Hopkins University from 1953 to 1972.

The new discipline of comparative literature varied a lot from university to university, but it was given credence by being established at elite universities like Harvard and Yale. Harry Levin did this at Harvard, and the émigré scholars Eric Auerbach and René Wellek were largely responsible for doing this at Yale, with some help eventually from younger émigré scholars like Peter Demetz, Geoffrey Hartman, and Paul de Man. In spite of the fact that such scholars all had English as a second language, comparative literature tended to have an implicit nationalism by giving one language predominance, English in Yale's case and in the United States generally. Wellek's monumental *A History of Modern Criticism: 1750–1950* (1955–1992), in eight volumes, translates all its citations into English, even though his native language was Czech. He appends his citations in the original languages in small print at the end of each volume. For René Étiemble, on the contrary, the leading comparatist in France, French was the dominant language. Many departments of comparative literature, most notably the one at Yale, became centers of literary theory. Comparative literature at Yale was the center of the writing and teaching of the so-called Yale Critics.[3] World literature has developed in opposition to the Eurocentrism of most Western comparative literature departments.

The present context for the development of world literature as an academic discipline also responds to the many facets of globalization today that make Eurocentrism obsolete. I say more about these conditioning contexts in other chapters in this book.

The recent, impressive development of a new discipline called world literature seems pretty far from climate change, the World Wide Web, and the recent financial meltdown, but I think it can be shown to be a somewhat different version of a pattern of inadvertent reversal evident in those forms of globalization. The renewed emphasis on the teaching and study of world literature has, without doubt, been a response to manifold forms of technological and economic globalization. Another quite different response is the widespread takeover of literature departments by those kinds of social studies called cultural studies, postcolonial studies, ethnic studies, women's studies, film studies, and so on. These developments are to a considerable degree a good thing. It is harder and harder to justify the separate study of supposedly homogeneous national literatures, or to justify the isolated study of literature separately from other cultural forms. Widespread migration from all over the world to all over the world has meant that more and more people worldwide live in ethnically diverse communities where many languages are spoken, if you can any longer call them communities. In one section of Montreal, so I am told, an astonishing fifty-six different languages are spoken. It seems natural and inevitable these days to look at literature globally.

Doing that, however, differs radically from the shift to cultural studies and their ilk. These fields of study tend to take for granted that print literature is playing a smaller and smaller role in most people's lives, as new media like film, television, Facebook, and video games replace printed novels, plays, and poems.

The ethos of fewer and fewer people worldwide is determined to any large extent by reading literature in the traditional Western sense of printed novels, poems, and plays. This transformation is no doubt occurring unevenly around the globe, but it is happening to some degree everywhere.

I wish this were not so, but the evidence shows that it is the case. As I said in my part of the introduction to this book, statistical evidence shows the astounding number of hours a day many people spend surfing the web or using a smartphone or playing video games. Such people do everything but read Shakespeare or Jane Austen, even in e-text versions. Literature, in the old-fashioned sense of printed books, moreover, is migrating to e-readers like Amazon's Kindle or Apple's iPad.

Literature, in the traditional sense, tends to be marginalized in cultural studies, as it is in the lives of the mostly younger scholar-teachers who "do cultural studies." The new discipline of world literature, on the contrary, might be seen as a last-ditch effort to rescue the study of literature. It does this by implicitly claiming that studying literature from around the world is a way to understand globalization. This understanding allows one to become a citizen of the world. If I study world literature in a course or in a textbook, I will become a cosmopolitan, not just a citizen of this or that local monolingual community. In the course of developing the new world literature, however—through the planning of courses, the publication of textbooks, and the training of competent teachers—some problems arise. Here are three important challenges to the new discipline of world literature.

One: the challenge of translation. No single student, teacher, or ordinary reader can master all the hundreds of languages in which world literature is written. Any literary work in a given language can be translated into any other language, but difficulties of translation always exist. Will world literature have a single master language, such as Chinese or English, into which a given textbook will translate all the selections? That would appear to be a form of cultural imperialism. How can world literature avoid being dominated by some single, national academic culture? This issue arises in Ranjan Ghosh's use in his chapter 5 of a complex integument of Sanskrit words to express his reading of Wordsworth's "Daffodils." Those Sanskrit words sound, in transcriptions of the originals into English letters, quite strange to a Westerner like me. Sahitya? Ghosh gives English meanings of those words. These are of great help. But just having a rudimentary vocabulary of Sanskrit poetics with translations of those words is not at all the same thing as reading key texts in Sanskrit poetics in the original language and then internalizing those texts in the form of an embodied attitude toward reading literature. Ghosh has apparently done that, as his chapters in this book indicate, though it is only part of his larger project of developing a transcontinental (in)fusion approach to literature that draws together sources from all over the world.

Two: the challenge of representation. A scholar can spend his or her whole life studying a single national literature and still not master it. World literature will, of necessity, for example, in textbooks or courses, work by way of relatively brief selections from the literature of many countries or regions. Such selections will always be to some degree biased or controversial. How can this bias be avoided as much as possible? Who will have the authority to decide which works in a given language or in a given national literature belong to world literature? What will be the criteria for the decisions to include or exclude? Does Franz Kafka, for example, belong to world literature? The book on Kafka by Gilles Deleuze and Félix Guattari is subtitled *Toward a Minor Literature*.[4] Is that a true description? Does being minor mean Kafka's works do not belong to world literature? How would you know for sure one way or the other?

David Damrosch, in the brilliant introductory essay to his *What Is World Literature?* touches with wisdom and impressive learning on all the issues I am raising. He sidesteps the problem of setting a canon of world literature by saying that "world literature is not an infinite, ungraspable canon of works but rather a mode of circulation and of reading."[5] Does that mean that any literary work that is circulated and read globally automatically becomes part of world literature?

Teachers of world literature and editors of textbooks on world literature still need to decide, however, which works to help circulate and get read. Such experts also need to decide what to tell students about a work from a culture that is different from their own. Damrosch identifies succinctly the challenges to doing this. "A specialist in classical Chinese poetry," he says, "can gradually, over years of labor, develop a close familiarity with the vast substratum beneath each brief T'ang Dynasty poem, but most of this context is lost to foreign readers when the poem travels abroad. Lacking specialized knowledge, the foreign reader is likely to impose domestic literary values on the foreign work, and even careful scholarly attempts to read a foreign work in light of a Western critical theory are deeply problematic."[6] Would that mean that reading a Western poem in the light of Sanskrit theory is also problematic? That is a dialogical question I hereby pose to Ghosh.

Three: the challenge of defining what is meant by *literature*. Goethe, in one of those famous conversations with J. P. Eckermann about world literature, serenely affirms his belief that literature is a universal. It is something possessed by every human culture, everywhere at all times. When Eckermann, Goethe's fall guy or straight man, resisted reading Chinese novels by asking whether the one they have been discussing is "perhaps one of their most superior ones," Goethe responded firmly:

> "By no means," said Goethe; "the Chinese have thousands of them, and had when our forefathers were still living in the woods."
>
> "I am more and more convinced," he continued, "that poetry is the universal possession of mankind. . . . the epoch of world literature is at hand, and everyone must strive to hasten its approach."[7]

What Goethe says here is echoed by Ghosh's epigraph from Tagore in chapter 5. This indicates that the notion that poetry is the universal possession of mankind is by no means limited to one culture or another. But even within a relatively homogeneous, though multilingual, culture, such as that of Western Europe and America, literature is not quite so easy to define or to take for granted as Goethe makes it sound. Nonetheless, one might say of literature what a United States Supreme Court Justice famously said about pornography: "I can't define it, but I know it when I see it." Literature, in its modern Western form, is not even three centuries old. Is it legitimate to globalize that parochial notion of what is meant by *literature*, to make it valid for all times and places, for all cultures? The modern Western idea of literature is parochial in the sense of being limited to Western culture during one historical time—the time of the rise of the middle class, of increasing literacy, and of the printed book. It seems unlikely that what we Westerners have meant by *literature* for the last couple of centuries would hold true worldwide. How can a discipline of world literature respect the many different conceptions of literature in different times and places throughout the world? Damrosch recognizes that literature means something different in each culture, but he says, in a circular formulation, that we can define literature as whatever people in diverse times and places take as literature. All of us, in all our diversity of cultures and conceptions of literature, know a piece of literature when we see one.

The effort to globalize literary study, admirable though it is, encounters through its deployment intrinsic features in so-called literature that unglobalize the project. These features of diversity tend, or ought to tend, to return literary study not so much to the dispersed and self-enclosed investigations of national literatures in a given language in a given time and place as to the one-by-one reading of individual works that we have decided are examples of literature. The narrowness of segregated national literature study is just what the redevelopment of world literature was trying to escape. Comprehensive study of even a single national literature, however, is a Herculean, perhaps impossible, task. In the end, no literary work, it may be, fits the periodizing or generic generalizations that can be made about it. To speak of "the Victorian novel" is a mystified projection of unity where immense variation actually exists.

The new discipline of world literature, I conclude, problematizes itself, or ought to problematize itself, through rigorous investigation of the presuppositions that made the development of world literature as an academic discipline possible and desirable in the first place. Does that mean it is not worthwhile to read a few pages of Chinese, Hindu, Arabic, Kenyan, or Czech literature in English translation, with succinct expert commentary? Would it be better not to read bits of those literatures at all? By no means. The challenges to world literature I have identified do mean, however, that one should not exaggerate the degree to which courses in world literature are any more than a valuable first step toward giving students knowledge of literatures and cultures from all corners of the earth.

I have stressed the challenges and difficulties faced by world literature as a discipline concomitant with the new forms of globalization. That does not mean world literature should not flourish. Shakespeare, in the various plots of *As You Like It* (1600), shows pretty conclusively that love in the sense of sexual desire and love in the sense of spiritual affection may not by any means be reconciled. They form an aporia, an impasse. No bringing together of lust and love. The play ends triumphantly, however, with four marriages. These break through the impasse. Let world literature thrive, say I, just as Shakespeare's mad King Lear says, "Let copulation thrive."[8]

This chapter, up to this point, was presented in an earlier form as part of my presentation at a conference in Shanghai, "Comparative Literature in the Phase of World Literature: The Fifth Sino-American Symposium on Comparative Literature" (August 11–15, 2010). As I expected, I learned much from all the papers. By meeting and hearing so many of the leaders worldwide in the new discipline of world literature, I learned that this discipline is thriving globally and that a consensus is beginning to emerge about what world literature is and what it does, what its conventions and protocols are.

I found, however, especially relevant to my own reflections about world literature Thomas Beebee's paper asking "What in the World does Friedrich Nietzsche have against *Weltliteratur?*" I found Beebee's paper extremely provocative, not least by way of the citations from Nietzsche's *The Birth of Tragedy* and *Beyond Good and Evil*, the exegesis of which generated his essay. I had so much to say about both Beebee's paper and the citations on his handout that I refrained from commenting at the time he presented his paper for fear of impolitely taking up too much time in the discussion. The following remarks, as a conclusion to this chapter, are my belated response to hearing Beebee's admirable paper.

Just what does Nietzsche have against *Weltliteratur*? In order to be brief and to avoid an interminable exegesis, I limit myself almost completely to the citations from Nietzsche in Beebee's handout. Readers of the major essays on Nietzsche's *The Birth of Tragedy* by Paul de Man, Andrzej Warminski, Carol Jacobs, and Thomas Albrecht will know how complex, contradictory, and controversial *The Birth of Tragedy* is.[9] Warminski, in "Reading for Example," gives an example of the problems of translation I have mentioned. He shows that Walter Kaufmann, in the standard translation of *The Birth of Tragedy*, misleadingly translates the German word *Gleichnis* as "symbol." Kaufmann thereby imports the whole Romantic ideology of symbol into Nietzsche's text, whereas Gleichnis actually means "parable," or "figure," or just plain "image," in the sense of "likeness," which is, after all, what Gleichnis literally means (Warminski, *Readings*, xliv–xlv).

What Nietzsche says in the striking passage from *The Birth of Tragedy* Beebee began by citing adds one more challenge to the enterprise of world literature to the three I identify and discuss above. Readers of Nietzsche's "Vom Nutzen und Nachtheil der Historie für das Leben" will remember that Nietzsche argues, paradoxically and even scandalously, that it is healthy to forget history so we can get on with living productively in the present.[10] We need to start afresh without the great weight of history on our shoulders. Nietzsche's title has been translated in many different ways, in exemplification of what I say above about translation and world literature, but my German dictionary gives "advantage" and "disadvantage" as the primary meanings of *Nutz* and *Nachtheil*, not "utility" and "liability," as the Richard Gray translation I cite has it.

This essay is Nietzsche's version of James Joyce's definition of history as "the nightmare from which I am trying to awake." Nietzsche's and Joyce's views of history seem paradoxical and scandalous to us humanities professors who have given our lives to studying the history of literature, including, for many now, the history of world literature. Nietzsche himself was charged with an obligation to study and teach literary history as an Ordinarius Professor of Classical Philology at the University of Basle. Appointed at twenty-four, he was one of the youngest ever called to such a post. The Nietzschean view is the opposite of the by no means implausible and now proverbial counterassertion that those who forget history are condemned to repeat it.

Nietzsche's basic assumption, in the extracts from *The Birth of Tragedy* and *Beyond Good and Evil* Beebee discusses, is that we now live trapped in the meshes of what he calls an "Alexandrian" culture: "Our whole modern world is entangled in the net of Alexandrian culture. It proposes as its ideal the theoretical man equipped with the greatest forces of knowledge, and laboring in the service of science, whose archetype and progenitor is Socrates."[11] Just what do these two sentences mean? They mean that, like the citizens of Alexandria in the twilight of the ancient Greek world, we in the modern world know everything and have accumulated all knowledge, such as was gathered in the famous library of Alexandria, or as was collected in the great European university libraries of Nietzsche's time, or as does the Internet encompass today. In these days of global telecommunications, anyone can get information about almost anything by Googling it from almost anywhere in the world, that is, wherever one has an Internet connection that allows one to open Google. Use of Google is by no means globally allowed. Moreover, even our art, in Nietzsche's view, has been enfeebled by becoming imitative. It is cut off from fresh sources of inspiration. Our poets and artists know too much about the histories of poetry and art. This is Nietzsche's version of what Harold Bloom, in the late twentieth century, was to call "the anxiety of influence."[12]

Nietzsche takes a dim view of this situation. Why? Why does Nietzsche define the power of knowing everything as like being entangled in a net? It might seem a wonderful asset to have knowledge of everything under the sun at one's fingertips. On the contrary, Nietzsche holds that just as a wild animal, a fish, or a bird caught in a net is deprived of the ability to live its life freely, so Alexandrian people are paralyzed. They are prevented from living a normal human life by knowing too much, just as we today, it may be, are made Alexandrian by being entangled in the immense knowledge provided by the Internet. Nietzsche's concept of a proper human life is to live and act in the present, in a particular situation with present problems. We must live oriented toward the future, forgetting the past. One of Beebee's citations quotes Nietzsche's citing of Goethe's praise of Napoleon to Eckermann as the type of the non-theoretical man who embodies "a productiveness of deeds."[13] Normal human beings dwell within a local culture. This culture includes indigenous literature and other art forms. Such a culture is sequestered from other cultures and takes its assumptions, as well as its native language, as universals. The Greeks saw everyone who did not speak Greek as barbarians. It sounded as if they were stammering "bar . . . bar . . . bar," not speaking anything intelligible. Learning another language seemed pointless or dangerous to the Greeks. It would lead to dissonance, to the multiplication and dissolution of the self.

The word *dissonance* appears in the second of Beebee's citations. It is taken from the last section of *The Birth of Tragedy*, section 25. The word *dissonance* appears with increasing frequency toward the end of *The Birth of Tragedy*. "If we could imagine dissonance become man—and what else is man?—this dissonance, to be able to live, would need a splendid illusion that would cover dissonance with a veil of beauty [einen Schönheits-schleier über ihr eignes Wesen]."[14] A more literal translation would say "spread a veil of beauty over its own being." "*Ihr*," "its," could refer either to dissonance or to man, but Nietzsche's argument, after all, is that man is essentially dissonance. They are the same. Man is dissonance in living human form. (Present-day readers are likely to note, by the way, the imperturbable sexism of Nietzsche's formulations. He speaks of dissonance become man, not man and woman. *Mensch* apparently includes everyone, both men and women. Sexual difference does not matter to Nietzsche, at least not in these citations. *Birth* is used in the title without apparent reference to the fact that only women can give birth.)

Just what is Nietzsche's dissonance? Thomas Beebee was perhaps too reticent or too intellectually chaste to say anything, so far as I can remember his oral presentation, about that dissonant can of worms, the vexed opposition between the Dionysian and the Apollonian that ambiguously organizes the whole of *The Birth of Tragedy*. That opposition is especially salient as the leitmotif of section 25. In incautiously opening that can of worms, I say the opposition ambiguously organizes *The Birth of Tragedy*. The opposition is ambiguous because, though at first it seems that the Dionysian and the Apollonian are clear opposites, it turns out that matters are not quite so simple. The Dionysian, it appears, refers to the underlying cacophony of the universal Will (an echo of Schopenhauer), "the Dionysian basic ground of the world."[15] Music and Greek tragedy (Sophocles and Aeschylus, but not Euripides) are direct expressions of this Dionysian "basic ground of the world."[16] "Music and tragic myth are equally expressions of the Dionysian capacity of a people, and they are inseparable."[17]

The full title of Nietzsche's book, after all, is *The Birth of Tragedy out of the Spirit of Music*. Just why Nietzsche says "spirit of music" rather than just "music" is a difficult question to answer. Apparently the spirit of music precedes actual musical compositions, such as those operas by Wagner that are Nietzsche's prime example of the modern Dionysian. The spirit of music and music, Nietzsche's phrasing implies, are two different things. In any case, the Apollonian seems clearly opposed to the Dionysian. "Man" cannot face the Dionysian directly and go on living. It has to be covered over with a veil of beautiful illusion: "This dissonance [that is, dissonance become man in a *Menschwerdung*], in order to be able to live, would need a splendid illusion that would spread a veil of beauty over its own being." As T. S. Eliot puts this, "Human kind / Cannot bear very much reality."[18]

This opposition seems clear enough. It has an Apollonian, reasonable clarity. The more one reads carefully, however, everything Nietzsche wrote about the Dionysian and the Apollonian, including the abundant notes written prior to *The Birth of Tragedy*, Nietzsche's letters of the time, the recanting "Attempt at a Self-Criticism," written for the third edition of the book (1886), and the comments on *The Birth of Tragedy* in *Ecce Homo* (written 1888, published 1908), the more complicated matters become. The edition of 1886 even had a different title: *Die Geburt der Tragödie, oder: Griechenthum und Pessimismus* (The Birth of Tragedy, or: Hellenism and Pessimism). More and more, the careful reader comes to recognize that the Dionysian and the Apollonian, even at the time of the first edition of *The Birth of Tragedy* (1872), are not opposites. They are, to borrow Jacobs's word, "stammering" permutations of one another as slightly different "transfigurations" or figurative displacements of an original dissonance that, pace Schopenhauer, can never be expressed directly.

That dissonance can only be figured by one or another catachresis, that is, by a borrowed word or phrase used to name something that has no proper name. Dissonance, after all, is not music but the absence of music in clashing sound, just as stammering is language that is not language but the product of a speech impediment that produces repetitive dissonant sounds, like "bar, bar, bar." Already in section 25 of *The Birth of Tragedy* the same word, *transfiguration*, is used to define what Dionysiac music, tragic myth, and Apollonian illusion all do in different ways: "Music and tragic myth are equally expression of the Dionysian capacity of a people, and they are inseparable. Both derive from a sphere of art that lies beyond the Apollonian; both transfigure a region in whose joyous chords dissonance as well as the terrible image of the world fade away charmingly."[19] Only Apollonian form, apparently, can save us from the formlessness of the Dionysian: "Of this foundation of all existence—the Dionysian basic ground of the world—not one whit more may enter the consciousness of the human individual than can be overcome again by this Apollonian power of transfiguration."[20]

The reader is left, in the end, with an opposition not between the Dionysian and the Apollonian, but between the primordial, underlying dissonance, on the one hand, and, on the other, both the Dionysian and the Apollonian in all their various permutations as forms of the transfiguration (in the sense of turning into figures) of what mankind cannot face directly and go on living. These apparently clear figures, however, betray their origin in their own stammering dissonance. Carol Jacobs has in her brilliant essay "The Stammering Text: The Fragmentary Studies Preliminary to *The Birth of Tragedy*" conclusively demonstrated this in her admirable reading of the notebooks (especially notebook 9) preliminary to *The Birth of Tragedy*.[21] Her essay culminates in an exegesis of Nietzsche's use of the word *stammeln* (stammer) both in the notebooks and once in *The Birth of Tragedy* itself.[22] Jacobs's difficult insight might be summarized by a slight extension of her epigraph from *The Birth of Tragedy* itself: "Thus the intricate relation of the Apollonian and the Dionysian in tragedy may really be symbolized by a fraternal union of the two deities: Dionysus speaks the language of Apollo; and Apollo, finally the language of Dionysus."[23]

In truth, Nietzsche, as Albrecht and others of the scholars listed in my endnotes argue, saw both the Dionysian and the Apollonian as generating out of their own stammering dissonance the illusion of primordial dissonance, rather than just being figurative transfigurations of it. My word *catachresis*, as I said in chapter 4, the tropological name for a "forced or abusive transfer," hints at this possibility.[24] I refrain from pursuing this rabbit any further down its rabbit hole. It is a good example of the way an innocent-looking word, *dissonance*, can lead to a virtually interminable reading that ultimately includes everything the author wrote and its dissonant (and therefore resistant to totalization) intellectual, cultural, and linguistic context.

Nietzsche's harsh judgment of Goethe's *Weltliteratur* is a concomitant of this larger set of contextual assumptions. Specialists in world literature know many languages, many cultures, many literatures. They set these all next to one another in simultaneity, as exemplary of a universal or global literature that began thousands of years ago and that still flourishes everywhere in the inhabited world. The efflorescence of world literature as an academic discipline today is clearly a concomitant of globalization, as I began this chapter by asserting. Nietzsche in *Beyond Good and Evil* (1886) saw this, ironically, as civilization, humanizing, progress, or "the *democratic* movement in Europe," that is, as "an immense *physiological* process . . . the slow emergence of an essentially *super-national* and nomadic species of man, who possesses, physiologically speaking, a maximum of the art and power of adaptation as his typical distinction."[25] This process has now reached a hyperbolic level. The new, nomadic species of man takes many forms today, but it might be personified in the scholar who travels much of the time all over the world by jet plane, as I used to do, to attend conferences and to give papers that are heard by participants who come from all over the world, the globe compacted to the size of a lecture hall.

In the light of this brief establishment of a wider context for world literature, as Nietzsche saw its "disadvantage" for life, I now turn back to the first citation Thomas Beebee made from *The Birth of Tragedy*. The narrower context of Nietzsche's putdown of world literature is Goethe's celebration of it in that famous interchange with Eckermann, already cited, about Chinese novels as a manifestation of world literature. The Chinese, Goethe told Eckermann, had novels when we Europeans were still living in the woods. "The epoch of world literature is at hand, and everyone must strive to hasten its approach," said Goethe with his usual somewhat ironic cheerfulness. It is coming anyway, so why not hasten its coming, or, rather, we *should* therefore hasten its coming. Goethe, as opposed to Nietzsche, saw no danger in world literature. In his serene and sovereign imperturbability, he welcomed its coming, perhaps because he was sure he would be part of it, as has certainly turned out to be the case.

Nevertheless, the effects on Goethe's Faust of total knowledge should give the reader pause. Beebee's citations include a reference in *The Birth of Tragedy* to Goethe's Faust as the type of modern man's omniscience turning against itself in a perpetual dissatisfaction: "How unintelligible must *Faust* [He means Goethe's Faust], the modern cultured man, who is in himself intelligible, have appeared to a true Greek. . . . Faust, whom we have but to place beside Socrates for the purpose of comparison, in order to see that modern man is beginning to divine the limits of this Socratic love of knowledge and yearns for a coast in the wide waste of the ocean of knowledge."[26]

Well, just what does Nietzsche have against Weltliteratur? Here is the crucial passage Beebee cites. It must be scrutinized closely: "Our art reveals this universal distress: in vain does one depend imitatively on all the great productive periods and natures; in vain does one accumulate the entire 'world-literature' around modern man for his comfort; in vain does one place oneself in the midst of the art styles and artists of all ages, so that one may give names to them as Adam did to the beasts: one still remains eternally hungry, the 'critic' without joy or energy, the Alexandrian man, who is at bottom a librarian and corrector of proofs, and wretchedly goes blind from the dust of books and from printers' errors."[27]

Just what is the "universal distress," the unassuaged need for "comfort," the eternal hunger that modern man suffers? The passage just cited from *The Birth of Tragedy*, as well as other passages from Nietzsche's writings, indicate that it is the distress of a successful Socratic, Faustian, or even a Kantian or Hegelian, search for total knowledge, empirically verified and epistemologically sound. This search has turned against itself through its very success. This reversal has left modern man in a state of universal distress, typified by the eternal dissatisfaction of Goethe's Faust. The dissatisfying superabundance of knowledge that causes Faust grief is exemplified today by the more or less limitless knowledge about everything under the sun, and beyond the sun, available on the Internet.

The immediate context of the passage just cited from section 18 of *The Birth of Tragedy* affirms clearly that this superabundance of knowledge is the cause of universal distress. The whole section, however, is complex and would demand a lengthy exposition. To put what Nietzsche says in an oversimplifying nutshell, the search by theoretical, scientific, or scholarly man for the power and equanimity granted by a comprehensive knowledge has reversed itself by reaching the irrational and illogical, from which theoretical man recoils in fear:

> It is certainly a sign of the "breach" of which everyone speaks as the fundamental malady of modern culture, that the theoretical man, alarmed and dissatisfied at his own consequences, no longer dares entrust himself to the terrible icy current of existence: he runs timidly up and down the bank.[28] So thoroughly has he been pampered by his optimistic views that he no longer wants to have anything whole, with all of nature's cruelty attaching to it. Besides, he feels that a culture based on the principles of science must be destroyed when it begins to grow *illogical*, that is, to retreat before its own consequences.[29]

In this extraordinary passage, rational knowledge is said to overreach itself and become dangerously illogical, irrational. This is the "distress" of which Nietzsche speaks in the opening sentence of the first citation Beebee discussed: "Our art reveals this universal distress."

Just how, for Nietzsche, does this revelation through the art of the present moment, that is, the moment of the late nineteenth century in Europe, occur? It happens, says Nietzsche, through the Alexandrian derivative and imitative quality of today's art. Present-day artists and poets know too much literary history and too much art history to produce other than feeble imitations of the great productive artists and poets of the past. Nietzsche's formulations take place, you will have noticed, through a cascade of phrases beginning with "in vain." It is as a member of this sequence that the failure of world literature to give modern man comfort in his distress is asserted. Categorizing art styles and periods in the literature of all ages and countries (for example, speaking of Baroque, Romantic, or Victorian styles), work all we literary historians perform, is as arbitrary and ungrounded as are, to a skeptical eye, those names Adam gave to all the beasts.

The bottom line is that for Nietzsche world literature, far from giving modern man comfort in his distress, fails completely to do that. In fact, turning to world literature is one of the signal ways that distress manifests itself and is exacerbated. As far as Nietzsche is concerned, it would be better not to know, better to forget all those alien literatures that swarm around the globe. It would be better to live as Nietzsche implies Athenian Greeks did, that is, in joyful possession of a narrow local culture that ignored all other cultures and literatures and saw them as barbarous.

Nietzsche's view of Greek culture is not quite so simple, however. *The Birth of Tragedy* ends with paragraphs asserting that Athenian Apollonian beauty was a compensation for Dionysian madness: "In view of this continual influx of beauty, would he [someone today imagining himself a curious stranger in ancient Athens] not have to exclaim, raising his hand to Apollo: 'Blessed people of Hellas! How great must Dionysus be among you if the god of Delos [Apollo] considers such magic necessary to heal your dithyrambic madness.'"[30] Nietzsche imagines an old Athenian's responding, "But say this, too, curious stranger: how much did this people have to suffer to be able to become so beautiful!"[31] The Dionysian causes suffering. The Apollonian is beautiful.

Nietzsche's forceful rejection of world literature already manifests in hyperbolic form the reversal that was the climax of the paper I gave at the Shanghai Symposium (that is, the original version of the first part of this chapter). The new discipline of world literature, I said, "problematizes itself, or ought to problematize itself, through rigorous investigation of the presuppositions that made the development of world literature as an academic discipline possible and desirable in the first place." One of the bad effects of the discipline of world literature, Nietzsche implies, is that it transforms scholars into something like what Nietzsche became or feared becoming as a professor of classical philology. Nietzsche's description is memorably sardonic. It recalls George Eliot's description in *Middlemarch* of Edward Casaubon and his futile pursuit of the Key to All Mythologies. Here again is Nietzsche's description: "The 'critic' without joy or energy, the Alexandrian man, who is at bottom a librarian and corrector of proofs, and wretchedly goes blind from the dust of books and from printers' errors." It may have been in part fear of becoming like this critic that led Nietzsche to resign his professorship. His main, overt reason was trouble with his eyesight. Here is Eliot's description of Casaubon: "Poor Mr. Casaubon himself was lost among small closets and winding stairs, and in an agitated dimness about the Cabeiri, or in an exposure of other mythologists' ill-considered parallels, easily lost sight of any purpose which had prompted him to these labors."[32] What circulates in Casaubon's veins is neither blood nor passion but marks of punctuation, just as Nietzsche's dry-as-dust scholar spends his time with misprints. As Mrs. Cadwallader, one of Casaubon's sharp-tongued neighbors, says, "Somebody put a drop [of his blood] under a magnifying-glass, and it was all semicolons and parentheses."[33] For both Nietzsche and Eliot, culture as enshrined in texts is reduced to concern with the materiality of the letter or of punctuation marks, such as have preoccupied me in revising and footnoting this essay. Friedrich Nietzsche, the precociously brilliant young professor of classical philology, may have written an outrageously unorthodox first book (*The Birth of Tragedy*) as a way to avoid becoming just another classical philologist.

I make one final observation. I intended to make a few brief comments about Thomas Beebee's admirable paper and about the citations from Nietzsche on which he focused. As I might have foreseen, my comments have got longer and longer and might be yet longer. They extend themselves indefinitely. What Thomas Beebee, and then I, following in his footsteps, have said about Friedrich Nietzsche's theory of Weltliteratur indicates that theoretical statements about world literature require as much contextualizing exposition as do works of world literature themselves. Such statements must be read, and they must be contextualized.

I do not think we can ever go back to a world of isolated societies, each with its own indigenous culture. To wish we could all be like the putatively happy ancient Athenians, as Nietzsche sometimes seems to do, is, in my view, a form of unproductive nostalgia. We must make do with what we have, which is a worldwide Alexandrian culture. The new efflorescence of world literature as an academic discipline is a natural concomitant of this.

Its great value is that even if it does not give "comfort," it does help us to understand and to live productively in the new, uncomfortable world of global telecommunication and global wandering that Nietzsche calls nomadism. The encounters between me and Ranjan Ghosh in the alternating chapters of this book are attempts to exemplify in another way such an "understanding and living productively."

Though Ghosh and I agree in putting the new discipline of world literature in question, our questioning comes from opposite directions. Our chapters 1 and 2 somewhat unexpectedly ended in my recognition of a consonance, or at least resonance, between Ghosh's concept of *Sahitya*, which is one version of his sacredness of literature, and my only slightly ironic allegiance to "the imaginary" as expounded by Wolfgang Iser and Maurice Blanchot. Our chapters 5 and 6 are not so happily in tune, even though in both cases the exposition is structured as a juxtaposition of a theory section and a section "close reading" a text, a poem by Wordsworth in Ghosh's chapter, a passage from Nietzsche's *The Birth of Tragedy* in my chapter. Ghosh challenges the new discipline of world literature in the name of the more than global, that is, in the name of a complex theory of literature based on both Eastern and Western sources that works as well for Wordsworth's "Daffodils" as it would for any poem in Chinese, Sanskrit, Hindi, or Bengali. I challenge world literature in the name of the irreducible idiosyncrasy and specificity of each literary work, for example, Wordsworth's "Daffodils." That individuality can, I claim, be assimilated neither to a more than global theory nor to whatever may be said about the characteristics of English Romantic literature or even of Wordsworth's poetry. The most important features of "Daffodils" are sui generis. Moreover, my "theory section" in this chapter by no means takes Nietzsche, much less Goethe, as solid foundations for a theory of world literature. Both Goethe and Nietzsche, I hold, must be read with a critical eye and with close attention to problematic linguistic details in what they wrote, not as solid foundations on the basis of which a correct more than global theory of literature might possibly be constructed.

PART IV

Teaching Literature

REINVENTING THE TEACHING MACHINE
Looking for a Text in an Indian Classroom

Everything in the seminar must, in principle, begin at fictive zero point of my relation to the audience: as though we were all "complete beginners" the whole time.
—Jacques Derrida

One cannot without intellectual dishonesty assimilate the "production" of
texts . . . to the production of goods by factory workers: writing and thinking are
not alienated labor in that sense, and it is surely fatuous for intellectuals to seek to
glamorize their tasks . . . by assimilating them to real work on the assembly line.
—Fredric Jameson

Entering my postgraduate Indian classroom of seventy-odd students
to teach Samuel Beckett's *Endgame* is taking a plunge into a cocktail of
challenge and fun. The classroom becomes atmospheric in billowing expectations constructed on the pillars of existential philosophy, modernist
aesthetics, European dramatic tradition, and certainly Beckettian philosophy and ethics of writing. So theoretically *Endgame* has already had its
rules of interpretive gaming ready and formed and my presence in the
classroom stays entrenched in a prefigured circulation where the students
and the teacher function as satellites around a heliocentric textual gravity.
However, once I decide to activate the battle lines across disciplines, the
"throb" in the classroom changes and teaching, a beginning conducted at
fictive zero point, generates "desire lines" that demand able and prescient
protection from official and sanctioned pathways of communication and
travel.[1] My teaching tries to sniff out how differences across cultures of
understanding and traditions of thought can be the strength of communication, the nutrition of good learning and understanding. What Marjorie
Garber calls "discipline envy" becomes for me the "disciplinary eros" in the
classroom. Garber observes: "But I use *envy* here to designate a mechanism,
a kind of energy, an exhilarating intellectual curiosity as well as what Ve-
blen called emulation. Envy in this sense is not the same as jealousy ('fear

of losing some good through the rivalry of another; resentment or ill will toward another on account of advantage or superiority'). Rather it corresponds to older notions of the word that are generally positive rather than negative: a 'desire to equal another in achievement or excellence; emulation' and (a sense derived from the French *envie*) a 'wish, desire, longing; enthusiasm.' "[2]

What if I import transcultural envy into the classroom? How does that change the desire lines, introduce a sense of loss and limit, create problems in the identification of paradigms of understanding, *schadenfreude*, the pleasure at the expense of someone's discomfort and unease? But what gain does this unease bring? Pursuing and practicing humanities in the classroom is setting out on a search for the "blue bird." Garber refers to the symbolist play by the Belgian writer Maurice Maeterlinck called *The Blue Bird*, where two children embark on a quest for a special blue bird. Garber writes: "The children set out on their journey. In the space of what they think is a year but what turns out to be a long Christmas night's dream, they travel to the Land of Memory, the Palace of Night, the Graveyard, and the Kingdom of the Future, but although they often glimpse a bluebird, they can never quite capture it."[3] They return home only to discover that their pet turtle dove, a caged bird they paid scant attention to, is indeed blue in color. Garber rightly notes "that the children of this story needed to travel around the world, and to the worlds of the past and the future, in order to recognize that what they had been seeking was at home with them all along. They had neglected or failed to value it, because it seemed so ordinary. Their bluebird, when they finally put it to work in the world, giving it to the neighbor's child and curing the child's illness, ultimately escapes."[4] I would like to argue that any literary text in a classroom has a blue bird that actually is the link, the continuum, the vestibule, the unease, between what the text possesses and the critical peregrinations that occur around it. The blue bird occasions exciting angles and turns in a text that, again, are not what strictly define a text. It enhances the choices that a text delivers, the points around which the text vanishes and reappears; the text somehow eludes captivity.

It has to be agreed that "any pedagogy that eliminates the classroom text from its questioning repeats the colonizing gesture. Critical problematizing should therefore interrogate the authority relations that seem at once so stereotypical and so natural."[5] So a text dynamically inscribed into the notion of the uncanny (the transcultural uncanny as elaborated in chapter 5) cannot be immured within the dialectic of the center and the periphery, which has influenced facetiously our universals of critical understanding. Rather, a "new universalism" is under critique and awaits appropriation where the West and the East have ceased to sit on either side of the fence in a triumphalist and imperialist way; interestingly, de-centered thinking has come to change our discourses in an equation where Pozzo and Lucky (characters from Beckett's *Waiting for Godot*), as representatives of crosscultural epistemic and conceptual parameters, as it were, are not master-slaves changing batons, but become proficient and productive in their exchanges for each other's configurative identities. The "contact zone" speaks of inequality in power, values, and ideologies; but such inequalities result in freedom, echoing Alexis de Tocqueville, to create spaces to test the limits and frontiers of negotiation.[6] Equality constrains and, hence, the transcultural planetization of reading and reception is about breaking norms, courting the "unpeace": the meaning it makes is both within and beyond us. This is not without rules, rules that lend rationality to understanding and interpretive claims, but must take into account the ability of the interpreter to reframe few rules, reinvest his or her critical understanding to bend the game to his or her advantage, to rally home a point, or winsomely score from a deft, perceptive nexus of ideas, leaving behind a trail of surprise and serendipity.

Within such a restless aesthetic, a kind of "revenge of the aesthetic," Beckett's *Endgame* has a disquiet that beckons transcultural momentum and movement, provocatively dislocating the play from its Eurocentric anchorage by relating it uncannily to a world with which its apparent relation looks contradictious and ambiguous. How pertinent is the paradigm of archetypal existentialism in our understanding of *Endgame* even after the play has crossed the borders of the Indian subcontinent and invited a renewed epistemic achievement? So let me begin by arguing that Beckett's works are about the human condition and, hence, cannot avoid being dialogic with different worldviews. They bring in their wake ambivalence and the splitting of concepts that only transculturalism, with its odd mix of congruence and contradiction, can generate. Thus, within the dynamics of "border-art," the play, when read and performed in India, can predominantly, albeit arguably, remap itself within a Hindu worldview.[7] This attitude is contrary to what Rukmini Bhaya Nair calls the "lotus eater syndrome," one that "the typical English literature teacher is guilty of perpetuating." She writes (indeed, an appropriate observation whose reality has not changed much between the time her piece was published and a general Indian literature classroom today): "The English literature classroom in Indian universities is one such well-defined cultural context in which pre-selected texts are placed before us, sign-posted as it were, explained with the help of earlier deified generations of critics, positively evaluated in terms of other non-canonical texts, and thus raised to full glory before the bemused eyes of students. . . . [Students] have so internalized the received explanations, comparisons, definitions and deifications that their own linguistic awareness is silenced or suppressed."[8] My reading of Beckett's *Endgame* here is a demonstration of how such intellectual faineance in the classroom can be overcome with all its attendant complications and spin-offs.

Producing a New Object

The blue bird is the provocation to think outside disciplines, the meaningful inspiration for transdisciplinary mobility and momentum. It does not belong to anyone, is not to be understood as "purely on its own terms," exists to multiply the color of a text and enthuse a maieutic reception.[9]

Louis Menand notes:

> What humanities departments should want is not interdisciplinarity or postdisciplinarity, and they should definitely not want consilience, which is a bargain with the devil. What they need to do is hunt down the disciplines whose subject matter they covet and bring them into their own realm. To the extent that programs and particularly graduate programs consist of a guided tour of the Norton Anthology, literature programs are perpetuating their isolation. Why aren't all literature majors required to take a course on the sociology of literature? Or a course on literature and philosophy, or literature and science? Why do students of literature have to take their history courses in history departments when literature departments could offer them history for literature students? This seems a minor curricular point, but it goes to the fear academics have that their fields will be dumbed down if they stray from their traditional boundaries. It's the boundaries themselves that are dumbing us down. Interdisciplinarity begins at home.[10]

Academic freedom, whether in a classroom or outside it, does not necessarily invest in disciplinary disciplehood—a typical Indian provincial university syndrome—daunted by disciplinary dictates and communal fealty. Working under the arch of a discipline is espousing sheltered freedom, structured and well premised. The autonomy that such spaces constitute primarily sponsors a negotiation between a critical purveyor and the integrity of disciplines. A literary critic, for instance, need not be swamped by a continental philosopher, for each of them is committed to safeguard disciplinary integrity and independence. However, academic freedom inspires opening onto each other, with a Derridean impiety, with a mind that has caution, critical care, innovation, invention, experiment, audacity, a kind of "step careful and step careless" attitude (to appropriate Robert Frost). Douglas Steward notes that we might pastiche Derrida: "there is no outside-the-humanities." He observes:

> The pastiche may seem flippant, but in the age of genocide and terror- ism the notion that *nothing human could be alien to us as humanists* in the world's sole superpower could not be more relevant. This relevance is exactly what many in the humanities have wanted to engage when they have been accused of impertinent politicking in the classroom: to ask if language can be more adequate to the truth; to ask if history has been recounted truthfully; to discern the alien as human; to learn the lan- guage and culture of the other; to explore the history of the inhuman/e in the human/e; to demand an expansion of human rights; to interro- gate the border rather than the human being at the border; to discover what rhetorics of language and image mobilize a border around who counts as human; to question who is patrolling the border and with what ends. These questions can only be impious.[11]

Herein lies the need to *create* a new ethics of an Indian undergradu- ate and postgraduate classroom for teaching literature, the need to in- terlocute impious questions that would form a genuine part of academic freedom and would not perniciously threaten interdisciplinarity. I agree with Miller on the strategic strangulation that a common core curriculum can produce, which is why college and university teachers in India are sub- jected to a "syllabus" approved by a central committee trusted to unleash a near common program of reading for students across the country, under the aegis of the University Grants Commission. The question is heavily centered on what we should read to get a degree that would enable and endow a professional career. The agony is probably less in being strapped under a generally agreed syllabic sky than when a teacher encounters a text in a classroom. The common Indian graduate and postgraduate class- room-teaching has a direct connection with the kinds of questions that end-of-semester examinations would demand of the students. Students *should* read a particular text, and teachers should teach the text in a partic- ular way because questions should be set in a particular way. It is difficult, if not impossible, for Beckett's *Endgame* to manifest on the students in the way it exists in this chapter because the autonomy and design of teaching literature in a general Indian classroom is much prescribed, unfortunately mapped and formalized through generational transmission, collective parity, and subservience to a consensually settled standard.

But should teaching and the experience of literature be what most teachers in India are familiar with and immune to? Literary texts should be reinvented in the classroom through the conjoined commitment derived out of the patience and curiosity of the students and the desire and indulgence of the teachers. Disciplinizing interdisciplinarity, then, is making allowance for an entangled discursivity where the "already spoken" builds on and polemicizes the "not yet spoken"—a "smooth" classroom milieu caught in dialogized consciousness. As I have argued elsewhere in this book, the entangled generation of meaning is not always something that we figurize or extrapolate; it already exists in a life of its own, within a self-sustaining chamber (Beckett's thoughts about life and humanity at large peremptorily coexisted with or superposed Hindu ethics and certain paradigms of Hindu philosophy, existing before what I thought I had unraveled for my students in the classroom).

Rey Chow observes that ultimately "aesthetic judgment involves a reflection of the terms of the reflecting activity (or subjectivity) from within rather than only a reflection of the external object it judges, bringing with it a potential for dismantling those terms precisely as the reflecting activity (or subjectivity) tries to reach for the universal. Defined along these lines, aesthetic or reflective judgment seems poignantly germane to those areas of knowledge production in which problems of radical otherness are the most acute."[12] A classroom must encourage aesthetic and reflective judgments that stay circumscribed by cultural difference and the denationalization of literature. There is, thus, an "instant" in such an attitude, the pursuit of an instant in its radical presentness. It works on the gains of a fraught now, the hope that its perpetual pregnancy generates, "intermittently eclipsed by an awareness of the present as deferment, as an empty excited openness to a future which is in one sense already here, in another sense yet to come."[13] Being unavailable to itself, the instant is continually under pressure to lose its instantness. By wrestling with the now, transcultural poetics keeps diverse subjects in company, enfolds one present into the other and stays ironically "present imperfect." This is about routing the uncanny in the classroom, which turns into a literary zone, a zone that Vilashini Cooppan describes as the "disjunctive merging of the familiar and the strange, the present and the past, the repressed and the returned," where no text is pure and original and no work can avoid being "inserted into the globalized processes of migration, borrowing, adaptation, and retelling." Cooppan adds, "Temporally, it haunts, ghosting new texts with the residual presence of older ones, or indeed, old texts with the anticipatory presence of new ones. Because the time line of the uncanny is not chronological, it invites us to resist the impulse to read only some texts—usually modern, postcolonial, emergent, or otherwise belated texts—in the shadow of their greater others, and to recognize instead a ghostly alienness animating every text."[14]

Let me unveil, at this point, the teaching of *Endgame* within an uncanny transcultural eros. Working within the ambit of Hindu ethics and philosophy, one may begin the class by arguing that it is the problematization of the dharma of existence that deeply informs many of Samuel Beckett's plays, particularly *Waiting for Godot* and *Endgame*. And so it might be worthwhile to ask: what is dharma? The word comes from *dhr*, which means to form, sustain, and support, and "in its widest sense," as John Koller observes, "it refers to that which sustains and holds together the universe itself."[15] Sarvepalli Radhakrishnan interprets dharma as the right action. He points out that "in the *Rg Veda rta* is the right order of the universe. It stands for both the *satya* or the truth of things as well as the dharma or the law of evolution."[16] In fact, to hold and sustain order, the observance of the necessary acts becomes essential; it helps to keep the order of the world.[17] Hence, it is karma, action, that eventually becomes the determinant for the sustenance of order. Every form of life cannot deny its dharma of existence, the law of its being, and this concern with order—the order of being, the being-in-the-world, the ever-impinging world of alien entanglements, the order of values—brings us to interrogate the text in the classroom with a host of questions: to what extent have Hamm and Clov honored the dharma of their being as evolutionary and generative? Do Hamm and Clov suggest everything that life represents or does not represent? Within the limitations of their mutilated selves, how far can we consider them to be the representatives of all humanity? Are we to assume that there is no other side to this benumbing world of the play? Can we not look into the substratum of this enervating predicament and finger the nerves that evoke this hellish milieu? How can we perspectivize the prevalence of "evil" spacing itself out in such an existential configuration? Despite Hamm's self-reflexive moves to change the horizon of existence, the inherent immovability of suffering remains the "unyielding sureness of reality," which does not fail to cross our will. Why this persistent suffering and what is the suffering for? Does *Endgame* provide us with the means by which we can judge the reality and vitality of suffering? How do we account for such a dismembered and disjointed world? Is it the collapse of dharma, the loss of order, in every conceivable sphere of existence? It is worthwhile to see how ideas emerging from Indian knowledge systems argue a case for the play, putting forth a critique pronouncedly removed from what we have come to accept as inherited modes of reception.

The *samkhya-karika* sees three kinds of suffering, bodily or physical, environmental, and mental. It is virtually impossible to remove suffering: "From the torment by three fold misery arises the enquiry into the means of terminating it; if it be said that it is fruitless, the means being obvious to us, we reply no, since in such means there is no certainty or finality."[18] Suffering, in *Endgame*, cannot end "the abject and indigestible husks of direct contact with the material and the concrete."[19] Spinoza, who had a great influence on Beckett, has this to say in his "On the Improvement of the Understanding":

> After experience had taught me that all the usual surroundings of social life are vain and futile, seeing that none of the objects of my fear contained in themselves anything either good or bad, except in so far as the mind is affected by them, I finally resolved to inquire whether there might be some real good having power to communicate itself, which would affect the mind singly, to the exclusion of all else: whether, in fact, there might be anything of which the discovery and attainment would enable me to enjoy continuous, supreme, and unending happiness.[20]

Beckett's *Endgame* seems to be shorn of any "good"; *sarvam duhkham* (universal suffering), the classically elemental, unimpassioned ritual of agony, permeates every crevice of the play. This *sarvam duhkham* charts out value-bereft lives for both Hamm and Clov as it does to all of us on earth. If we take Patanjali's thesis in *Yoga-Sutra* (2.15) and *Visuddhimagga* we find that *duhkha* is born out of the agony of the search, the dissatisfaction and the rebutted craving. But *duhkha*, as embedded in the searching conditions in *Endgame*, is not plain corporeal suffering or mental affliction. It is not a state of paranoia about a loss of pleasure and also not a hedonistic concept that could be critiqued in conflation with *sukha* (pleasure or happiness). *Duhkha* in *Endgame* is, rather, a realization that we are essentially in a conditioned state where there is a complete lack of freedom (compare the *samskara-duhkha* of the *Visuddhimagga*). In our conditioned state, there is a marked awareness of this utter absence of freedom and it is what makes *duhkha* a profound realization. Buddhist philosophy would have us believe that everything is suffering because everything is conditioned and is in a state of impermanence and flux. The Nyaya school would instruct us to judge everything as pain, for we do not have any experience of unmixed pleasure, or *sukha*. The Hindu concept of suffering argues this phenomenon as an "eternal return of events." There is no harm either in being tempted to perceive a kind of eternal recurrence of the same monotonic life-activities in *Endgame*, which simultaneously engender ennui and enigma. Arthur Danto elaborates: "Imagine having endless times to go through what we all have gone through once, the mastering of our bodies: learning to walk erect, learning to control our bowels and going through all the same stages of emotional awakening again and again with all its embarrassments, all the torments. . . . I think the knowledge would be shattering. The mere tedium of it all could not be borne."[21] This is the Hindu view of a despairing life that records the very depths of Beckett's world.

There is no escape for Hamm and Clov from this loop of *duhkha*. The absurdity of the situation is heightened by the fact that while they can take this view and realize what they do in life is arbitrary and meaningless, they cannot disengage themselves from life by this awareness. It may be said that we realize the truth while we remain, as we must, immersed in the ocean of untruth. This immersion in the sea of untruth is very difficult to rationalize: an inertial force powerful enough to defy systematic rationalization takes over. Even if they choose to undertake a self-transcendental step backward, they are regressed by the question about the available freedom to do so. Are they really free to make a move? But is the truth of suffering the only reality that Hamm and Clov are faced with? Can we argue that the submergence in a sea of untruths is what makes the experience of suffering for both a ceaseless and encompassing phenomenon? We can within the classroom concur to argue that the situation in the play is not as depressing and calamitous as it seems on the surface. The prospects of karma lie implicit within; it, thus, triggers karmic possibilities, unrealized on most occasions, of freedom and positive authenticity against the grain of a soul-deadening suffering that stays conspicuously written into the very heart of the play. Could they then invent a transcendental meaning, a value within their arbitrary, hollow, and purposeless life? One must admit here that when *duhkha* exists as a persistent and insuperable reality the responsibility rests with man's weakness, what Hindu ethics would term as the "untruth," and not with God. Is *sarvam duhkham* a child of man's incompetence to realize his predicament? Are the weaknesses and untruths enough of a hindrance to preclude the rationalization of absurdity?

Pain, argues Rabindranath Tagore in *Sadhana*, is the feeling born out of our finiteness, our incompetences: "It is what error is in our intellectual life." The embedded evil in the circumambient situation precludes Hamm and Clov from consorting with the "whole" or the dharma of existence. "Evil is ever moving," writes Tagore. It becomes characteristic of man "to represent statically what is in motion" and "in the process things assume a weight in our mind which they have not in reality."[22] Evil and suffering are the manifestations of the imperfections in our knowledge, our available power, and in the application of our will. Beckett's protagonists have revealed their weaknesses to themselves, resulting in choking depression. Human life is drawn up within a narrow frame in which miseries and failures are made to loom large and limitations are allowed a dominant voice. Failing to hold the core of things ("Am I right in the centre?"[23] questions Hamm), they hit the self hard in a confounded state of understanding that brings them before an unavoidable "hollowness." Hamm: "Do you hear? . . . Do you hear? Hollow bricks! . . . All that's hollow!"[24] They fail to realize that the ideal of truth is not in the narrow present, not also in our immediate sensations, but in the consciousness of the whole that gives us a taste of what we should have in what we do have.

> HAMM: . . . Put me right in the centre!
> CLOV: I'll go and get the tape.
> HAMM: Roughly! Roughly! . . . Bang in the centre!
> CLOV: There!
> HAMM: I feel a little too far to the left. . . . Now I feel a little too far to the right. . . . I feel a little too far forward. . . . Now I feel a little too far back.[25]

This wobbly, indecisive state, informed by a struggle to remain at the center, comes from an incomplete sense of the self. Beckett's world, with its elusive focal point, cuts at the root of a deep inner growth that we may describe as the liberating enterprise to "work at ourselves."[26] Dharma, in Hindu ethics, demands a self that has a proper sense of the center, becomes the totality of our functional resources, and is not built on reason or feeling alone. It encourages the development of a knowledgeable self that can tell the right from the wrong, the beautiful from the ugly.[27] The "ought" of dharma gets appropriately responded to by an "I ought." The answer emerges from one's awareness and conscience to explore the poise at the center, a belief that leads us back to the deep-welling foundations of life that I would like to qualify as "being-needs."[28] It is the demand on the self to remain in accord with a wider system of values, a demand to look beyond survival needs.

One pole of Hamm and Clov's being, in the words of Tagore, is hitched to "stocks and stones." They are faced with a reality that has an inexpugnably dictating and compulsive presence. However, when the searchlight is on the other pole of their being, the identity of their existence takes on a kind of alethic truth. This pole is "separate from all." "There," as Tagore explains, "I have broken through the cordon of equality and stand alone as an individual. I am absolutely unique, I am I, I am incomparable."[29] There is a discernible lack of individuality in the atmosphere that hangs grimly over the play. We notice that the characters, within the ethics of their existence, struggle to maintain themselves against the "tremendous gravitation of all things"—the centripetality of an abyss of dead matter. The individual is sorely out of place. But can we perceive Hamm as being possessed with a discernible mission to trace his individuality? Is the struggle worth the isolation that provides the meditative space to rethink Beckett's man-world nexus? Hamm tries; at least, he dares to. He fails; he tries again. Beckett, it must be admitted, wills his failure to an appreciable extent. By willing it, however, Beckett, it may be argued, unearths the need for a superstructure of the self that would revel in a karmic thrust. The drugged dimension of existence is willed to unconceal some vital promises that can thus encounter the regnant disabilities of a normalized inert existence. This elemental, existential bankruptcy stems from a desiccation of individuality, something that we can call our very own. What Hamm and Clov do not—rather cannot—imbibe is a relation between the "I" and the "they" that intersubjectively enriches our existence. A communion with the other and the world at large is sustained through continual reformulation of the internal laws of the self, the smithy of the "I." The predicament of every human is a misplaced understanding of gaming without ends, when one gets busy with the nets and neglects fishing. As part of this philosophical rejoinder to the *Endgame* crisis, one can argue that the problem is not in being able to unlearn the knowledge of "imperfection"; there is no effort to burn up the error that could set free the light of unshackled existence. Hamm and Clov are all too self; they fail miserably to encourage and establish such an understanding and knowledge with their "own" and what exists outside of their own. The confusion springing from the strug-gle to come to grips with the state of things, thus, persists unabated.

> HAMM: Do you know what's happened?
> CLOV: When? Where?
> HAMM: (violently) When! What's happened! Use your head, can't you! What has happened?[30]

They fail to widen the limit of the self. It is the misconstrual and lack of understanding of the "life of the self" that causes all such complications and contradictions, upstaging the dharma of their present. Beckett's play hinges on a dialectical tension between the self trying to think positive thoughts and the persistent opposition that it faces to snuff out any sem-blance of hope. For me the text builds itself on this "growing out while collapsing in" principle that nourishes a tension and makes an oppressive life less tortuous in nature and potency. The sense of self grows out of the consciousness of sin, of the benignity of grace, and of the self's very atmospheric existence. Hamm's radius of the self is not defined on such lines of consciousness. To what extent does Hamm realize that he has been degrading himself, that his sense of the self has been inadequate and non-discriminatory (*viveka-yuktena-manasa*)? The evil and ennui confronting Hamm emerge from his inability to redefine his self-identity. The contin-gent, atmospheric stress dominates him in that the limit of contraction becomes the limit of blindness. In a dehumanized set up, tethered to the dead weight of the finite, Hamm fails both to evoke and participate in the "peak experiences." These peak experiences (one needs to note what Hamm means by trying to have an "idea," a "bright idea!")[31] shape the self into being decently volitional, strengthening it in the process. However, it is what could have turned the situation of Hamm and Clov into both axiogenetic and axiosoteric.[32]

Does Hamm demonstrate certain signs of a prospective generation of "values" indicative of a positive resistance to the great neutralizing enterprise of absurd existence? Hamm, for me, has made some meaning-ful efforts, the consequences of which may belie the initial thrust of will. Yet Hamm shoots through with a positive desire—hoping for a "gull," the "sea," the "sky"—amid the crippling limitations of the present.

> HAMM: No gulls?
> CLOV: (looking) Gulls!
> HAMM: And the horizon? Nothing on the horizon?[33]

In Hamm we record a certain fluctuation in mental attitudes—a waxing and waning of hope, desire and effort. This desire is for a vital or higher existence that may offer a contrast to the profaneness of a soul-numbing finitude. Hamm says: "If I could sleep I might make love. I'd go into the woods. My eyes would see . . . the sky, the earth. I'd run, run, they wouldn't catch me."[34] Such an urge to romanticize, to sail beyond the repressive encapsulation of reality, must be read as a positive commentary on the need to reinterrogate the dharma of existence. Hamm's perennial "act of sitting" is the reflective part of our existence, the reflectiveness that chooses to impose questions on our predicament. Hamm evinces the human capacity of self-consciousness (karmic possibilities) as he takes a step backward to reflect on life and the futility, the absurdity of our strivings, hopes, aspirations and evaluations. But Hamm's psychic state, in its reflective awareness, radiates a reflexive dynamicity to find a place for imagination, a possibility of hope and a curiosity for a horizon. The karmic propensities to rationalize a way out of the depressive undertow of events cannot be ruled out. Attempts made by Hamm, albeit abortive, are nonetheless attempts to determine a choice; these are efforts to look at the other side of hell to see whether the possibility of happiness can be raised. Hamm's effort to unleash himself becomes a truncated, though promising, projection of an image of man repeatedly thwarted and disclaimed. So being decisively dwarfed cannot avoid manifesting the culpability of silence and inaction. Hamm proposes to write out a meaning and in the process opens up the possibility of reframing the reality of absurdism and the politics of normalized given.

But such karmic affirmations are sparse as they die out under the heft of a relentless surge of dead energy (the *tamasic* state in Hindu philosophy). Herman Keyserling, applying the Hindu doctrine of karma, perceives the activism of the self, which in "what is free in it" becomes a significant component of the agent. Efforts made to overcome the given is a way to self-transcendence. [35] The *Gita* ascribes it as *dhriti*, the conative persistence, the rigor to signal a growth of being. But the karmic propensities in the play could not be realized in concrete acts; the world of the play lacks proper "navigators" whose growth, at best, is stunted and whose discourse of growth does not have the gestaltic relationship between the self and the world.

HAMM: I am asking you is it very calm?
CLOV: Yes.
HAMM: It's because there are *no more navigators*.[36]

The anxiety of living in *Endgame* is traumatic. The will to navigate and the freedom to step into the shoes of a navigator are decimated. Perhaps the specter of deindividualization in the soul-killing suffering sparks a propensity to dream of the gulls, the sail, the seas and the urge to look down, over the window. When Hamm says—"Let's go from here, the two of us! South! You can make a raft and the currents will carry us away, far away,"[37] we realize their urge to experience "what is free" in the self, the desire to realize "being-needs" over "survival needs." It is the urgency to "build the raft" that matters (Hamm: "Get working on that raft immediately"[38]). Hamm and Clov need to build the raft and learn to navigate. [39]

Thomas Nagel writes: "We cannot live human lives without energy and attention, nor without making choices which show that we take some things more seriously than others. Yet we have always available a point of view outside the particular form of our lives, from which the seriousness appears gratuitous. These two inescapable viewpoints collide in us, and that is what makes life absurd. It is absurd because we ignore the doubts that we know cannot be settled, continuing to live with nearly undiminished seriousness in spite of them."[40] Clov does tend to live this absurdity with seriousness. But Hamm, entrapped by an overpowering disability, generates some energy to make a choice that points to another version of seriousness. This seriousness interrogates the other side of the prevailing predicament but is countermanded by the "seriousness of absurdity" that Clov cannot avoid representing. This is what makes for the *duhkha* in life, resulting in dissatisfaction embedded in valuelessness. The value judgments that would otherwise have come from questioning life or existence "seriously" are annulled deterministically. Karma is a spiritual necessity which makes one judgmental and adjudicatory, forging a way through the *maya* (illusion) and *avidya* (ignorance) of life. *Niskarmakrita* (remaining inactive) means contravening dharma. *Gita* describes karma as something that springs from *guna* (dispositions). It is, however, difficult to find *gunas* in Hamm and Clov that are strong enough to challenge *niskarmakrita*. *Gunas* have manifested in brief bursts; desire for karma raises, at best, a transient promise. But circumstantial immovability has not allowed the self to grow. The world of Hamm and Clov cannot produce the mechanism to raise the self by the self, the existent self raised by the karmic self. The Hamm-Clov ensemble puts forth a self that requires a construction through the establishment of another self; it is reinvesting one's prevalent self, says the *Gita*, through the karmic potency of another self, adding to a genuine sense of it and *vidya* (knowledge). Hamm needs to keep Clov affected by the choice (as pointed out earlier) to extend the dimensions of his choices within the ambit of the existentialist enigma of *duhkha*.

Human existence that fails to combine the reflective karma with the dynamic karma is fated to get weighed down in schism and sickness. The karmic reflexivities that we notice in Hamm do not lead him to an orderly and poised dharma of existence and certainly not to any deeper realization of values and order. Addled efforts of Clov, significantly under Hamm's direction, to reach up to the sight beyond the window (the symbol of the ladder is significant) can be ascribed as the bid to appropriate truth—an entity that lies beyond the world of appearances as incomprehensible and indescribable. In fact, what can be seen through Murphy, Moran, and Molloy is a perception of the core that, however, is a fugitive entity delimited by a mere glimpse of the idea and the inability to realize it. Hamm's effort then becomes an emaciated plowing of the surface without digging enough into any formative stage of understanding.[41] Hamm's spasmodic efforts (a fleeting intimation of self-transcendence: "What? A sail? A fin? Smoke?")[42] are hopelessly caught midway between an alleged determinism of circumstances (nothing can happen) and an ever-mounting self-thwarting conservatism of the individuals (since nothing can happen inaction remains the only possible action). Such consciousness of an overpowering eventuality makes the absence of freedom the defining signature of their lives. Hamm and Clov also dread "waking" (an alive, alert consciousness of circumambient reality) and, therefore, cannot evade espousing the *avidya* or *avidyas*; this allows the deception to continue unabated. What lies amiss in the *Endgame* world is *jnana* (the emancipatory wisdom) that is a "realized" and realizable experience. If the arrival of Godot is an eagerly awaited event, looking beyond the window for sights that would rejuvenate the prevalent levels of existence is also an intense requirement.[43] Hamm and Clov fail to reach the desired dharma because their will is not informed by the knowledge of the potential of the self. The self must act centripetally, pedaling within, to wade across the muck that engulfs them both from without; it is also about enjoining the sundered notes within, piecing the shards together, to trigger an initiation toward some vital and redemptive moments. Both Hamm and Clov, in their *adharmic* patterns of existence, have chosen to flinch from the boy's presence, failing to explore a possibility of redemption and deliverance. Steeped in *avidya* (the ignorance springing from the lack of sense of self) they are not ready to accept the generative impact of a new procreative force. The boy offers a possibility to mend walls and is the beckoning to *vidya* that promises to replace the self-debilitating life of the mind and soul with a true emancipatory one, an inner emigration. Tagore, in *Gitanjali*, characterizes this situation poetically: "I am ever busy building this wall all around; and as this wall goes up into the sky day by day, I lose sight of my true being in its dark shadow."[44] Blinded to the reality and potential of true being, the *Endgame* world awaits redemption. So the prevalent strains of *adharma* in Hamm and Clov's lives do not allow a wholesome perspective on existence, disrupting in the process the integrality that lies enshrined in the conceptualization of dharma. Within this aspect of Hindu thought we find a refusal to appeal to a whole human being, a denial to speak to an integrative worldview. The entropic disability in Hamm and Clov's predicament points to an abuse of life, a life that leaves no door open for modes of liberation and enlightenment. Perhaps Beckett's world in *Endgame* has denounced the rebel in the human; it loses sight of or, rather, is denied the sight of, the internal revolution in every human; the betrayal of self, thus, is the violation of the dharma of existence.

Finally, I am tempted to refer to *Gita* (section 18) again to my students to analyze the five factors—*adhishthanam* (the matrix of action), *karta* (agent), *karanam* (the diverse instruments of action), *chesta* (coordinated, well-meaning effort), and *daivam* (the wider expanse of action beyond the immediate). The disabled *karta* (Hamm and Clov) and their enfeebled *chesta* contribute to the *tamasic* state (the dark state of suffering). Inhibited thus, it fails to achieve the *daivam*, which I interpret here as the world beyond the immediate consequence of objective karma—the zone of being-needs. It is the *karta* or doer's intensive *karanam* (modes of action) that discloses a world beyond the causal existential web. Dharma through good action and voluntary action becomes the inner law of being. Hamm and Clov prove a failure and the failure signals the collapse of dharma and the consequent relapse into *tamas* (darkness). So the evil remains and the *tamasic* state continues. This evil, unfortunately, does not allow suffering to be seen as positive—the positive suffering, or *duhkha*, that encourages molting, the act of sloughing off the self that meekly surrenders to absurdity. Differently argued, it may be pointed out that the mere fact of our continuing in existence proves that existence is worthy of continuance. Within the world of the play, a Hindu view of life would seek to question and problematize this worthiness to continue living. The classroom can converge on the fact that Hindu philosophy of dharma can make a "difference"—somewhat radical, though—to our transcultural under-standing of the play, educating ourselves differently on Beckett to produce a "new object."

Resetting the Teaching Machine

Endgame in the classroom then splits into two texts: a pedagogic one that is more oriented to the conventional teaching machine devised and encoded for the writing examination and consequent grading; perhaps our repres-sive ways of grading and examination system maim our teaching ways in the classroom. Our illocutionary and pedagogical persuasions drive us to experience a literary text within certain conditions that a classroom straps on us, conditions that are at once constitutional and institutional. Texts are usually tried in their syllabic and received constitutional coun-tenances, within laws that have made them look similar every semester, every year, in every encounter. Most Indian literature classrooms avoid working as pedagogical outlaw; they are heavily daunted by disciplinary envy that might thicken the air of teaching with less visible or discernible lighthouses. Classrooms promote a parody of reading and replication of reading strategies that dodge individualism for a collective critical con-sciousness. A student rarely reads but duplicates the rituals of learning inscribed within institutional modes of instruction and performance ap-praisal. The second part of the split is the "performative," which challenges the cultural and affective bounds of learning literature, becoming a happy victim of the teacher-critic's desire-lines. Are we then conflating and con-trasting two different kinds of textual disciplines in the classroom?

On what possible lines can a modernist text speak to students in the classroom? Or should I rephrase the question: In what "erotic" ways can a modernist text articulate itself to students attending a literature class? The performative classroom, then, is always interdisciplinary, a source and space for "intersubjective vitality," where teaching comes as a "task verb."[45] Although we cannot ignore disciplined interdisciplinarity, we must prefer delicate randomness of connection—the "transgression of law," the mon-ster that Alain Badiou instructs us to seek—that might just choose to trip over the strictness of righteous disciplinary claims.[46] Outlawing literature has its value and the fun owes a lot to some law deficit. This is a kind of "guerrilla pedagogy" that Jody Norton argues is "dislocative, decentering, confounding and clarifying. . . . mobile, improvisational, contingent, and unpredictable."[47] She writes:

There are two crucial ways in which guerrilla pedagogy is unlike guerrilla theater. First, whereas guerrilla theater presented explicitly radical messages, guerrilla pedagogy does not have an agenda, other than textual analysis, ideological critique, and self-examination. Conservatives can interrogate and affirm (or modify) their own ideas and values as easily as liberals or radicals. The guerrilla teachers are open about their politics, but work hard to keep authority separate from belief systems, so that the latter must convince or not on their own merits. . . . Secondly, whereas guerrilla theater, operating rapidly in noisy public areas, had a practical need for "simplicity of tactics" and was self-consciously "not subtle" . . . , guerrilla pedagogy, carried on over eighty minutes in the quiet, private space of the classroom, can afford as much complexity and difficulty as the discussants can generate and absorb.[48]

Outlawing the teaching machine is inscribed in the abilities and valence of translation, the repeated demands on one's background, cultural consciousness, and the complex negotiations with textual alienation that such consciousness infuses. There is a vibrant tangle between the vernacular that my students speak—the multilingual Indian classroom—and the medium of classroom instruction, which is English. So when *Endgame* comes to enliven the classroom in its polydiscursivity, we cannot ignore how different linguistic backgrounds deliver different levels of affect and connotative understanding. The textual affect here deepens and widens in its singularity. The whole game I am implicating here is worked out on a unique axis that has to appreciate that I am not teaching *Endgame* in translation (say, in Hindi or Bengali) but in English interpreted through concepts and paradigms that are imported from the non-Anglophone tradition. How does the text adjust to sitting on these transcultural crosspoints of meaning generation? But this teaching across traditions and cultural consciousness produces its own affect that transcends the language in which the reading was executed. The textual affect might become, for instance, Buddhist or Hindu or Zen without being required to have it "translated" into Tibetan, Japanese, or Hindi. This becomes a kind of denial of language, rather, an overcoming of the language to generate a radiantly different experience of textual impact and textual density. Tejeswani Niranjana notes appropriately:

If English literature is indeed being transformed—at home and abroad—into English studies, it seems pertinent to consider the gap between the roles we as teachers are prepared to play and that we may choose and then prepare to play. The first is a result of conditioning and envisages our own role as that of a catalyst—unchanging but capable of transforming others. The second involves using our alien selves as prisms and filters to explore and understand our historical situation. It is one of the few privileges that our discipline affords us—a painful but promising way out of the canonized readings of our texts and ourselves.[49]

So the teacher's self in this new classroom is seriously complexified, in that a nonnative English speaker reads a text written in English or translated from French into English with a big group of students whose native language is not English, with diverse cultural and linguistic backgrounds. The text in the classroom is read in English but *thought* both in English and in non-English ways, a continual process of remapping conducted both consciously and unconsciously, a unique vein of sensitiveness to the text that refuses to "use a torque wrench at 65 pounds of pressure to bolt Idea A into Student's B brain."[50]

The things that Miller wants a Chinese reader or a video-games-playing Western young man or a student in an Indian classroom to know to appreciate W. B. Yeats's "Cold Heaven" (see chapter 8) are precise and perceptive. I agree with Miller that reading a poem, as much as reading a play, requires a roadmap, a cartographic familiarity with context, stylistics, sociocultural peculiarities, and certain other sets of information that are instrumental in building the pathway to the province of the poem. But is our knowing the kind of bird the rook is or the kind of flower daffodils are always insurmountably essential to the understanding of a poem? My students would have little idea about the Irish landscape (the materiality or embodied understanding of the poem) and, in this case, the sights and sounds of the train-journey that Yeats undertook from Manchester to Norwich on February 21, 1911, when he drafted the poem. In many ways, a poem or a play or a novel set in a European context is in all likelihood a step away—a bit withdrawn and reclusive—from my students in the Indian classroom. The sociocultural displacement of a text in a classroom is a reality that the reading and experience of literature have to encounter. I agree mostly with the fifteen points that Miller makes about knowing the poem, but what I still stay interested in is the worlding that a poem provides in the classroom, both in its aesthetic and postaesthetic ways. Yeats, with his proven familiarity with Indian and Chinese philosophy, Japanese drama, and Zen Buddhism, occult practices, Goethe, Winckelmann (he did not know German), Tagore (he did not know Bengali), and

Upanishadic thought, magic, theosophy, and other fields of interest endow his poetry with the profound potentialities for worlding. The across factor is high and decisive when we find Arabia, as part of Yeats's engagement with Asia, making a presence in his poetic sensibility.[51] His acquaintance with Alfārābi and Avicenna, of whom he wrote in *Rosa Alchemica*, teachings of Arab en Shemesh, Arabic folklore, Charles Doughty's book *Arabia Deserta*, T. E. Lawrence's book *Seven Pillars of Wisdom*, and enthusiastic explorations into *The Arabian Nights* develop several avenues of communication that brought his Irish consciousness to flank notes and queries into Arabia, explorations into Chinese thought, Japanese ways of life and action, incursions into Upanishad and Vedic thought: a febrile and fecund association in trans-now. The more than global impetus must try to make a variety of (in)fusionist inroads into Yeats and Arabia beyond poems like "The Gift of Harun Al-Rashid," "Solomon to Sheba," "Solomon and the Witch," "The Second Coming," and "Michael Robartes and the Dancer," which have Arabia or Arabic influences as conspicuous categories of reference. Yeats notes, "Certain typical books—Ulysses, Mrs. Virginia Woolf's Waves, Mr. Ezra Pound's Draft of XXX Cantos—suggest a philosophy like that of the *Samkara* school of ancient India, mental and physical objects alike material, a deluge of experience breaking over us and within us, *melting limits* whether of line or tint; man no hard bright mirror dawdling by the dry sticks of a hedge, but a *swimmer*, or rather the waves themselves."[52] Under (in)fusion-trans-now can the classroom read "The Cold Heaven" within the philosophy of Daimon or the artifice and apocalypse of Mirror? Why cannot our ways—one of them Miller's predominantly rhetorical method and the other being my emphatically philosophical, transcultural ways of reading—be brought into a dialogic plexus to re-premise the experience of a literary text in a classroom? Our "whys" are not divergences but synergic peaks of contrastive studies.

A democratic community in the classroom, then, acknowledges that cultures are unequal as much as forms of class-life, text-life, and student-teacher life are continuously under mediation and resuscitation. The classroom of literature is parrhesic and stays alive through a lively dialogue both with the past that a student brings and the critical consciousness that a teacher imports. Such forces synergize to argue how a text can come alive in the present—a performative narrative caught between the pulls of tradition and the creative accents of individuality. The subjectivities of students then become both multiple and democratic, composite and anti-essential. Students dwell genitively in such spaces with both oppositional and transformative consciousness. So the experience of reading literature is both humanist and skeptical, never beyond criticism and dialogue; it is aware of the limits of reason and committed to the defense of reason, encouraging subject positions implicated in intersections of power, knowledge, politics, desire, and affect. However, the dynamics between the teacher and the student are subjected to "pedagogy effect," which Gregory Ulmer qualifies as "a kind of symbolic violence."[53] It becomes a submission to "magisterial effect," which, without the depropriation of authority the teacher privileges over the students, quite disingenuously cuts off the participation of the students in the discursive domain of the classroom. *Endgame*'s interpretive articulation predominantly emerges from the teacher's end. But teachers cannot be completely neutral either. Perhaps knowledge-generation in the classroom has an imbalance to it, calling for participation but not without its own scale-tilting, where the slant is more on the freshness that the teacher can bring.

Teaching literature is perhaps always a failure—the inadequacies in making literature get taught. We pedagogize, paradoxically, in effective failure. Shosana Felman, in discussing Lacan and Freud on pedagogy, speaks of a "pedagogical imperative" that is inimical to "desire," the desire to speak otherwise, removed from established protocols of teaching.[54] The classroom is held in the cusp of repression and license, the seriously vexed borderline between conventional pedagogy and the desire to undo it. This sets us up with the "impossibility" of teaching, the "doing away with pedagogy," and the concomitant challenge that refuses to die out. Ignorance in the classroom is a reality that refuses to get dislodged under the mounting attainment of knowledge because the untotalizable quotient of learning and teaching cannot be ignored. Teaching Beckett expressly addresses the consciousness of the text, its uncanny ways and haunted terrains, but cannot forget its career stewed in ignorance, in regimes of thought that stay at the realm of the unconscious, the unarticulated voices, the domain of teaching or thought that the teacher would not be able to reach or access. Felman explains:

> Ignorance is thus no longer simply opposed to knowledge: it is itself a radical condition, an integral part of the very structure of knowledge. But what does ignorance consist of, in this new epistemological and pedagogical conception? If ignorance is to be equated with the a-totality of the unconscious, it can be said to be a kind of forgetting-of forgetfulness: while learning is obviously, among other things, remembering

and memorizing ("all learning is recollection," says Socrates), ignorance is linked to what is not remembered, what will not be memorized. But what will not be memorized is tied up with repression, with the imperative to forget—the imperative to exclude from consciousness, to not admit to knowledge. Ignorance, in other words, is not a passive state of absence—a simple lack of information: it is an active dynamic of negation, an active refusal of information.[55]

Resistance to the learning and teaching of a text comes with its profits. It combines ignorance at both levels of the interlocutor and the recipient. Roger Simon argues: "What is to be recognized in a dialogic pedagogy is that both student and teacher are doubly ignorant, not only of their structured resistances but as well of the knowledge of what it is that resists in the other. Given this doubled structure of ignorance in a pedagogical encounter, each then must listen for the silence in the other, helping each other to knowledge that is inaccessible. This knowledge is not in the teacher; it cannot be given. It is only to be acquired in the conversation between the teacher and students as coinvestigators of each other's resistances."[56] The passion of the classroom is both knowledge and ignorance. I teach *Endgame* reveling both in ignorance and knowledge as a pedagogue and antipedagogue because teaching is also about the impossibility to teach and think all that teaching can do. Deficit is ignorance, which inversely is the excess that keeps the passion in the classroom going.

SHOULD WE READ OR TEACH LITERATURE NOW?

An entire epoch of so-called literature, if not all of it, cannot survive a certain technological regime of telecommunications (in this respect the political regime is secondary). Neither can philosophy, or psychoanalysis. Or love letters.
—Jacques Derrida, "Envois," in *The Post Card*

This chapter is more or less an extended endnote to what Derrida says in the epigraph above, about what happens to literature in our age of ubiquitous digitalization. Let me begin with a dialogic response to Ranjan Ghosh's chapter 7. Having now read it carefully, I understand much better than even with the help of his chapters 1, 3, and 5 the most salient features of his commitment to teaching English literature in India. Ghosh centers his account of teaching English literature in India on an example, Samuel Beckett's *Endgame*. The reader of Ghosh's chapter gets a good idea of just what Ghosh would have to say about Beckett's play in a class at the University of North Bengal of seventy-odd "post-graduates," that is, of what we would call "graduate students."

Ghosh, in his chapter 7, emphasizes the way he teaches *against* the Indian equivalent of the common core curriculum in the United States. He observes at one point that some of his students are not native English speakers. He has informed me by e-mail, however, to my surprise, that many of them have learned excellent English in convent schools. I had not known convent schools were so important in India or at least in Bengal. My surprise shows how little I know about contemporary India. Ghosh's solution to the actual situation in his classroom when he walks in to teach Beckett's *Endgame* is innovative. It successfully resists, moreover, the expectations of general institutional teaching methodologies in Indian universities and colleges, just as I believe much good teaching of literature in the United States these days resists the procedures of the common core curriculum. Ghosh presents a reading of Beckett's play by way of the Hindu or Sanskrit tradition in the *Gita* and elsewhere of dharma and other related Hindu or Sanskrit concepts. His Hindu reading is augmented or "(in)fused," as is characteristic of his writing, with a wide array of citations from a variety of Western sources.: Wai Chee Dimock, Shoshana Felman, Rey Chow, Terry Eagleton, and others. I should stress that Ghosh sees Hindu dharma not as fundamental or "best," but as just one element in the complex transcultural combination he calls the (in)fusion approach. To use dharma in that particular classroom situation, however, is a good way to teach Beckett's *Endgame* to those particular students (and to interpret it for me, too, I should add).

Ghosh's chapter has as one of its goals an energetic challenge to traditional ways of teaching English literature in India. This customary way, so he tells his readers, is according to a standardized method of reading and teaching a given work. In place of that, and with augmentation from numerous citations of recent Western essays and books that are in one way or another consonant with his own position, Ghosh argues persuasively for reading Beckett's play in an Indian classroom in the context of an elaborate "transcultural" theory of literature that sees each literary work as giving hints of a transcendent spiritual power that can only be glimpsed indirectly. That theory of literature, as his earlier chapters already have shown, is an important part of the perennial Hindu religious tradition, with its roots in Sanskrit writings. As Ghosh shows, that tradition depends on a lot of key words in Sanskrit that are exceedingly hard to translate into English, as I discover when I look them up in Wikipedia.

I tend, in opposition to Ghosh's procedure, to take for granted that I should read Yeats's "The Cold Heaven" in the context of Yeats's own tradition, whatever may be my own opinions about that tradition. I give a good bit of factual "background" information about my example, "The Cold Heaven," including its relation to Chinese thought. I cite the entire poem, which is one reason I chose a short text for discussion in a lecture originally given before a Chinese audience. (I by no means assume, by the way, that an Indian academic audience is all that much like a Chinese one.) Whereas Ghosh makes some short citations from here and there in Beckett's *Endgame*, I wanted my Chinese audience to hear the whole poem read aloud, from that marvelous first line to the disquieting end: "Suddenly I saw the cold and rook-delighting heaven. . . . and stricken / By the injustice of the skies for punishment." My outline of a reading of "The Cold Heaven" remains in the tradition of the "close reading" or "rhetorical reading" done in the United States, with a close focus on linguistic detail, formal features, and figurative language as generators of meaning. I stress

Yeats's own tradition more than Ghosh does Beckett's personal tradition. Yeats, as Ghosh observes, belonged not only to a native Irish tradition that was Protestant Christian, but also to a perennial tradition he learned from his reading in esoteric sources like Madame Blavatsky. As Ghosh correctly observes, Yeats did much reading in Arabic, Indian, and Chinese traditions. This mixture was Yeats's own tradition, just as Irish Anglicanism was Beckett's native tradition. Hindu religious theories of literature can hardly be said to have been decisively formative for Beckett, at least so far as I know. Ghosh's reading is therefore an example of what the great American critical theorist Kenneth Burke called "perspective by incongruity." Ghosh's use of Hindu theories of literature to read *Endgame* in an Indian classroom tacitly presumes that such transcultural readings, readings by way of what he calls "across," is sometimes the best way to go.

Tradition: the word means in our readings what was passed on by parents and early schooling, and then augmented by further education, reading, and friendships. In Beckett's case, one important adult influence was his long acquaintance and collaboration with James Joyce in Paris. Joyce, both in *Ulysses* and, especially, in *Finnegans Wake*, infuses with a vengeance terms and traditions from all over the world, often by way of what are called portmanteau words, words, that is, that superimpose words from different languages and traditions in a single complex word that you will find in no dictionary. A portmanteau word is like a lot of incongruous things packed in a single suitcase. Such words are Ghosh's (in)fusion approach in a nutshell, so to speak. Here is just one example out of an immense number, since portmanteau words are the vocabulary of the whole of *Finnegans Wake*, from the title on. I give a bit of the context for the one word I have most in mind: "This is brave Danny weeping his spache for the popers. This is cool Connolly wiping his hearth with brave Danny. And this, regard! How Chawleses Shewered parparaparnelligoes between brave Danny boy and the Connolly. Upanishadem! Top. Spoken hath L'arty Magory. Eregobragh. Prouf!"[1]

It would take pages and pages to unsnarl this palimpsest, even if I had learning enough to do so. It mixes figures of Irish politics: James Connolly, a leader of the Easter uprising (1868–1916); Charles Stewart Parnell, Irish nationalist political leader, whose scandalous private life ruined his political career (1846–1891); Daniel O'Connell (1775–1847), Irish political leader and the "Great Emancipator," who fought for Catholic Emancipation and Irish independence. The passage alludes to Irish popular music such as "Danny Boy," and to Irish esoteric spiritualism, folklore, and aesthetics.

"L'arty Magory" may be a reference to Yeats's friend Lady Gregory. All these are superimposed in "Upanishadem." *Upanishads* is the name of one of the greatest of Hindu spiritual texts, written in Sanskrit, of course. Here, if I read it right, the word becomes not only a reference to Irish esoteric spiritualism, but an exclamation directed at brave Danny Boy, Connolly, Parnell, and the rest. "Upanishad" means "sitting at the foot or feet of." Sit at the feet of the whole lot of them! "Upanishad" is a reference to the way the Upanishads are made of questions and answers between master and disciple.

I add one final important dialogic response to Ghosh's chapter 7. Reading Ghosh's chapter makes me, "suddenly," aware of a big difference in our "subject positions," as I have been taught to call them, especially in relation to literature in English, which we both teach. It is perhaps not without significance that both of us have chosen as our examples of literary texts in chapters 7 and 8 of this book Irish authors originally from a Protestant background: Samuel Beckett and W. B. Yeats. Ghosh is an Indian citizen. I am a United States citizen. We have both inherited the effects of British colonialism in the countries we live in, but in far different ways. My ancestors came in the late eighteenth century from a German-speaking part of Europe (Hesse) to the new United States, just as the latter was being established in a successful war of revolution against the British colonizing occupation of one part of North America. My paternal ancestor was a Hessian soldier recruited (or perhaps "impressed" is a better word) by the British army to fight in North America against the rebelling colonists. He surrendered to the American army, probably at the Battle of Saratoga, 1777, where 5,895 British and Hessian troops laid down their arms. He then settled in the new United States, after being freed from a prisoner of war camp in the new state of Virginia. English is my native language, though my ancestors on both sides were German-speaking immigrants. English literature feels as though it belongs to me, in spite of the absurdity, about which I say something later in this chapter, of building our literature teaching in the United States on works written by a people we defeated in a War of Independence. We descendants of transplanted Europeans, moreover, though we remember the shame of slavery, tend to forget or minimize the way the creation of the United States was accompanied by the equally shameful, genocidal elimination of almost all American Indians. These were the ironically so-called Indians (because Columbus mistakenly thought he had reached the East Indies). Those peoples were in America as diverse tribes for thousands of years before the Europeans arrived.

India, too, was invaded, occupied, and colonized by the British, but its native inhabitants were by no means almost completely exterminated, though many were killed over the years. Huge differences exist, of course, between Indian cultural, intellectual, and religious traditions, on the one hand, and American Indian ones, on the other. When India was finally liberated, in 1947, about one hundred and fifty years after the liberation of the United States from British colonialism, the abundantly surviving native Indian peoples took control. Though Indian history and culture is immensely complex, down to the present day, Ranjan Ghosh is one example in language and culture of a large group living in India today.

The comparison seems somehow grotesquely inappropriate, but it is a little as if in the United States British and European power were to have been eliminated, leaving the Iroquois, the Seneca, the Sioux, and all the other American Indian tribes in possession of their ancestral homeland. Those American Indians would then have been able to bring back, though in different circumstances, their own cultural assumptions as exemplified in their beliefs, practices, oral traditions, and writings. That this did not happen in North America makes it quite different from India, to say the least.

Gauri Viswanathan, in a remarkable book, *Masks of Conquest: Literary Study and British Rule in India* (1989), has demonstrated that the discipline of English literature study, more or less as we knew it until recently in the United States and around the world, was invented as a way to teach Indian natives in British occupied India about English culture. This was perhaps on the assumption that the imperialistic occupation would last indefinitely. It is no wonder that Ranjan Ghosh opposes the traditional way of teaching English literature in India as it still exists. His opposition goes by way of innovative reading strategies that straddle multiple continents—a kind of no-centric approach. Ghosh wants forcefully to reassert the importance of the great Hindu and Bengali intellectual traditions in all his chapters in this present coauthored book. I have nothing at all comparable that "belongs to me" in the way Ghosh's Hindu texts on literature belong to him. I have nothing parallel to which I can appeal as an alternative to Anglo-American intellectual traditions. Ghosh wants to show, under the aegis of *sahitya*, the power of Sanskrit traditions to provide a strong and valid way to read even texts in English and American literature, for example, Beckett's *Endgame*. One must always keep in mind, however, that sahitya is only one aspect of that much more comprehensive, trans-continental, "more than global" complex, the materials from all over the world that Ghosh's approach infuses and fuses.

Ghosh's chapter 7 has given me an opportunity to see, and I hope at least partially to understand, the differences and similarities between what it means to read and teach British literature in India as opposed to reading and teaching it in the United States, as I have done for so many years.

The first draft of this chapter, written in 2010, included the paragraphs that follow this one. Now, in the last days of June 2015, I will go on to up-date these opening remarks as they were changed again in late 2014, and augment them still further. The context within which literature is taught in United States colleges and universities has changed markedly since 2010.

By "we" in my title ("Should We Read or Teach Literature Now?") I mean we students, teachers, and the ordinary citizens of our "global village," if such a term still means anything. By *read* I mean careful attention to the text at hand, that is, "close reading." By *literature* I mean printed novels, poems, and plays. By *now* I meant initially the hot September of 2010, the culmination of the hottest six months on record, clear evidence for those who have bodies to feel that global warming is not a fiction. Much of what I say here, however, still applies in early 2016. I mean the time after a global financial crisis and worldwide deep recession whose effects have not yet wholly disappeared in 2016. I mean the time of desktop comput-ers, the Internet, iPhones, iPads, DVDs, MP3s, Facebook, Twitter, Google, video games by the thousand, television, and a global film industry. I mean the time when colleges and universities are, in the United States at least, losing funding and are shifting more and more to a corporate model. As one result of these changes, over 70 percent of university teaching in all fields is now done by ill-paid adjuncts, that is, by people who not only do not have tenure but who also have no possibility of getting it. They are not "tenure track." I mean a time when calls on all sides, both by President Obama and his colleagues in the government and by the media left and right, are being made for more and better teaching of science, technol-ogy, engineering, and math (*STEM*), while hardly anyone calls for more and better teaching in the humanities. The humanities, as a high administrator at Harvard, perhaps its then president, Lawrence Summers, is reported to have said some years ago now, "are a lost cause."

Often ill-paid adjuncts are deliberately kept at appointments just below half-time, so they do not have medical insurance, pension contributions, or other benefits. All three of my children have doctorates, as does one grandchild, but none of the four has ever held a normal tenure-track teaching position, much less achieved tenure. Tenure-track positions in the humanities are few and far between, with hundreds of applicants for each one, and an ever-accumulating reservoir of unemployed humanities PhDs. Books by Marc Bousquet, Christopher Newfield, Frank Donoghue, and Jeffrey J. Williams, among others, have told in detail the story of the way U.S. universities have come to be run more and more like business corporations governed by the financial bottom line, or, as Peggy Kamuf puts it, the "bang for the buck."[2] The humanities cannot be shown to produce much bang of that sort at all.

The weakening of American public universities has been accompanied by a spectacular rise in for-profit and partly online universities like the University of Phoenix. These are openly committed to training that will get you a job. John Sperling, the head of the Apollo Group, which developed the University of Phoenix, said some time ago, "[the University of Phoenix] is a corporation. . . . Coming here is not a rite of passage. We are not trying to develop [students'] value systems or go in for that 'expand their minds' bullshit."[3]

Richard Levin, an economist and still president back in 2010 of Yale University, in a lecture given before the Royal Society in London, enthusiastically praised China for more than doubling its institutions of higher education (from 1,022 to 2,263), for increasing the number of higher education students from one million in 1997 to more than 5.5 million in 2007, and for setting out deliberately to create a number of world-class research universities that will rank with Harvard, MIT, Oxford, and Cambridge.[4] The numbers Levin cites are no doubt far higher now. Levin's emphasis, however, is all on the way China's increased teaching of science, technology, engineering, and math will make it more highly competitive in the global economy than it already is. Levin, in spite of Yale's notorious strengths in the humanities, says nothing whatsoever about humanities teaching or its utility either in China or in the United States. Clearly the humanities are of no account in the story he is telling.

It is extremely difficult to demonstrate that humanities departments bring any financial return at all ("bang for the buck") or that majoring in English is preparation for anything but a low-level service job or a low-paying job teaching English. (I wonder, by the way, what Ghosh's English major students at the University of North Bengal characteristically go on to do when they graduate.) Many students at elite places like Yale can safely major in the humanities because they will take over their father's business when they graduate, or will go on to law school or business school and get their vocational training there. Lifelong friendships with others who would come to be important in business, government, or the military are often for Yale students more important than any vocational training. The presidential race between George W. Bush and John Kerry in 2004 was, somewhat absurdly, between two men who did not do all that well academically at Yale but who were members of Yale's most elite secret society, Skull and Bones. Whoever won, Yale and the political power of the Skull and Bones network would win.

Enrollments in humanities courses and numbers of majors have in the United States, not surprisingly, especially at less elite places than Yale, shrunk to a tiny percentage of the undergraduate and graduate population. Only composition and beginning language courses plus some required distribution survey courses are doing well in the humanities. Legislators, boards of trustees, and university administrators took advantage of the Great Recession to exercise more control over universities, to downsize, and to manage what is taught. The state of California, for example, essentially went broke during the recession that began in 2008. That meant for a while frozen positions, reduced adjunct funding, and salary reductions for faculty and staff in the University of California system of between 5 percent and 10 percent, depending on rank. Teaching loads were increased for above-scale professors, that is, for the ones who have done the most distinguished research and who have been rewarded by being given more time to do that. The humanities especially suffered because so many people believed they were less important than *STEM* courses and research.

That was what I said in 2010, slightly revised now in 2016. What can I say about the "now" of April 2016, as a context within which literature must today be read and taught? The situation has changed quite a bit in the intervening four years, and by no means always for the better. The United States is still hell-bent on autoimmune self-destruction. *Autoimmunity* is Jacques Derrida's term for the way a community or a nation destroys itself through its own self-protection mechanisms. Derrida's figure is drawn from autoimmune diseases in the human body that turn the body's immune system against itself, for example, in the pancreatic cancer that killed Derrida himself.

I put the self-destructive autoimmune forces at work in the United States today under six interrelated rubrics. They constitute the context now for reading or teaching literature in my country: (1) education; (2) the media; (3) economics; (4) politics; (5) foreign wars; and (6) climate change. Except for putting education first, since it is the main topic in this book, my list is not in any hierarchical or causal order. Each demands and has elsewhere received, from me and from many others, lengthy treatment, with abundant facts and statistics. I have written something about them in early chapters of this book. Here I shall merely sketch the context for any discussion of literature teaching in the United States now in 2016. I have said my six rubrics are interrelated. What binds them together, I claim, is the different ways each of them is fundamentally inflected these days by the digital revolution, a transformation that is, with astonishing rapidity, changing every corner of our lives.

One, education: What I said back in 2010 about the diminished role of the humanities in higher education is still true, as is the shift to teaching by adjuncts in all fields. Though the funding for higher education has improved somewhat as the Great Recession has gradually receded, though tuition and other costs have continued to increase rapidly, the emphasis on more spending for STEM courses, as opposed to humanities and social sciences, has increased. Our colleges and universities are more and more becoming trade schools, preparing students directly for technological jobs, as opposed to what they used to be: liberal arts institutions preparing young people to live better lives because they know something about all fields, science and mathematics as well as philosophy, history, literature, and economics. Higher education used also to teach students the critical thinking that might help them to resist being taken in by the lies with which they are bombarded from all sides these days by the media.

Though literature is still widely taught by a great many gifted and devoted teachers, and though an immense number of books and essays on literature, such as this one, are still published, nevertheless, the actual role of literature either in the sense of printed books or in the sense of online e-texts has become more and more peripheral. All of Anthony Trollope's novels are available as e-texts, to give one example of literature's availability these days in nonprint forms. People can read Trollope novels on their smartphones or iPads if they wish, but almost all, and not just in the United States, use them for other purposes instead. They use Facebook (an amazing average of seventeen hours, fifty minutes daily, per online visitor in September 2014), Twitter, Google, BuzzFeed, etc.[5] That irresistible, magical little, gadget you can hold in your hand has, even more than in

2010, to a large extent replaced printed books. It is an amazing cultural and psychological transformation. By five years from now an estimated 5.9 billion people worldwide will own smartphones.[6]

The final change since 2010 in our colleges and universities is the incredibly rapid development of various digital substitutes for actual face-to-face teaching in a classroom: online courses; universities without buildings; MOOCs, or "massive, on-line, open courses," and the like. Why should I, or my family, pay hundreds of thousands of dollars to send me to Oberlin or Harvard, if I can get the "same education" almost for free, sitting at my computer at home? The old-fashioned university, with class-room buildings and residential dormitories, is rapidly being outmoded by the digital revolution, and with it the traditional ways of teaching lit-erature (face-to-face lecture courses, seminars, tutorials, and the like).

The controversial common core curriculum, now being widely adopted in the United States, with its standardized lists in the literature section of books to read and with its prescriptions of what constitutes correct American English, along with standardized exams, is a creature of the dig-ital revolution through and through. In spite of its attempts to be flexible and to encourage give and take in the classroom, it pays little attention to differences among teachers or students in a given classroom. Applying the common core throughout the country gives great opportunity for adver-tent or inadvertent ideological indoctrination, just as did the traditional teaching of English literature in British India. In my judgment, on the contrary, the independent literature classroom is a great place to teach students to think for themselves as well as a place for the teacher to find out what works best for a particular set of students, including which liter-ary texts work best.[7]

Two, the media: I have mentioned the new digital media that are so rapidly replacing the printed-book medium and even old-fashioned radio, television, and films shown in theaters: Facebook, Twitter, YouTube, and a host of other digital media. People watch Fox News on their handhelds. Judgments about courtship, marriage, how to vote, and the like are influ-enced or even determined these days by these new digital media, no longer by novels. Novels, poems, even, for the highly educated, Greek and Latin classics, played to a considerable degree that role in Victorian England, at least for middle-class citizens.

What can one say about the content of these new media, streamed into the smartphones of so many millions of people? To put it briefly: that content is for the most part pretty awful. It facilitates a major dumbing-down of the American people. The "news," say in TV format on Fox News, but also on NBC, and even on PBS, is full of lies and distortions. It is also constantly interrupted by commercials, the same ones shown over and over again, day after day. Those ads are even more distorted, for example, the claim in ads by the American Petroleum Institute, that until recently were shown over and over, night after night, on NBC News, that "fracking" (recovery of oil and gas from shale deposits) is safe, clean, and will gain us "energy independence." Nothing is said in such ads about how fracking and the burning of its products will markedly increase disastrous global warming, nor about the fact that fracking is not at all safe. The news stresses violence, sex, the imminent threat of contagious disease, and the latest happenings among media celebrities, as do our films and news applications for smartphones, like BuzzFeed. I watch NBC Evening News on television from 6:30 to 7:00 PM. Twenty minutes of it is made up primarily of brief stories about the latest disasters from around the world, often with dead bodies and visible blood. The other ten minutes are made up of ads, often of great sophistication. Much of our poetic and cinematic talent goes into inventing these ads. Since NBC TV news is intended primarily for old folk like me (younger people get their news from smartphone sites), many such ads are for medicines that promise to alleviate such diseases as diabetic nerve pain, shingles, dry eye, pneumonia, loss of bladder control, erectile disfunction, or atrial fibrillation. The video parts show happy people whose lives have been changed by Cialis or Restasis or whatever. Meanwhile, the voice-over, accompanied by subtitles, intones, as required by law, the horrible side effects of each medicine. These lead me to resolve never to take any one of them if I can help it. Such news and the accompanying ads appear calculated to keep the American people in a perpetual state of abject terror, anxiety ("Am I coming down with shingles?"), and distraction. This is perhaps so we won't notice that our civil liberties are disappearing into a constant state of surveillance both by the government and by the media themselves (the latter for marketing purposes). "Big Brother is watching you!" as George Orwell has his fascist authorities' posters say in his prescient novel, *1984*.

In spite of all these negative features of the new dominant media, Internet sites like Google, Wikipedia, and Project Gutenburg give people studying literature, teaching it, or writing about it enormous resources available at a few clicks of a mouse. The Internet has quietly revolutionized literary study, as my use of it for this book indicates.

Three, economics: Since 2010 the Great Recession has receded somewhat, with a lower unemployment rate, though little increase in wages for ordinary workers. The stock market is at historic highs, with the Dow over eighteen thousand again, though it has fluctuated a lot recently. The disparity between rich and poor has never been higher, however, with 40 percent of national wealth in the hands of the top one percent. The "recovery" has not greatly helped the ordinary ill-paid worker at, say, Walmart. The recession was brought on and prolonged to some degree by a false belief in the beneficial effects of government austerity (reduction in expenditures for things like school lunches, medical care, education, and road building) and by unregulated use by banks and other financial institutions of digital programs to speculate with depositors' money, for example in subprime mortgages. No effective regulation of banks has yet been imposed. Banks, hedge funds, and the like are now at it again. Sooner or later, another disastrous crash will likely come. The economy is at this point completely dependent on digitization, for example, on the possibility of making thousands of computer-programmed stock market trades in a fraction of a second, buying, selling, and then buying again to make almost innumerable tiny profits that add up to billions.

Four, politics: the United States these days, I am sorry to say, is more and more becoming a postdemocracy, a plutocracy. To a large degree, this depends once more on computer programs. In this case, it is programs that allow the hiding or obfuscation of a political contribution's actual source. Such programs keep the money circulating so fast that no one can identify where it originally came from. The very rich have bought our federal politicians, especially the Republicans in Congress. They have bought also many state and local elected officials from state governors on down. The very rich, through their often somewhat covert ownership of the media, for example Fox News, have succeeded in getting voters to believe in a lot of lies, for example, that the Affordable Health Care Act ("Obamacare") is a terrible piece of legislation, whereas it has given health care already to over sixteen million citizens who did not have it. Obamacare is working very well, in spite of Republican attempts to sabotage it at every step of the way. Another set of lies is what the media, bought and paid for, have kept on saying against Obama, that he is ineffective and vacillating, that everything he has done is bad or unconstitutional, that he ought to be impeached, that he is not really an American citizen in any case, and so ineligible to be president, etc., a constant litany of abuse. Against these lies, Paul Krugman, in a recent *New York Times* op-ed piece, has presented a substantial list of important good things Obama and our federal government did just in 2014: handling the Ebola threat; bringing about further economic recovery in jobs and growth; bringing Obamacare successfully into operation; confronting Vladimir Putin's threats without rushing into war.[8] When I revised this once more, in mid-September 2015, the dozen or so Republican candidates for president were holding periodic debates, with the dangerous buffoon Donald Trump the center of attention and the leader of the polls. Each and every one of them tells such a collection of lies and makes such disastrous proposals as would make any of them a catastrophic president both in domestic policy and in their support for perpetual foreign wars. Now, in April 2016, it looks as if Donald Trump, the worst of the lot, will actually be the Republican candidate for president.

Five, foreign wars: the United States is committed to a perpetual "War on Terror" that was first enunciated by President George W. Bush after the bombing of the Twin Towers on 9/11/2001. That is part of the context in which any teaching of literature must take place in the United States today. We spend a huge percentage of our annual gross domestic product on military costs, 40 percent of the entire world's military expenditures, a patent absurdity. We are armed to the teeth. Our disastrous invasions of Iraq and Afghanistan have cost at least two trillion dollars all told. Think how many schools could have been built with that money or how many new bridges and new roads to repair our decaying infrastructure! The ten miles of paved and numbered state road (Route 15) between my winter home in Sedgwick, Maine, and the nearest town of any size (Blue Hill) has been, until recently, more or less unusable in the winter because of frost heaves and potholes. Now a new surface has been applied that makes it a rollercoaster rather than a series of big bumps. President Obama has withdrawn our troops from Iraq and Afghanistan. The formal end of the War in Afghanistan was declared December 28, 2014, thirteen years after our initial invasion, but of course we still kept "advisory" troops there, as we do in Syria. American soldiers are still dying in these countries. Obama acquiesces too easily to our generals, for example, in authorizing the bombing of ISIS in Syria and Afghanistan. This is a futile enterprise that has hardly given ISIS pause, but has already produced many civilian casualties and has made us hated even more than we were before by many in the Middle East. Afghanistan, Iraq, and Syria are all, in April 2016, in one way or another in political and social chaos. The forms these disastrous conditions have taken are to a considerable degree the result of our invasions of the first two and everything short of invasion of the third.

Our bombing of ISIS "targets" is an example of a new kind of digital war, terrifying in its impersonality. This is not only because all our military might, warplanes for example, depends on digital programming, as does communication among soldiers, but also because much of our warfare is carried on now by unmanned, digitally operated drones that are controlled from command centers in the United States. Some military officer watching a screen in the military base in Grand Forks, North Dakota, presses a button on his computer mouse, and a large number of people thousands of miles away in Syria are killed with "pinpoint precision." He then presumably goes home in the evening with a clear conscience and in more or less complete safety to join his wife and children at his home on the military base. Similar equipment is used to monitor our borders against "illegal aliens." Such border guards, like our soldiers, are often trained through video games like World of Warcraft or Call of Duty. About these much could be said. The players of such games (millions of them) participate by digital manipulation in an imaginary world of the utmost violence. They thereby become inured to deaths that they have themselves caused in that cyberspace world. What would Wordsworth, Dickens, Trollope, or Elizabeth Gaskell have thought of such replacements for reading poems and novels? I have not forgotten that there is a lot of killing in Homer and Shakespeare, too! Think of Macbeth, Hamlet, or Achilles.

Six, climate change: human-caused global warming is in many ways the paradigmatic example of "auto-co-immunity," as Derrida calls it. In all of my examples what is intended to save or help the community works to destroy it. To recall one example, banks, which are supposed to keep our money safe and pay us fair interest for it, lose our money in wildly speculative investments. All of my examples are ways the digital revolution facilitates collective self-destruction. Global warming, however, is the most extreme example. Carbon technology (coal, oil, and gas) brought many good things to our culture: automobiles, central heating, electricity for all, etc. Unbeknown to us, however, until recently, burning these fuels was emitting sufficient carbon dioxide into the atmosphere to warm the planet enough to melt Arctic and Antarctic ice as well as glaciers everywhere they still exist, to flood our coastlines and coastal cities, and ultimately, in not all that many decades, to bring extinction to many species of life on earth, including perhaps homo sapiens. We in the United States are already experiencing floods, violent storms, forest fires, prolonged droughts, rising sea levels, and the warmest years on record. We have known for several decades now the facts about global warming and that it is anthropogenic. Nevertheless, the use of digital technology in media propaganda by oil companies and others to spread the lie, known by them to be a lie, that global warming is a hoax has meant that so far nothing sufficient has been done by governments around the world to mitigate climate change. We are now on the cusp of irreversible climate change. It is most likely already too late.

Should or ought we to read or teach literature in a "now" that is in so many ways an extreme crisis situation? Is it a civic obligation to do so? If so, which works? How should these be read and taught? One tempting answer would be to say that "the humanities are a lost cause." We do not have time, in our dire straits, to spend on something so trivial and so peripheral as reading George Eliot's *Middlemarch* or any other "great work of literature." I shall later on in this chapter give, however, a different and somewhat more hopeful answer.

During the nineteen years I taught at The Johns Hopkins University, from 1953 to 1972, I would have had ready answers to the questions about whether or not we should read or teach literature, and how. These answers would have represented our unquestioned consensus at Hopkins about the nature and mission of the humanities. A (somewhat absurd) ideological defense of literary study, especially study of British literature, was pretty firmly in place at Hopkins during those years. We in the English Department at Hopkins had easy consciences because we thought we were doing two things that were good for the country: teaching young citizens the basic American ethos and doing research that was like that of our scientific colleagues in that it was finding out the "truth" about the fields covered by our disciplines: languages, literatures, art, history, philosophy. *Veritas vos liberabit*, the truth shall make you free, is the motto of Hopkins. It is a quotation from the Bible, by the way, something said by Jesus (John 8: 32). By *truth* Jesus hardly meant scientific truth, as it for the most part did at Hopkins in my time there. *Lux et veritas*, light and truth, is the motto of Yale. Just plain *veritas* is Harvard's slogan. Truth, we at Hopkins believed, having forgotten the source of our motto, included objective truth of every sort, for example, the truth about the early poetry of Alfred Tennyson or about the poetry of Barnaby Googe. Such truth was a good in itself, like knowledge of black holes or of genetics. Our research and teaching was focused primarily on the literature of a foreign country, England, which we defeated in a revolutionary War of Independence. The absurdity of some of the presuppositions behind that project only recently got through to me. We in "the land of the free" had gone on acting like a colony in our teaching of literature. More and more, in the years since the

1950s, a shift has occurred toward teaching predominantly American literature rather than British literature.

Hopkins, as is well-known, was the first exclusively "research university" in the United States. It was founded on the model of the great German research universities of the nineteenth century. In literary study that meant inheritance of the German tradition of Romance philology, Germanic philology (which included English literature), and classical philology, all of which flourished at Hopkins. No comparative literature at Hopkins in those days. Such research needed no further justification beyond the intrinsic value accorded to the search for truth and the not entirely persuasive assumption that humanities scholars who were doing that kind of research would be better teachers of literature as the precious repository of our national values. The word *research* was our collective leitmotif. Every professor at Hopkins was supposed to spend 50 percent of his (we were almost all men) time doing research in his field of specialty. That included humanities professors.

Hopkins was to an amazing degree run by the professors, or at least it seemed so to us. Professors made decisions about hiring, promotion, and the establishment of new programs through a group of professors called the "Academic Council." They were elected by the faculty. Though there was no established quota, the council always included humanists and social scientists as well as scientists. That means the scientists, who could have outvoted the humanists, were cheerfully electing humanists. Outside support for research at Hopkins came not from industry, but primarily from government agencies like the National Science Foundation, the National Institutes of Health, the National Defense Education Act, and the National Endowment for the Humanities. We benefitted greatly from the Cold War mentality that thought the United States should be best in everything, including even the humanities. None of the teaching was done by adjuncts, though graduate students taught composition and discussion sections of large lecture courses. Most students who received the PhD obtained good, tenure-track appointments. Misleading statistics even indicated that a shortage of PhDs in the humanities was about to happen, so the English department at Hopkins briefly instituted a three-year PhD in that field. Two of my own students finished such a PhD and went on to hold professorships at important universities. That shows a PhD in English need not take twelve years or more, the average time today.

Hopkins was, in my time there, a kind of paradise for professors who happened to be interested in research as well as in teaching. Hopkins then was the closest thing I know to Jacques Derrida's nobly idealistic vision in

2001 of a "university without condition," a university centered to a considerable degree on the humanities and devoted to a disinterested search for truth in all areas.[9] It is a great irony that Derrida's little book was delivered as a president's lecture at Stanford University, since Stanford is one of the great elite, private universities in the United States that is and always has been deeply intertwined with corporate America and, by way of the Hoover Institution, located at Stanford, with the most conservative side of American politics.

Well, what was wrong with Hopkins in those halcyon days? Quite a lot. Practically no women were on the faculty, not even in nontenured positions—not a single one in the English department during all my nineteen years at Hopkins. Our protocols at Hopkins for teaching literature in English seem from my perspective now to have been narrowly ideological and sexist. We downplayed American literature and taught literature mostly by British men. The education of graduate students in English was brutally competitive, with a high rate of attrition, often by way of withdrawal by the English department faculty of fellowship funds, initially granted to students who were later judged not to be performing well. Some students whom we "encouraged to leave" took PhDs elsewhere and had brilliant careers as professors of English. Hopkins, finally, was up to its ears in military research at the Applied Physics Laboratory. The Johns Hopkins School of Advanced International Studies was not then, and still is not today, to put it mildly, what one would call a model of democratic thinking. Even so, Hopkins seemed to me in the fifties and sixties a wonderful place to be a professor of the humanities.

Now, over fifty years later, everything is different in U.S. universities and colleges from what it was at Hopkins when I taught there. Even in the fifties and sixties, Hopkins was the exception, not the rule. I have described the not entirely cheerful situation in which my questions, "Should we read or teach literature now? Do we have an obligation to do so?" must be asked and an attempt to answer them made. How did this disappearance of the justification for literary study happen? I suggest three reasons:

> The conviction that everybody ought to read literature because it embodies the ethos of our citizens has almost completely vanished. Few people any longer really believe, in their heart of hearts, that it is necessary to read *Beowulf*, Shakespeare, Milton, Samuel Johnson, Wordsworth, Emerson, Dickinson, Whitman, Dickens, Woolf, Stevens, and Conrad in order to become a good citizen of the United States.

A massive shift in dominant media away from printed books to all forms of digital media, what I call "prestidigitalization," has meant that literature, in the old-fashioned sense of printed novels, poems, and dramas, plays a smaller and smaller role in determining the ethos of our citizens. Middle-class readers in Victorian England, as I have said earlier, learned how to behave in courtship and marriage by entering into the fictive worlds of novels by Charles Dickens, George Eliot, Anthony Trollope, Elizabeth Gaskell, and many others. Now people satisfy their needs for imaginary or virtual realities by watching films, television, DVDs, playing video games, and listening to popular music. It was announced as long ago as July 19, 2010, by Amazon that for the first time they are selling more e-books to be read on iPads or Kindles than hardcover printed books. A high point of the summer of 2010 for a colleague and friend of mine in Norway, a distinguished humanities professor, was his trip to Rotterdam to hear a Stevie Wonder concert at the North Sea Jazz Festival, followed by a repeat performance of the same concert in his home town of Bergen. He e-mailed me with great excitement and enthusiasm about these concerts. Stevie Wonder has obviously great importance in shaping this humanist's ethos. Whenever I gave a lecture on some literary work in any place in the world, members of my audience, especially the younger ones, always wanted to ask me questions about the film of that work, if a film had been made. They knew the film, not the book.

The rise of new media has meant more and more the substitution of cultural studies for old-fashioned literary studies. It is natural for young people to want to teach and write about things that interest them, for example, film, popular culture, women's studies, African American studies, and so on. Many, if not most, departments of English in the United States these days are actually departments of cultural studies, whatever they may call themselves. Less and less literature is taught these days in American departments of English. Soon, Chinese or Indian students of English literature, American literature, and worldwide literature in English will know more about these than American students do. A list not long ago of new books published at the University of Minnesota Press in "Literature and Cultural Studies" did not have one single book on printed literature proper.

Just to give three examples out of hundreds of career-orientation shifts: Edward Said began as a specialist on the novels and short stories of Joseph Conrad. He went on to write a book that is theory-oriented, *Beginnings*, but his great fame and influence rests on political books like *Orientalism, The Question of Palestine*, and *Culture and Imperialism*. Second, a quite different example: Joan DeJean is a distinguished professor of romance languages at the University of Pennsylvania, but she does not write about French literature in the old-fashioned sense of plays by Racine, novels by Pierre de Marivaux or Flaubert, poems by Baudelaire, or novels by Duras (all men but Duras, please note). Her influential books include, among others, *The Essence of Style: How the French Invented High Fashion, Fine Food, Chic Cafes, Style, Sophistication*, and *The Age of Comfort: When Paris Discovered Casual—and the Modern Home Began*. In short, Professor DeJean does cultural studies, with a feminist slant, not literary studies. Third example: Frank Donoghue began his career as a specialist in eighteenth-century English literature. He published in 1996 a fine book on *The Fame Machine: Book Reviewing and Eighteenth-Century Literary Careers*. Around 2000, Donoghue shifted to an interest in the current state of the humanities in American universities. In 2008, he published *The Last Professors: The Corporate University and the Fate of the Humanities*. He then began lecturing frequently as an expert on the corporatizing of the American university.

I have briefly sketched the present-day situation in the United States within which the question "Should We Read or Teach Literature Now?" must be asked: smaller and smaller actual influence of literature on common culture; fewer professors who teach literature as opposed to cultural studies; fewer tenured professors of literature in any case; fewer books of literary criticism proper published, and tiny sales for those that are published; reduced enrollment in literature courses in our colleges and universities; the reduction of literature departments toward being service departments teaching composition and, in even fewer universities, the rudiments of foreign languages and foreign cultures. The attitude toward languages other than English seems to be, "What, me worry? Everybody everywhere speaks and reads English anyhow, or ought to do so. Why worry about teaching French, German, Italian, or Russian?"[10]

The usual response by embattled humanists is to wring their hands, become defensive, and say literature ought to be taught because we need to know our cultural past, or need to "expand our minds," or need the ethical teaching we can get from literary works. Presidents of the Modern Language Association of America (MLA) have in their presidential addresses over the decades echoed what Matthew Arnold said about the need to know, as he puts it in *Culture and Anarchy* (1869), "the best that has been thought and said in the world." Robert Scholes, for example, in his MLA Presidential address delivered in 2004, asserted: "We need to show that our learning is worth something by . . . broadening the minds of our students and helping our fellow citizens to more thoughtful interpretations of the crucial texts that shape our culture. . . . We have nothing to offer but the sweetness of reason and the light of learning."[11] "Sweetness and light" is of course Arnold's repeated phrase, in *Culture and Anarchy*, for what culture gives. That book was required reading in the freshman English course all students took at Oberlin College when I became a student there in 1944.

I think the noble, Arnoldian view of the benefits of literary study is pretty well dead and gone these days, in spite of Ranjan Ghosh's spirited defense of Arnold in his dialogic response to my chapter 10. For one thing, we now recognize more clearly how problematic and heterogeneous the literary tradition of the West actually is. It by no means teaches some unified ethos. Many of its greatest works are hardly uplifting in the usual sense of the term. That includes, for example, Shakespeare's *King Lear*, Melville's *Moby Dick*, and many others. About reading *King Lear*, Keats said in a sonnet, "On Sitting Down to Read King Lear Once Again": "For once again the fierce dispute, / Betwixt damnation and impassion'd clay / Must I burn through."[12] Nor is American literature much better. Of one of our great classics, *Moby-Dick*, its author, Herman Melville, said, "I have written a wicked book." As for Keats's own writings, Matthew Arnold found Keats's letters deeply troubling. Arnold wrote to his friend Clough, "What a brute you were to tell me to read Keats' letters. However, it is over now: and reflexion resumes her power over agitation."[13] Furthermore, it is not at all clear to me how reading Shakespeare, Keats, Dickens, Whitman, Yeats, or Wallace Stevens is any use in helping our students to deal with the urgent problems that confront us all these days in the United States: I have discussed six of these earlier in this chapter. Young people in the United States now need, or think they need, to get training that will help them get a job and be able to pay for housing and food. As I shall argue in a little more detail at the end of this chapter, students might benefit from courses that would teach them how to tell truth from falsehood on Internet postings.[14]

Well, why in the world should we read and teach literature now, in these dire circumstances? In order to make this question less abstract, I shall confront my question by way of a short poem by Yeats. I greatly admire this poem. It moves me greatly. It moves me so much that I want not only to read it but also to teach it and talk about it to anyone who will listen. The poem is called "The Cold Heaven." It is from Yeats's volume of poems of 1916, *Responsibilities*. It is available in a number of sites online. Here is the poem:

THE COLD HEAVEN

Suddenly I saw the cold and rook-delighting heaven
That seemed as though ice burned and was but the more ice,
And thereupon imagination and heart were driven
So wild that every casual thought of that and this
Vanished, and left but memories, that should be out of season
With the hot blood of youth, of love crossed long ago;
And I took all the blame out of all sense and reason,
Until I cried and trembled and rocked to and fro,
Riddled with light. Ah! when the ghost begins to quicken,
Confusion of the death-bed over, is it sent
Out naked on the roads, as the books say, and stricken
By the injustice of the skies for punishment? [15]

I long ago wrote a full essay on this poem.[16] I discussed it briefly again once more in 2010 at a conference on world literature at Shanghai Jiao Tong University. At Jiao Tong I used Yeats's poem as an example of how difficult it is to transfer a poem from one culture to a different one. Now I want to consider the poem as a paradigmatic exemplification of the difficulties of deciding whether we should read or teach literature now. Should I read or teach this poem now?

My first answer is that there is no should about it, no compelling obligation or responsibility. I can read or teach it if I like, but that decision cannot be justified by anything beyond the call the poem itself makes on me to read it and teach it. Least of all do I think I can tell students or administrators with a straight face that reading the poem or hearing me teach it is going to help them find a job, or help them mitigate climate change, or help them resist the lies told by the media, though I suppose being a good reader might conceivably aid resistance to lies, as I shall later in this chapter argue. Reading the poem or teaching it is, however, a good in itself, an end in itself, as Kant said all art is.

The mystical poet Angelus Silesius (1624–77) affirmed, in *The Cherubic Wanderer*, that "the rose is without why."[17] Like that rose, "The Cold Heaven" is without why. The poem, like a rose, has no reason for being beyond itself. You can read it or not read it, as you like. It is its own end. Young people these days who watch films or play video games or listen to popular music do not, for the most part, attempt to justify what they do. They do it because they like to do it and because it gives them pleasure. My academic friend from Bergen did not try to justify his great pleasure and excitement in hearing at great expense the same Stevie Wonder concert twice. He just e-mailed me his great enthusiasm about the experience. It was a big deal for him, just as reading, talking, or writing about Yeats's "The Cold Heaven" is a big deal for me. That importance, however, is something I should not even try to justify by its practical utility. If I do make that attempt I am bound to fail.

A natural response when I see a film I like or hear a concert that moves me is to want to tell other people about it, as my correspondent in Bergen wanted to tell everybody about those Stevie Wonder concerts. These tellings most often take the form, "Wow! I saw a wonderful movie last night. Let me tell you about it." I suggest that my desire to teach Yeats's "The Cold Heaven" takes much the same form: "Wow! I have just read a wonderful poem by Yeats. Let me read it to you and tell you about it." That telling, naturally enough, is to pass on what I think other readers might find helpful to lead them to respond to the poem as enthusiastically as I do.

I list, in an order following that of the poem, some of the things that might need to be explained not only, for example, to a Chinese reader, but also, no doubt, mutatis mutandis, to a video-games-playing Western young person ignorant of European poetry, or to a student in an Indian classroom. David Damrosch recognizes with equanimity, as do I, that when a given piece of literature circulates into a different culture from that of its origin, for example by translation, it will be read differently.

I am not talking here, however, about a full, culturally embedded reading, or the sort of (in)fusionist, transcultural reading Ranjan Ghosh sketches out in his dialogic response to this section of my chapter, or about a reading that might arise from a classroom discussion, but just about making sense of Yeats's poem. This need to make sense might arise, for example, in teaching this poem to an undergraduate or graduate class in a U.S. university. Here are some things it might be good to know when trying to understand "The Cold Heaven":

Something about Yeats's life and works.

An explanation of the verse form used: three iambic hexameter quatrains rhyming ABAB. Is it an odd sort of sonnet in hexameters rather than pentameters, and missing the last couplet?

Knowledge of the recurrent use of *sudden* or *suddenly* in Yeats's lyrics, as in the first lines of his poem, "Leda and the Swan": "A sudden blow: the great wings beating still / Above the staggering girl."

What sort of bird a rook is and why they are delighted by cold weather.

The double meaning of *heaven*, as "skies" and as the supernatural realm beyond the skies, as in the opening of the Lord's Prayer, said daily by millions of Christians: "Our Father who art in heaven"; compare "skies" at the end: "the injustice of the skies for punishment."

An explanation of oxymorons (burning ice) and of the history in Western poetry of this particular one.

Attempt to explain the semantic difference between "imagination" and "heart," as well as the nuances of each word.

Explanation of "crossed" in "memories . . . of love crossed long ago," both the allusion to Shakespeare's Romeo and Juliet as "star-crossed lovers," that is, as fated by the stars to disaster in love, and the reference to the biographical fact of Yeats's disastrous love for Maud Gonne. She turned him down repeatedly, so it is to some degree absurd for him to take responsibility for the failure of their love. He did his best to woo her.

Account of the difference between "sense" and "reason" in "I took the blame out of all sense and reason," or is this just tautological? A. Norman Jeffares cites T. R. Henn's explanation that "'out of all sense' is an Irish (and ambiguous) expression meaning both 'to an extent far beyond what common sense could justify' and 'beyond the reach of sensation.'"[18]

Explanation of the double meaning of the verb "riddle" in the marvelous phrase, "riddled with light": *riddle* as punctured with holes, like a sieve, and *riddle* as having a perhaps unanswered riddle or conundrum posed to one. Being riddled with light is paradoxical because light is supposed to be illuminating, not obscuring.

Unsnarling of the lines centering on "quicken" in "when the ghost [meaning disembodied soul] begins to quicken, / Confusion of the death bed over." *Quicken* usually refers, in one of its meanings, to the coming to life of the fertilized egg in the womb, so an erotic love-bed scene is superimposed on the death-bed one.

"As the books say": which books? The esoteric and Irish folklore ones Yeats delighted to read.

One would need to relate "injustice of the skies for punishment" to the usual assumption that heaven only punishes justly, gives us our just deserts after death. Why and how can the skies be unjust? By blaming him for something that was not his fault? This would need to be related to Greek and later tragedy. It is not Oedipus's fault that he has killed his father and fathered children on his mother, or is it? Are we all guilty in Freud's sense of having an Oedipus complex or an Electra complex?

Why is the last sentence a question? Is it a real question or a merely rhetorical one? Would the answer find its place if the blank that follows the twelve lines of this defective sonnet were filled? The poem seems both too much in line lengths and too little in number of lines.

Finally, readers might like to know, or might even observe on their own, that Yeats, like other European poets of his generation, was influenced in this poem and elsewhere by what he knew, through translations, of Chinese poetry and Chinese ways of thinking. The volume *Responsibilities*, which contains "The Cold Heaven," has an epigraph from someone Yeats calls, somewhat pretentiously, "Khoung-Fou-Tseu," presumably Confucius: "How am I fallen from myself, for a long time now / I have not seen the Prince of Chang in my dreams"[19] Readers might have a lot to say about this Chinese connection and about whether or not it makes "The Cold Heaven" a work of world literature.

All this information would be given to my hearers or readers, however, not to expand their minds, but in the hope that it might help them admire the poem as much as I do and be moved by it as much as I am. Yeats's poem can hardly be described as uplifting, since its thematic climax is a claim that the skies are unjust and punish people for things of which they are not guilty. That is a terrifying wisdom. Telling others about this poem is not something I *should* do but something I cannot help doing, something the poem urgently calls on me to do.

In an actual U.S. classroom, depending a bit on whether it was an undergraduate or a graduate course and on how many students there were in the class, my contextual information and rudimentary reading would be followed or accompanied by questions and discussion from the students, and perhaps lead to papers, long or short, in which students would present their own readings. Large lecture courses on literature in the United States, such as the introductory literature major courses at Yale, which I taught in for many years, are often augmented by small "discussion sections" taught both by the senior faculty and by graduate students. In those, students engage in the give and take of reflection on the material presented in the lectures. Some form of student participation is a fundamental part of teaching literature in the United States, though I believe, as against the conviction of some teachers these days, that faculty members have an obligation not to hide their knowledge and their own ways of reading particular works. The fine line between handing down the law and failing to help students learn to read for themselves must be walked by each teacher as best she or he can.

Do I think much future exists in United States colleges and universities or in our journals and university presses for such readings and modes of teaching? Not as much as I would wish. Even many of those who could teach literature, who were hired to do so, choose, rather, to teach cultural studies instead: fashion design, or the history of Western imperialism, or film, or some one or another among those myriad other interests that have replaced literature.

I add in conclusion, however, somewhat timidly and tentatively, one possible use studying literature and literary theory might have, or ought to have, "in these bad days" (an echo of Matthew Arnold's early sonnet "To a Friend."). Citizens, in the United States at least, are these days inundated with a torrent of distortions and outright lies from politicians, the news media, and advertising on television and radio, for example, commercials for oil companies, or assertions in Donald Trump's campaign speeches, which have been rated as only 9 percent accurate.

Learning how to read literature rhetorically is primary training in how to spot such lies and distortions. Students might benefit from literature courses that would teach them how to tell truth from falsehood in Internet postings. This is partly because so much literature deals thematically with imaginary characters who are wrong in their readings of others, for example, Elizabeth Bennett in her misreading of Darcy in Jane Austen's *Pride and Prejudice* or Dorothea Brooke's misreading of Edward Casaubon in George Eliot's *Middlemarch*, or Isabel Archer's misreading of Gilbert Osmond in Henry James's *The Portrait of a Lady*. (My choice of these heroines does not mean that it is only women who make such mistakes in Victorian novels. Think of Pip in *Great Expectations* or of Lydgate in *Middlemarch* or of Conrad's *Lord Jim*!)

Literature is also training in resisting lies and distortions in the skill it gives in understanding the way the rhetoric of tropes and the rhetoric of persuasion works. Such expertise as literary study gives might be translated into a savvy resistance to the lies and ideological distortions politicians and talk-show hosts promulgate, for example the lies of those who deny climate change, or the lying claims, believed by high percentages of Americans, that Barack Obama is a Muslim, a socialist, and not a legitimate president because he was not born in the United States. The motto for this defense of literary study might be the challenging and provocative claim made by Paul de Man in "The Resistance to Theory." "What we call ideology," says de Man, "is precisely the confusion of linguistic with natural reality, of reference with phenomenalism. It follows that, more than any other mode of inquiry, including economics, the linguistics of literariness is a powerful and indispensable tool in the unmasking of ideological aberrations, as well as a determining factor in accounting for their occurrence."[20]

The chances that literary study would have this benign effect on many people are slim. One can only have the audacity of hope and believe that some students and teachers who read and study literature and literary theory might be led to the habit of unmasking ideological aberrations such as those that surround us on all sides in the United States today. The chances are slim because of the difficulty of transferring what you might learn by a careful reading, say, of *The Portrait of a Lady* to unmasking the dominant ideologies that mean a thoughtful person should only vote Republican if her or his income happens to be in the top two percent of all Americans and if maximizing your wealth in the short term is your only goal. Another great difficulty is the actual situation in American universities today, as I have described it. Derrida's *The University without Condition* was not exactly greeted with shouts of joyful assent when he presented it as a lecture at Stanford. In spite of their lip-service to teaching so-called critical thinking, the politicians and corporate executives who preside today over both public and private American colleges and universities are unlikely to support something that would put in question the assumptions on the basis of which they try to make decisions about who teaches what. As I have argued earlier in this chapter, they think they need colleges and universities these days, if at all, primarily to teach math and science, technology, engineering, computer science, basic English composition, and other skills necessary for working in a technologized capitalist economy. The ability to do a rhetorical reading of *Pride and Prejudice* and transfer that skill to politicians' and advertisers' lies is not one of those necessities. I have never yet heard President Barack Obama so much as mention literary study in his eloquent speeches about the urgent need to improve education in the United States.

PART V

Ethics and Literature

THE ETHICS OF READING SAHITYA

But true art is never fixed, but always flowing.
—Ralph Waldo Emerson

Dissonances are only the remote consonances.
—Arnold Schoenberg

Human life . . . is composed of two heterogeneous parts which never blend. One part is purposeful, given significance by utilitarian and therefore secondary ends; this part is the one we are aware of. The other is primary and sovereign . . . it evades the grasp of our aware intelligence.
—Georges Bataille

The ethics of sahitya (literature) are inscribed in a variety of hunger. Sahitya creates its own hunger, the desire to feed on the "other" and be fed upon. It is formed out of a hunger to explicate ways of human experience and engagements with emotions. It is anchored in a hunger that is its *eros*, its creative aesthesis, its power of sustenance and motivation. The inherent hunger of sahitya calls for at once imaginative ventures of crossdisciplinarity and the understanding of human values born out of philosophic designs, both conceptual and experiential. Sahitya has the ability to operate beyond the point of a direct act of perception. This is what lends freedom to individual interpretive journeys, furthering intelligible aesthetic experiences. We encounter new interpretive behaviors with potentially realizable values springing out of a certain premise of inheritance, a literary heritage, ideas nourished by a certain intellectual climate, cultural and symbolic accumulation, and also some unfulfillments that keep sahitya alive against the reificatory modes of subjugation. Hunger satiated is hunger generated. Hunger attended is hunger made possible. Hunger is experience realized; hunger is responsibility awaiting fulfillment. The ethics of sahitya argue for various incarnations of hunger, both at the level of the aesthetic and the postaesthetic.

Emotion, Hunger, and (In)fusion

The success of interpretation is most often a lie. The text, in its reticulated existence, brings the disenfranchised others to bear on its signification. For me this "aesthetic of hunger" in sahitya is about forming, foregrounding, and fictionalizing the "other." This other is born out of an urge and need to feel for a variety of discourses and thoughts across cultures and traditions. Hunger is a "mark," the "referentiality," and the otherity that sahitya is possessed by and embedded in. The literary critic as a disciplinary scofflaw, a Barthean "joiner," appreciates the ineliminable hunger in sahitya to evolve greater modes of meaning and deeper enclaves of sense, and this hunger is integral to sahitya's survival.

The (in)fusion approach respects both the nontranscendent and the transcendent aspects of what we understand as sahitya, and literarity builds on the intentional acts that, without being merely projective and subjective, can also be figured out within certain networks of meaning and an abiding consciousness of limits and restrictions. In fact, the invention that Derrida looks into in relation to his understanding of literature is somewhere close to what the (in)fusion approach commits to perform—a certain restiveness with essence, a certain restless agony with dogmatism. But in its transdiscursivity and transcultural propensities the (in)fusion approach raises the notion of accountability and responsibility to create and invent hunger in literature. This is a responsibility toward the other that is, as Derek Attridge argues, "also a responsibility towards the future since it involves the struggle to create within which the other can appear beyond any of our programs and predictions, can come to transform what we know or think we know."[1] Looking at a text (in)fusionally does not mean that meaning can multiply endlessly with the promotion of radical linguistic skepticism and textual permissiveness. (In)fusion approach looks at the "reality" of the text and "thinks out" the ways of thought, the intricacies of the concepts, the possibilities of theory to explore this "reality" or the "tissues of textualities." It is the reality of the theory-paradigm interface, the viability of conceptual trafficking and the interconnectivity among traditions of interpretation or critical thought that concern an (in)fusionist. This spells out a "discretion" which springs from our deep and meticulous understanding of critical paradigms, concepts, or theoretical orientation; the understanding teaches us or validates our interpretative orientation to stretch and extend the "infusionist space" and sanction an awareness of the limit. (In)fusion approach in its acts of "homecoming festival"[2] cannot oversight a certain submission to tell a truth, an obedience before a law and an acceptance without flagrant contempt of a court of certain receptive modes of acknowledged competences and comprehension. Sahitya then is a "strange coupling, the coming together of two orders, one chaotic, the other ordered, one folding and the other unfolding, one contradiction and the other dilation."[3] It is a way of forming a "composed chaos."[4]

The complex dynamics between hunger and the other throw us into the fury and force of literary cannibalism. The Brazilian modernist poet Oswald de Andrade's "Manifesto da poesia pau-brasil" (1924) (Manifesto of Brazilwood poetry) and Manifesto Anthropofago (1928) talk about a deep tension that "challenges the dualities civilization/barbarism, modern/primitive, and original/derivative, which had informed the construction of Brazilian culture since the days of the colony." The import of modernist aesthetic projects and national and nativist identities are held in a "playful, polemical theory of cultural cannibalism," where the cannibal metaphor develops the idea of devouring—the consuming of the other—in that one's literature adapts the strength of the other and incorporates them into the native self.[5] The ethics of anthropophagy bring into play participatory consciousness: "I am only concerned with what is not mine. Law of Man. Law of the cannibal."[6] An implicit refigurative spirit constructed as a challenge to authority and authenticity is revealed in expressions like "the world's single law. Disguised expression of all individualism, of all collectivisms. Of all religions. Of all peace treaties."[7] Kenneth Jackson observes that "from Freud, Oswald absorbed the transformation of tabu into totem and blended the concept with Nietzsche's metaphor (in A Genealogy of Morals) of man as an animal that assimilates interior and exterior conflicts. From Keyserling the idea of technological savagery would be mixed with Spengler's conclusion about the victory of the machine and lead Oswald to the theory of a 'revolucao caraiba' [supernatural and indigenous revolution]. This Brazilian revolutionary synthesis would replace indigenous originality and pau-brasil [Brazilwood] simplicity with the cannibalistic instinct of rebellion."[8] So anthropophagus reason makes allowance for the continual mastication of the other to produce what I may argue is the regurgitated aesthetics of reading, which is about setting new transpoetical orders, politics of relationality, and planetization. Pointing to the new literary combinatorics, Rachel Galvin notes that "the poetics of cannibalism have pointed politico-aesthetic implications: ingesting and devouring describe the ludic recombination of preexisting cultural elements—or what might be called, more neutrally, innovation through engagement with tradition."[9] Anthropophagia disembeds what stays latent in the philosophy of revisionism and the across. The literary capital built out of such transcreative hunger has its own power and politics of insertion, interference, and assimilation. Hunger inspires recycling, reimagining, and recombinatory energy.

It is worthwhile to see how this cannibalistic hunger, in its ways of coupling—folding and unfolding, hiding and revealing—*speaks* through a poem as well known as Matthew Arnold's "The Scholar-Gipsy" (1853). V. S. Seturaman points out that Arnold's mind was preoccupied with thoughts from the *Bhagavad Gita* (the principles of *dwandwas* [dialectic, contrariety] and also a state of consciousness which transcends all dualism).[10] Commenting on Arnold's interests in oriental wisdom, Seturaman observes that for Arnold

> the secret of life was not joy but peace. Peace, however, is not sad patience but something that passes beyond the *Dwandwas*. . . . As for his attitude to Oriental wisdom it must be clear to every reader of his Note-Books that it was one of respect and devotion. The entries in the Note-Books mark, in the words of the editors, "Arnold's consecration to a life larger than that of the poet and essayist. Whatever one thinks of his studies in religious subjects, few men have tried harder to attend to the great language of faith and to make it the word of their daily lives."[11]

And there are as many as half a dozen entries from Oriental scriptures like *Manava dharma shastra*, the *Bhagavad Gita*, and Buddhist works. The orientalist "tremors" and tendrils are the poem's inherent hunger. Hunger hides its own hunger. It is a locked away hunger that has always fascinated and fostered crisis. It has made the other feel the necessity of its emergence, the necessity that encourages the strength to break through the lock, the secret of inheritance. The "hiding" is, thus, its own incitement and enticement, too. Working beyond ascriptive modes of interpretative behavior, this poem throws itself in imaginative sympathy into the lives and desires of other disciplinary and discursive formations. Hunger thus invokes traveling theory—its travails and truths—as it moves across cultures and experiential domains inviting channelization and reproduction (all my chapters are a potential mix of hunger and the traveling differential). This is theory as it might exist or configure itself to exist within spatialities determined by the particular effectivities and intensities of different traditions and cultures. There is a mourning over the "loss" of traditional ideas into a "hunger of a new becoming," and it is what makes the experience of reading sahitya provocative. The hunger of literature is born, thus, amid the duality of a loss and an excess. This can be what Derrida would call "demi-deuil," half-mourning, which installs a kind of interruption within the motivation that literary analysis has toward a teleological fulfillment. Half-mourning is about the incompleteness and insatiety of hunger that calls for strife between the imperiousness of ontological questions, established protocols of signification, and what Derrida would ascribe as "commentary." *Alors, qui êtes-vous?*

What does the hunger do to the poem? Whom does the poem become? Seturaman points out that Arnold "deliberately calls his poem The Scholar Gipsy—a scholar who has chosen to become a gipsy. He stands surely for a new kind of awareness, a new poise, for such values as concentration, detachment, a unified functioning of the faculties."[12] Arnold's belief in the "integrated vision" incarnates the gipsy-scholar with a *sattvic* nature which, thus, empowers him to understand the unity of the world better. He has attached a new meaning to his "wandering." There is no happiness for the man who does not travel, says the *Aitareya brahmana*. This is in meaningful contrast to the mad rush of the common Victorians. The Scholar-Gipsy, in a Kierkegaardian undertone, discovers the meaning of *walk* and with it the possibility of the "spark" falling from heaven. He ensures walking himself into a state of well-being and walking away from every illness. This walk and a certain elusiveness attached to it prepare him for the moment when the spark ("And waiting for the spark from heaven to fall") from heaven would fall. In a trans-now dynamic, the spark can come to mean the infinite consciousness that is omnipresent, pure and tranquil, an experience after which one stops feeling the "lapse of hours" ("The Scholar-Gipsy"). It is a light without fire, a spirit without body that illuminates our inner being. It is the moment of joy that one experiences by abandoning the transient (the concealed *ananda*, joy, in the Vedic sense of the term). It is a vision that comes through "inner Emigration" and from this inwardness one gets the glimpse of some abiding reality. So the spark can fall as revelation of truth that might teach the Victorians the precepts of dharma, help them to reach the heart of the matter, establish the supreme necessity of invocation, grow an awareness of the inner being, and emphasize the means of purification of the soul. It can also mean the flame of a single lamp about which the Buddha pontificates in *Sutra of Forty Two Sections*. I am also tempted to look at this moment as the hour of the "spiritual revolution" that Sri Aurobindo emphasizes. The trouble with the

Victorians has been the defective organization of the inner being. With the descent of the spark, the Victorians would stop being rebellious to the higher law and consent to be spiritualized. Arnold realizes, "More strictly, then, the inward judge obey!" ("The Better Part"). He admits, "The aids to noble life are all within" ("Worldly Place"). So the spark is the "mark of everlasting light" above the ebb and flow of howling senses ("East London"), something that renders worth to one's labor through the night. It turns man "composed, refresh'd, ennobled, clear" ("A Wish"). He writes: "Leave then the Cross as ye have left carved gods, / But guard the fire within!" ("Progress"). This fire fights against all efforts to obliterate the "unregarded river of our life." The unspeakable desire resides in the waiting for the moment:

> After the knowledge of our buried life;
> A thirst to spend our fire and restless force
> In tracking out our true, original course ("The Buried Life")

The spark is a way of tracking the "original course" within. It can descend as perfect tranquility when one transcends both life and extinction and overcomes the contrary pull of the desirable and the undesirable—the *dwandwas* of the *Gita* that Arnold was so interested in. In Hindu religious philosophy, it is the moment when the mind becomes a blank sheet, when one gives himself and demands nothing. It is the inspiration that seeks to assimilate the many. The spark is a possible resolution to the *dwandwas*, an exit from "anarchy." I see it as a hope for a new birth among antinomies and existential striations—a lesson that He is in the spark and all sparks are in Him. It is a promise for liberation, a culture of existence when ironically one has been made captive by the "mighty moment." The spark can also be a divine mandate, a promise to preserve his devotees, an hour to manifest His majesty and a vocation to establish every assembly which stood for Him with "*one* aim, *one* business, *one* desire" ("The Scholar-Gipsy"). It is the hour when our faculties work together in harmony, choosing culture over anarchy. The spark can also mean the moment of peace (seen in keeping with Arnold's philosophy of integralism) that comes from spiritual rehabilitation and a feeling of oneness with nature, leaving aside a self-gratifying, mechanized existence. Distanced from the spark, the Victorians, as "ignorant armies" clashing by night (the *tamasic* state, according to the Hindu view of life), keep playing in the three cities of waking, dreaming, and deep sleep. They are far away from the state of "unclouded joy" and betray a misconception about the true nature of a spiritual culture.

Miller's observations on Arnold's views on idea and fact in the next chapter goad me to see the politics and aesthetics of hunger even further. Not that I have any disagreement with the kind of ethical position that Miller demonstrates; this chapter, as a contrast to his position, is intentioned to explore the other dimensions in which I think sahitya can exist to ethicalize. Miller's response to my discussion on "The Scholar-Gipsy" invites a dialogic intervention that intends to work out Arnold's ideas on tradition and comparison. For a man to whom impersonality, disinterestedness, seriousness, and renouncement were significant ideas that went into formulating his ethics of reading and living, the impertinence of individuality and the "saturnalia of personal passions" could never be provinces of art and poetry.[13] "Doing as one likes" (the liberty of "ordinary selves") cannot be the ground and cause for ethical action and thinking. Discipline of conduct is close to Arnoldian ethos. I agree with Miller, as with Arnold, that disinterested endeavor to know the best that has been thought and known in the world cannot be left in the abstract (confined to the "athletes of logic," systematic philosophy, and dogmatic theologists) but must find a way to connect with life, become a criticism of life, generating a sense of creativity.[14] But Arnold was not committed to uphold British civility; instead, he invested his life and thought into creating a culture. Unlike his German counterpart Johann Gottfried Herder (*Kulturgeschichte*), for whom the self-sufficiency of a nationalist whole dominated the cultural, literary discourse, Arnold thought of a perfection where walking alone was courting anarchy and being *with* others organically and symbiotically spelled culture. Deep interest in comparative education— Arnold's reports on the education system in France, Italy, Germany, Holland, and Switzerland are works of an educational prophet—demonstrates his eagerness to know "how others stand" and "to know how we ourselves stand."[15] Arnold writes:

> In short, it is expedient for the satisfactory resolution of these educational questions, which are at length beginning seriously to occupy us, both that we should attend to the experience of the Continent, and that we should know precisely what it is which this experience says. Having long held that nothing was to be learned by us from the foreigners, we are at last beginning to see, that on a matter like the institution of schools, for instance, much light is thrown by a comparative study of their institution among other civilised states and nations. To treat this comparative study with proper respect, not to wrest it to the requirements

of our inclinations or prejudices, but to try simply and seriously to find what it teaches us, is perhaps the lesson which we have most need to inculcate upon ourselves at present.[16]

A critical comparative negotiation between the self and the other, the native and the foreign, the insider and the outsider, is what forms culture. Rhetoric and emotional exuberance over triumphalist, racist, ethnic, and nationalist braggadocio clogs the mind into an unvital space, disabling all spiritual progression. Arnold points out that "everywhere there is connexion, everywhere there is illustration: no single event, no single literature, is adequately comprehended except in its relation to other events, to other literatures."[17] The ethics of thinking and doing are recognizing the "connection," the *sahit* (the other name for hunger), that contributes to the idea of perfection and "modernity," the intellectual maturity and orientation to observe facts with a critical spirit, not prejudice or caprice. *Tradition* is the word that holds the desired tenancy. Shirley Letwin explains that Arnold's thinking in terms of tradition can be illustrated through the example of Palladian architecture. Palladian buildings bear traces of classical tradition but Palladio maintained a certain sense of order, a sense of the parts connecting to the formation of the whole. Palladio learned a "classical theory of proportion through his studies in the circle around the humanist, Trissino." But he made sure to add his own contribution, supplemented through his reading of Alviso Cornaro, the Bolognese theorist, Sebastiano Serlio, Italian designers like Brunelleschi and Michelangelo, and others. Letwin argues that "all this Palladio absorbed and reformulated so that out of a repertoire drawn from many diverse sources, he produced buildings that look as if they have grown out of the ground on which they stand. Though there is good reason for describing Palladio as classical, he was not classical in the same way as Bramante, Sangallo, Sansovino, or Raphael. He has created a style of his own, the Palladian building."[18] This accent on comparison and synthesis leaves us to confront hunger in the understanding of art: the hunger that does not stay immured in the nationalist bunkum but develops its traveling potential across systems, cultures, and continents. Hunger is not in being "ought" but is in the "is"; being British is becoming British with the German, Italians, and the French. There is a hunger for the idea of wholeness but formed not with parts that are monochromatic and dogmatically affiliated to an inflexible core. Parts are distinct; they have their own hunger that combines cosmopolitically and transpoetically to produce an idea. This idea is the "being with"—discovering oneself, not just "how to live" but also what makes living. Tradition is a failure if deemed rigid and transcendental; tradition is life and "sweetness" when it outlives any imposed dogmatism to start believing in incorporation, a connective momentum across borders. Hunger is the propriety of literary conduct that becomes both the authority and the order, transgression and culture.

Literature's indigence is in ignoring the other. Hunger is literature's insecurity. It encounters the distress and anxiety of being trapped in the holy (the interpretation of the word *spark* moves beyond the economy of the sacrosanct meanability of the poem per se), the constrictions of understanding life and its relation to art within certain restrictive paradigms that prevent sublimation and outreaching. Literature "presents" and, at the same time, embellishes the "not-yet-present." Funded meanings drawn from established codes and motivations are not discounted; rather, the "secondary imaginary" is created with a renewed purposiveness. Hunger, then, is aesthetic reordering, a rapport with disciplines and indispensabilities of the medium without being oblivious to the continual striving to aesthetic re-creation. It is scarcely absolutist (as the interpretation of the poem shows) and makes for a critical intelligence that enhances its sociocultural participation and outdoes the intellectual egoism and immurement. Imaginative and intentional sympathies with the author and his art cannot nudge out values that provide the aesthetic distance required for the interventionist other to function. The exegesis on the spark is a demonstration in that direction. This is the catholicity that hunger in literature is capable of foregrounding, combining fresh patterns of belief, pervasive human attitudes, and also appraisals of a heritage that every work under investigation cannot avoid betraying.

Franz Kafka's "A Hunger Artist" is an example of literature's abilities for aesthetic refigurations. Brenda Machosky notes: "Ontologically, literature is present in the very moment of its experience, in reading it. The hunger artist is a figure for the writer, for literature itself, and for the reader, because hungering, even more than fasting, manifests presence. Hungering depends on each moment. It does not matter if you hungered yesterday, or if you will hunger tomorrow. Hungering, unlike fasting, is not a matter of will or desire. In German, there are two verbs for fasting: *fasten* and *hungern*. Kafka consistently chooses *hungern*."[19] Machosky adds that literature "remains in crisis because it continually poses itself as a question" and to "respond to the question of literature can be terrifying enough to keep us from ever proceeding beyond the practicalities of the institution of literature. When we sustain ourselves with the question, we hunger. Literature demands hunger, and we cannot fast in the presence of literature any more than we can feast on it."[20] Miller, in chapter 2, through his reading of Blanchot and Iser, reaches at a hunger, too. This is the hunger that produces the critical perspectives on the real, the hunger that makes literature transpose the real into the fictive, and the hunger that makes literature generate the pleasure of going beyond itself. The imaginary that Miller talks about is the hunger both for the materialization of the imaginary and the approach to the unapproachable imaginary which inheres in ambiguity and undecidability. The Iserian imaginary is also a kind of hunger, with its embeddings in human self-cultivation and plasticity. Hunger is also implicated in Blanchot's "unknown, obscure, foreign, dangerous point from which the *récit* begins." Sahitya's hungry sacredness is the empty space waiting to be rented and stays perennially advertised for repeated occupancy.

Sahitya, in its openness to critical understanding, releases a certain amount of energy, an excess that comes from a loss of meaning. This unutilized energy (as evidenced through the potency that the spark sparked off) is what makes sahitya's hunger continue, defying interpretive, productionist strategies of understanding. The hunger of sahitya, then, is about a complementarity struck between strategies to normalize meaning and becoming-meaning. However, hermeneutic caution calls for a careful understanding of the general economy of hunger. The understanding of the spark shows that hunger reads into the causality of events and emotions, works out a coordination between thoughts and processes, seeks out an understanding of a wholeness, coherence, logic, and yet looks for a suspension of meaning, destabilization, and redefinition. Sahitya, in its general economy, provokes the aesthetics of labor, combining investment with energy, capital with product, force with value, and invention with revelation.

What crisis can this hunger create? Is it about the aesthetic, cognitive, ethical, and the intentional? Is this at once about being-literature and becoming-literature? The hunger is both science and art having an ethics peculiar to its situatedness within certain cultural, political, and historical persuasions and premises. The strict domains of the inside and the outside of textual desire are difficult to pin down. The space of hunger is scarcely neutral. In fact, our inabilities and, hence, frustrations to understand the hunger on several occasions result in fostering a greater set of competences. Is this journey toward unraveling the known and unknown a kind of religious pursuit akin to man's fervency to decipher the mysteries in the face of the unknowable and the uncontrollable? Certain hungers mollify further curiosities by getting identified and satiated. But a few of them are tantamount to a tryst with wilderness, and it is in such acts of inconclusive and indeterminable eventualities that surprise and rapture reside.

Hunger not generated is suffering; hunger not met is suffering, too. Does sahitya's hunger then grow out of a law of love, a love of difference, love of being refuted and polemicized, love of the unreadable, love of being one among many, love of resisting fake, love of inheritance and tradition? Sahitya is a personal act, an answerable act, and yet inscribed in certain notions of irresponsibility. Hunger is desire and love—a catholic agape and eros—which turns into a kind of attention and acknowledges the "composite manifoldness" of an event or a thing. This hunger does not stir all in equal measure for love, like suspicion, varies. (In)fusion-trans-now makes suspicion across borders act as love for neighbors. This is a risky task to perform where hunger cannot be omnivorous in nature but has to be discriminatory, in that the neighbor can shun the love, refuse it, and leave the hunger thwarted. The hermeneutics of hunger cannot be righteousness without trial; it is seldom a ceaseless empowerment to proceed and project—something I would term as "bigotry of écriture." The negotiation born out of hunger cannot singularly be an endowment in self-knowledge but it has a future in a charitable mutuality that becomes life-giving to both the self and the other. The hunger proceeding from a point for the other mutates into a hunger of the other for the point from which it all began. The happiness in meaning-expansion is salvific. The hunger in Arnold's poem is an unselfing attention to the kenosis of literary merit: the phenomenon where the sacralization of divine attributes are relinquished by Christ to embrace the experience of human suffering forms a close analogy to the desacralization of literary meaning in "The Scholar-Gipsy," which makes the poem espouse a suffering in hermeneutic, crosscultural hunger.

Hunger is neither banality nor free love. This is the excitement of sinning on an eroticism where emotions are most often affection, virtuosity, exultation, exchange, and protests. And in a Nietzschean erotic transfiguration, this interpretive eros erupts less out of the attractive and the desirable and more from the unlovable and the unreadable (a deeper understanding of the case study on the spark demonstrates this phenomenon). This hunger is both conditional and unconditional and subjected at times to an accountability that requires high proficiency of paradigm and epistemic competence. Paradigms cause each other to appraise sahitya's hunger, but that does not always typically follow a forwardish accretional or incremental movement in meaning, which we understand as an extension of what existed for us to proceed from. This "causing" upon each other is both backward and forward, where the circumambient and the flitting lock horns amid the interstices of heritage and invention. I would like to see this import of the other through the emotion of sacrifice (from the Latin *sacrificium*, root of *facere*, "to do, perform," primarily used in the sense of "something given up for the sake of another"). Sacrifice would mean giving up on something for the benefit of the other. But here the otherness invested in the trans-now hunger is meant to be a sacrifice whose benefit extends to both the parties in play. It is a hunger (like the meaning of *spark* that feeds on Hindu, Buddhist philosophy and Arnold's consciousness of the Victorian spiritual crisis) that is constructed around a sacrifice ranging across ideas, ideology, experiment, perceptions to produce a cosmopolitan experience of intermeshing discourses. This can be argued as being ambitious for each other, being organismic when required, and becoming the health that grows, as Nietzsche would like to see: continually growing because acquirement comes from giving up again and again and the intent to give up to survive and thrive.[21] The health and volume (in the Gadamerian sense of the word) of the poem have grown in a process of giving up or sacrificing reified meaning for the hospitable accommodation of the other, consequently sponsoring role-perplexities between guests (the Hindu and Buddhist intonations) and the hosts (Arnold's spiritual and cultural figurations). Phenomenologically, this hunger is intersubjective in the sense that the parent and target literature and theory come into a communion where the hunger of one is increased by being hungry for the other, in recognizing and sensing the hunger in the other for oneself. This is collaborative, dialectical hunger, more aggressive and combative than Socrates would have liked. Indeed, my (in)fusion-trans-now is epitomized and conceptualized in a hospitality, which, far from being a snug shelter of established protocols of meaning, provides hospitality to the unsheltered, the "stalking-talking-stranger," that keeps literary studies alive. This is both conditioned and unconditioned hospitality whose specificities are difficult to determine and that often refuse to work under fettered conditions of signification. It lends dignity to the rights of the stranger, the foreigner: the host text's hunger is also a responsibility that needs critical attendance and commentary.

Taking a cue from Derrida's *Monolingualism of the Other* (1992), I would like to argue that the foreigner, which (in)fusionism brings into the court of interpretation of a text, is vulnerable to both exclusion and rejection. The trans-now inputs that invest the reading of the poem are apparently the "absolute other," which is always under the risk of disenfranchisement under the literary, cultural, and contextual rights that the text under discussion promotes and tries to establish. The hospitality of the hunger legitimizes the right to speak and also a freedom to receive, accept, and suffer. The interpretation that builds on the spark is a kind of pervertibility, a dignity of meaning whose legitimacy rests more on unconditional laws of hospitality. This dignity is not sovereignty, not a Kantian universal, but what (in)fusionism, in a Derridean way, can often do is *demi-dignité* (the possibility of validating a hunger). Hunger in such cases of unprogrammability becomes an event. In its iterability the thoughts on the spark become an event.

Hunger is the potency that sahitya possesses where affirmation is both conservation and the expenditure of energy. But the (in)fusion approach, despite the kind of reflexivity that it whips up, admits the possible confrontation with a "sacredness" of meaning (it is not necessary that all acts of interpretation become sacrifice or subversive). So the (in)fusion approach, despite being aware of its limits (head-brushing with sanctioned significance of the sacred), justifies a "will"—a will to empower, otherize— and an erotic dynamics (corresponding with Derrida's "re-mark") for a general economy of discharge and energetic dissipation. The critical exposition centering on the spark lives on a hunger that functions transpoetically but cannot sever its inherent connection with the context that gave birth to it (the Victorian malaise that Arnold was deeply troubled by). It is an example of interpretive hunger that expends and yet saves what it emerges from. The conditional commitment to Arnold's originary intentions are not discounted; rather, the (in)fusionized progression calls for an articulated desire to move beyond Arnold's predictable and established conventions of thinking and belief into the moment of a pregnant neighborhood of the other. This is the name-calling of the other, the other's ability to write the event.

Hunger, Ethics, and Things

Sahitya, in its creation and in the construction of the life-worlds, is never closed off from the "things" that constitute it. On one hand, we have things represented as literary, in the form of a plant, a table, a piece of wood, a hammer, a stone, and many other things; on the other, there is the unrepresented matter in the form of things that preexist sahitya but exist, as I shall argue, in the making of sahitya. For instance, while writing this chapter I encountered things like the table and the chair that I sat and wrote on, the window, the curtains, the floor, the décor, the lights, the wood, the dust, the breeze that blew across my study and so on. The ethics of creativity address both states of things, the classical and the quantum, one that is visible in its representation (the intended, conscious encounters), and the other that is invisible and imperceptible (unintended) because they go unrepresented in the final form of a text. Sahitya would know its matter (substance), the things (here meant as objects, *dravya*) that help make it matter (the subject, *visaya*), but most often fails to be distinctly conscious about the materiality (how matter matters both in the sense of how it is made to matter—the "pressure of prejudice," as Edmund Husserl points out, and how matter matters on its own) that contributes to its "coming into being."[22] I am not arguing for a state of postrepresentationalism, rather, a state of invisible representation, a material ontology of creation whose uncanny worth lies in a disturbing dialectic where not being represented is not about undermining its significant contribution to the processes of literary production or representation. Sahitya is not just a construction of the mind created out of the writer's imagination, emotions of wonder, curiosity, and private considerations and perspectives. There are ways sahitya is "thingized" in its formation and finality. Sahitya is obtained out of a complexity that is built on how a writer reacts to the things around him (the mentalization of matter as revealed through the writer's use of the narrative, images, metaphor, and rest) and how things in their independence and necessity serve to form the writing. This, I argue, is an entanglement where the mind and the body come into a complex play: the writer thinks through the faculties of his mind and is also affected by the things he uses or accesses to make his thinking find shape and consequence, an ethics of copresence meshed in invisibility.

Sahitya thus begins in a chaos of things, chaotic in its undetermined and underdetermined patterns of interaction in which the computer, its battery, its memory, the power connection, the strokes on the keyboard, the mouse, the light on the screen, the display of the text on it, do not additively contribute to the writing material but combine and recombine every moment in the growth of the matter as a manuscript. The materiality of the matter is not intrinsically chaotic and the apparent order, as represented in the coherence of sahitya itself, does not arise magically.

Rather, there is a pattern in the intra-actions that is not "relata" but an intricate combination that we struggle to make much sense of, where our accountability fails and intuitive knowledge takes over. It is here that the "bottom of things" surface: when things are seen beyond their anthropocentric utility and understanding.[23] There is a butterfly effect (in the words of chaotologists) in sahitya—order, but not preordained, at the edge of chaos, not what Ian Stewart has described as "cake-mix periodicity/aperiodicity."[24] The chaos that sahitya has to negotiate is not about knowing a preconceived order, but knowing a law that apparent lawlessness conceals. Something happens on a minor scale (the flapping of the wings of the butterfly) to effect a dramatic change or event later (for instance, a storm off the coast of India). In the course of the construction of a text, there are chances that one of my paragraphs can hurry into emergence under the pressure of a failing battery found reeling under a sudden power cut. It is highly likely that this paragraph that I hastily script will have forgotten its point of origin when the text becomes finally ready. There are no disputes as to the contribution of the mind toward the construction of this paragraph, which we might eventually judge as extraordinary. But this extraordinariness, I would like to argue, results from an entangled effect of a dwindling battery and the sudden shift, probably intensification, in the levels of my concentration because I did not want to lose out on my thoughts under the specter of the computer's dying on me any moment. These *things* undoubtedly contribute to the making of sahitya (*dravya-visaya*, coconstitutive enactments). The chair I sit on to write is the welcome support I need to make my writing progress comfortably; it, like the table or the other objects associated with my writing, adds to the security and convenience of my literary business, which is tagged irrevocably to constructions within finitude. That the object we designate as a chair affects my thoughts through its principled contribution in the form of comfort and convenience cannot be denied because writing without a chair like object or an object like a chair is not an easy deal—sitting on the floor or on the bare earth may not always be gleeful alternatives. The object as chair is coextensive with the processes of my writing: *dravya* in imperceptible ligatures with *visaya*, a kind of processual relating, an unavoidable mangle.

Although I call these thing-forces and thing-effects the order on the edge of chaos, they cannot become fixed determinants in the corpuscular growth of the text. Things working independently and in their particular order can influence their human other in a variety of ways. Sahitya, as a kind of order, is constructed through a force field of things that does not have any visible and formal contribution to make (within the ambit of human comprehension, the sinking battery or the power cut or the display on the screen will suffer from an indifference, not considered as ever having a role to essay in the formation and existence of sahitya). The subjectivity of objects is lost out to the autonomy of things resulting in, to appropriate John Casti, nothing less than a "surprise."[25] Sahitya is not magicalized into being but it has its own encounters of surprise. As a product of entangled fields—within principles of quantum understanding there is a demon in the atom—sahitya is thingized. Metaphorically, the bibliography does not produce a book; it is just a part of the creation (the mind that reads and processes) and the other part owes to the book's being produced by a variety of things. So the book is both a literary thing and a thing.

I would like to identify in sahitya a different consciousness that tries to find the link between form (configurations that develop through interactions with matter) and empiricism (direct contact with things). The consciousness that develops the form or the content or the aesthetic of sahitya changes our awareness of the physicality of sahitya's formation. This calls for a unique participation in the nature and configuration of reality and matter. To think of sahitya as emerging separately from mind and matter is to miss the character of entanglement I am arguing about. Ralph Waldo Emerson is right to note that "every property of matter is a school for the understanding—its solidity or resistance, its inertia, its extension, its figure, its divisibility. The understanding adds, divides, combines, measures, and finds nutrient and room for activity in this worthy scene. Meantime, Reason transfers all these lessons into its own world of thought, by perceiving the analogy that marries Matter to Mind."[26] The ethics of sahitya develop in the convergences that differential forces of the mind and matter effectuate, a kind of "holography" or "sympoesie."

Ethics of sahitya are not always manifest in the represented, because *sahitya* has always had her trouble with the external world, the trouble being in its agential dynamicity to annihilate or consume the world through representation and normativism and, again, its subsequent, niggling failure to remain content with the represented congeries of knowledge. With the slant on Descartes, we can argue that although our claim to a privileged access to ideas is confident, our communication with material objects is constricted and inscribed in a "deficit making" (we understand things in a reality we are generally confident about), resulting in asymmetric understanding that is quintessential to sahitya. The ethics of sahitya inhere in a materiality whose possibilities or conditions of emergence are not necessarily prefigured in the politics and poetics of linguistic representations. The problematic of critical understanding, then, is hubbed in an entangled creativity whose points of origin are difficult to locate and whose represented product—genetic and constellative through factors that are human, nonhuman, materialist and nonmaterialist—is challenging and intriguing in its pretence to an integrated wholesomeness of meaning.

There is a fullness of materiality whose presence and imperceptible presence (not a real absence) contribute to the performativity of sahitya. Barad observes:

> It is difficult to imagine how psychic and sociohistorical forces alone could account for the production of matter. Surely it is the case—even when the focus is restricted to the materiality of "human" bodies—that there are "natural," not merely "social," forces that matter. Indeed, there is a host of material-discursive forces—including ones that get labeled "social," "cultural," "psychic," "economic," "natural," "physical," "biological," "geopolitical," and "geological"—that may be important to particular (entangled) processes of materialization.
>
> If we follow disciplinary habits of tracing disciplinary-defined causes through to the corresponding disciplinary-defined effects, we will miss all the crucial intra-actions among these forces that fly in the face of any specific set of disciplinary concerns.[27]

Sahitya is a phenomenon that is ethicized through "agentially intra-acting components."[28] Its boundaries of ethics are not created through the influence of preexisting relations; rather, they are created through agential intra-actions, "relata-within-phenomena," which result in an "interdeterminacy" that is not fully linguistic.[29] The table is not simply the cause that supports the writing pad or the computer of the author; its exteriority to the subject does not limit its function and agency. The table undergoes agential cuts in presencing entanglements that are local in nature, which is about taking its causality beyond what we think a table and the author are connected and mediated by. This increases the possibility of the table as an object and aggravates its contribution toward the ethics of writing and experiencing literature. An ethics of literature is produced, then, through the nonhuman, without the relata and with the materiality of the matter. They are not, as Barad argues, "set in place" before the constitutive mechanisms of sahitya begin, the matter as phenomena. "Boundaries do not sit still."[30] And the intra-actions result in the cultivation of the immanence through a separate understanding of time and space:

> The world is a dynamic process of intra-activity in the ongoing reconfiguring of locally determinate causal structures with determinate boundaries, properties, meanings, and patterns of marks on bodies. This ongoing flow of agency through which "part" of the world makes itself differentially intelligible to another "part" of the world and through which local causal structures, boundaries, and properties are stabilized and destabilized does not take place in space and time but in the making of spacetime itself. The world is an ongoing open process of mattering through which "mattering" itself acquires meaning and form in the realization of different agential possibilities.[31]

The ethics, then, are in feeling the materiality of experiencing sahitya: reading literature through the materiality of matter and the workings of the body. Reading literature matters in how the body of the reader reads it—a book in hard and paperback, the cover design and its affects, the font size, read in iPad or PDF (the electronic aesthetics of reading), the position and state in which the reading was conducted (reclining on an armchair or standing with the book kept on a high table or sitting on a chair with the book on the table or sitting on a quiet park bench). It is significant for us to realize how a pathographical treatise or pathography read by a patient recuperating through her illness in the hospital bed and read again when she is home in her armchair, cheerful in body in its post-illness state, deliver differing levels of affect. Such soma-humanist ways of reading are loyal to intra-active formations, reject relata but are sensitive to sahitya's reception and experience dwelling both in the materiality and biologics of the body and what supports the body through a chair, a bed, a writing table, the lamp, the décor and state of the room, the windows and carpet and other equipmental impingement.

So sahitya is produced through entanglements in the nonhuman: Keats's "Ode on a Grecian Urn" owes its creation as much to his creative imagination as to the Hellenic frieze that he saw. Tagore's poems are produced through a contribution of the table he worked on, the windows that allowed gusts of summer breeze to blow across the room, the other equipments that his room had, the door that he ensured was locked to seal him off from human contact when he was writing, and the arrangement or décor of the room that Tagore is known to have changed very often to stave off boredom. A poem on a tropical, subcontinental summer, written in the intense heat and dust of Santiniketan during his time, with no facility for electricity, cannot be similar semantically, imagistically, and affectively to another poem on summer unleashed, for instance, within the confines of a snug room powered by an air conditioner or soothed by the blessing of ceiling fans. This is what I argue is the intrusion of the nonhuman on the human body to produce art (the nonhumanization of the human)—a fact that, most often, theories of aesthetic production ignore. Tourists visit Tagore's house at Santiniketan to see where the poet might have written his poems and stories but invariably miss how the materiality of his writing-space contributed to the production of art. There is a disjuncture in the history of the setting and the aesthetics of production (the things around and with which the book got written and the book as a work of art): the ethics of sahitya are about making a critical call on this disjuncture, trying to see how the material history of writing contributes to the aesthetic history of literary production.

The famous Indian scientist Jagadish Chandra Bose (1858–1937) is quoted to have said that when we eat vegetables we also eat the sun. This comment is relevant to what I am trying to argue. We cannot eat the sun and can enjoy eating the vegetables only; but in a deep entanglement the sun as the nondiscursive and the nonrepresentational other is inscribed in the discursive and the real (vegetables). This is a complicated version of the material that is not merely the vegetable but the sun-installed and sun-inscribed materiality of eating. Much in the same way, literature cannot be a mere vegetable but has a sun to it, in the form of the nonhuman and the material that contributes to its making. When we eat, rather annihilate, consume, and experience literature, we just don't stay confined to the aesthetic, the social, the cultural, and the imaginary; we also consume the nonhuman that went into its making. Intra-action in sahitya is not just in seeing the background or the historical, aesthetic conditions of productions but in trying to experience the diffractive materiality, a vibrant presence in absence beyond the humanist center of literary production. Unfortunately, sahitya veils a continent while offering it to be experienced, because sahitya does not know how its acknowledgment of things in their nonanthropomorphized reality can be manifested or represented. This is the disjuncture (sahitya's mattering as against matter needs rethinking) that our ethics of reading sahitya has to identify. The ethics of sahitya are about this awareness, this continent of things that does not illuminate any area of our consciousness beyond disciplinary and normative categories of understanding. To miss understanding this disjuncture is to miss reading the surplus that things imperceptively generate in their production of sahitya. The art historian and artist James Elkins, in his book *What Painting Is*, writes:

> But I know how strong the attraction of paint can be, and how wrong people are who assume painters merely put up with paint as a way to make pictures. I was a painter before I trained to be an art historian, and I know from experience how utterly hypnotic the act of painting can be, and how completely it can overwhelm the mind with its smells and colors and by the rhythmic motions of the brush. Having felt that, I knew something was wrong with the delicate dry erudition of art history, but for several years I wasn't sure how to fit words to those memories.[32]

In the entangled relationship of paint and painting the paint loses its thingness to structures of understanding, the planes of transcendence, the foundations of thought that exist external to paint as a thing and consider it as the means to painting. Elkins pans across 8,900 books catalogued in the Library of Congress on the history of art, art criticism, and techniques of painting to discover that less than six "address paint itself, and try to explain why it has such a powerful attraction *before* it is trained to mimic some object, *before* the painting is framed, hung, sold, exhibited and interpreted."[33] Losing sight of this disjuncture means we are handed a lost game, a missed encounter, between matter and materialization, thing and thingification.

Hunger and the Postaesthetic

The ethics of sahitya has a postaesthetic hunger: a hunger for and in the postaesthetic. It is like looking into the picture and getting arrested by an uncertainty; it is about a failure to methodize the experience of seeing; it is a wrestle with an indefinable, secret understanding, the nature of which is rarely in the loop of interpretive modes. My understanding of this secret is at the level of the ineffable and the asymmetrical understanding of literary experience: a negotiation between the emotive, reflective, and the intangible. This speaks of the inability to hermeneuticize hunger definitively, becoming "for once, and then something."

> Once, when trying with chin against a well-curb,
> I discerned, as I thought, beyond the picture,
> Through the picture, a something white, uncertain,

Something more of the depths—and then I lost it.
Water came to rebuke the too clear water.
One drop fell from a fern, and lo, a ripple
Shook whatever it was lay there at bottom,
Blurred it, blotted it out. What was that whiteness?
Truth? A pebble of quartz? For once, then, something.[34]

I am tempted to see such experience and discernment as something close to Husserl's *epochē*, the suspension of existence, which leaves the object as existing independent of the perceiver and external to the domain of universally presupposed interpretive factor. This experience is about the transport and the delight that certain conditions of understanding lend to the constitution of the self. It has a strange quality beyond the presuppositiveness of methodicity. An investiture that cannot decide between the pebble and the quartz and yet tenaciously delights in the ripple that blurs and blots is once something and then becomes something else: "I lost it." This experience inaugurates without a method, a flighty, spontaneous emanation, expiring in a hint of a structure that is dourly loose at its ends and impermanent in nature. The postaesthetic of sahitya, for me, is deeply invested in emotion, its speaking, and its ability to draw narration out of the self.

What happens, for instance, when one reads the first two stanzas of Wordsworth's "By the Sea" with no knowledge of the poet and his aesthetics, staying oblivious of all the conceptual parameters informing a tradition that can help one to prise the poem open methodologically? Expressions like "the holy time is quiet as a nun" and "the gentleness of heaven is on the sea: / Listen! the mighty Being is awake" can put the whole economy of sahitya to test, igniting an experience that moves and defies all explanation frameworked through the metaphorics of interpretive boundaries and conceptual structures. What ethics of sahitya am I talking about if I say, "I don't know why it feels this way?" What happens when a universe of discourses fail to "horizon" my literary experience? Here the hermeneutical and heuristically unutilized, rather, never-to-be-utilized energies are losses that write off a gain whose emergence is clearly out of step with conventional means of understanding and intellectual consumption. Literary worlds are also produced beyond what I have come to see as the (in)fusionized domain of literary hunger: experiences relished in the tremble, the unperceived undulation of the text, and the resonant volume that it silently mounts on us.

If Graham Harman's "object oriented ontology" is brought to bear on our understanding of the ethics of sahitya, we are faced with seeing a text as neither getting dissolved "upward into its readings or downward into its cultural elements." There is no access to a method, whether New Critical, feminist, or poststructuralist. If all reading is a method, then such an approach is always a countermethod, in the sense that the experience of a text becomes a resistance to any such dissolution or annihilation within the bounded frames of analysis. Harman writes:

> All efforts to embed works exhaustively in their context are doomed to failure for some fairly obvious reasons, though one usually avoids stating them because they are often associated with people whose motives are viewed with suspicion. One of those obvious reasons is that to some extent, the social conditions under which authors produced *The Epic of Gilgamesh* or *Frankenstein* are not entirely relevant to these works themselves. For one thing, these works travel well across space and time—and generally the better the work, the better it travels. If literary canons have been dominated by white European males, then this may be cause for shaking up the canons and reassessing our standards of quality, not for dissolving all works equally into social products of their inherently equal eras. We are all at our best not when conditioned by what happens around us, but when an inner voice summons us to take a courageous stand, walk in a different direction, or do the most outstanding work of our lifetimes.[35]

Any courageous stand resulting in an unconditioned reading of a text is hunger of a different level, generated both by the text on the reader and the reader's "innocent" desires on the text. Hunger is not merely the generative and productive index of certain social, historical, materialist, cultural, and traditional forces subservient to a certain period in time and space; it is also the product of forces that are never registered or recorded in our formal understanding of a text's travel down the ages and times. Harman is right to note that more than connection it is the "nonconnections" that can be considered as influences on literature. Instead of proposing that since a text is demonstrative of a certain aspect in cultural history or political thought or social discourse, let us examine where and why is the connection. We must ask why there is no connection between a text and another segment of history or culture.[36] Precisely what we consider as nonconnection is what Harman considers the premise to begin with.

What interests me about nonconnections is the way a text withdraws from itself. Deconstructionists would see a text as withdrawing from the reader every time he wants to conquer it with an irrefutable sovereignty of meaning. This results in the text's slipping away from the reader and emerging in a variety of meaning-experiences. But here the argument is about making the text withdraw from being a text, disclosing an experience that does not stay limited to what the text has to offer. "Beauty is truth, truth beauty" is a text that withdraws from Keats's "Ode on a Grecian Urn" per se: a withdrawal that indicates that the ontology of the line has a unique indifference to the poem as a whole, neither making the line emerge as a kind of mounting conceptual climax nor making the line take the poem climactically to a different altitude. The line's ontological value is in redundancy, a recurrence in meaning even outside the poem's intended or established meaning, a retrojection whose void is in fullness.

So why are we prodded to explain things always or provide heuristic frameworks for all experiences? Can't experiences cease, impermanently though, to be agential, intentional, and moralistic? What is the goodness of being "good for nothing?" Jerry Foder writes:

> It's very hard to get this right because of our penchant for teleology, for explaining things on the model of agents with beliefs, goals, and desires is inveterate and probably itself innate. We are forever wanting to know what things are for, and we don't like having to take Nothing for an answer. That gives us a wonderful head start on understanding the practical psychology of ourselves and our conspecifics; but it is not of the (no doubt many) respects in which we aren't kinds of creatures ideally equipped for doing natural science. Still I think that sometimes out of the corner of an eye, "at a moment which is not action or inaction," we can glimpse the true scientific fission: austere, tragic, alienated and very beautiful. A world that isn't for anything; a world that is just there.[37]

The ethics of sahitya are in realizing that literary experiences are sometimes austere, bare, and alienated. It redefines the understanding of the beautiful by offering "nothing" in response to any interrogation as to what makes something beautiful. There is an indifference to the principles of aesthetic formations and understanding, dropping the coins of "how" and "why" deep down into the well of non-reckoning. This surely is also a way to rethink nonconnections.

If one, instead of describing space as "the boundless, three-dimensional extent in which objects and events occur and have relative position and direction," writes, "space is a doubt," what kind of an experience does that project?[38] The words *space* and *doubt* ooze a thought, leaving behind room for reflection that is unstructured, most often method-defying, and more in the nature of a provocation. This provocation does not prod one to labor on theories of space; rather, it becomes an experience that settles on our self and grows on us with a sense of confusion and ignorance that we may take delight in and very rarely feel embarrassed about. This is about "feeling" the thought out, implicating a difference that we make between the delight of the odor of a rose and a high fashion perfume with an inscription of its chemical composition. Sahitya frees itself up in the postaesthetic when the trenchant rigor and regimes of aestheticization are discounted in favor of a pretheoretical state. The experience of the postaesthetic signifies a mobility beyond a given horizon of expectations, vectoring into an excess, discoursing about which is, most often, difficult. I would like to term this phenomenon as "becoming aesthetic." This tendency to conjoin with the habits of the postaesthetic is what sahitya provokes us to salvage, a bargain power that supposedly was lost on literature in the compulsive duress of interpretation. If *écriture* has made deeper inroads into sahitya's manifestation of its hunger, the postaesthetic has its phantom presence, feeding on its own uncanny ability to salvage experiences beyond what methodological stridency and (in)fusionist astuteness allow. It is about feeling the hunger and not rationalizing, logicalizing, and historicizing it. Becoming aesthetic is when sahitya speaks, speaking from an indwelling power (its sacredness) whose nature is unstructured, unpredictable, asymmetrical, and yet uninterruptedly provocative. Sahitya, on such occasions, moves rather than constructs and signifies. Becoming aesthetic owes to sahitya's ability for deviancy, detouring competences in the form of an "imposed aesthetic" or trained habits of aesthetic response. Sahitya makes itself vulnerable in the premises of the literary, and vulnerability is its fate in the postliterary, also.

The postaesthetic of hunger is the excess of energy that leaps beyond the interpreter's mortal, limiting abilities to submit to a signification; it is a separate sort of uselessness that sahitya exudes without the slightest aim to become ascribed and inscribed. Uselessness is a hunger whose manifest gain is in a senseless loss, in being unremarkable to a *sensus communis* (common sense). It emerges in a moment of readerly transaction without being obligated to reemerge in a similar way to the following reader or any succeeding readerly intervention. Sahitya has its own unreserved expenditures in the sense of the prelogical and pretheoretical as distinguished from the preontological. The postaesthetic is built around a "coyness" with no apotheosis of meaning or determined identity. This is the zone of the "radical aesthetic," which is an experience where torture is mixed with the delight of having felt something and yet not being able to unveil what it felt like. It is an experience that sahitya grows on us where even a mild, probing spirit can expire into a helpless smile of inexplicability. This is "becoming aesthetic," whose constituents and experiential relish are ever so elusive and, at best, translucent.

Is the secret of the aesthetic and the postaesthetic of sahitya integral to its own survival? Does it make sahitya unique in its democratic forbearance and endurance, letting upon itself multiple discourses in a carnival of power and knowledge? What is it that makes sahitya readable, yet intangible, sometimes unreadable and, hence, provocative and *rapportable* and yet not wholly presentable? In sahitya's strangeness lies its hunger. The mystery is its hunger. In a way, its hunger mystifies it. Miller and I have been left troubled in this book by sahitya's hunger—one in a dominantly rhetorical way and the other (in)fusionally caught within the trans-now phenomenon of literary experiences. Committed to our contrastive habits of doing literature, we found our own aesthetic and politics of reflection within a canvas that did not allow antagonism but sponsored a rhythm, a rhythm both in contrariety, rupture, and *sambandha* in much desired and inevitable estrangement. We walked across each other in nodding acknowledgment of our distinctness of thought and literary habits and settled on the across to rediscover together the changing climate of values, affect, hunger, and ethics around us—a sahit across continents that I hope the reader will discover and appreciate.

LITERATURE AND ETHICS
Truth and Lie in Framley Parsonage

Poets are the unacknowledged legislators of the world.
—Percy Bysshe Shelley

Ranjan Ghosh and I have agreed to center our last pair of essays on ethics in relation to his *sahitya* and to my *literature*. The reader should remember that these two key words are synonyms. *Sahitya*, Ghosh tells me in an e-mail, is "a Sanskrit, Bengali, Hindi word and simply means what we in the West call literature." Literature, for me, means primarily printed poems, plays, novels, and short stories, as in the term *Victorian literature*, so I assume sahitya means the same. Using the word *literature*, as we in the West do, is a relatively recent event. The word gets its modern sense only with the full shift to a print culture in the eighteenth-century. Neither Sophocles nor Shakespeare would have said they were writing literature, in the modern sense of the word. The term originally meant anything written in letters. Our present-day meaning is more restricted.

What the two of us mean by *ethics* in relation to sahitya or to literature differs to some degree from one to the other of us. Ghosh means by the ethics of sahitya, to oversimplify quite a bit, sahitya's insatiable "hunger" (his word) for a relation to the other as manifested in sahitya. *Hunger* is a key word in Ghosh's chapter 9. As he tells me in that same e-mail, "I meant the hunger that is inherent in *Sahitya*. Hunger is desire, motivation, intention, and dynamicity. *Sahitya* is impregnated with hunger and functions, sometimes, independent of the readerly hermeneutics." Sahitya is here said to have independent hunger. It is hungry on its own, without any intervention by the reader, for example, any attempt to understand a given example of sahitya. Ghosh calls that attempt to understand "hermeneutics." The word *hunger* is surely, at least obscurely, a personification, as is "impregnated." A given poem or novel has a life of its own. The reader must carefully follow Ghosh's argument in his chapter 9 to get an answer to the obvious question, "What is sahitya hungry for?" Its hunger is clearly, in any case, an outward orientation that Ghosh names "desire, motivation, intention, and dynamicity."

I mean by "the ethics of literature" a version of what the word *ethics* has meant in the West since Aristotle, that is, the issue of how to act or choose rightly. For me, the ethical dimensions of a given literary work involve a work's ethical authority over me, that is, its ability to influence my ethical acts and judgments. The ethics of a work include the author's ethical responsibility to his readers. Writing a novel or poem is, among other things, an ethical act. Moreover, the ethics of a work involve the narrator's or the poem's speaker's ethical obligations to her or his or "its" imagined characters and to the projected readers the narrator or speaker of the poem addresses. In a novel, this is the narrator's obligation to tell the truth about the imaginary characters in the story. My reading later in this chapter of Anthony Trollope's *Framley Parsonage* will elaborate this issue further. Finally the representation, within the work, of the characters' ethical choices or acts constitutes a work's internal ethical dimension. Is, for example, Lucy Robarts's lie to Lord Lufton, in *Framley Parsonage* ("I cannot love you.") ethically defensible? My concept of the ethical dimension of literature is, you can see, somewhat different from Ghosh's "ethics of reading sahitya," as I shall now go on to specify.

I can only indicate a few features of Ghosh's chapter 9 here. I shall especially stress the way Ghosh's procedures differ considerably from mine, in an attempt to fulfill our contract to be "dialogical." Though Ghosh is not against close reading or the establishment of context, historical, biographical, or otherwise, for him sahitya carries its own authority and is to a considerable degree independent of any originating contexts.

Ghosh's references and citations are wide-ranging, including as they do many Western essays and books, among them a relevant section on books by Georges Bataille, but also including references to Hindu and Sanskrit sources that may especially interest Western readers of this book. He gathers these sources together, into a complex "transcultural poetics of meaning and understanding."

I would stress, in a way somewhat different from Ghosh's synthesizing propensities, the profusion of different ideas about the ethics of literature in the West. Each work, for me, is unique. Each has a different idea of the ethics of literature from the ones that preside over each of the other works. No single concept of the ethics of literature dominates, for example, even in something so relatively circumscribed and homogeneous as Victorian English literature. Works in that group may nevertheless have what Ludwig Wittgenstein called a "family resemblance." Still, you must learn to read each work carefully for itself and expect it to be sui generis. You must derive its ideas about ethics, that is, correct and incorrect conduct, from the work itself. I shall try to do that later on in this chapter for Trollope's *Framley Parsonage*.

It follows naturally from our somewhat different premises that our interpretative procedures differ greatly. My conclusions aim to be based on a careful and more or less comprehensive close reading of whatever work I am discussing. This reading includes formal or rhetorical features as well as thematic statements, as you will see in my reading of *Framley Parsonage*. Ghosh, on the contrary, abstracts details from the literary works he cites to support the transcultural poetics of meaning and understanding that he has been developing for years and that he calls the (in)fusion approach. I feel my way inductively toward any generalizations I make, whereas Ghosh's style is full of formulations like the following: "So the 'spark' can fall as revelation of truth that might teach the Victorians the precepts of dharma, help them to reach the heart of the matter, establish the supreme necessity of invocation, grow an awareness of the 'inner being,' and emphasize the means of purification of the soul."

Ghosh here appropriates Arnold's line about "waiting for the spark from heaven to fall," from his long poem "The Scholar-Gypsy," as an example of the poetics of sahitya. He makes this appropriation on the basis of an article he cites by V. S. Seturaman that focuses on something most Arnold scholars will have noticed, namely that Arnold knew and was influenced by oriental scriptures like the *Bhagavad Gita*. He was especially taken by the Gita's development of "the principles of 'dwandwas'" [a musical debate] and the *Gita*'s advocacy of "a state of consciousness which transcends all dualism," for example, the oppositions of dwandwas. In my view, by the way, Arnold did to some degree wish he could believe in the *Gita*, but was unable quite to do so. More central to Arnold's thinking, in my judgment, are the famous assertions at the beginning of "The Study of Poetry" (1880):

> There is not a creed which is not shaken, not an accredited dogma which is not shown to be questionable, not a received tradition which does not threaten to dissolve. Our religion has materialized itself in the fact, in the supposed fact, and now the fact is failing it. But for poetry the idea is everything: the rest is a world of illusion, of divine illusion. Poetry attaches its emotion to the idea; the idea *is* the fact. The stron-

gest part of our religion to-day is its unconscious poetry. . . . More and more mankind will discover that we have to turn to poetry to interpret life for us, to console us, to sustain us.[1]

If we had world enough and time, I'd dearly like to engage in a serious dialogue with Ranjan Ghosh about how he reads this passage, especially the opposition between "fact" and "idea," in the context of the rest of Arnold's essay, not to speak of the rest of Arnold's voluminous work. For me, Arnold meant by *idea* something akin to "imaginary fiction" or "literary fiction." Ghosh has responded in a dialogic entry in his chapter 9 to what I say here about Arnold, with an assertion of his more positive way of reading Arnold's writing as an example of sahitya.

What does it mean to believe, choose, or act "on the ethical authority of literature?" Where does a text said to be literature get its ethical authority? What is that authority's source, ground, or guarantee? Who or what validates it or authenticates it, signs off on it, takes responsibility for it? The author? The reader? Some divine or supernatural power? The circumambient society? The work's sources or influences? Some preexisting reality the work accurately copies, imitates, or represents? Can a work perhaps be self-authorizing? Just what would that mean, "self-authorizing?" All these ways of ascribing authority to literary works have had valence in the Western tradition, often at the same time, in incoherent profusion, down to the present day. An essay I have already published, "On the Authority of Literature," discusses, with some help from Henry James, Proust, and many others, the permutations in the West of answers to the questions I have just posed.[2] My exploration in that essay of the various ways authority has been claimed for literature culminates in a recognition that this authority derives from a performative use of language artfully begetting in the reader, as James puts it, a disposition to take on trust the virtual reality the reader enters when he or she reads a given work. That certainly happens. It happened to me, for example, when I read *The Swiss Family Robinson* as a child. Since my "On the Authority of Literature" is easily available, I shall not repeat its arguments here, but turn straight to Anthony Trollope's *Framley Parsonage* in order to investigate the way it exemplifies my various categories of the ethics of literature.

Anthony Trollope's *Framley Parsonage* (1861) is the fourth of the six so-called Barsetshire novels. These novels are about an extended community of clergymen and their families in an imaginary English shire. The same characters return from novel to novel in this sequence, but the focus in each is on one or two family stories among the members of that imaginary community. *Framley Parsonage* was first published serially in the *Cornhill Magazine* (a coup for Trollope and a turning point in his writing career) from January 1860 through April 1861, and in book form (three volumes) by the publisher Smith, Elder, in 1861. It was his first conspicuous success as a novelist. Both the serial edition and the three-decker book edition had six admirable illustrations by a distinguished artist of the pre-Raphaelite school, John Everett Millais. I have cited the standard, modern Oxford World's Classics edition,[3] since it has pagination, but it does not include the illustrations. The original edition with the illustrations included is available as a Gutenberg e-text, to be read for free on your computer. I mention these details to put the novel in its historical context of Trollope's writing and in the context of the history of the book. All forty-seven of Trollope's novels, plus his nonfiction books, seventy-seven books all told, are available as Gutenberg e-texts for free.

Earlier in this chapter, I identified four ethical dimensions of a given literary work. The first dimension is the work's ethical authority over the reader, its power to determine the reader's ethical acts and judgments. That is certainly the case for me with *Framley Parsonage*. When I read it, a vivid imaginary world opens up for me. Just what is that imaginary world like? It is different for each work and no doubt for each reader or for each reading by the same reader. What my inner imaginary world is like when I read *Framley Parsonage* is a complex question. It is also one not much talked about, even in recent research in cognitive science about what happens in reading. Cognitive science tends to measure what parts of my brain light up when I read such and such a work, rather than trying to study subjective sensory images as the reader reports them: "Now I am seeing my idea of a long drawing room with many fashionably dressed people standing or sitting in it." Pedagogical theories about how best to teach people to be good readers tend to assume that reading is primarily a matter of making sense of the words, a matter of vocabulary, grammar, and syntax.

My imaginary space for *Framley Parsonage*, it happens, is relatively rich in visual images. I make up in my mind the topography of Barsetshire and the décor of rooms in the houses on the basis of the sparse details Trollope gives. He claims to have had the topography of the whole imaginary shire vividly in his mind and to have made a map of it. My mental images are also influenced by the map of Barsetshire devised by Mgr. Ronald Knox and available at the beginning of the relatively new illustrated paperback edition of *The Warden* (1952) and in the reissued Oxford World's Classics edition (1991). *The Warden* was originally published in 1855. In spite of that help, my subjective image of the space between Framley Parsonage and Lady Lufton's mansion is quite different from Knox's schematic map, with dots for villages and lines for roads. I imagine trees, fields, fences, hedges, and roadbeds, to a considerable degree on the basis of my experience of rural England. My subjective images are also to some degree influenced by the admirable Millais illustrations. Here is the one showing a meeting between Lord Lufton and Lucy Robarts early in the novel, followed by the one showing the memorable meeting at Miss Dunstable's reception between Lady Lufton and her great enemy, the Duke of Omnium, with the hostess Miss Dunstable between them:

Much as I admire the Millais illustrations and believe they accurately show period costume and Victorian hairstyles and fashion, they do not agree with my mental images of those characters, perhaps because I read the novel long before I saw the original illustrations. Trollope, in *An Autobiography*, praises them for their accurate rendition of what he had in mind. Millais and Trollope had their mental images. I have mine. The difference is that Millais was a genius at turning his interior visions into graphic representations, whereas my visions mostly remain secret, private, uncommunicated. This is because of my inability to do what Millais did in drawing, or what Trollope did with words. My interior visual images, in any case, exceed the data. I have my own mental images of what the characters look like, for example, images of Lucy Robarts, or of her brother Mark, or of Lady Lufton. These images are aided by clues in the narrator's discourse, for example, the narrator's report that Lucy was "brown," "short," and had wonderfully flashing eyes. I am also constantly aware, at least subliminally, that I am free at any time to reenter that mental space, either in memory or by rereading the novel. It remains available at any time, in an odd sort of perdurability.

To an unusual degree, however, my subjective experience when reading *Framley Parsonage* is auditory rather than visual. I hear the almost continuous voice of the narrator, who is very much present as a speaker throughout and who speaks, strangely enough, in my own voice, as though I were reading the novel out loud to myself. Moreover, I enter into the characters' interiorities by way of the narrator's masterful use of indirect discourse. I hear what they are thinking, feel what they are feeling, as though their consciousnesses had a miraculous ability to turn themselves into eloquent language. That language seems to have been spoken within their minds

Figure 10.1 Millais's illustration of meeting between Lord Lufton and Lucy Robarts in *Framley Parsonage* (1861).

Figure 10.2 Millais's illustration of meeting between Lady Lufton and her enemy, the Duke of Omnium, in *Framley Parsonage* (1861).

in the first-person present tense and then reported by the clairvoyant or telepathic narrator in the third-person past tense by way of that remarkable kind of language that linguists and narratologists call free indirect discourse. These interiorities are then reduplicated in my own mind and feelings. As a result, in reading *Framley Parsonage* I come to feel that I know the characters even better than I do my own family and friends, since I have no direct access to the interiorities of the real people around me such as the narrator of *Framley Parsonage* provides me for the characters in the novel. By way of this wholly imaginary intimacy with characters who exist only as words on the page, I come to care a lot about what happens to them.

The novel, moreover, by way of the stories Trollope's narrator tells about these entirely imaginary Victorian personages, Mark Robarts, Lucy Robarts, Lady Lufton, Mr. Sowerby, and so on, certainly influences my ideas about correct or incorrect ethical behavior. That happens even if I try to place these characters back in another country and an earlier time that, some would claim, since it is historically conditioned, has relatively little relevance to my own ethical actions and decisions.

The second dimension I listed is the author's ethical responsibility to his readers. Trollope himself writes eloquently about this in *An Autobiography*, as I have demonstrated in more detail in previous essays, though never in relation to *Framley Parsonage*. I have never written anything about that novel before now. In *An Autobiography*, written in 1875–76, though published posthumously, Trollope tells how, as a poor day student, he was treated as a pariah at those fashionable public schools, Harrow and Winchester. In compensation, and in striking confirmation of Freud's theory of art as expressed in a wonderful passage at the end of the twenty-second of his *Lectures on Psychoanalysis*, Trollope developed a habit that lasted many years of daydreaming long continuous narratives. These were carried on from day to day, from month to month, and from year to year. He bound himself down, as he says, "to certain proportions and proprieties and unities."[4] He was, he says, "his own hero": "I was a very clever person, and beautiful young women used to be fond of me. I strove to be kind of heart and open of hand and noble in thought, despising mean things and altogether a much better fellow than I have ever succeeded in being since."[5] Trollope's imaginary self-image was, in short, a highly ethical person.

Trollope, in accordance with what many parents would still tell their children, goes on to say, "There can, I imagine, hardly be a more dangerous mental practice."[6] Daydreaming is dangerous, I suppose, because, like novel-reading, daydreams are a means of escaping from the real world and its duties. Nevertheless, continues Trollope, "I have often doubted whether, had it not been my practice, I should ever have written a novel. I learned in this way to maintain an interest in a fictitious story, to dwell on a work created by my own imagination, and to live in a world altogether outside the world of my own material life. In after years I have done the same,—with this difference, that I have discarded the hero of my early dreams, and have been able to lay my own identity aside."[7] One might argue, contra Trollope, that something very like his own identity is present in his narrators, conspicuously, for example, in the narrator of *Framley Parsonage*.

The passage I have cited is, in any case, striking evidence that in Trollope's case, his novel-writing was a displacement of his penchant for guilty daydreams. His novels, moreover, had their origin in a wish to be ethically good. A later passage in *An Autobiography* gives an amazing description of the way Trollope dwelt within the fictitious worlds created by his own imagination. The novels proper were the writing down as words on paper of a rendition of what was initially solitary, secret, and subjective. His best work has been done, he says, "at some quiet spot among the mountains,—where there has been no society, no hunting, no whist, no ordinary household duties." He concludes, "And I am sure that the work so done has had in it the best truth and the highest spirit that I have been able to produce. At such times I have been able to imbue myself thoroughly with the characters I have had in hand. I have wandered alone among the rocks and woods crying at their grief, laughing at their absurdities, and thoroughly enjoying their joy. I have been impregnated with my own creations till it has been my only excitement to sit with the pen in my hand and drive my team before me at as quick a pace as I could make them travel."[8]

I have elsewhere discussed the purport of the not-all-that-obscure sexual imagery in this passage. The reader will note, for my purposes here, however, Trollope's insistence on his responsibility for "the best truth" in his novel-writing. This ethical obligation to make his novels improve his readers' morals is made explicit in the last citation I shall make from *An Autobiography*. In this case, Trollope is writing explicitly about *Framley Parsonage*. Here the image of self-impregnation is turned into an image of impregnating his readers with ethical goodness. Speaking of Nathaniel Hawthorne's praise of Trollope's novels as hewing a lump out of the real earth and following the people on that lump of earth as they go about their daily lives, Trollope says:

I have always desired to "hew out some lump of earth," and to make men and women walk upon it just as they do walk here among us,— with not more of excellence, nor with exaggerated baseness,—so that my readers might recognize human beings like to themselves, and not feel themselves carried away by gods or demons. If I could do this, then, I thought, I might succeed in impregnating the mind of the novel reader with a feeling that honesty is the best policy, that truth prevails while falsehood fails; that a girl will be loved as she is pure and sweet and unselfish;—that a man will be honored as he is true and honest and brave of heart; that things meaning done are ugly and odious, and things nobly done beautiful and gracious. . . .

There are many who would laugh at the idea of a novelist teaching either virtue or nobility,—those, for instance, who regard the reading of novels as a sin, and those who think it to be simply an idle pastime. They look upon the tellers of stories as among the tribe of those who pander to the wicked pleasures of a wicked world. I have regarded my art from so different a point of view that I have ever thought of myself as a preacher of sermons, and my pulpit as one which I could make both salutary and agreeable to my audience. I do believe that no girl has risen from the reading of my pages less modest than she was before, and that some may have learned from them that modesty is a charm well worth preserving. I think that no youth has been taught that in falseness and flashiness is to be found the road to manliness; but some may perhaps have learned from me that it is to be found in truth and a high but gentle spirit. Such are the lessons I have striven to teach, and I have thought that it might best be done by representing to my readers characters like themselves,—or to which they might liken themselves.[9]

Well, there you have it! I know no other passage that expresses so well the Victorian ideology of realistic fiction and so eloquently praises its power to teach ethical principles and conduct to its readers. Trollope also pays his respects to those Victorians who thought reading novels was sinful or a waste of time. My readers will notice the unabashed sexism of what Trollope says. Girls should be modest and do their best to wait passively for some eligible man to fall in love with them. An example is (apparently) Lucy Robarts in *Framley Parsonage*. Trollope says of her in *An Autobiography*: "I think myself that Lucy Robarts is perhaps the most natural English girl that I ever drew,—the most natural at any rate of those who have been good girls."[10]

Youths, as opposed to girls, should be true and have a high but gentle spirit. Lord Lufton is the example of that in *Framley Parsonage*. I might also mention at this point Trollope's unashamed and deplorable anti-Semitism, as in the dishonest and lying moneylenders, the Tozers, in *Framley Parsonage*. It is all very well to say that such anti-Semitism was an essential part of Victorian ideology, as in Dickens's Fagin in *Oliver Twist*. That it was more or less universal in that time, place, and culture does not make it any the less reprehensible and dangerous. Hitler capitalized on the habitual anti-Semitism of some German people to lead them to condone the Holocaust.

That Trollope wanted his novels to inculcate ethics is clear enough. The question now is whether he succeeded and, if so, by way of what thematic and narratological devices. That takes me to the final two dimensions of literature and ethics as they are exemplified in *Framley Parsonage*. These are, you will remember, the narrator's ethical obligations to her, or his, or its characters and to the projected readers the speaker addresses. In a novel, this is the narrator's obligation to tell the truth about the characters. The final ethical dimension is the representation, within the work, of ethical choices or acts by the characters.

First, the narrator of *Framley Parsonage*: it is all too easy to assume that the narrator is Anthony Trollope himself. The narrator speaks of himself as an "I." He uses the same "voice" and style as does, for example, the writer of *An Autobiography* when Trollope is narrating the misery of his childhood experiences. To put this the other way, reading *An Autobiography* sometimes seems like reading yet another novel by Trollope. Many of the same narrative devices are used and the same self-irony is present. Autobiographies, we know, are always to some degree fictional reconstructions.

A little reflection, however, will lead one to recognize that Anthony Trollope and the narrator of *Framley Parsonage* are quite different. Trollope's life experiences really happened in the real world and are therefore capable of being judged as true or false by a process of comparison with external evidence. Nothing of the sort is possible for *Framley Parsonage* because the whole thing is a made-up fiction. No Barsetshire ever existed, no Lord Lufton, no Lucy Robarts, none of the events and choices the novel records. The narrator of the novel, however, speaks in the first person as if they all existed and happened. Trollope, the author, could have made it up in any way he liked. The narrator, on the contrary, speaks as if bound to tell the truth about real historical events and personages, as when he says about one event, "I here declare, on the faith of an historian, that the rumor spread abroad . . . was not founded on fact."[11] That seems really weird, when you think of it, as when the narrator says of some dingy law chambers, "I once heard this room spoken of by an old friend of mine, one Mr. Gresham of Greshambury."[12] Here the narrator speaks as if he were a real person in the fictional world of the novel, as real as Lucy Robarts or Lord Lufton. I conclude that the narrator of *Framley Parsonage* is best thought of as one of the fictitious characters in this work of fiction. He is perhaps even the most important one, since the reader is entirely dependent on the narrator's telepathic powers for her or his knowledge of the (fictitious) events and persons of the novel.

The narrator's ethical responsibilities go in two directions, toward the reader and toward the characters. In both orientations the primary obligation is truth-telling. *Magna est veritas*, "great is truth," is the title of chapter twenty-four. The phrase is echoed several times in the text. In one place, the narrator says: "Being desirous, too, of telling the truth in this matter, I must confess that Lucy did speculate with some regret on what it would have been to be Lady Lufton."[13] The narrator has an ethical obligation to tell the whole truth about the characters to the reader. He also has an obligation to the characters to be scrupulously accurate in reporting their speech, thoughts, feelings, and actions. This truth-telling, please remember, all takes place within the imaginary world in which the characters are taken as real people. In one sense, everything the narrator says is a lie, since it asserts as historical fact what was no such thing.

Just what storytelling devices or forms of discourse does the narrator employ to fulfill that double ethical responsibility? I identify four. Of course, they overlap. More than one is often used in the same paragraph. Other modes are also used, for example, the verbatim printing of private letters. Letters sent by post were the Victorian version of our e-mail, telephone, and other means of private communication at a distance. As everyone knows who has read *An Autobiography*, Trollope worked for the British Post Office for many years. These four salient methods of storytelling are by no means unique to Trollope among Victorian novelists or among novelists in general, but Trollope has brilliant mastery of them. He uses them in ways and with a power that are unique to him. Given a citation in any of his modes, an adept reader would likely be able to tell whether or not it was by Trollope.

Here are the four most common narrative modes Trollope uses. Each is pervaded in one way or another by an ironic tinge that is a particular feature of Trollope's style.

Much of the *Framley Parsonage* is made up of dialogue. This give and take usually has little commentary beyond some variant of "he said" or "she said." Most often, but not always, the dialogue is between just two of the characters. Such dialogue is a chief means of getting the story told.

The narrator of *Framley Parsonage* presents a good bit of descriptive or ruminating discourse here and there along the way. You could call it "sermonizing." These narrative interventions are about many topics, for example, parliamentary politics in the England of Trollope's time. Trollope's narrator is by no means impersonal or detached.

Much of the stylistic texture of *Framley Parsonage* is made up of that peculiar form of language called by linguists free indirect discourse. Trollope is a great master of this common Victorian narrative form. In free indirect discourse the narrator enters into the mind, feelings, interior monologue, and bodily sensations of one or another of the characters. The narrator speaks in the third-person past tense of what was for the characters either altogether unworded or a secret interior speech in the first-person present tense. It is a basic and entirely "unrealistic" assumption in *Framley Parsonage* that the narrator has full "telepathic" knowledge of what is going on in the interiorities of almost all the characters. It is "unrealistic" because such direct insight into the minds and feelings of others in my judgment happens only in fictions, not in real life. I borrow Nicholas Royle's wise suggestion that "telepathic narrator" is a better term than "omniscient narrator." "Omniscient" has irrelevant and misleading theological implications. The characters, on the contrary, have only a partial and imperfect insight into what the other characters are thinking and feeling. No total clairvoyance of others for them.

Trollope, finally, often presents explicit ethical analysis by the narrator of a character's nature, behavior, and choices. Did he or she choose and act rightly? What was the process whereby choice and act came to happen in a given case? Trollope's narrator in *Framley Parsonage* does not hesitate to pass ethical judgment on what the characters think and do.

In order to keep this chapter to reasonable length, I shall concentrate on the love story between Lucy Robarts and Lord Lufton for my examples. That story is, moreover, the most interesting from my chosen perspective of ethics and literature. Trollope initially intended the story of the reverend Mark Robarts' disastrous entanglement in moneylenders to be the central story. He planned the novel to be "a morsel of the biography of an English clergyman who should not be a bad man but one led into temptation by his own youth and by the unclerical accidents of the life around him."[14] Trollope asserts in *An Autobiography* that Lucy's story gradually became the main plot: "Out of these slight elements I fabricated a hodge-podge in which the real plot consisted at last simply of a girl refusing to marry the man she loved till the man's friends agreed to accept her lovingly."[15]

Nevertheless, the reader should remember that *Framley Parsonage*, like almost all of Trollope's novels and like most Victorian novels, is a multi-plotted concoction or hodge-podge of somewhat analogous stories. It was also originally published, as I have said, in parts in the *Cornhill Magazine*, so it is an example of that common Victorian genre, the serial novel. The first readers encountered the novel in installments, with time breaks between each segment. The story of Lucy's love is interwoven with a whole set of other stories that in one way or another are entangled with it. This set includes not only the Mark Robarts story, but the story of Mr. Nathaniel Sowerby's loss of his ancestral estate, Chaldicotes, and the large fortune that goes with it, as well as his seat in parliament, through his spendthrift ways. This plot has attendant political stories of other MPs, prime ministers, and England's imperial possessions. The reader learns much about the power of Tom Towers and the great newspaper, *The Jupiter* (read the *London Times*), for which Tom writes "leaders." A moving subplot is the story of Miss Dunstable. She has inherited an enormous fortune from her father's (and then her own) sales of a quack medicine, the "Oil of Lebanon." In the end she comes to marry a poor country doctor, Dr. Thorne. Intertwined with the courtship of Lord Lufton and Lucy Robarts is the story of Lady Lufton's unsuccessful attempt to get her son, Lord Lufton, to marry the statuesque but empty-headed Griselda Grantly, the daughter of Archdeacon and Mrs. Grantly. Griselda's actual marriage to Lord Dumbello, whose name fits his nature (what a pair!), is a separate story. Lord Dumbello is the next in line in the Hartletop family and will be a Marquis. Griselda will become a Marchioness, much higher in the social scale than Lucy as the wife of Lord Lufton, a mere Baron. Trollope, finally, includes in *Framley Parsonage* episodes about the life of the miserably impoverished Mr. Crawley and his wretchedly underfed and barely clothed family. Crawley is the perpetual curate of the small parish church at Hogglestock. He is the central figure in a later Barsetshire novel by Trollope, *The Last Chronicle of Barset* (1867).

All those plots make a hodge-podge all right, but thematic and figurative resonances or analogies bind all these stories together. This is generally the function of multiple plots in a work of fiction, especially Victorian fiction, but it is also the case with the multiple marriage plots of Shakespeare's plays, such as *As You Like It*.

In the course of reading *Framley Parsonage*, the reader learns by way of Trollope's often ironic transposition of the real Victorian social context into an imaginary fiction all sorts of things about the Church of England in the mid-nineteenth century. The reader also learns about the immense complexities of the British class structure, especially in its relation to money. Miss Dunstable, for example, is enormously wealthy, but she is below the extremely poor Reverend Crawley in the social scale, as well as below the man she marries, Dr. Thorne. Crawley has gone to Harrow and Cambridge. He knows Greek and Latin, while Miss Dunstable is the daughter of a seller of quack medicine. The reader also learns about British imperialism at that stage of it (1860). He or she also learns about the bewildering complications of England's mode of parliamentary and monarchal governance. *Framley Parsonage*, finally, shows in action the crucial Victorian assumption that falling in love was an absolute and permanent change in a person.

One might sum up much of this context by saying that Victorian fiction most commonly centered on love stories because what interested Victorians most was the question of who would marry this or that marriageable maiden and so rearrange, at least to some degree, the present distribution of rank and money. Lucy Robarts, the daughter of a country physician and the sister of a mere parish clergyman, becomes Lady Lufton, a Baroness. Her first son will inherit Lord Lufton's barony. The large Lufton fortune will pass on to the next generation, Lucy's children, either in part as dowries, if they are girls, or through outright inheritance by the first son. This will happen by the strange English law of primogeniture. At least it seems strange to an American reader like me. Primogeniture leaves second or third sons penniless, forced to enter the army or to become clergymen. If money and rank mattered most to the Victorians, primarily of the middle class and the upper class, who read novels, it is easy to see why the marriage plot so fascinated Victorian readers, and why the ethical issues involved in courtship and marriage were so important to them. Lucy has to prove herself worthy to become the next Lady Lufton. She must do that in the context of all those assumptions about class and money I have specified.

Lucy's marriage, as is often the case with courtship and marriage in Victorian novels, takes place against the vigorous opposition of parents, of guardians, of all those responsible for Lucy's care as a maiden of marriageable age. Her marriage is a species of exogamy, almost like the marriage to an Israelite of the Moabite Ruth, in the Book of Ruth, in the Old Testament. Lucy's socially forbidden union, however, is necessary to the constant renewal of the community that marriage brings about. The marriage of the insipid Griselda Grantly to the vapid Lord Dumbello simply perpetuates a feeble aristocracy.

All of this concern for class and rank is exceedingly difficult for an American reader to understand, since our class structure is so different. For example, we have no aristocracy. A lack of money is not a big obstacle to marriage. Divorce is easy. Parental approval for a marriage is by no means so universally required. An American student reading *Framley Parsonage* is likely to say, "What's the problem? If they are in love with one another, why don't they get on with it?"

The story of Lucy's and Lord Lufton's love for one another is told in a series of discrete episodes presented at intervals interleaved with episodes from the other plots. To single these out and make a direct sequence of them is greatly to falsify the way Victorian (and modern day) readers encountered and now encounter that story. *Magna est veritas*, but I can only hope that my readers will forgive my unforgivably untrue truncation. It allows me to focus on the major example of truth-telling and lying as ethical events in *Framley Parsonage*. A full and detailed account of the way the novel works might take hundreds of pages.

I identify eleven stages or episodes in the Lucy Robarts story as Trollope tells it. The first comes when Lucy goes with her brother and sister-in-law, Mark and Fanny Robarts, to a dinner party at Lady Lufton's grand house, Framley Court. Lady Lufton is Mark's rich patroness, who has given him his living as the vicar of the church at Framley. Lucy feels completely out of place. She wishes she had never come. I cite part of a sequence that occurs in the drawing room after dinner as the guests talk and listen to Fanny Robarts play and sing, Griselda Grantly play, and Lord Lufton sing. The episode goes on for a couple of pages. I cite it in part because it is an admirable example of Trollope's remarkable ability to interweave with ease all the modes of narration I identified above. Just try to do it yourself, dear reader, and you'll see what amazing skill it hides in its apparent informality. Its subtlety is beguilingly simple in appearance, but difficult to analyze. It is also difficult to describe in words the scene of two characters in dialogue that forms itself in my mind as I read. That imaginary scene is no doubt different for each reader.

There she sat, still and motionless, afraid to take up a book, and thinking in her heart how much happier she would have been at home in the parsonage. She was not made for society; she felt sure of that; and another time she would let Mark and Fanny come to Framley Court by themselves. . . . Lucy sat alone, turning over the leaves of a book of pictures. She made up her mind fully, then and there, that she was quite unfitted by disposition for such work as this. She cared for no one, and no one cared for her. Well, she must go through with it now; but another time she would know better. With her own book and a fireside she never felt herself to be miserable as she was now. She had turned her back to the music for she was sick of seeing Lord Lufton watch the artistic motion of Miss Grantly's fingers, and was sitting at a small table as far away from the piano as a long room would permit, when she was suddenly roused from a reverie of self-reproach by a voice close behind her: "Miss Robarts," said the voice, "why have you cut us all?" and Lucy felt that, though she heard the words plainly, nobody else did. Lord Lufton was now speaking to her as he had before spoken to Miss Grantly.

"I don't play, my lord," said Lucy, "nor yet sing."

"That would have made your company so much more valuable to us, for we are terribly badly off for listeners. Perhaps you don't like music?"

"I do like it,—sometimes very much."

"And when are the sometimes? But we shall find it all out in time. We shall have unraveled all your mysteries, and read all your riddles by— when shall I say?—by the end of the winter. Shall we not?"

"I do not know that I have got any mysteries."

""Oh, but you have! It is very mysterious in you to come and sit here—with your back to us all—"

"Oh, Lord Lufton; if I have done wrong—!" and poor Lucy almost started from her chair, and a deep flush came across her dark cheek.

"No—no; you have done no wrong. I was only joking. It is we who have done wrong in leaving you to yourself—you who are the greatest stranger among us."

"I have been very well, thank you. I don't care about being left alone. I have always been used to it."

"Ah! but we must break you of the habit. We won't allow you to make a hermit of yourself. But the truth is, Miss Robarts, you don't know us yet, and therefore you are not quite happy among us."

"Oh! yes, I am; you are all very good to me."

"You must let us be good to you. At any rate, you must let me be so. You know, don't you, that Mark and I have been dear friends since we were seven years old. His wife has been my sister's dearest friend almost as long; and now that you are with them, you must be a dear friend too. You won't refuse the offer, will you?"

"Oh, no," she said, quite in a whisper, fearing that tears would fall from her tell-tale eyes.[16]

By the time I reach this passage in my reading, I have a mental image of Lady Lufton's long drawing room at Framley Court, even though the details Trollope provides are pretty sparse. We know there is a sofa, a piano, a table where Lucy sits "as far away from the piano as a long room would permit," but I am left to my own imagination to provide the rest. The passage begins with an example of the narrator's descriptive mode: "There she sat." It rapidly modulates into an example of the narrator's extraordinary ability to enter into the imaginary subjectivities of most of the characters: "Thinking in her heart how much happier she would have been at home in the parsonage." "Thinking in her heart" seems to be the narrator's locution for unworded thinking. That modulates quickly again to an example of indirect discourse, in which, as I have said, the narrator transposes the character's interior monologue into third-person past tense. "She was not made for society; she felt sure of that; and another time she would let Mark and Fanny come to Framley Court by themselves," is a transposition of "I am not made for society; I feel sure of that; and another time I will let Mark and Fanny come to Framley Court by themselves." In indirect discourse, the reader gets two minds superimposed, that of the character and that of the narrator. The latter has telepathic knowledge of what the character is saying to herself or to himself. Indirect discourse generates, always, to some degree, however slight, an ironic distance from the character. Lucy, that distance leads the reader to think, is being a bit silly in denigrating herself, however much we are meant to admire her maidenly modesty, her reticence, and her sense of being of a lower class than the other guests. The irony in the indirect discourse indirectly tells the reader all that. It gives the reader an outside perspective on Lucy's interiority. The effect would be quite different if

Lucy's thoughts were given as interior monologue, like Molly Bloom's soliloquy in *Ulysses*.

The indirect discourse for Lucy is picked up on the next page, when I start my citation again after a break: "She made up her mind fully, then and there, that she was quite unfitted by disposition for such work as this. She cared for no one, and no one cared for her.[17] Well, she must go through it now; but another time she would know better."

Lucy's bitter meditation is interrupted by Lord Lufton's speaking quietly to her from behind her as she sits alone turning the leaves of a book of pictures with her back to the room: " 'Miss Robarts,' said the voice, 'why have you cut us all?' " What follows is a characteristic example of Trollope's brilliant use of what the Greeks called "stichomythic" dialogue, the rapid give and take of dialogue, often brief questions and answers. No careful reader can fail to note that what begins as apparently just polite conversation soon becomes something almost approaching lovemaking, or at least serious flirtation, on Lord Lufton's part: " 'His [Mark Robarts's] wife has been my sister's dearest friend almost as long; and now that you are with them, you must be a dear friend too. You won't refuse the offer, will you?' 'Oh, no,' she said, quite in a whisper."

The passage I have cited is a good synecdochic sample of the mixture of narrative discourses that characterizes *Framley Parsonage* in general, and the rendition of the love story between Lucy Robarts and Lord Lufton in particular. It is atypical in having only one brief example at the beginning of the frequent short or sometimes quite long interpolations of description, or of ethical interpretation and judgment, or of ruminative digression by the narrator's speaking for himself in his own voice, in direct address to the reader. Here is one example: "That girls should not marry for money we are all agreed. A lady who can sell herself for a title or an estate, for an income or a set of family diamonds, treats herself as a farmer treats his sheep and oxen—makes hardly more of herself, of her own inner self, in which are comprised a mind and soul, than the poor wretch of her own sex who earns her bread in the lowest stage of degradation [that is, becomes a prostitute]."[18]

Trollope's quite distinctively brilliant use of the major forms of Victorian narrative techniques continues throughout the various episodes telling Lucy's story. These episodes are distributed at uneven intervals through the novel.

In the next episode in the series after Lucy and Lord Lufton first meet, Lady Lufton warns Fanny Robarts that her son Lord Lufton may be spending too much time talking intimately to Lucy. This is followed in the same chapter by Fanny's warning to Lucy against "flirting" with Lord Lufton[19] (ch. 13, "Delicate Hints"). Then comes chapter 16 in which Lord Lufton makes his first proposal to Lucy and she tells her lie in refusing him, since she is deeply in love with him: " 'Lord Lufton,' she said, 'I cannot love you' "[20] ("Mrs. Podgens' Baby").

Five chapters later comes the episode in which Lucy flogs the pony Puck (a significant Shakespearean name) when she is driving the pony carriage with Fanny. She does this in exasperation at hearing that Lord Lufton is probably to marry Griselda Grantly, thereby giving away to Fanny that she is secretly in love with him (ch. 21, "Why Puck, the Pony, Was Beaten"). The next episode in the series shows Lucy confessing in a self-mocking irony ("It was his title that killed me.")[21] her love for Lord Lufton to her sister-in-law Fanny Robarts and confessing also that she lied to him: "I told him a lie"[22] (ch. 26, "Impulsive"). Five chapters later Lord Lufton tells Lucy's brother Mark that he loves Lucy and intends to come the next day to propose to her again, a visit Lucy refuses (ch. 31, "Salmon Fishing in Norway").

In chapter 34, "Lady Lufton Is Taken By Surprise," Lord Lufton tells his mother that he means to make Lucy his wife. In just the next chapter, "The Story of King Cophetua," Lucy out-smarts Lady Lufton and tells her that though she is deeply in love with Lord Lufton and he with her, she will only agree to marry him when Lady Lufton asks her to do so. In chapter 41, "Don Quixote," Trollope shows Fanny Robarts defending Lucy to Lady Lufton: "I have not given any advice; nor is it needed. I know no one more able than Lucy to see clearly, by her own judgment, what course she ought to pursue. I should be afraid to advise one whose mind is so strong, and who, of her own nature, is so self-denying as she is."[23] Chapter 43, "Is She Not Insignificant?" tells how Lady Lufton tried unsuccessfully to persuade her son, Lord Lufton, that Lucy is too "insignificant" to be his wife. In chapter 46, "Lady Lufton's Request," Lady Lufton gives in and asks Lucy to marry Lord Lufton: "And now I have come here, Lucy, to ask you to be his wife." Lucy sends by Lady Lufton a one word message to him, "simply yes."[24]

Chapter 48, "How They Were All Married, Had Two Children, and Lived Happy Ever After," tells how Lucy, shortly before her marriage, refuses to admit to Lord Lufton that she lied to him when she told him she could not love him: " 'Ludovic, some conjuror must have told you that.' She was standing as she spoke, and, laughing at him, she held up her hands and shook her head. But she was now in his power, and he had his revenge [presumably an embrace and kiss]—his revenge for her past falsehood and her present joke."[25]

This recapitulation is no substitute for reading the novel, but it will give my readers some sense of the way the course of this true love does not run smooth, but has a happy ending nevertheless. Readers will also see from the chapter numbers that the episodes telling the story of how Lucy came to marry Lord Lufton are distributed throughout the novel at intervals of about five chapters. These episodes are interspersed with many chapters about the other plots. They are, moreover, included in different serial sections. The initial Victorian readers would have received Lucy's story with two different kinds of interruption along the way.

Lucy's story turns on several different kinds of speech acts or performative utterances.[26] I shall now conclude this chapter with a brief commentary on these. Each would merit a lengthy analysis and elucidation. Each performative in Trollope's telling of Lucy's story works differently. Lord Lufton's iterated proposals to Lucy are speech acts. They force her to respond in some way, even if only by silence. Lucy's lie to Lord Lufton is a speech act, as, in a different way, is her confession to Fanny that she loves Lord Lufton dearly and has lied to him. Lucy's "verdict" that she will marry her suitor only if Lady Lufton asks her to do so is a performative utterance that forms a turning point in the story. Any utterance that can be called a "verdict" is a speech act, a use of words to make something happen, in this case to put the ball in Lady Lufton's court, so to speak. Lady Lufton's ultimate request to Lucy, followed by Lucy's ratifying "simply yes" are two more speech acts. Lucy's refusal to confess her lie to Lord Lufton is, in a somewhat strange way, yet another performative. As J. L. Austin recognized, speech acts take many different forms, sometimes quite peculiar ones that may masquerade as apparently statements of fact, "constatives."

A lie, a confession, a proposal of marriage, a "verdict" or decision, a request, a "yes," with its implicit, "I promise to do that," a refusal to confess: each of these is a different way of doing things with words, not a constative assertion. Each differs from the others in its mode of working, but each demands some kind of answering response from the person to whom it is spoken. For example, Lord Lufton goes away in deep disappointment and dejection when Lucy says, "I cannot love you." Her lie works as an efficacious speech act. It makes something happen.

Lucy's love story, as you can see, proceeds through a cascade of performative utterances that make salient the ethical issues her story raises.

These issues are made explicit in the novel, either by the narrator or by one or another of the characters. Most obviously Lucy's story turns on the question of whether or not a lie is ever justified, as well as on the performative force of her assertion that she will only consent to marry Lord Lufton if his mother asks her to accept him: "Tell him, that if his mother asks me I will—consent."[27] This is a speech act in the sense that it forces Lady Lufton to respond in one way or another. Lady Lufton must either accept or refuse. Doing nothing is a virtual speech act in response. *Magna est veritas*. The novel repeatedly, in the various plots, stresses the importance of strict truth-telling and the perfidy of lying. Mr. Sowerby, for example, is a congenital liar. He is punished as a consequence: "It is roguish to lie, and he had been a great liar."[28]

J. L. Austin affirms, truthfully enough, that all performative statements have a constative dimension, and vice versa. A true statement is a classic example of a constative utterance, since it is in correspondence with an extraverbal state of affairs. Its performative dimension is minimal. A lie is a peculiar form of speech act. Its constative value is nil, since it does not correspond to a true state of affairs. Its performative force, however, can be decisive if it is believed. When Lucy replies to Lord Lufton's proposal with her "I cannot love you," her lie is an efficacious speech act because he believes her and goes away disappointed and, as he says, "wretched." She is motivated by "pride," which forbids her to endure Lady Lufton's violent disapproval and her inevitable belief that Lucy has entrapped Lord Lufton, that she is, as she thinks to herself, a "horrid, sly, detestable, underhand girl."[29] The whole Lucy Robarts love story turns on the consequences of her lie and on the question of whether a lie is ever justified. This is the chief ethical question her story forcefully dramatizes.

After uttering her lie to Lord Lufton, Lucy goes to her room, throws herself on her bed, and asks herself, in another example of the indirect discourse so pervasive in the novel: "Why—oh! why had she told such a falsehood? Could anything justify her in a lie? Was it not a lie—knowing as she did that she loved him with all her loving heart? But, then, his mother! and the sneers of the world, which would have declared that she had set her trap, and caught the foolish young lord! Her pride would not have submitted to that. Strong as her love was, yet her pride was, perhaps, stronger—stronger at any rate during that interview. But how was she to forgive herself the falsehood she had told?"[30] Later on she says to herself, "And now she had thrown all that aside because she could not endure that Lady Lufton should call her a scheming, artful girl! Actuated by that fear she had repulsed him with a falsehood, though the matter was one on which it was so terribly important that she should tell the truth."[31]

This ethical dilemma comes up explicitly again later on in the novel, when Lucy tells all her story up to then to Fanny, with a mixture of solemnity and self-deprecating irony:

> "I lied to him, and told him that I did not love him."
>
> "You refused him?"
>
> "Yes; I refused a live lord. There is some satisfaction in having that to think of, is there not? Fanny, was I wicked to tell that falsehood?'
>
> . . .
>
> "I know that it is better as it is; but tell me—is a falsehood always wrong, or can it be possible that the end should justify the means? Ought I to have told him the truth, and to have let him know that I could almost kiss the ground on which he stood?"
>
> That was a question for the doctors [meaning Doctors of the Church, theologians, or, by analogy, interpreters of the ethical dimensions of literature, like me] which Mrs. Robarts would not take it upon herself to answer. She would not make that falsehood matter of accusation, but neither would she pronounce for it any absolution. In that matter Lucy must regulate her own conscience.[32]

That is the question, all right: Is a lie ever justified? Fanny's appeal to Lucy's conscience is not sufficient. At least it does not satisfy me. Kant's famous example is about the person who, according to Kant, should not lie when asked whether a fugitive has taken shelter in his house, even though telling the truth will likely lead to the capture or death of the fugitive. For Kant a lie is never justified.[33] And yet Lucy's falsehood was uttered for the most high-minded and self-denying of reasons.

I think in the end that Trollope, or Trollope's narrator, leaves it to the reader to decide this ethical question. That question presides over the whole of the Lucy Robarts's plotline. It arises for Mark Robarts when he learns that Lord Lufton has proposed to Lucy and has been refused, but intends to ask her again: "And then, he would have said, Lord Lufton would have been the last to fall in love with such a girl as his sister. And now, what was he to say or do? What views was he bound to hold? In what direction should he act?"[34]

To tell the truth, I'm not sure what my own judgment is about Lucy's lie. It is a question for the doctors to decide. But a return in conclusion to

Lucy's other determining speech act may help me reach a decision, or at any rate may clarify to some degree what is at stake.

Lucy's "Tell him, that if his mother asks me I will—consent" can be seen in at least two ways, as can her story as a whole. What she says is characterized by the narrator in the formal language of a courtroom decision. It is a "verdict," that is, etymologically, "true speech," or "saying the truth": "Such was her verdict, and so confident were they both [Mark and Fanny Robarts] of her firmness—of her obstinacy Mark would have called it on any other occasion,—that neither of them sought to make her alter it."[35] A little earlier, the narrator says of Lucy, "She had still, in some perversely obstinate manner, made up her mind against that result [becoming the next Lady Lufton]."[36] On the one hand, Lucy believes, or thinks she believes, that Lady Lufton will never consent. Her verdict is an example of the meek self-denial and modesty that we commonly associate with Victorian heroines. On the other hand, it can be seen as a brilliant ploy by the highly intelligent and strong-willed Lucy Robarts to fulfill her love and marry Lord Lufton. Lufton knows that his mother, who loves him inordinately, will eventually give in and welcome Lucy as his daughter-in-law. Lucy, the reader is encouraged to imagine, may have known Lady Lufton well enough to have foreseen somewhere "in her heart of hearts" that outcome. Her verdict certainly works as a "felicitous speech act," in Austin's phrase, to produce that result.

Lucy's whole story is double in that way. On the one hand, it is a prime example of the typical Victorian, fictional love story in which the modest, self-denying maiden keeps her love secret, but nevertheless in the end marries her beloved and above her class origins. She thereby, through her children, participates in the reassignment of money and class that was the way Victorian society renewed itself. On the other hand, many hints and details indicate that Trollope is actually critical of the ideological assumptions of that standard plot. The satirical parallels with such models as Scott's *The Bride of Lammermoor* and, more explicitly, the ballad of "King Cophetua and the Beggar Maid." The latter is used as the title of the chapter in which Lucy confronts Lady Lufton and wins the battle of wills with her by invoking once more her verdict.[37] Trollope's narrator uses to some degree in telling Lucy's story the ironic distancing that, as I have said, is intrinsic to indirect discourse. That distancing is also present in the conspicuous irony that is constantly used by Lucy herself in telling her story, especially in the way she tells it to Fanny:

"What you tell me so surprises me, that I hardly as yet know how to speak about it," said Mrs. Robarts.

"It was amazing, was it not? He must have been insane at the time; there can be no other excuse made for him. I wonder whether there is anything of that sort in the family?"

"What; madness?" said Mrs. Robarts, quite in earnest.

"Well, don't you think he must have been mad when such an idea cane into his head? But you don't believe it; I can see that. And yet it is as true as heaven. . . ."

. . .

"And what shall I do next?" said Lucy, still speaking in a tone that was half tragic and half jeering.

"Do?" said Mrs. Robarts.

"Yes, something must be done. If I were a man I should go to Switzerland, of course; or, as the case is a bad one, perhaps as far as Hungary. What is it that girls do? they don't die nowadays, I believe [as Lucy Ashton does, melodramatically, in *The Bride of Lammermoor*]."[38]

The Lucy story in *Framley Parsonage* is two stories in one: the first is a straightforward version of the typical Victorian love plot. The other, present in the irony of language and in the ironic allusions to famous previous examples of such stories, deconstructs, if I may dare to use that word, by way of its rhetoric, the "straight" story. It puts the solemnity of that story radically in question. It does so subtly but unmistakably, if the reader follows the clues given by the "poetics" of *Framley Parsonage*, that is, the way things are said. Poetics are opposed to "hermeneutics," that is, the identification of what things are said by way of overt thematic statements. The novel's poetics reveals it to be a devastatingly comic parody of the conventional sentimental love plot, as well as a brilliant rendition of it. Lucy's story in *Framley Parsonage* superimposes and interweaves two different narratives. It is, to use the vernacular, a "twofer," two for one.

That duplicity is exposed in the double meanings of Lucy's word "conjuror." The happy marriage of Lord Lufton and Lucy Robarts is based on a lie kept secret by Lucy from her husband to be. It is a permanent secret between the two. The happy ending is founded on a falsehood that Lucy refuses to confess that she has uttered. The figure of speech she uses in making that refusal seems extremely odd, if you think a little about it: " 'Ludovic, some conjuror must have told you that.' She was standing as she spoke, and, laughing at him, she held up her hands and shook her head."

Lucy's word "conjuror" is only used jestingly. The narrator calls it a "joke." It is a lighthearted figure of speech. I know of no evidence that Trollope believed words could, as Shakespeare's Hotspur puts it, "call spirits from the vasty deep." Nevertheless, Lucy's use of the word is highly suggestive. Speech acts are, after all, like a conjuror's sleight-of-hand tricks. They make something happen with words, by an "abracadabra!" or an "open sesame!"

Conjuror, as well as meaning "magician," which everyone knows is someone adept at misleading prestidigitations, also means someone who invokes spirits by magic spells or incantations. The Latin *con* or *com*, "with," plus *jure*, "swear" means "to swear with." The word also means, as early as the 1580s, when used in the phrase "conjure up," "cause to appear in the mind as if by magic, by invocation, or spell."[39] Lucy's "conjuror" will have revealed her secret lie, by conjuring it up within Lord Lufton's mind. Lord Lufton will then be able to read the magician's words or can read what is betrayed in Lucy's holding up her hands and shaking her head, in an act of conjuration or perhaps of banishment, exorcism: "Now you see it, now you don't." And of course the narrator as conjuror or spirit medium has conjured up for the readers, with words used as invocations, all the characters, events, and settings of the novel. "I hereby invoke Lucy Robarts." In particular, the narrator has told Lucy's secret to the reader by way of reporting his magical, telepathic knowledge that she has confessed her lie to herself in interior monologue and in overt speech to Fanny Robarts.

I claim to have shown in a salient example how the ethics of literature works in my interpretation of it. Have I fulfilled my ethical obligation to tell the truth about *Framley Parsonage*? This I can never know for sure, as is the case in all realms of ethical responsibility, decision, and action. I can only say truthfully that I have done my conscientious best.

My version of the relation between ethics and literature, as this chapter shows, is different from Ranjan Ghosh's "The Ethics of Reading Sahitya," though resonances exist. Our book's final pair of chapters constitutes a concluding demonstration of two ways to think literature across continents.

RANJAN GHOSH

EPILOGUE

Every tradition and system of thought and knowledge belonging to a particular culture and community must begin by offering its ideas and thoughts to the other; this welcome and potential indulgence creates opportunities to experiment with such offerings, inspiring our walking the untrodden paths. "Taking" is the openness to accept and assimilate what others have to offer and this also initiates a separate level of coordination and contact. Giving and taking unleash a variety of "circulation"—the complexity emerging out of constraints and enablings—generating a host of entanglements in our enunciation and enframing of literature. Our life of dialogue, which began about fifteen years ago, was inscribed in a poetics of taking, a poetics about how close we could get to listening to literature and listening to each other's thinking about literature across canons, continents, and cultures. The book, promoting positions that were conflationary and contrastive, combined an astute and genuine listening that enabled a patient growth of the other, an encouragement to get tolerant with the other, in a domain of altogether, a togetherness that we suppose flourished because we realized our separation in communication, dislocations in convergences. Our transactional listening to each other has, hopefully, opened literature as a democratic community where readers are welcome to install and invest their inputs through a separate level of listening that may not be docile always.

The book, then, is an out-of-habit project. Streams of thought on an exuberantly wide range of issues will rush onto the reader's encounter with the book, a ceaseless across-momentum of thoughts and positions, an unavoidable yet cheerful obligation to listen to multiple voices and vocabularies made available through a celebration of literary thoughts and communities. Such acts of listening are a challenge to our habitual encounters with books usually authored, edited, and coauthored. The Miller-Ghosh presence and the authors' interface at every juncture of the unfolding is a way to alert the reader about two books building in conjunction, in colloquy, listening to each other in their mutual substantiation and relishing the inability to author and authorize the final word on a particular subject, be that ethics or world literature or teaching literature or reading poetry. This will leave readers in the midst of three books, one by Ghosh, another by Miller, and the third by Ghosh-Miller. The chapters were not just intended to follow each other but coexist. Our voices were individual and collaborative; our consciousnesses were singularly articulated and participatory. So the book will make the readers see the disturbance that dialogism brings, a process of thinking where difference becomes understanding. Arguments across a variety of subjects, colored and informed by different kinds of training and intellectual establishments, do not have an impositional totality, for Hillis and I germinated this project knowing our indentificatory and ideological differences and kept discovering ourselves productively as we progressed through time with meticulous mapping and scrupulous patience. Dialogism, conversational becomings at different levels of literary affect and epistemic concretizations, is the pith of this project and it prevented us from overlaying the carefully crafted canvas built over the last four years with our literary prejudices. Dialogues through chapters and other modes of innumerable exchanges made us rethink our positions and perspectives and become accommodative about the impetus and impingement of the other. The book is formally "one from many" constructed out of co-particulars, and every chapter can be signposted as Miller-Ghosh.

Are we directing readers to a future of literature? Perhaps not. To call on a future is to allow a settlement on a bolus of steady accretion, a penultimate point of literature's evolution that is more telic than configurative. What, perhaps, we ended up doing, to an extent, is stirring the pot, bringing the sedimented to the surface and allowing the once settled to sink away in the stir at different points in the container. Our dyadic and dialogic investments went beyond the stir also, ensuring fresh formations on the meaning-effect of literature, the world in world literature, the teaching-affect of literature, ethics and postaesthetics of literature, and many other issues. Sitting by the fireplace in the playhouse of literature, we have also allowed things to grow in silence. Perhaps this silence is what the book urges on its readers, triggering their own explorative ways; the meditation that the book is intended to generate effectuates the stirring of continents and the silences that such stirrings have left behind rather unavoidably for readerly ascension and tenancy.

Becomings are secret, as Deleuze and Guattari were right to observe. The book's being is its becoming.

NOTES

Introduction

Epigraphs: Rabindranath Tagore, *Letters to a Friend. Rabindranath Tagore's Letters to C.F. Andrews* [1928] (New Delhi: Rupa, 2002), 119. Emphasis mine. Quoted from John G. Rudy, *Wordsworth and the Zen Mind* (Albany: State University of New York Press, 1996), 49. See Michel Deguy, *Recumbents: Poems* (Middletown, CT: Wesleyan University Press, 2005), 84.

1 Rodolphe Gasché, "Alongside the Horizon," in *On Jean-Luc Nancy: The Sense of Philosophy*, ed. Darren Sheppard, Simon Sparks, and Colin Thomas (London: Routledge, 1997), 136.

2 Martta Heikkilä, *At the Limits of Presentation* (Frankfurt: Peter Lang, 2008), 103.

3 Jean-Luc Nancy, *Birth to Presence* (Stanford, CA: Stanford University Press, 1993), 155–56.

4 Dictionary.com, s.v. "Trans," accessed March 13, 2016, http://dictionary .reference.com/browse/trans. For more on trans-habit, see my *Transcultural Poetics and the Concept of the Poet: From Philip Sidney to T. S. Eliot* (London: Routledge, 2016). Chapter 1 from this book elaborates what I theorize and mean by trans-habit.

5 Deguy calls this an "affair of ference," and we are in the midst of the ag-glomerated force of inter-ference, con-ference, de-ference, di-ference, and in-ference (suffix, *ferre*, "to carry"), in the words of Deguy, "quotable/Defer-ence preference difference/Afference." See "Memorandum," in Michel Deguy, *Gisants* (Paris: Gallimard, 1985), translated as *Recumbents: Poems* (Middle-town, CT: Wesleyan University Press, 2005).

6 See John Phillip Williams, "Hodos Infusion and Method," in *Romancing Theory, Riding Interpretation: (In)fusion Approach, Salman Rushdie*, ed. Ranjan Ghosh (New York: Peter Lang, 2012), 73.

7 See Karen Barad, "Intraactions," *Mousse*, 2012, 34.

8 See Gilles Deleuze, *Foucault*, trans. S. Hand (Minneapolis: University of Minnesota Press, 1988), 23–44.

9 Tim Cresswell, *In Place/Out of Place: Geography, Ideology, Transgression* (Minneapolis: University of Minnesota Press, 1996), 11.

10 Karen Barad, "Diffracting Diffraction: Cutting Together-Apart," *Parallax* 20, no. 3 (2014): 168.

11 Barad, "Diffracting Diffraction," 169.

12 Deleuze, *The Fold*, 76, 78.

13 See my *(In)fusion Approach: Theory, Contestation, Limits* (Lanham, MD: University Press of America, 2006).

14 Elizabeth Grosz, *The Nick of Time* (Sydney: Allen and Unwin, 2004), 9.

15 Elizabeth Grosz, *Chaos, Territory, Art: Deleuze and the Framing of the Earth* (New York: Columbia University Press, 2008), 8.

16 See Rene Girard's introduction to Michel Serres, *Detachment*, trans. Genevieve James and Raymond Federman (Athens: Ohio University Press, 1989), viii.

17 Robert Frost, "Mending Wall," accessed November 10, 2015, http://www.poetryfoundation.org/poem/173530.

18 Michel Serres, *Genesis*, trans. Genevieve James and James Nielson (Ann Arbor: University of Michigan Press, 1995), 2.

19 Serres, *Genesis*, 3.

20 Serres, *Genesis*, 6.

21 See Michel Serres, *The Parasite*, trans. Lawrence R. Schehr (Baltimore: Johns Hopkins University Press, 1982).

22 Gilles Deleuze, *The Logic of Sense*, trans. M. Lester and C. Stivale, ed. C. Boundas (New York: Columbia University Press, 1990), 37. Also see Gilles Deleuze, "How Do We Recognize Structuralism?" in *Desert Islands and Other Texts, 1953–1974*, trans. M. Taormina (New York: Semiotext(e), 2004), 170–92.

23 Deleuze, *Essays Critical and Clinical*, 133, 132.

24 Gilles Deleuze, and Félix Guattari, *A Thousand Plateaus: Capitalism and Schizophrenia*, trans. Brian Massumi (Minneapolis: University of Minnesota Press, 1987), 21.

25 Gilles Deleuze and Félix Guattari, *Kafka: Toward a Minor Literature* (Minneapolis: University of Minnesota Press, 1986), 83.

26 Andy Merrifield, *Guy Debord* (London: Reaktion Books, 2005), 51.

27 Globalization as "unitotality" suppresses world-forming, which is indeed a conceptual catastrophe. See Jean-Luc Nancy, *The Creation of the World or Globalization*, trans. Françoise Raffoul and David Pettigrew (Albany: State University of New York Press, 2007).

28 Bruno Latour, "The Enlightenment without the Critique: A Word on Michel Serres's Philosophy," in *Contemporary French Philosophy*, ed. A. Phillips Griffiths (Cambridge: Cambridge University Press, 1987), 90–91.

1 Louis Althusser, "Ideology and Ideological State Apparatuses (Notes towards an Investigation)," *Lenin and Philosophy and Other Essays*, trans. Ben Brewster (New York: Monthly Review Press, 1972), 127–86. Paul de Man, "The Resistance to Theory," *The Resistance to Theory* (Minneapolis: University of Minnesota Press, 1986), 3-20.

2 Michael Shermer, "Skeptic: Scientia Humanitatis," *Scientific American*, June 2015, 80. Shermer is publisher of *Skeptic* magazine.

3 Rens Bod, *A New History of the Humanities: The Search for Principles and Patterns from Antiquity to the Present* (Oxford University Press, 2014).

4 Wikipedia, s.v. "Donation of Constantine," accessed June 4, 2015, https://en .wikipedia.org/wiki/Donation_of_Constantine.

5 Paul de Man, "The Resistance to Theory," 10.

6 Google "fake scientific papers" for a long list of websites on this topic, for example, an essay in *Nature* entitled "Publishers withdraw more than 120 gibberish papers" (http://www.nature.com/news/publishers-withdraw-more -than-120-gibberish-papers-1.14763, accessed June 3, 1015). Other fake papers claim to be based on scientifically conducted research that never occurred, for example, a recent, notorious one claiming with fake evidence that just talking to people will cure them in a few minutes of their opposition to gay marriage.

7 My Chinese correspondent cited the two sentences I have quoted here from the preface in Chinese to the Chinese translation of my *Fiction and Repetition*. They come originally from my "The Critic as Host," in *Deconstruction and Criticism*, ed. Harold Bloom (New York: Seabury Press, 1979), 251. The short paragraph from which these two sentences are drawn begins with an unequivocal assertion that "the word 'deconstruction' has misleading overtones or implications" (251). Any careful reader should see that my figure of the dismantled watch is an ironic parody of what many people mistakenly think deconstruction is.

8 See Wikipedia's entry for "pun" for a valuable entry on the different forms of *pun* along with a brief history of examples. *Paronomasia*, as the pun is called in Greek, itself contains a multiple pun on antithetical meanings, since the prefix "para," sometimes, as in this case, shortened to "par," means "beside; next to, near, from; against, contrary to." (Wikipedia, s.v. "Pun," accessed June 6, 2015, http://en.wikipedia.org/wiki/Pun.)

9 An immense number of editions of the Alice books exist. I cite the one I read as a child and still have in my library. It is much battered and worn from having been read by generations of children. It has the Tenniel illustrations, which were, and are, essential to my "rhetorical reading" of the two Alice books: Lewis Carroll, *Alice's Adventures in Wonderland and Through the Looking-Glass* (New York: A. L. Burt, n.d.), 12.

10 Carroll, *Alice's Adventures in Wonderland and Through the Looking-Glass*, 30–32.

11 "'Then you should say what you mean,' the March Hare went on.

'I do,' Alice hastily replied; 'at least—at least I mean what I say—that's the same thing, you know.'

'Not the same thing a bit!' said the Hatter. 'You might just as well say that "I see what I eat" is the same thing as "I eat what I see"!'

'You might just as well say,' added the March Hare, 'that "I like what I get" is the same thing as "I get what I like"!'

'You might just as well say,' added the Dormouse, who seemed to be talking in his sleep, 'that "I breathe when I sleep" is the same thing as "I sleep when I breathe"!'" (Carroll, *Alice's Adventures in Wonderland and Through the Looking-Glass*, 82).

12 "Trolling 'Anthropos'—Or, Requiem for a Failed Prosopopeia," in *Twilight of the Anthropocene Idols*, ed. Tom Cohen, Claire Colebrook, and J. Hillis Miller (London: Open Humanities Press, 2016), 20–80.

13 de Man, *The Resistance to Theory*, 51.

14 de Man, *The Resistance to Theory*, 27–53; Paul de Man, *The Rhetoric of Romanticism* (New York: Columbia University Press, 1984), 239–62.

Chapter 1: Making Sahitya Matter

Epigraphs: Anthony Earl of Shaftesbury, *Characteristics*, ed. John M. Robertson (London: Grant Richards, 1900), vol. I, 189; *Ontogeny and Phylogeny* (Cambridge, MA: Belknap Press of Harvard University Press, 1977), 289.

1 Tagore, "Sadhana," in *The English Writings of Rabindranath Tagore*, ed. Sisir Kumar Das, vol. 2 (New Delhi: Sahitya Academy, 1999), 322–23.

2 Wai-Lim Yip, *Diffusion of Distances: Dialogues between Chinese and Western Poetics* (Berkeley: University of California Press, 1993), 140–41.

3 Raghavan, "Sahitya," in *An Introduction to Indian Poetics*, ed. V. Raghavan and Nagendra (Bombay: Macmillan, 1970), 82.

4 Paul Hernadi, "Why Is Literature: A Coevolutionary Perspective on Imaginative Worldmaking," *Poetics Today* 23 (spring 2002): 22.

5 D. C. Lau, *Lao Tzu Tao Te Ching* (Harmondsworth, UK: Penguin Books, 1963), 3.

6 See D. C. Lau, *Lao Tzu Tao Te Ching*, accessed September 26, 2015, http://terebess .hu/english/tao/lau.html.

7 Prabas Jiban Chaudhury, *Tagore on Literature and Aesthetics* (Calcutta: Rabindra Bharati, 1965), 12.

8 Immanuel Kant, *Critique of Judgment*, vol. 1 (Oxford: Oxford University Press, 1911), 59.

9 Chaudhury, *Tagore on Literature and Aesthetics*, 13. Tagore writes in "Sahityer Swarup": "There is no need in art to settle a problem, its business is to perfect its form. To untie the knot of a problem is an achievement of the intellect but to give perfection to some form is the work of creative imagination. Art dwells in this realm of imagination and not in the realm of logic" (45). I hope I have been able to problematize literary judgment as elucidation and the analysis of literature.

10 Tagore, *Personality* (London: Macmillan, 1945), 16.

11 Tagore, "Sristrir Adhikar," in *Rabindra Rachanabali* (Calcutta: Visva Bharati, 1965), 451.

12 For further elaboration, see Tagore's "Sahityer Pathe," in *Rabindra Rachanabali*, vol. 10, 435–561.

13 *Rabindranath Tagore: Selected Poems* (Delhi: Penguin Books, 1985).

14 Tagore, *Personality*, 17.

15 Tagore, *Personality*, 8.

16 Ghose, ed., *Angel of Surplus*, 101.

17 Tagore, *Personality*, 29.

18 Tagore, *Personality*, 69.

19 Chaudhury, *Tagore on Literature and Aesthetics*, 17.

20 Chaudhury, *Tagore on Literature and Aesthetics*, 38.

21 Chaudhury, *Tagore on Literature and Aesthetics*, 39.

22 Chaudhury, *Tagore on Literature and Aesthetics*, 39.

23 *Personality*, 83–84; Tagore, "The Religion of an Artist," cited in Chakravarty, *A Tagore Reader* (New York: Macmillan, 1961), 234.

24 Chakravarty, *A Tagore Reader*, 234–35.

25 Tagore, *Personality*, 60.

26 Ming Dong Gu, "The Divine and Artistic Ideal: Ideas and Insights for Cross-Cultural Aesthetic Education," *Journal of Aesthetic Education* 42, no. 3 (fall 2008): 68.

27 Ming, "The Divine and Artistic Ideal," 68–69.

28 Yip, *Diffusion of Distances*, 205.

29 Arthur Danto, *The Philosophical Disenfranchisement of Art* (New York: Columbia University Press, 1986), 67.

30 Jacques Rancière, "The Politics of Literature," *SubStance* 33, no. 1 (2004): 14–15.

31 Rancière, "The Politics of Literature," 15.

32 Cleanth Brooks, *The Well Wrought Urn* (San Diego: Harcourt Brace, 1975), 72–73.

33 Robert Frost, "Birches," accessed October 14, 2015, http://www .poetryfoundation.org/poem/173524.

34 James Joyce, *Portrait of the Artist as a Young Man* (New York: Viking, 1964), 169.

35 Thomas Mann, *The Magic Mountain* (New York: Knopf, 1955), 653.

36 See Thompson Clarke, "The Legacy of Skepticism," *Journal of Philosophy* 69 (1972): 754–69.

37 This approximates Annie Dillard's "Teaching a Stone to Talk," wherein Larry makes meaning by teaching a small stone to talk. The apparent absurdity of the proposition is denied when we come to understand Dillard's suggestions that talking is about attending to the silence that a stone has. See Dillard, "Teaching a Stone to Talk," in *Teaching a Stone to Talk* (New York: Harper Perennial, 1992), 87.

38 Dillard, "Teaching a Stone to Talk," 87.

39 Hans-Georg Gadamer, *Truth and Method* (New York: Continuum, 1998), 112–13.

40 Laurent Dubreuil, "What Is Literature's Now?" *New Literary History* 38, no. 1 (winter 2007): 66.

41 Martin Heidegger, "Hölderlin and the Essence of Poetry," in *Existence and Being*, ed. Werner Brock (London: Vision, 1968), 295–96.

42 Heidegger, "Hölderlin and the Essence of Poetry," 295–96.

43 Dubreuil, "What Is Literature's Now?," 66.

44 Heidegger, "Hölderlin and the Essence of Poetry," 310.

45 Rancière, "The Politics of Literature," 22.

46 Quoted from the preface in Arvind Sharma's *The Philosophy of Religion* (New Delhi: Oxford University Press, 1995).

Chapter 2: Literature Matters Today

1 Simona Sawney, *The Modernity of Sanskrit* (Minneapolis: University of Minnesota Press, 2008).

2 Alfred Lord Tennyson, "Tears, Idle Tears," accessed January 3, 2015, http://www.poemhunter.com/poem/tears-idle-tears/.

3 J. Hillis Miller, "Temporal Topographies: Tennyson's Tears," *EurAmerica* 21, no. 3 (1991): 29–45.

4 Paul de Man, "Conclusions: Walter Benjamin's 'The Task of the Translator,'" in *The Resistance to Theory* (Minneapolis: University of Minnesota Press, 1986), 87–88.

5 Jacques Derrida, "Forcener le subjectile," in *Antonin Artaud: Dessins et portraits* (Paris: Gallimard, 1996), 55–108; Jacques Derrida, "To Unsense the Subjectile," in *The Secret Art of Antonin Artaud*, trans. Mary Ann Caws (Cambridge, MA: MIT Press, 1998), 59–157.

6 J. Hillis Miller, *The Medium Is the Maker: Browning, Freud, Derrida, and the New Telepathic Ecotechnologies* (Brighton, UK: Sussex Academic Press, 2009).

7 Jacques Derrida, *Passions* (Paris: Galilée, 1993), 64–68; Jacques Derrida, "Passions: 'An Oblique Offering,'" in *On the Name*, ed. Thomas Dutoit (Stanford, CA: Stanford University Press, 1995), 28–30.

8 Jacques Derrida, "Envois," in *La carte postale: De Socrates à Freud et au-delà*, 5–273 (Paris: Flammarion, 1980), 212; Jacques Derrida, "Envois," in *The Post Card: From Socrates to Freud and Beyond*, trans. Alan Bass (Chicago: University of Chicago Press, 1987), 197.

9 French, 114–15; English, 104.

10 J. Hillis Miller, "Anachronistic Reading," *Derrida Today* 3 (10): 75–91.

11 Walter E. Houghton, *The Victorian Frame of Mind, 1830–1870* (New Haven, CT: Yale University Press, 1957); E. M. W. Tillyard, *The Elizabethan World Picture* (London: Chatto and Windus, 1943).

12 Paul de Man, "Conclusions," 87–88; Walter Benjamin, "Die Aufgabe des Übersetzers," in *Illuminationen: Ausgewählte Shrifte*, ed. Siegfried Unseld (Frankfurt am Main: Suhrkamp, 1955), 56–69; Walter Benjamin, "The Task of the Translator," in *Illuminations*, trans. Hannah Arendt (New York: Schocken Books, 1969), 69–82.

13 Jacques Derrida, "This Strange Institution Called Literature," in *Acts of Literature*, ed. Derek Attridge (London: Routledge, 1992), 44.

14 William Shakespeare, *Hamlet*, accessed January 4, 2015, http://shakespeare.mit.edu/hamlet/full.html.

15 John Milton, *Paradise Lost*, accessed January 4, 2015, http://www.literature.org/authors/milton-john/paradise-lost/chapter-01.html.

16 Jane Austen, *Pride and Prejudice*, accessed January 4, 2015, http://www.pemberley.com/janeinfo/ppv1n01.html.

17 William Wordsworth, "A Slumber Did My Spirit Seal," accessed January 4, 2015, http://www.poetryfoundation.org/poem/174822.

18 Tennyson, "Tears, Idle Tears."

19 Herman Melville, *Moby-Dick; or, the Whale*, accessed January 4, 2015, http://etext.virginia.edu/etcbin/toccer-new2?id=Me12Mob.sgm&images=images/modeng&data=/texts/english/modeng/parsed&tag=public&part=1&division=div1.

20 Anthony Trollope, *The Last Chronicle of Barset*, accessed January 4, 2015 at www.gutenberg.org.

21 W. B. Yeats, "The Cold Heaven," accessed January 4, 2015, http://www.poetryfoundation.org/poem/172059.

22 Marcel Proust, *À la recherche du temps perdu*, accessed January 5, 2015, http://beq.ebooksgratuits.com/vents/Proust_A_la_recherche_du_temps_perdu_01.pdf.

23 Wallace Stevens, 2011. "Oak Leaves Are Hands," accessed January 5, 2015, http://www.geegaw.com/stories/oak_leaves_are_hands.shtml.

24 Maurice Blanchot, "La voix narrative (le 'il,' le neutre)," in *L'Entretien infini* (Paris: Gallimard, 1969), 556–67; Maurice Blanchot, "The Narrative Voice (the 'He,' the Neutral)," in *The Infinite Conversation*, trans. Susan Hanson (Minneapolis: University of Minnesota Press. 1993), 379–87.

25 For a wonderful essay contrasting Japanese and German personal pronouns as a topic in Yoko Tawada's "Eine leere Flasche," see John Namjun Kim, "Ethnic Irony: The Poetic Parabasis of the Promiscuous Personal Pronoun in Yoko Tawada's 'Eine leere Flasche' (A Vacuous Flask)," *The German Quarterly* 83, no. 3 (2010): 333–52.

26 Paul de Man, "Sign and Symbol in Hegel's Aesthetics," in *Aesthetic Ideology*, ed. Andrzej Warminski (Minneapolis: University of Minnesota Press, 1996),

91–104; G. W. F. Hegel, *Enzyklopädie der philosophischen Wissenschaften*, in *Werke in zwanzig Bänden*, vols. 8–10 (Frankfurt am Main: Suhrkamp, 1979), 8:80, 8:74.

27 Nicholas Royle, "The 'Telepathy Effect': Notes toward a Reconsideration of Narrative Fiction," in *The Uncanny* (Manchester: Manchester University Press, 2003), 256–76.

28 Maurice Blanchot, "Les deux versions de l'imaginaire," in *L'espace littéraire*, (Paris: Gallimard, 1955), 266–77; Maurice Blanchot, "Two Versions of the Imaginary," in *The Gaze of Orpheus and Other Literary Essays*, trans. Lydia Davis (Barrytown, NY: Station Hill Press, 1981), 79–89; Maurice Blanchot, "Le chant des Sirènes," in *Le livre à venir* (Paris: Gallimard, 1959), 7–34; Maurice Blanchot, "The Song of the Sirens," in *The Book to Come*, trans. Charlotte Mandell (Stanford, CA: Stanford University Press, 2003), 1–24.

29 Wolfgang Iser, *Das Fiktive und das Imaginäre: Perspektiven literarische Anthropologie* (Frankfurt am Main: Suhrkamp, 1991); Wolfgang Iser, *The Fictive and the Imaginary: Charting Literary Anthropology* (Baltimore: Johns Hopkins University Press, 1993).

30 Iser, *Das Fiktive*, 1991, 21; Iser, *The Fictive*, 1993, 3.

31 Iser, *Das Fiktive*, 1991, 46; Iser, *The Fictive*, 1993, 18.

32 Iser, *Das Fiktive*, 1991, 24; Iser, *The Fictive*, 1993, 4

33 Iser, *Das Fiktive*, 1991, 38; Iser, *The Fictive*, 1993, 13.

34 Iser, *Das Fiktive*, 1991, 45; Iser, *The Fictive*, 1993, 17.

35 Iser, *Das Fiktive*, 1991, 46; Iser, *The Fictive*, 1993, 18.

36 Iser, *Das Fiktive*, 1991, 48; Iser, *The Fictive*, 1993, 19.

37 Iser, *Das Fiktive*, 1991, 51; Iser, *The Fictive*, 1993, 20–21.

38 Iser, *The Fictive*, 1993, xviii–xix; not in the German foreword.

39 Blanchot, "Le chant des Sirènes," 1959, 22; Blanchot, "The Song of the Sirens," 2003, 14.

40 See, for example, Blanchot's important essay "Literature and the Right to Death," in *The Work of Fire* (Stanford, CA: Stanford University Press, 1995), 300–344; Maurice Blanchot, *La part du feu* (Paris: Gallimard, 1949), 291–331.

41 Blanchot, "Le chant des Sirènes," 1959, 12–13; Blanchot, "The Song of the Sirens," 2003, 6–7.

42 Blanchot, "Le chant des Sirènes," 1959, 11–12; Blanchot, "The Song of the Sirens," 2003, 5.

43 Homer, *Odyssey*, trans. Robert Fitzgerald (Garden City, NY: Doubleday, 1963), 1.

Chapter 3: The Story of a Poem

Epigraphs: Mansour Àjami, *The Alchemy of Glory: The Dialectic of Truthfulness and Untruthfulness in Medieval Arabic Literary Criticism* (Washington, DC: Three

Continents Press, 1988); Wan Keping, *Spirit of Chinese Poetics* (Beijing: Foreign Language Press, 2008), 9; Joy Goswami, *Selected Poems: Joy Goswami* (New York: Harper Perennial, 2014), n.p.

1 Christopher Clausen, "Poetry in a Discouraging Time," *Georgia Review* 35, no. 4 (winter 1981): 703.

2 Dana Gioia, "Disappearing Ink: Poetry at the End of Print Culture," *Hudson Review* 56, no. 1 (spring 2003): 49.

3 Gioia, "Disappearing Ink: Poetry at the End of Print Culture," 49.

4 Clausen, "Poetry in a Discouraging Time," 708.

5 Dana Gioia, "Can Poetry Matter?" accessed August 16, 2015, www.danagioia .net/essays/ecpm.htm.

6 Edwin Muir, *The Estate of Poetry: Essays by Edwin Muir* (Minneapolis: Graywolf Press, 1993).

7 Wendell Berry, "The Specialization of Poetry," *Hudson Review* 28, no. 1 (spring 1975): 26.

8 Berry, "The Specialization of Poetry," 27.

9 Mary Oliver, "For the Man Cutting the Grass." *Georgia Review* 35, no. 4 (winter 1981): 733.

10 *Rasa* (Sanskrit: "essence," "taste," or "flavor," literally "sap" or "juice") is the "Indian concept of aesthetic flavour, an essential element of any work of visual, literary, or performing art that can only be suggested, not described. It is a kind of contemplative abstraction in which the inwardness of human feelings suffuses the surrounding world of embodied forms. The theory of rasa is attributed to Bharata, a sage-priest who may have lived sometime between the 1st century BCE and the 3rd century CE. It was developed by the rhetorician and philosopher Abhinavagupta (c. 1000), who applied it to all varieties of theater and poetry. The principal human feelings, according to Bharata, are delight, laughter, sorrow, anger, energy, fear, disgust, heroism, and astonishment, all of which may be recast in contemplative form as the various rasas: erotic, comic, pathetic, furious, heroic, terrible, odious, marvelous, and quietistic. These rasas comprise the components of aesthetic experience. The power to taste rasa is a reward for merit in some previous existence." Rasa, Indian Aesthetic Theory, accessed October 1, 2015, http://www.britannica .com/EBchecked/topic/491635/rasa.

"It may be pointed out here," writes Sushil Kumar De, "that [the] subtle conception of *Rasa* makes it difficult to express the notion properly in Western critical terminology. The word has been translated etymologically by the terms 'flavour,' 'relish,' 'gustation,' 'taste,' 'Geschmack,' or 'saveur'; but none of these renderings seems to be adequate. The simpler word 'mood,' or the term 'Stimmung' used by Jacobi may be the nearest approach to it, but the concept has hardly any analogy in European critical theory." See *History of Sanskrit Poetics*, 2nd ed. (Calcutta: Firma K. L. Mukhopadhyay, 1960), 2:135.

11 Lu Ji, "A Descriptive Poem on Literature," in *Early Chinese Literary Criticism*, ed. Sui-kit Wong (Hong Kong: Joint Publishing Company, 1983), 40–41.

12 Jibanananda Das, *Kobiter katha* [The story of a poem] (Kolkata: Signet, 1994), 7–8. The translation is mine.

13 See Andrea Gerbig and Anja Muller-Wood, "Trapped in Language: Aspects of Ambiguity and Intertextuality in Selected Prose and Poetry of Sylvia Plath," *Style* 36, no. 1 (spring 2002): 82.

14 Eliseo Vivas, "What Is a Poem?" *Sewanee Review* 62, no. 4 (October–December 1954): 594.

15 J. A. Honeywell, "The Poetic Theory of Viśvanatha," *Journal of Aesthetics and Art Criticism* 28, no. 2 (winter 1969): 172.

16 Ramaranjan Mukherjee, "Doctrine of Dhvani in Practical Application," in *East West Poetics at Work*, ed. C. D. Narasimhaiah (New Delhi: Sahitya Akademi, 1994), 124.

17 Mukherjee, "Doctrine of Dhvani," 128–29.

18 James J. Y. Liu, *Language-Paradox-Poetics: A Chinese Perspective* (Princeton, NJ: Princeton University Press, 1988), 42.

19 Liu, *Language-Paradox-Poetics*, 48.

20 Keping, *Spirit of Chinese Poetics*, 16–17.

21 Keping, *Spirit of Chinese Poetics*, 71.

22 Keping, *Spirit of Chinese Poetics*, 76. Jiang Kui writes: "A poem depends entirely on the last line; this is like stopping a galloping horse. When both the meaning and the words come to an end, it is like 'overlooking the water to see off someone going home'; when the meaning comes to an end but the words do not, it is like 'spiralling with a whirlwind'; when the words come to an end but the meaning does not, it is like the returning boat on the Shan stream; when both words and the meaning have no ending, it is like [meeting] Wenbo Xuezi" (73).

23 Charles Simic, "Notes on Poetry and Philosophy," *New Literary History* 21, no. 1 (autumn 1989): 218.

24 Brett Bourbon, "What Is a Poem?" *Modern Philology* 105, no. 1 (August 2007): 32.

25 Bourbon, "What Is a Poem?" 35.

26 Bourbon, "What Is a Poem?" 39.

27 Bourbon, "What Is a Poem?" 39.

28 Vincent Colapietro, "A Poet's Philosopher," *Transactions of the Charles S. Peirce Society* 45, no. 4 (fall 2009): 553.

29 George Santayana, *Little Essays* (London: Constable, 1924), 140.

30 William H. Poteat, "What Is a Poem About?" *Philosophy and Phenomenological Research* 17, no. 4 (June 1957): 547.

31 Jacques Maritain, "Poetic Experience," *Review of Politics* 6, no. 4 (October 1944): 393.

32 K. D. Sethna, *Talks on Poetry* (Pondicherry: Sri Aurobindo International Centre of Education, 1989), 330.

33 D. Semah, "Muḥammad Mandūr and the 'New Poetry,'" *Journal of Arabic Literature* 2 (1971): 151.

34 Semah, "Muḥammad Mandūr and the 'New Poetry,'" 152.

35 See Jean-Jacques Lecercle, *Badiou and Deleuze Read Literature* (Edinburgh: Edinburgh University Press, 2010), 100.

36 Maritain, "Poetic Experience," 398.

37 See Robert Frost, "The Figure a Poem Makes," accessed August 12, 2015, http://www.mrbauld.com/frostfig.html.

38 Holly Stevens, ed., *Letters of Wallace Stevens* (New York: Knopf, 1966), 319.

39 Samuel French Morse, ed., *Opus Posthumous* (New York: Knopf, 1957), 219–20.

40 Morse, *Opus Posthumous*, 226–27.

41 Wallace Stevens, *The Necessary Angel: Essays on Reality and the Imagination* (New York: Knopf, 1951), 58.

42 H. Stevens, *Letters of Wallace Stevens*, 544.

43 Aristotle writes: "The greatest thing by far is to be a master of metaphor. It is the one thing that cannot be learnt from others; and it is also a sign of genius, since a good metaphor implies an intuitive perception of the similarity in dissimilar." See Aristotle, *Poetics* (New York: Modern Library, 1954), 1459a, 255.

44 William Wordsworth, *The Prelude* [1850], book 2, "School Time," 11, 382–86.

45 Ali Asghar Seyed-Gohrab, ed., *Metaphor and Imagery in Persian Poetry* (Leiden: Brill, 2012), 9.

46 Michelle Yeh, "Metaphor and Bi: Western and Chinese Poetics," *Comparative Literature* 39, no. 3 (summer 1987): 245.

47 Yeh, "Metaphor and Bi," 246.

48 Kapil Kapoor, *Language, Linguistics, and Literature: The Indian Perspective* (Delhi: Academic Foundation, 1994), 126–27.

49 P. K. Mishra, trans., *Sahityadarpana* (Delhi: Motilal Banarsidass, 1967), 10, 28.

50 Hyde Cox and Edward Connery Lathem, eds., *Selected Prose of Robert Frost* (New York: Holt, Rinehart, and Winston, 1966), 77.

51 For more on this subject, see my "The Figure that Robert Frost's Poetics Make: Singularity and Sanskrit Poetic Theory," in *Singularity and Transnational Poetics*, ed. Birgit Kaiser (London: Routledge, 2015), 134–54.

52 Stevens writes in "Effects of Analogy": "A poet writes of twilight because he shrinks from noonday." Stevens, *The Necessary Angel*, 122.

53 Stevens, *The Necessary Angel*, 77.

54 Gadamer, *Truth and Method*, 238.

55 William H. Matchett, "What and Why Is a Poem?" *College English* 27, no. 5 (February 1966): 355.

56 Matchett, "What and Why Is a Poem?" 358.

57 H. G. Gadamer, "Composition and Interpretation," in *On the Relevance of the Beautiful* (Cambridge: Cambridge University Press, 1986), 67.

58 H. G. Gadamer, "Reflections on My Philosophical Journey," *Philosophy of Hans-Georg Gadamer* (Chicago: Open Court, 1997), 39.
59 Gadamer, "Reflections on My Philosophical Journey," 39.
60 See Christopher Lawn, "Gadamer on Poetic and Everyday Language," *Philosophy and Literature* 25, no. 1 (April 2001): 113–26.
61 George Santayana, *Interpretations of Poetry and Religion* (New York: Scribner's, 1900), 255–56.
62 Manuel Durán, "Octavio Paz: The Poet as Philosopher," *World Literature Today* 56, no. 4 (autumn 1982): 594.
63 Jonathan Mayhew, "Jorge Guillén and the Insufficiency of Poetic Language," *PMLA* 106, no. 5 (October 1991): 1146–55.
64 Gérard Genette, *Mimologiques: Voyage en cratylie* (Paris: Seuil, 1976).
65 Daniel H. H. Ingalls et al., trans. and ed., *The Dhvanyaloka of Anandavardhana with the Locana of Abhinavagupta* (Cambridge, MA: Harvard University Press, 1990), 19.
66 G. T. Despande, *Indian Poetics* (Mumbai: Popular Prakashan, 2009), 259.
67 Despande, *Indian Poetics*, 260–61.
68 Ming Dong Gu, *Chinese Theories of Reading and Writing: A Route to Hermeneutics and Open Poetics* (Albany: State University of New York, 2005), 47.
69 Liu, *Language-Paradox-Poetics*, 84.
70 S. K. De, "Kuntaka's Theory of Poetry," in *An Introduction to Indian Poetics*, ed. V. Raghavan and Nagendra (Bombay: Macmillan, 1970), 51.
71 Sethna, *Talks on Poetry*, 317–18.
72 Poteat, "What Is a Poem About?," 550.
73 See Sri Aurobindo, *Future of Poetry: Letters on Poetry, Literature and Art* (Pondicherry: Sri Aurobindo Ashram, 1972).
74 Liu, *Language-Paradox-Poetics*, 81.

Chapter 4: Western Theories of Poetry

1 Wallace Stevens, *Opus Posthumous*, ed. Samuel French Morse (New York: Knopf, 1957), 219–20.
2 Wallace Stevens, *The Collected Poems* (New York: Vintage, 1990), 285–408.
3 Stevens, *The Collected Poems*, 288.
4 Aristotle, *The Poetics*, trans. W. Hamilton Fyfe (Cambridge, MA: Harvard University Press, 1991), 1459a, 22:16–17, 90–91.
5 Wallace Stevens, *The Necessary Angel: Essays on Reality and the Imagination* (New York: Knopf, 1951); Wallace Stevens, *Opus Posthumous*.
6 Stevens, *Opus Posthumous*, 169.
7 Cleanth Brooks and Robert Penn Warren, *Understanding Poetry*, 4th ed. (New York: Holt, Rinehart and Winston, 1976).

8 Paul de Man, "Conclusions: Walter Benjamin's 'The Task of the Translator,'" in *The Resistance to Theory* (Minneapolis: University of Minnesota Press, 1986), 86, 88.

9 I have written elsewhere in detail about de Man's "The Resistance to Theory," which is in *The Resistance to Theory* (Minneapolis: University of Minnesota Press, 1986), 3–20. See J. Hillis Miller, "Reading Paul de Man While Falling into Cyberspace: In the Twilight of the Anthropocene Idols," in *Twilight of the Anthropocene Idols*, ed. Thomas Cohen, Claire Colebrook, and J. Hillis Miller (London: Open Humanities Press. 2016), 126–93.

10 Stevens, *The Collected Poems*, 9–10.

11 Stevens, *The Collected Poems*, 372–78.

12 Stevens, *Opus Posthumous*, 179.

13 Walter Benjamin, "Die Aufgabe des Übersetzers," in *Illuminationen: Ausgewählte Schriften* (Frankfurt am Main: Suhrkamp, 1969), 67; Walter Benjamin, "The Task of the Translator," *Illuminations* (New York: Schocken Books, 1969), 80.

14 See Aristotle, *The Poetics*, 1457b, 14–15, 81–83: "Sometimes there is no word for some of the terms of the analogy but the metaphor can be used all the same. For instance, to scatter seed is to sow, but there is no word for the action of the sun in scattering its fire. Yet this has to the sunshine the same relation as sowing has to the seed, and so you have the phrase 'sowing the god-created fire.'" Theology appears here once more, in this case in Aristotle's example of what is called, though Aristotle does not use the word here, a catachresis. Jacques Derrida, in his magisterial "La mythologie blanche" (white mythology), by far the greatest twentieth-century essay on metaphor, makes much of this passage in Aristotle and of the general role in theories of metaphor of the diurnal rising and setting of the sun. See Jacques Derrida, "La mythologie blanche: La métaphore dans le texte philosophique," *Marges de la philosophie* (Paris: Les Éditions de Minuit, 1972), 247–324; Jacques Derrida, "White Mythology: Metaphor in the Text of Philosophy," in *Margins of Philosophy*, trans. Alan Bass (Chicago: University of Chicago Press, 1982), 207–71. It is tempting to make a detour into a reading of Derrida's wonderful essay, but that would add a great many more pages, perhaps a hundred or so, to this essay, and I have sworn to keep my eye on Stevens's poem.

15 Stevens, *The Collected Poems*, 165, 373. The full sentence that contains the phrase about metaphor as evasion is a self-exhortation that says the reverse of what is said about (and done with) metaphor in "The Motive for Metaphor": "Let's see the very thing and nothing else, / Let's see it with the hottest fire of sight. / Burn everything not part of it to ash. / Trace the gold sun about the whitened sky / Without evasion by a single metaphor." The hot fire of the sun is here transferred by metaphor to the poet's eyesight, his ability to see what is really there, without evasion, by a lambent refinement like the purifying of metal in a forge. The figure of a forge appears in "The Motive

for Metaphor," though not explicitly in "Credences of Summer." In the latter poem, the sky is whitened not just because a bright, sunny day does that, but because the sun purifies the sky of the blue of imagination, source of metaphorical evasions. Stevens's locutions match the example in Aristotle about sun "sowing the god-created fire." The sun, it might be said, is, in the Western tradition from Aristotle on, the closest thing you can have to a visible sign of that fatal, dominant X named at the end of "The Motive for Metaphor." The reader will note that just as Aristotle imports a catachresis, *sowing*, to name what has no proper name, that is, "the actions of the sun in scattering its fire," so Stevens evades the nameless brightness of the sun by calling it gold. Gold is the most precious of metals and the measure of all other values, as in "gold standard." An exploration of these connections would take me far and would repay the doing, but would, once again (as have Aristotle, de Man, Derrida, and Stevens in his prose tempted me to let happen), divert me by way of attractive displacements and evasions from trying to see "The Motive for Metaphor" with the hottest fire of sight. So I desist, with difficulty.

16 A steel, by the way, is a small, cylindrical object made of serrated steel you hold in your hand as a tool to sharpen knives.

Chapter 5: More than Global

Epigraphs: See K. A. Subramania Iyer, ed., *The Vakyapadiya of Bhartrhari* (Delhi: Motilal Banarsidass, 1977); Pheng Cheah, "What Is a World?: On World Literature as World-Making Activity," *Daedalus* 137, no. 3 (summer 2008): 29; Tagore, "Visva-Sahitya" [1907], *Journal of Contemporary Thought* 34 (2011): 223, 213–25.

1 Djelal Kadir, "To Compare, to World: Two Verbs, One Discipline," *Comparatist* 34 (2010): 5. Reminded of Édouard Glissant's approach to problems of "world-totality," I see a chaos in our tryst with the global. That tryst leads to the contradictions and conflicts of strange pairings and moorings and conglomerates. The harmony among such "relational identities," working across borders, translocomoting through terrains of varied cultures, speaks both of intellectual vigilance, doubt, and opens the way to a proactive essence (the Deleuzian way). See Édouard Glissant, "The French Language in the Face of Creolization," in *French Civilization and Its Discontents: Nationalism, Colonialism, Race*, ed. Tyler Stovall and Georges van den Abbeele (Lanham, MD: Lexington Books, 2003), 108, 109, 112.

2 Wai Chee Dimock, "Planetary Time and Global Translation: 'Context' in Literary Studies," *Common Knowledge* 9, no. 3 (fall 2003): 489.

3 See Jean-Luc Nancy, *The Creation of the World or Globalization* (Albany: State University of New York, 2007), 28, 50.

4 Karen Barad, "Diffracting Diffraction: Cutting Together-Apart," *Parallax* 20, no. 3 (2014): 168. Also see Karen Barad, *Meeting the Universe Halfway: Quan-*

tum Physics and the Entanglement of Matter and Meaning (Durham, NC: Duke University Press, 2007).

5   Karen Barad, "Posthumanist Performativity: Toward an Understanding of How Matter Comes to Matter," *Signs: Journal of Women in Culture and Society* 28, no. 3 (2003): 815.

6   S. H. Rigby, *Marxism and History: A Critical Introduction* (Manchester, UK: Manchester University Press, 1998), 195.

7   See Jean-Paul Martinon, "Im-Mundus or Nancy's Globalizing-World-Formation," in *Nancy and the Political*, ed. Sanja Dejanovic (Edinburgh University Press, 2015). I thank Professor Martinon for sharing this chapter with me.

8   Victor Li, "Elliptical Interruptions," CR: *The New Centennial Review* 7, no. 2 (fall 2007): 148.

9   Jean-Luc Nancy, *Being Singular Plural* (Stanford, CA: Stanford University Press, 2000), xvi.

10   Nancy, *Being Singular Plural*, xvi.

11   Nancy, *Being Singular Plural*, 3.

12   Martta Heikkilä, *At the Limits of Presentation: Coming-into-Presence and Its Aesthetic Relevance in Jean-Luc Nancy's Philosophy* (Helsinki: Helsinki University Printing House, 2007), 116.

13   Zhang Longxi, *Mighty Opposites: From Dichotomies to Differences in the Comparative Study of China* (Stanford, CA: Stanford University Press, 1998), 83.

14   Henk Oosterling, "From Interests to 'Inter-esse': Jean-Luc Nancy on Deglobalization and Sovereignty," *SubStance* 34, no. 106 (2005): 85.

15   Serres, *The Five Senses: A Philosophy of Mingled Bodies* (London: Continuum, 2008), 258, 240.

16   Serres, *The Five Senses*, 262.

17   Serres, *The Five Senses*, 264.

18   Serres, *The Five Senses*, 271.

19   For a detailed analysis of the development of comparative world literature program and studies, see *Comparative Literature in the Age of Multiculturalism*, ed. Charles Bernheimer (Baltimore: Johns Hopkins University Press, 1995); A. Owen Aldridge, *The Reemergence of World Literature: A Study of Asia and the West* (Newark: University of Delaware Press, 1986); Robert J. Clements, *Comparative Literature as Academic Discipline: A Statement of Principles, Praxis, Standards* (New York: Modern Language Association of America, 1978); Claudio Guillén, *The Challenge of Comparative Literature*, trans. Cola Franzen (Cambridge, MA: Harvard University Press, 1993); John Pizer, *The Idea of World Literature: History and Pedagogical Practice* (Baton Rouge: Louisiana State University Press, 2006); John David Pizer, "Toward a Productive Interdisciplinary Relationship: Between Comparative Literature and World Literature," *Comparatist* 31 (May 2007): 6–28; Emily Apter, *The Translation Zone: A New Comparative Literature* (Princeton, NJ: Princeton University

Press, 2006), 41–64; David Damrosch, *What Is World Literature?* (Princeton, NJ: Princeton University Press, 2003); Gayatri Chakravorty Spivak, *Death of a Discipline* (New York: Columbia University Press, 2003); Steven Totosy de Zepetnek, ed., *Comparative Literature and Comparative Cultural Studies* (West Lafayette, IN: Purdue University Press, 2003).

20 Jonathan D. Culler, "Whither Comparative Literature?" *Comparative Critical Studies* 3, nos. 1–2 (2006): 89.

21 Fernando Cabo Aseguinolaza, "Dead, or a Picture of Good Health?: Comparatism, Europe, and World Literature," *Comparative Literature* 58, no. 4 (fall 2006): 419.

22 Jonathan Arac, "Anglo-Globalism?" *New Left Review* 1, no. 6 (July–August 2002): 35–45.

23 The concern is about resurrecting literature from the fuss and fizz of world literature. I want to see it freed from the uncritical comparative modes of doing literature, from Franco Moretti's sweeping categorizations, and from the seeming authority of acknowledged universals of "global literature." Anders Pettersson's observations come very close to my concerns here: "Not only do I think that Moretti fails to analyze the concept of world literature, and that he fails, a fortiori, to derive a method for the study of world literature from the analysis, but I already regard it as a mistake to pose the question of what world literature 'is' as a factual question." "Transcultural Literary History: Beyond Constricting Notions of World Literature," *New Literary History* 39, no. 3 (2008): 473.

24 See Lesley Sharpe, ed.,*The Cambridge Companion to Goethe* (Cambridge: Cambridge University Press, 2002); Fritz Strich, *Goethe and World Literature* (New York: Hafner, 1949); Alec G. Hargreaves, Charles Forsdick, David Murphy, *Transnational French Studies: Postcolonialism and Littérature-monde* (Liverpool: Liverpool University Press, 2010); John D. Pizer, *Imagining the Age of Goethe in German Literature, 1970–2010* (Rochester: Camden House, 2011); Elke Sturm-Trigonakis, *Comparative Cultural Studies and the New Weltliteratur* (West Lafayette, IN: Purdue University Press, 2013).

25 Zhang Longxi, *Unexpected Affinities: Reading across Cultures* (Toronto: University of Toronto Press, 2007), 55.

26 See Rosi Braidotti, *Transpositions: On Nomadic Ethics* (Cambridge: Polity, 2006).

27 Steven G. Yao, "The Unheimlich Maneuver; or the Gap, the Gradient, and the Spaces of Comparison," *Comparative Literature* 57, no. 3 (summer 2005): 252.

28 Nicholas Royle, *Veering: A Theory of Literature* (Edinburgh: Edinburgh University Press, 2011), 3.

29 Royle, *Veering*, 4.

30 Paul Celan, *Collected Prose*, trans. Rosemarie Waldrop (Manchester, UK: Carcanet, 1986), 35.

31 Didier Coste, "Is a Non-Global Universe Possible?: What Universals in the Theory of Comparative Literature (1952–2002) Have to Say about It," *Comparative Literature Studies* 41, no. 1 (2004): 47.

32 Tagore, "Visva-Sahitya," 213.

33 Tagore, "Visva-Sahitya," 214 (my emphases).

34 Tagore, "Visva-Sahitya," 217.

35 Bill Ashcroft, "Transcultural Presence," *Storia della Storiografia* 55 (2009): 76. Also see Ranjan Ghosh and Ethan Kleinberg, eds., *Presence: Philosophy, History, and Cultural Theory for the 21st Century* (Ithaca, NY: Cornell University Press, 2013).

36 Jean-Luc Nancy, *The Birth to Presence* (Stanford, CA: Stanford University Press, 1993), 2.

37 Nancy, *The Birth to Presence*, 4.

38 Wai Chee Dimock, "A Theory of Resonance," PMLA 112, no. 5 (1997): 1061.

39 T. R. Sharma, *Toward an Alternative Critical Discourse* (Shimla: Indian Institute of Advanced Study, 2000), 10–11.

40 Raimundo Pannikar, "What Is Comparative Philosophy Comparing?" In *Interpreting Across Boundaries: New Essays in Comparative Philosophy*, ed. Gerald J. Larson and Eliot Deutsch (Princeton, NJ: Princeton University Press, 1988), 116–36. He writes: "Diatopical hermeneutics is an art as much as a science, a praxis as much as a theory. It is a creative encounter, and there is no blueprint for creativity" (133). The more than global does not have any blueprint either.

41 G. N. Devy, *After Amnesia: Tradition and Change in Indian Literary Criticism* (London: Sangam Books, 1992), 78–82.

42 For more on these lines, see Ranjan Ghosh,"Institutionalised Theory, (In)fusion, Desivad," *Oxford Literary Review* 28 (2006): 25–36.

43 Dorothy Wordsworth, *Journals of Dorothy Wordsworth*, 2 vols. (New York: Macmillan, 1941), April 15, 1802, 1:131.

44 William Wordsworth, *The Poetical Works of William Wordsworth*, 2d ed. (Oxford: Clarendon, 1952–59), 2:507n, 187.

45 Urs Stäheli, "The Outside of the Global," CR: *The New Centennial Review* 3, no. 2 (summer 2003): 14.

46 See S. Radhakrishnan, *Principal Upanisads* (New Delhi: HarperCollins, 2006).

47 Steve Odin, *Process Metaphysics and Hua-yen Buddhism: A Critical Study of Cumulative Penetration vs. Interpenetration* (Albany: State University of New York Press, 1982), 5.

48 See Michel Deguy, "Apparition du nom," in *Actes* (Paris: Gallimard, 1966), 245–47. Also see Jacques Derrida, "Comment nommer," in *Le poète que je cherche à être*, ed. Yves Charnet (Paris: Table Ronde, 1996), 189.

49 Arthur Rimbaud, "Je est un autre." In *Illuminations* (New York: New Directions, 1957), xxvii.

50 Sankaracarya, *Brahma Sutra Bhasya*, trans. Swami Gambhirananda (Advaita Ashram, 2000).

51 Rabindranath Tagore, "Sense of Beauty." In *Angel of Surplus*, ed. Sisir Kumar Ghose (Calcutta: Visva-Bharati, 1978), 54.

52 B. C. Hutchens, *Jean-Luc Nancy and the Future of Philosophy* (Montreal: McGill-Queen's University Press, 2005), 12.

53 Hutchens, *Jean-Luc Nancy and the Future of Philosophy*, 38.

54 Oosterling, "From Interests to 'Inter-esse,'" 86, 88.

55 See James J. Y. Liu, *Language-Paradox-Poetics: A Chinese Perspective* (Princeton, NJ: Princeton University Press, 1988), 21; emphasis mine.

56 Quoted from John G. Rudy, *Wordsworth and the Zen Mind* (Albany: State University of New York Press, 1996), 28.

57 "Criticism must be transcendental, that is, must consider literature ephemeral and easily entertain the supposition of its entire disappearance," Ralph Waldo Emerson, journal, May 18, 1840, quoted in *The Fateful Question of Culture*, ed. Geoffrey Hartman (New York: Columbia University Press, 1997), 5.

58 Nancy, *Hegel: The Restlessness of the Negative* (Minneapolis: University of Minnesota Press, 2002), 44.

59 Oosterling, "From Interests to 'Inter-esse,'" 94–95.

60 Hutchens, *Jean-Luc Nancy and the Future of Philosophy*, 51.

Chapter 6: Globalization and World Literature

1 Karl Marx and Friedrich Engels, "The Communist Manifesto," accessed January 24, 2015, http://www.marxists.org/archive/marx/works/1848/communist-manifesto/.

2 Claire Colebrook, in an essay entitled "A Globe of One's Own: In Praise of the Flat Earth," which I have seen in manuscript, sent me back to Satan's space-travel in Milton. Her essay has been provocative for me in other ways, too, as have recent manuscript essays on "Critical Climate Change" by Tom Cohen.

3 See J. Hillis Miller, "Tales out of (the Yale) School," in *Theoretical Schools and Circles in the Twentieth-Century Humanities: Literary Theory, History, Philosophy*, ed. Marina Grishakova and Silvi Salupere (New York: Routledge, 2015), 115–32.

4 Gilles Deleuze and Félix Guattari, *Kafka: Toward a Minor Literature*, trans. Dana Polan (Minneapolis: University of Minnesota Press, 1986).

5 David Damrosch, *What Is World Literature?* (Princeton, NJ: Princeton University Press, 2003), 5.

6 Damrosch, *What Is World Literature?*, 4–5.

7 Johann Wolfgang von Goethe, *Conversations with Eckermann*, ed. J. K. Morehead, trans. John Oxenford (London: Everyman, 1930), 132. The conversations with Eckermann originally occurred between 1823 and 1832.

8 *King Lear*, 4.6.16.

9 Paul de Man, "Genesis and Genealogy (Nietzsche)," in *Allegories of Reading: Figural Language in Rousseau, Nietzsche, Rilke, and Proust* (New Haven, CT: Yale

University Press, 1979), 79–101; Andrzej Warminski, "Reading for Example: A Metaphor in Nietzsche's Birth of Tragedy," in *Readings in Interpretation: Hölderlin, Hegel, Heidegger* (Minneapolis: University of Minnesota Press, 1987), xxxv–lxi; Andrzej Warminski, "Terrible Reading (Preceded by 'Epigraphs')," in *Responses: Paul de Man's Wartime Journalism* (Lincoln: University of Nebraska Press, 1989), 386–96; Carol Jacobs, "The Stammering Text: The Fragmentary Studies Preliminary to The Birth of Tragedy," in *The Dissimulating Harmony: The Image of Interpretation in Nietzsche, Rilke, Artaud, and Benjamin* (Baltimore: Johns Hopkins University Press. 1978), 1–22; Thomas Albrecht, "A 'Monstrous Opposition': The Double Dionysus and the Double Apollo in Nietzsche's Birth of Tragedy," in *The Medusa Effect: Representation and Epistemology in Victorian Aesthetics* (Albany: State University of New York Press, 2009), 51–70.

10 Friedrich Nietzsche, "Vom Nutzen und Nachtheil der Historie für das Leben," in *Sämtliche Werke*, ed. Giorgio Colli and Mazzino Montinari (Munich: Walter de Gruyter, 1988), 1:243–334; Friedrich Nietzsche, "On the Utility and Liability of History for Life," in *Unfashionable Observations*, vol. 2 of *The Complete Works*, 83–167 (Stanford, CA: Stanford University Press, 1995).

11 Friedrich Nietzsche, *The Birth of Tragedy and The Case of Wagner*, trans. Walter Kaufmann (New York: Vintage, 1967), 110; Friedrich Nietzsche, "Die Geburt der Tragödie," in *Sämtliche Werke*, ed. Giorgio Colli and Mazzino Montinari (Munich: Walter de Gruyter, 1988), 1:9–156. The German original of the citation is on p. 116.

12 Harold Bloom, *The Anxiety of Influence: A Theory of Poetry* (New York: Oxford University Press, 1973).

13 Nietzsche, *The Birth of Tragedy*, 111.

14 Nietzsche, *The Birth of Tragedy*, 143; Nietzsche, "Die Geburt der Tragödie," 155.

15 Nietzsche, *The Birth of Tragedy*, 143.

16 Nietzsche, *The Birth of Tragedy*, 143.

17 Nietzsche, *The Birth of Tragedy*, 143.

18 T. S. Eliot, "Burnt Norton," in *The Collected Poems and Plays: 1909–1950* (New York: Harcourt, Brace, 1952), 118.

19 Nietzsche, *The Birth of Tragedy*, 143.

20 Nietzsche, *The Birth of Tragedy*, 143.

21 Jacobs, "The Stammering Text"; Friedrich Nietzsche, "Nachgelassene Fragmente, 1869–1874," in *Sämtliche Werke*, ed. Giorgio Colli and Mazzino Montinari (Munich: Walter de Gruyter, 1988), 7:269–331.

22 Jacobs, "The Stammering Text," 20–22.

23 Nietzsche, *The Birth of Tragedy*, 130.

24 Warminski, in "Reading for Example," discusses catachresis in his reading of a metaphor in *The Birth of Tragedy* (liii–lxi).

25 *Jenseits von Gut und Böse*, in *Sämtliche Werke*, vol. 5, ed. Giorgio Colli and Mazzino Montinari, 9–243 (Munich: Walter de Gruyter, 1988), 182. I have used Beebee's unidentified translation.
26 Nietzsche, *The Birth of Tragedy*, 110–11.
27 Nietzsche, *The Birth of Tragedy*, 113–14.
28 Here appears again the figure of the tame shore as against the dangerous ocean of universal knowledge, or, in this case, the icy current of existence. "Knowledge" and "existence" are by no means the same, however. The import of the metaphor is reversed in the second example, as happens with so much else in the language of *The Birth of Tragedy*. In the first citation, universal Socratic knowledge is seen as bad, debilitating. In the second citation, man is seen as too timid to entrust himself, as he should do, to the icy waters of existence.
29 Nietzsche, *The Birth of Tragedy*, 113.
30 Nietzsche, *The Birth of Tragedy*, 144.
31 Nietzsche, *The Birth of Tragedy*, 144.
32 George Eliot, *Middlemarch* (Harmondsworth, UK: Penguin, 1974), 229. The Cabeiri were a group of Samothracian fertility gods, the note in the Penguin *Middlemarch* tells me, with Casaubon-like learning.
33 Eliot, *Middlemarch*, 96.

Chapter 7: Reinventing the Teaching Machine

Epigraphs: Jacques Derrida, "Where a Teaching Body Begins and How It Ends," in *Who Is Afraid of Philosophy?: Right to Philosophy I*, trans. J. Plug (Stanford, CA: Stanford University Press, 2002), 77; Fredric Jameson, *The Political Unconscious: Narrative as a Socially Symbolic Act* (Ithaca, NY: Cornell University Press, 1981), 45.

1 Marjorie Garber, *Academic Instincts* (Princeton, NJ: Princeton University Press, 2003), 53.
2 Garber, *Academic Instincts*, 60.
3 Marjorie Garber, "Good to Think With," *Profession* (2008): 12.
4 Garber, "Good to Think With," 13.
5 Suzanne Clark, "Discipline and Resistance," in *Margins in the Classroom: Teaching Literature*, ed. Kostas Myrsiades and Linda S. Myrsiades (Minneapolis: Minnesota University Press, 1994), 122.
6 See Joseph Epstein, *Alexis de Tocqueville: Democracy's Guide* (New York: HarperCollins, 2006), 119.
7 Also see Ranjan Ghosh, ed. *In Dialogue with Godot: Waiting and Other Thoughts* (Lanham, MD: Lexington Books, 2013), where I have provided a new reading of *Waiting for Godot* ("Waiting upon Each Other: Work and Play in Waiting for Godot") from an (in)fusionist perspective, keeping Hindu philosophy as the pervasive paradigm of intervention.

8 Rukmini Bhaya Nair, "Dissimilar Twins," in *The Lie of the Land*, ed. Rajeswari Sunder Rajan (Delhi: Oxford University Press, 1992), 265–66.

9 Roland Barthes noted that interdisciplinary approaches "consist in creating a new object, which belongs to no one." See Garber, "Good to Think With," 72. Also see Theodor Adorno, *Kant's Critique of Pure Reason*, ed. Rolf Tiedemann, trans. Rodney Livingstone (Stanford, CA: Stanford University Press, 2001).

10 Louis Menand, "Dangers within and without Author(s)," *Profession* (2005): 14.

11 Douglas Steward, "Taking Liberties: Academic Freedom and the Humanities," *Profession* (2008), 167; emphases mine.

12 Rey Chow, "The Old/New Question of Comparison in Literary Studies," ELH 71 (2004): 303.

13 Terry Eagleton, *Against the Grain: Selected Essays, 1975–1985* (London: Verso, 1986), 139.

14 Vilashini Cooppan, "Ghosts in the Disciplinary Machine: The Uncanny Life of World Literature," *Comparative Literature Studies* 41 (2004): 21.

15 John M. Koller, "Dharma: An Expression of Universal Order," *Philosophy East and West* 22 (1972): 134.

16 Sarvepalli Radhakrishnan, *The Hindu View of Life* (New Delhi: Indus, 1993), 56.

17 J. A. B. van Buitenen, "Dharma and Moksha," *Philosophy East and West* 7 (1957): 35–36.

18 *Samkhya-Karika*, verse 1, accessed August, 21, 2015, http://www.ivantic.net /Moje_knjige/karika.pdf.

19 Samuel Beckett, *Proust* (New York: Grove Press, 1931), 48. The problem is that there is no Russellian spirit as evidenced in "Free Man's Worship," or the spirit that Camus tries to foreground that suggests the effort to face agony, absurdity, vacuity, and "unpleasure" with stolid boldness. All references to the play are from *Endgame* (London: Faber, 1970).

20 Baruch Spinoza, *Works of Spinoza*, ed. and trans. R. H. M. Elwes, 2 vols. (New York: Dover, 1955), 2:3.

21 A. C. Danto, *Mysticism and Morality* (New York: Penguin Books, 1976), 56.

22 Rabindranath Tagore, *Sadhana* (Madras: Macmillan, 1979), 40.

23 Samuel Beckett, *Endgame* (London: Faber, 1970), 48.

24 Beckett, *Endgame*, 23.

25 Beckett, *Endgame*, 24.

26 See Karen Horney, *Neurosis and Human Growth* (New York: W. W. Norton, 1950). She clarifies the responsibility of consciousness where the "real self" forms the central inner core and becomes the deep source of growth. The question arises as to the extent to which Hamm and Clov have realized the significance of a generative center of being. A growth that combines both the vertical and the horizontal axes points to a harmonious development and unfolds itself sufficiently on the road of a self-enriching dharma of existence. For more pertinent references to Gita, see S. Radhakrishnan, *The Bhagavad Gita* (New Delhi: HarperCollins, 2011), especially sections 14, 16, and 18.

27 See Hannah Arendt, *The Life of the Mind* (New York: Harcourt Brace Jovanovich, 1978).

28 William E. Hocking, *Human Nature and Its Remaking* (New York: AMS Press 1976), 118–23.

29 Tagore, *Sadhana*, 57.

30 Beckett, *Endgame*, 47.

31 Beckett, *Endgame*, 33.

32 See Abraham H. Maslow, *Religions, Values, and Peak Experiences* (New York: Penguin, 1976); also by the same author, *Further Reaches of Human Nature* (New York: Viking, 1970).

33 Beckett, *Endgame*, 26.

34 Beckett, *Endgame*, 19.

35 Herman Keyserling, *From Suffering to Fulfilment*, trans. Jane Marshall (London: Selwyn and Blount, 1938), 122–24, 250–51, 257–58.

36 Beckett, *Endgame*, 43.

37 Beckett, *Endgame*, 28.

38 Beckett, *Endgame*, 28.

39 Mario Puglisi, *Prayer*, trans. Bernard M. Allen (New York: Macmillan, 1929), 211.

40 Thomas Nagel, *Mortal Questions* (Cambridge: Cambridge University Press, 1979), 14.

41 For Beckett, any perception of the "core" is problematic and very difficult to define. The "essence" of a thing remains elusive and defies formalization. Instances of this order are plentifully available in *The Unnamable* (1953). The sense of a fundamental unity is sorely lacking, which means that the metaphysical experiences of several of his protagonists are devoid of stability, permanence, and a transcendental joy. There is, thus, a relishing of passivity, an aspiration to revel in the freedom from the cardinal compulsion to cogit, "the great classical paralysis" (Molloy in *Three Novels* by Samuel Beckett [London: John Calder, 1956], 140). The inability to define the nature of reality and the virtual inexpressibility of the core of reality are the two issues that have primarily troubled me here; this means that the two characters cannot have the strength of the intellect to thrash out a significant view of the world. It is the "ordering" of the experiences and formalization of the chaos within that cry sorely for attention; despite the dim prospect of its eventual realization, the dharma of existence demands this inner reconstruction, which is what I ascribe to the inner emigration.

42 Beckett, *Endgame*, 25.

43 In the English translation, the boy is feared as "a potential procreator." There is a fearful possibility of his living on as the boy pushes at the horizons of a refigured dharma of existence where the possibility of a new order of life, a new cycle, and a new earth come to the fore, threatening to obviate the hith-

erto adharmic, existential coils. I believe that the significance of the "small boy" is more emphatically expressed in the French version.

44 Rabindranath Tagore, *Gitanjali* (London: Macmillan, 1921), 23.

45 K. Burch, *Eros as the Educational Principle of Democracy* (New York: Peter Lang, 2000), 180; see Gilbert Ryle, *The Concept of Mind* (London: Hutchinson, 1949).

46 Jane Gallop, "The Historicization of Literary Studies and the Fate of Close Reading," *Profession* (2007): 181–86.

47 Jody Norton, "Guerrilla Pedagogy: Conflicting Authority and Interpretation in the Classroom," *College Literature* 21, no. 3 (October 1994): 141.

48 Norton, "Guerrilla Pedagogy," 141.

49 Tejeswani Niranjana, "Siting the Teacher," in *The Lie of the Land*, 206.

50 Marshall Gregory, "Do We Teach Disciplines or Do We Teach Students? What Difference Does It Make?" *Profession* (2008): 127.

51 See Adnan M. Wazzan, "Arabia in Poetry," *Islamic Studies* 29, no. 1 (spring 1990): 93.

52 Yeats, "Note to the Only Jealousy of Emer," in *The Variorum Edition of the Plays of W. B. Yeats*, ed. Russell K. Alspach (New York: Macmillan, 1966), 568.

53 Gregory Ulmer, *Applied Grammatology: Post(e)-Pedagogy from Jacques Derrida to Joseph Beuys* (Baltimore: Johns Hopkins University Press, 1985), 169.

54 Shoshana Felman, "Psychoanalysis and Education: Teaching Terminable and Interminable," *Yale French Studies* 63 (1982): 23.

55 Felman, "Psychoanalysis and Education," 30.

56 See Roger I. Simon, *Teaching against the Grain: Texts for a Pedagogy of Possibility* (New York: Bergin and Garvey, 1992), 97.

Chapter 8: Should We Read or Teach Literature Now?

1 James Joyce, *Finnegans Wake* (New York: Viking Press, 1947), 303.

2 An enormous literature published over the last decades tracking this transformation exists. Among recent books and essays are Marc Bousquet, *How the University Works: Higher Education and the Low-Wage Nation* (New York: New York University Press, 2008); Christopher Newfield, *Unmaking the Public University: The Forty-Year Assault on the Middle Class* (Cambridge, MA: Harvard University Press, 2008); Frank Donoghue, *The Last Professors: The Corporate University and the Fate of the Humanities* (New York: Fordham University Press, 1998); Jeffrey J. Williams, *How to Be an Intellectual: Essays on Criticism, Culture, and the University* (New York: Fordham University Press, 2014). All these have extensive bibliographies. Peggy Kamuf, "Counting Madness," in *The Future of the Humanities: U.S. Domination and Other Issues*, a special issue of *Oxford Literary Review*, ed. Timothy Clark and Nicholas Royle, vol. 28 (2006): 67–77.

3   Quoted in Frank Donoghue, "Prestige," in *Profession* (New York: Modern Language Association of America, 2006), 156.

4   Richard C. Levin, "The Rise of Asia's Universities," January 31, 2010, The Royal Society, London, England, accessed April 29, 2016, http://communications .yale.edu/president/speeches/2010/01/31/rise-asia-s-universities.

5   See Mat Honan, "Fast, Loud, and Mostly True: Inside the All-New Buzz-Fueled American Media Machine," *Wired Magazine*, 23, no. 1 (January 2015): 67.

6   See Sam Frank's fascinating essay about one facet of the digital revolution, the springing up of visionary prophets predicting, among other things, a dangerous robotic future powered by computers. It is dangerous because the computers may begin thinking for themselves and turn against their human creators: "Come with Us If You Want to Live: Among the Apocalyptic Libertarians of Silicon Valley," *Harper's*, January 2015, 26–36.

7   A recent report, published April 2015, by a committee of the American Academy of Arts and Sciences, The State of the Humanities: Higher Education 2015 (available online at http://www.humanitiesindicators.org/binaries/pdf/HI _HigherEd2015.pdf) takes a somewhat more cheerful view, emphasizing, for example, that there has been no increase in the percentage of adjuncts and part-time faculty in the humanities (it is already over 70 percent), the increased number of students who do humanities as a second major, and an increase in course credits in the humanities even as the humanities' share of undergraduate degrees has been shrinking. The report is primarily based on statistical surveys, however. It would be interesting, for example, to know just what the content of those courses typically is. How many are in English composition, which is what most adjuncts in English departments primarily teach?

8   See Paul Krugman, "Tidings of Comfort," *New York Times*, December 26, 2014.

9   Jacques Derrida, *L'Université sans condition* (Paris: Galilée, 2001); Jacques Derrida, "The University without Condition," in *Without Alibi*, ed. and trans. Peggy Kamuf, 202–37 (Stanford, CA: Stanford University Press, 2002).

10 "What, me worry?" is the motto of that iconic nonworrier, Alfred E. Neuman, in *Mad Magazine*. See the Wikipedia entry for *Mad Magazine*.

11 Donoghue, "Prestige," 20.

12 John Keats, "On Sitting Down to Read King Lear Once Again," accessed September 6, 2010, http://www.poemhunter.com/poem/on-sitting-down-to-read -king-lear-once-again/.

13 Howard Foster Lowry, ed., *The Letters of Matthew Arnold to Arthur Hugh Clough* (London: Oxford University Press, 1932), 96.

14 For a proposal for such courses, see David Pogue's interview of John Palfrey, Harvard Law School professor and codirector of Harvard's Berkman Center for Internet and Society (accessed September 6, 2010, http://www.nytimes .com/indexes/2010/07/22/technology/personaltechemail/index.html).

15 W. B. Yeats, *The Variorum Edition of the Poems*, ed. Peter Allt and Russell K. Alspach (New York: Macmillan, 1977), 316.

16 J. Hillis Miller, "W. B. Yeats: 'The Cold Heaven,'" in *Others* (Princeton, NJ: Princeton University Press, 2001), 170–82.

17 The saying ("Die Rose ist ohne warum; sie blühet weil sie blühet") is cited in the original German by Jorge Luis Borges, "La cábala," *Siete Noches* (Mexico City: Fondo de Cultura Económica, 1980), 120–21; Jorge Luis Borges, "The Kabbalah," *Seven Nights*, trans. Eliot Weinberger (New York: New Directions, 1984), 94. See also Angelus Silesius, *The Cherubic Wanderer*, trans. Maria Shrady (New York: Paulist Press, 1986).

18 A. Norman Jeffares, *A Commentary on the Collected Poems of W. B. Yeats* (Stanford, CA: Stanford University Press, 1968), 146.

19 Yeats, *Variorum Edition of the Poems*, 269.

20 Paul de Man, "The Resistance to Theory," in *The Resistance to Theory* (Minneapolis: University of Minnesota Press, 1986), 11.

Chapter 9: The Ethics of Reading Sahitya

Epigraphs: B. J. Hiley and F. David Peat, eds., *Quantum Implications: Essays in Honour of David Bohm* (London: Routledge, 1991), 350; Georges Bataille, *Eroticism*, trans. M. Dalwood (London, 1987), 19.

1 Derek Attridge, ed., *Acts of Literature* (London: Routledge, 1992), 5.

2 Mikhail M. Bakhtin, *Speech Genres and Other Late Essays*, ed. Caryl Emerson and Michael Holquist, trans. Vern W. McGee (Austin: University of Texas Press, 1986), 170.

3 Elizabeth Grosz, *Chaos, Territory, Art*, 9.

4 G. Deleuze and F. Guattari, *What Is Philosophy?*, trans. Hugh Tomlinson and Graham Burchell (New York: Columbia University Press, 1994), 206.

5 Oswald de Andrade and Leslie Bary, "Cannibalist Manifesto," *Latin American Literary Review* 1, no. 38 (July–December 1991): 36.

6 Andrade and Bary, "Cannibalist Manifesto," 38, 39.

7 Andrade and Bary, "Cannibalist Manifesto," 38.

8 Kenneth David Jackson, "A View on Brazilian Literature: Eating the Revista de Antropofagia," *Latin American Literary Review* 7, no. 13 (fall–winter 1978): 3.

9 Rachel Galvin, "Poetry Is Theft," *Comparative Literature Studies* 51, no. 1 (2014): 20.

10 For some interesting documentation of Arnold's engagement with the Orient, see Martin William and R. Jarrett-Kerr, "Arnold Versus the Orient: Some Footnotes to a Disenchantment," *Comparative Literature Studies* 12, no. 2 (June 1975): 129–46.

11 V. S. Seturaman, "The Scholar Gipsy and Oriental Wisdom," *Review of English Studies* 9, no. 36 (November 1958): 413.

12 Seturaman, "The Scholar Gipsy and Oriental Wisdom," 412.

13 R. H. Super, ed., *The Complete Prose Works of Matthew Arnold* (Ann Arbor: University of Michigan Press, 1960–1977), 1:215.

14 Super, *The Complete Prose Works of Matthew Arnold*, 6:168.

15 Arnold, "On the Modern Element in Literature," *The Complete Prose Works of Matthew Arnold*, 1:21.

16 Quoted in Brendan Rapple, "Matthew Arnold and Comparative Education," *British Journal of Educational Studies* 37, no. 1 (February 1989): 58.

17 See Donald D. Stone, "Matthew Arnold and the Pragmatics of Hebraism and Hellenism," *Poetics Today* 19, no. 2 (summer 1998): 185.

18 Shirley Robin Letwin, "Matthew Arnold: Enemy of Tradition," *Political Theory* 10, no. 3 (August 1982): 338.

19 Brenda Machosky, "Fasting at the Feast of Literature," *Comparative Literature Studies* 42, no. 2 (2005): 290.

20 Machosky, "Fasting at the Feast of Literature," 304.

21 Friedrich Nietzsche, *The Gay Science*, trans. Walter Kaufmann (New York: Vintage, 1974), 382.

22 Edmund Husserl, "Philosophy as a Rigorous Science," in *Husserl: Shorter Works*, ed. Peter McCormick and Frederick A. Elliston (Notre Dame, IN: University of Notre Dame Press, 1981), 196.

23 See Mitchell Waldrop, *Complexity: The Emerging Science at the Edge of Chaos* (New York: Simon and Schuster, 1993), 146.

24 Ian Stewart, *Does God Play Dice?: The Mathematics of Chaos* (Cambridge, MA: Blackwell, 1989), 17.

25 John L. Casti, *Complexification: Explaining a Paradoxical World through the Science of Surprise* (New York: HarperCollins, 1994), 276; see also 170.

26 Ralph Waldo Emerson, "Nature," in *Selected Writings*, ed. Brooks Atkinson (New York: Random House, 1950), 20.

27 Karen Barad, "Posthumanist Performativity: Toward an Understanding of How Matter Comes to Matter," *Signs: Journal of Women in Culture and Society* 28, no. 3 (2003): 810.

28 Barad, "Posthumanist Performativity," 815.

29 Barad, "Posthumanist Performativity," 815.

30 Barad, "Posthumanist Performativity," 817.

31 Barad, "Posthumanist Performativity," 817.

32 David Baird, *Thing Knowledge: A Philosophy of Scientific Instruments* (Berkeley: University of California Press, 2004), 145.

33 Baird, *Thing Knowledge*, 146.

34 Robert Frost, "For Once, Then, Something," accessed September 19, 2015, http://www.poetryfoundation.org/poem/173528.

35 Graham Harman, "The Well-Wrought Broken Hammer: Object Oriented Literary Criticism," *New Literary History* 43, no. 2 (2012): 201–2.

36 The connections between Harman's object-oriented ontology and that ethics of sahitya as explicated in this chapter need further elaboration, which I hope to bring out someday. Some interesting recent additions to this line of scholarship dealing with humanities and OOO come from Richard Grusin,

ed., *The Non Human Turn* (Minnesota: University of Minnesota Press, 2015); Ming Xie, ed., *The Agon of Interpretations: Towards a Critical Intercultural Hermeneutics* (Toronto: University of Toronto Press, 2014); Timothy Morton, "An Object-Oriented Defense of Poetry," *New Literary History* 43, no. 2 (spring 2012): 205–24; Brian Kim Stefans, "Terrible Engines," *Comparative Literature Studies* 51, no. 1, *Special Issue: Poetry Games* (2014): 159–83.

37 Charles E. Scott, *Living with Indifference* (Bloomington: Indiana University Press, 2007), 5.

38 Lisa Robertson, "The Present," in *R's Boat* (Berkeley: University of California Press, 2010), accessed September 15, 2015, https://www.poets.org/poetsorg /poem/present.

Chapter 10: Literature and Ethics

1 Matthew Arnold, "The Study of Poetry," *Poetry and Criticism of Matthew Arnold*, ed. A. Dwight Culler (Boston: Houghton Mifflin Company, 1961), 306. "The Study of Poetry" was first published in 1880 as the general introduction to a four-volume anthology, *The English Poets.*

2 This essay is available as chapter 6 of J. Hillis Miller, *An Innocent Abroad: Lectures in China* (Evanston, IL: Northwestern University Press, 2015).

3 Anthony Trollope, *Framley Parsonage*, Oxford World's Classics edition (London: Oxford University Press, 1961).

4 Anthony Trollope, *An Autobiography*, ed. David Skilton (Harmondsworth, UK: Penguin Books, 1996), 32.

5 Trollope, *An Autobiography*, 33.

6 Trollope, *An Autobiography*, 33.

7 Trollope, *An Autobiography*, 33.

8 Trollope, *An Autobiography*, 115.

9 Trollope, *An Autobiography*, 96, 97.

10 Trollope, *An Autobiography*, 95. The whole paragraph about *Framley Parsonage* in *An Autobiography*, 94–95, gives Trollope's mature judgment of that novel. It will be discussed later in this chapter.

11 Trollope, *Framley Parsonage*, 514.

12 Trollope, *Framley Parsonage*, 293.

13 Trollope, *Framley Parsonage*, 229.

14 Trollope, *An Autobiography*, 94.

15 Trollope, *An Autobiography*, 95.

16 Trollope, *Framley Parsonage*, 126, 127–28.

17 This, by the way, is an example of Trollope's constant, covert use of uniden-tified citation or allusion. It echoes a passage many Victorian readers would perhaps have recognized, that is, what Sydney Carton says in Dickens's *A Tale of Two Cities* (published in 1859, a year before *Framley Parsonage* began to appear in periodical form), book 2, chapter 4: "I care for no man on earth and

no man on earth cares for me." Both Dickens and Trollope, however, may be echoing some folksong, popular song, or common saying. *Framley Parsonage* also contains, in my judgment, many covert echoes of Sir Walter Scott's *The Bride of Lammermoor*. Many of Trollope's readers would have known Scott's novel. Lucy Robarts is not called Lucy for nothing, since that is the name of Scott's heroine. Many parallels exist between the plots of the two stories. Lucy Robarts may be referring ironically to Scott's Lucy when, in a response to Fanny Robarts's question about how Lucy can joke about Lady Lufton's opposition to her marriage to Lord Lufton, she says: "I ought to be pale, ought I not? And very thin, and to go mad by degrees? I have not the least intention of doing anything of the kind" (Trollope, *Framley Parsonage*, 385). Or perhaps Trollope is satirically echoing Donizetti's opera, *Lucia di Lammermoor* (1835), based on Scott's novel, with its famous aria sung by Lucia in her madness.

18 Trollope, *Framley Parsonage*, 229.

19 Trollope, *Framley Parsonage*, 145.

20 Trollope, *Framley Parsonage*, 180.

21 Trollope, *Framley Parsonage*, 283.

22 Trollope, *Framley Parsonage*, 286.

23 Trollope, *Framley Parsonage*, 447.

24 Trollope, *Framley Parsonage*, 501, 502.

25 Trollope, *Framley Parsonage*, 524.

26 See J. L. Austin, *How to Do Things with Words*, 2d ed., ed. J. O. Urmson and Marina Sbisà (Oxford: Oxford University Press, 1980). See also J. Hillis Miller, *Speech Acts in Literature* (Stanford, CA: Stanford University Press, 2001).

27 Trollope, *Framley Parsonage*, 346.

28 Trollope, *Framley Parsonage*, 483.

29 Trollope, *Framley Parsonage*, 268.

30 Trollope, *Framley Parsonage*, 180–81.

31 Trollope, *Framley Parsonage*, 229.

32 Trollope, *Framley Parsonage*, 288, 289.

33 See Immanuel Kant, "On a Supposed Right to Lie from Altruistic Motives" (1797), translation by Lewis White Beck in *Immanuel Kant: Critique of Practical Reason and Other Writings in Moral Philosophy* (Chicago: University of Chicago Press, 1949; reprinted by New York: Garland Publishing Company, 1976).

34 Trollope, *Framley Parsonage*, 339.

35 Trollope, *Framley Parsonage*, 346.

36 Trollope, *Framley Parsonage*, 343.

37 The Wikipedia entry for "The King and the Beggar-Maid" mentions *Framley Parsonage* as one place among a great many in Western literature where the beggar-maid story appears.

38 Trollope, *Framley Parsonage*, 288–89.

39 See "conjure" in the *Oxford English Dictionary*.

BIBLIOGRAPHY

Adorno, Theodor. *Kant's Critique of Pure Reason*. Edited by Rolf Tiedemann. Translated by Rodney Livingstone. Stanford, CA: Stanford University Press, 2001.

Àjami, Mansour. *The Alchemy of Glory: The Dialectic of Truthfulness and Untruthfulness in Medieval Arabic Literary Criticism*. Washington, DC: Three Continents Press, 1988.

Albrecht, Thomas. *The Medusa Effect: Representation and Epistemology in Victorian Aesthetics*. Albany: State University of New York Press, 2009.

Aldridge, A. Owen. *The Reemergence of World Literature: A Study of Asia and the West*. Newark: University of Delaware Press, 1986.

Alspach, Russell K., ed. *The Variorum Edition of the Plays of W. B. Yeats*. New York: Macmillan, 1966.

Althusser, Louis. *Lenin and Philosophy and Other Essays*. Translated by Ben Brewster. New York: Monthly Review, 1972.

Apter, Emily. *Translation Zone: A New Comparative Literature*. Princeton, NJ: Princeton University Press, 2006.

Arac, Jonathan. "Anglo-Globalism?" *New Left Review* 16 (July–August 2002): 35–45.

Arendt, Hannah. *The Life of the Mind*. New York: Harcourt Brace Jovanovich, 1978.

Aristotle. *The Poetics*. Translated by W. Hamilton Fyfe. Cambridge, MA: Harvard University Press, 1991.

Arnold, Matthew. *The Letters of Matthew Arnold to Arthur Hugh Clough*. Edited by Howard Foster Lowry. London: Oxford University Press, 1932.

———. *Poetry and Criticism of Matthew Arnold*. Edited by A. Dwight Culler. Boston: Houghton Mifflin Company, 1961.

Aseguinolaza, Fernando Cabo. "Dead, or a Picture of Good Health?: Comparatism, Europe, and World Literature." *Comparative Literature* 58, no. 4 (fall 2006): 418–35.

Ashcroft, Bill. "Transcultural Presence." *Storia della storiografia* 55 (2009): 76–93.

Attridge, Derek, ed. *Acts of Literature*. London: Routledge, 1992.

———. *Singularity of Literature*. London: Routledge, 2004.

Aurobindo, Sri. *Future of Poetry: Letters on Poetry, Literature and Art*. Pondicherry: Sri Aurobindo Ashram, 1972.

Austin, J. L. *How to Do Things with Words*. Edited by J. O. Urmson and Marina Sbisà. Oxford: Oxford University Press, 1980.

Baird, David. *Thing Knowledge: A Philosophy of Scientific Instruments*. Berkeley: University of California Press, 2004.

Bakhtin, Mikhail M. *Speech Genres and Other Late Essays*. Edited by Caryl Emerson and Michael Holquist. Translated by Vern W. McGee. Austin: University of Texas Press, 1986.

Barad, Karen. "Diffracting Diffraction: Cutting Together-Apart." *Parallax* 20, no. 3 (2014): 168–87.

———. "Intraactions." *Mousse* 34 (2012). http://moussemagazine.it/mousse-34/.

———. *Meeting the Universe Halfway: Quantum Physics and the Entanglement of Matter and Meaning*. Durham, NC: Duke University Press, 2007.

———. "Posthumanist Performativity: Toward an Understanding of How Matter Comes to Matter." *Signs: Journal of Women in Culture and Society* 28, no. 3 (2003): 801–31.

Bataille, Georges. *Eroticism*. Translated by M. Dalwood. London: Marion Boyars, 1987.

Beckett, Samuel. *Endgame*. London: Faber, 1970.

———. *Proust*. New York: Grove Press, 1931.

———. *Three Novels*. London: John Calder, 1956.

Benjamin, Walter. "Die aufgabe des übersetzers." In *Illuminationen: Ausgewählte schrifte*, edited by Siegfried Unseld, 56–69. Frankfurt am Main: Suhrkamp, 1955.

———. "The Task of the Translator." In *Illuminations*, translated by Hannah Arendt, 69–82. New York: Schocken Books, 1969.

Bernheimer, Charles, ed. *Comparative Literature in the Age of Multiculturalism*. Baltimore: Johns Hopkins University Press, 1995.

Berry, Wendell. "The Specialization of Poetry." *Hudson Review* 28, no. 1 (spring 1975): 11–27.

Bhattacharya, R. "Siting the Teacher." In *The Lie of the Land*, edited by Rajeswari Sunder Rajan, 187–206. Delhi: Oxford University Press, 1992.

Blake, William. *The Poetry and Prose*. Edited by David V. Erdman. Garden City, NY: Doubleday, 1970.

Blanchot, Maurice. *The Book to Come*. Translated by Charlotte Mandell. Stanford, CA: Stanford University Press, 2003.

———. *The Infinite Conversation*. Translated by Susan Hanson. Minneapolis: University of Minnesota Press, 1993.

———. *La part du feu*. Paris: Gallimard, 1949.

———. "La voix narrative (le 'il,' le neutre)." In *L'Enretien infini*, 556–67. Paris: Gallimard, 1969.

———. "Le chant des sirènes." In *Le livre à venir*, 7–34. Paris: Gallimard, 1959.

————. "*Les deux versions de l'imaginaire.*" In *L'espace littéraire*, 266–77. Paris: Gallimard, 1955.

————. "Two Versions of the Imaginary." In *The Gaze of Orpheus and Other Literary Essays*, translated by Lydia Davis, 79–89. Barrytown, NY: Station Hill Press, 1981.

————. *The Work of Fire.* Translated by C. Mandel. Stanford, CA: Stanford University Press, 2004.

Bloom, Harold. *The Anxiety of Influence: A Theory of Poetry.* New York: Oxford University Press, 1973.

Bod, Rens. *A New History of the Humanities: The Search for Principles and Patterns from Antiquity to the Present.* Oxford: Oxford University Press, 2014.

Borges, Jorge Luis. *Seven Nights.* Translated by Eliot Weinberger. New York: New Directions, 1984.

————. *Siete Noches.* Mexico City: Fondo de Cultura Económica, 1980.

Bourbon, Brett. "What Is a Poem?" *Modern Philology* 105, no. 1 (2007): 27–43.

Bousquet, Marc. *How the University Works: Higher Education and the Low-Wage Nation.* New York: New York University Press, 2008.

Braidotti, Rosi. *Transpositions: On Nomadic Ethics.* Cambridge: Polity, 2006.

Brooks, Cleanth. *The Well Wrought Urn.* San Diego: Harcourt, Brace, 1975.

Brooks, Cleanth, and Robert Penn Warren. *Understanding Poetry.* New York: Holt, Rinehart and Winston, 1976.

Brunetière, Ferdinand. "La littérature européenne." In *Variétés littéraires*, 1–51. Paris: Calmann-Lévy, 1904.

Burch, K. *Eros as the Educational Principle of Democracy.* New York: Peter Lang, 2000.

Carroll, Lewis. *Alice's Adventures in Wonderland and Through the Looking-Glass.* New York: A. L. Burt, n.d.

Casti, John L. *Complexification: Explaining a Paradoxical World through the Science of Surprise.* New York: HarperCollins, 1994.

Celan, Paul. *Collected Prose.* Translated by Rosemarie Waldrop. Manchester, UK: Carcanet, 1986.

Chakravarty, Amiya, ed. *A Tagore Reader.* New York: Macmillan, 1961.

Charnet, Yves, ed. *Le poète que je cherche à être.* Paris: Table Ronde, 1996.

Chattarji, Sampurna, trans. *Selected Poems: Joy Goswami.* New York: Harper Perennial, 2014.

Chaudhury, Prabas Jiban. *Tagore on Literature and Aesthetics.* Calcutta: Rabindra Bharati, 1965.

Chow, Rey. "The Old/New Question of Comparison in Literary Studies." *ELH* 71, no. 2 (2004): 289–311.

Clarke, Thompson. "The Legacy of Skepticism." *Journal of Philosophy* 69 (1972): 754–69.

Clausen, Christopher. "Poetry in a Discouraging Time." *Georgia Review* 35, no. 4 (winter 1981): 703–15.

Clements, Robert J. *Comparative Literature as Academic Discipline: A Statement of Principles, Praxis, Standards*. New York: Modern Language Association of America, 1978.

Cohen, Tom, Claire Colebrook, and J. Hillis Miller. *Twilight of the Anthropocene Idols*. London: Open Humanities Press, 2016.

Colapietro, Vincent. "A Poet's Philosopher." *Transactions of the Charles S. Peirce Society* 45, no. 4 (fall 2009): 551–78.

Colebrook, Claire. "A Globe of One's Own: In Praise of the Flat Earth." *SubStance* 41, no.127 (2012): 30–39.

Cooppan, Vilashini. "Ghosts in the Disciplinary Machine: The Uncanny Life of World Literature." *Comparative Literature Studies* 41 (2004): 10–36.

Coste, Didier. "Is a Non-Global Universe Possible?: What Universals in the Theory of Comparative Literature (1952–2002) Have to Say about It." *Comparative Literature Studies* 41, no. 1 (2004): 37–48.

Cox, Hyde, and Edward Connery Lathem, eds. *Selected Prose of Robert Frost*. New York: Holt, Rinehart, and Winston, 1966.

Cresswell, Tim. *In Place out of Place: Geography, Ideology, Transgression*. Minneapolis: University of Minnesota Press, 1996.

Culler, Dwight, ed. *Poetry and Criticism of Matthew Arnold*. Boston: Houghton Mifflin, 1961.

Culler, Jonathan D. "Whither Comparative Literature?" *Comparative Critical Studies* 3, nos. 1–2 (2006): 85–97.

Damrosch, David. *What Is World Literature?* Princeton, NJ: Princeton University Press, 2003.

Danto, Arthur. *Mysticism and Morality*. New York: Penguin Books, 1976.

———. *The Philosophical Disenfranchisement of Art*. New York: Columbia University Press, 1986.

Das, Jibanananda. *Kobiterkatha*. Kolkata: Signet, 1994.

Das, Sisir Kumar, ed. *The English Writings of Rabindranath Tagore*. Vol. 2. New Delhi: Sahitya Academy, 1999.

De, S. K. *History of Sanskrit Poetics*. Calcutta: Firma K. L. Mukhopadhyay, 1960.

de Andrade, Oswald, and Leslie Bary. "Cannibalist Manifesto." *Latin American Literary Review* 1, no. 38 (July–December 1991): 35–37.

Deguy, Michel. *Actes*. Paris: Gallimard, 1966.

———. *Recumbants: Poems*. Translated by Wilson Baldridge. Middletown, CT: Wesleyan University Press, 2005.

Dejanovic, Sanja, ed. *Nancy and the Political*. Edinburgh: Edinburgh University Press, 2015.

Deleuze, Gilles, and Félix Guattari. *Essays Critical and Clinical*. Translated by D. W. Smith and M. A. Greco. Minneapolis: University of Minnesota Press, 1997.

———. *The Fold: Leibniz and the Baroque*. Translated by T. Conley. Minneapolis: University of Minnesota Press, 1993.

———. *Foucault*. Translated by S. Hand. Minneapolis: University of Minnesota Press, 1988.

———. "How Do We Recognize Structuralism?" In *Desert Islands and Other Texts, 1953–1974*, translated by M. Taormina, 170–92. New York: Semiotext(e), 2004.

———. *Kafka: Toward a Minor Literature*. Translated by Dana Polan. Minneapolis: University of Minnesota Press, 1986.

———. *The Logic of Sense*. Translated by M. Lester and C. Stivale. Edited by C. Boundas. New York: Columbia University Press, 1990.

———. *A Thousand Plateaus: Capitalism and Schizophrenia*. Translated by Brian Massumi. Minneapolis: University of Minnesota Press, 1987.

———. *What Is Philosophy?* Translated by Hugh Tomlinson and Graham Burchell. New York: Columbia University Press, 1994.

de Man, Paul. *Allegories of Reading: Figural Language in Rousseau, Nietzsche, Rilke, and Proust*. New Haven, CT: Yale University Press, 1979.

———. "Conclusions: Walter Benjamin's 'The Task of the Translator.'" In *The Resistance to Theory*, 73–105. Minneapolis: University of Minnesota Press, 1986.

———. *The Resistance to Theory*. Minneapolis: University of Minnesota Press, 1986.

———. *The Rhetoric of Romanticism*. New York: Columbia University Press, 1984.

———. "Sign and Symbol in Hegel's *Aesthetics*." In *Aesthetic Ideology*, edited by Andrzej Warminski, 91–104. Minneapolis: University of Minnesota Press, 1996.

Derrida, Jacques. *Du droit à la philosophie*. Paris: Galilée, 1990.

———. "*Forcener le subjectile*." In *Antonin Artaud: Dessins et portraits*, edited by Paule Thévinin and Jacques Derrida, 55–108. Paris: Gallimard, 1996.

———. *La carte postale: De Socrates à Freud et au-delà*. Paris: Flammarion, 1980.

———. "La mythologie blanche: La métaphore dans le texte philosophique." In *Marges de la philosophie*, 247–324. Paris: Les Éditions de Minuit, 1972.

———. *L'université sans condition*. Paris: Galilée, 2001.

———. *Marges de la philosophie*. Paris: Les Éditions de Minuit, 1972.

———. *Margins of Philosophy*. Translated by Alan Bass. Chicago: University of Chicago Press, 1982.

———. *Passions*. Paris: Galilée, 1993.

———. "Passions: 'An Oblique Offering.'" In *On the Name*, edited by Thomas Dutoit, 3–34. Stanford, CA: Stanford University Press, 1995.

———. *The Post Card: From Socrates to Freud and Beyond*. Translated by Alan Bass. Chicago: University of Chicago Press, 1987.

———. "This Strange Institution Called Literature." In *Acts of Literature*, edited by Derek Attridge, 33–75. London: Routledge, 1992.

———. "The Time of a Thesis: Punctuations." In *Philosophy in France Today*, edited by Alan Montefiore, 34–50. Cambridge: Cambridge University Press, 1983.

———. "To Unsense the Subjectile." In *The Secret Art of Antonin Artaud*, edited by Jacques Derrida and Paule Thévenin, 59–157. Cambridge, MA: MIT Press, 1998.

———. "The University without Condition." In *Without Alibi*, edited and translated by Peggy Kamuf, 202–37. Stanford, CA: Stanford University Press, 2002.

———. *Who Is Afraid of Philosophy?: Right to Philosophy I*. Translated by J. Plug. Stanford CA: Stanford University Press, 2002.

———. *Without Alibi*. Edited and translated by Peggy Kamuf. Stanford, CA: Stanford University Press, 2002.

Despande, G. T. *Indian Poetics*. Mumbai: Popular Prakashan, 2009.

Devy, G. N. *After Amnesia: Tradition and Change in Indian Literary Criticism*. London: Sangam Books, 1992.

Djelal, Kadir. "To Compare, to World: Two Verbs, One Discipline." *Comparatist* 34 (2010): 4–11.

Dillard, Anne. *Teaching a Stone to Talk*. New York: Harper Perennial, 1992.

Dimock, Wai Chee. "Planetary Time and Global Translation: 'Context' in Literary Studies." *Common Knowledge* 9, no. 3 (fall 2003): 488–507.

———. "A Theory of Resonance." PMLA 112, no. 5 (1997): 1060–71.

Donoghue, Frank. *The Last Professors: The Corporate University and the Fate of the Humanities*. New York: Fordham University Press, 1998.

D'Souza, Dinesh. "Illiberal Education." *Atlantic Monthly*, March 1991, 51–79.

Dubreuil, Laurent. "What Is Literature's Now?" *New Literary History* 38, no. 1 (winter 2007): 43–70.

Durán, Manuel. "Octavio Paz: The Poet as Philosopher." *World Literature Today* 56, no. 4 (autumn 1982): 591–94.

Eagleton, Terry. *Against the Grain: Selected Essays, 1975–1985*. London: Verso, 1986.

Earl of Shaftesbury, Anthony. *Characteristics*. Edited by John M. Robertson. London: Grant Richards, 1900.

Eliot, George. *Middlemarch*. Harmondsworth, UK: Penguin, 1974.

Eliot, T. S. *The Collected Poems and Plays: 1909–1950*. New York: Harcourt Brace, 1952.

Elwes, R. H. M., ed. and trans. *Works of Spinoza*. 2 vols. New York: Dover, 1955.

Emerson, Ralph Waldo. *Selected Writings*. Edited by Brooks Atkinson. New York: Random House, 1950.

Epstein, Joseph. *Alexis de Tocqueville: Democracy's Guide*. New York: HarperCollins, 2006.

Felman, Shoshana. "Psychoanalysis and Education: Teaching Terminable and Interminable." *Yale French Studies* 63 (1982): 21–44.

Frank, Sam. "Come with Us If You Want to Live: Among the Apocalyptic Libertarians of Silicon Valley." *Harper's*, January 2015, 26–36.

Gadamer, Hans-Georg. *On the Relevance of the Beautiful*. Cambridge: Cambridge University Press, 1986.

———. *Truth and Method*. Translated by Joel Weinsheimer and Donald G. Marshall. New York: Continuum, 1998.

Gallop, Jane. "The Historicization of Literary Studies and the Fate of Close Reading." *Profession* (2007): 181–86.

Galvin, Rachel. "Poetry Is Theft." *Comparative Literature Studies* 51, no. 1 (2014): 18–54.

Garber, Marjorie. *Academic Instincts*. Princeton, NJ: Princeton University Press, 2003.

———. "Good to Think With." *Profession* (2008): 11–20.

Genette, Gérard. *Mimologiques: Voyage en cratylie*. Paris: Seuil, 1976.

Gerbig, Andrea, and Anja Muller-Wood. "Trapped in Language: Aspects of Ambiguity and Intertextuality in Selected Prose and Poetry of Sylvia Plath." *Style* 36, no. 1 (spring 2002): 76–92.

Ghose, Sisir Kumar, ed. *Angel of Surplus*. Calcutta: Visva-Bharati, 1978.

Ghosh, Ranjan. "The Figure that Robert Frost's Poetics Make: Singularity and Sanskrit Poetic Theory." In *Singularity and Transnational Poetics*, edited by Birgit Kaiser, 134–54. London: Routledge, 2015.

———, ed. *In Dialogue with Godot: Waiting and Other Thoughts*. Lanham, MD: Lexington Books, 2013.

———, ed. *(In)fusion Approach: Theory, Contestation, Limits*. Lanham, MD: University Press of America, 2006.

———. "Institutionalised Theory, (In)fusion, *Desivad*." *Oxford Literary Review* 28 (2006): 25–36.

———. "Making Sense of Interpretation: Yes-ing and the (In)fusion Approach." *Parallax* 16, no. 3 (2010): 107–17.

Gioia, Dana. "Disappearing Ink: Poetry at the End of Print Culture." *Hudson Review* 56, no. 1 (spring 2003): 21–49.

Goethe, Johann Wolfgang von. *Conversations with Eckermann*. Edited by J. K. Morehead. Translated by John Oxenford. London: Everyman, 1930.

Gould, Stephen J. *Ontogeny and Phylogeny*. Cambridge, MA: The Belknap Press of Harvard University Press, 1977.

Gregory, Marshall. "Do We Teach Disciplines or Do We Teach Students?: What Difference Does It Make?" *Profession* (2008): 117–29.

Griffiths, A. Phillips, ed. *Contemporary French Philosophy*. Cambridge: Cambridge University Press, 1987.

Grosz, Elizabeth. *Chaos, Territory, Art: Deleuze and the Framing of the Earth*. New York: Columbia University Press, 2008.

———. *The Nick of Time*. Sydney: Allen and Unwin, 2004.

Grusin, Richard, ed. *The Nonhuman Turn*. Minnesota: University of Minnesota Press, 2015.

Gu, Ming Dong. *Chinese Theories of Reading and Writing: A Route to Hermeneutics and Open Poetics*. Albany: State University of New York Press, 2005.

———. "The Divine and Artistic Ideal: Ideas and Insights for Cross-Cultural Aesthetic Education." *Journal of Aesthetic Education* 42, no. 3 (fall 2008): 88–105.

Guillén, Claudio. *The Challenge of Comparative Literature*. Translated by Cola Franzen. Cambridge, MA: Harvard University Press, 1993.

Hahn, Lewis Edwin, ed. *The Philosophy of Hans-Georg Gadamer*. Chicago: Open Court, 1997.

Harman, Graham. "The Well-Wrought Broken Hammer: Object Oriented Literary Criticism." *New Literary History* 43, no. 2 (2012): 183–203.

Hartman, Geoffrey. *The Fateful Question of Culture*. New York: Columbia University Press, 1997.

Hegel, G. W. F. *Enzyklopädie der philosophischen wissenschaften*. Vols. 8–10. Frankfurt am Main: Suhrkamp, 1979.

Heidegger, Martin. "Hölderlin and the Essence of Poetry." In *Existence and Being*, edited by Werner Brock, 295–315. London: Vision, 1968.

Heikkilä, Martta. *At the Limits of Presentation*. Frankfurt: Peter Lang, 2008.

Hernadi, Paul. "Why Is Literature: A Coevolutionary Perspective on Imaginative Worldmaking." *Poetics Today* 23 (spring 2002): 21–42.

Hiley, B. J., and F. David Peat, eds. *Quantum Implications: Essays in Honour of David Bohm*. London: Routledge, 1991.

Hocking, William E. *Human Nature and Its Remaking*. New York: AMS Press, 1976.

Homer. *The Odyssey*. Translated by Robert Fitzgerald. Garden City, NY: Doubleday, 1963.

Honan, Mat. "All-New Media Machine." *Wired Magazine*. December 17, 2014.

———. "Fast, Loud, and Mostly True: Inside the All-New Buzz-Fueled American Media Machine." *Wired Magazine* 23, no. 1 (January 2015).

Honeywell, J. A. "The Poetic Theory of Viśvanatha." *Journal of Aesthetics and Art Criticism* 28, no. 2 (winter 1969): 165–76.

Horney, Karen. *Neurosis and Human Growth*. New York: W. W. Norton, 1950.

Houghton, Walter E. *The Victorian Frame of Mind, 1830–1870*. New Haven, CT: Yale University Press, 1957.

Hutchens, B. C. *Jean-Luc Nancy and the Future of Philosophy*. Montreal: McGill-Queen's University Press, 2005.

Ingalls, Daniel H. H., trans. and ed. *The Dhvanyaloka of Anandavardhana with the Locana of Abhinavagupta*. Cambridge, MA: Harvard University Press, 1990.

Iser, Wolfgang. *Das Fiktive und das Imaginäre: Perspektiven literarische Anthropologie*. Frankfurt am Main: Suhrkamp, 1991.

———. *The Fictive and the Imaginary: Charting Literary Anthropology*. Baltimore: Johns Hopkins University Press, 1993.

Jackson, Kenneth David. "A View on Brazilian Literature: Eating the Revista de Antropofagia." *Latin American Literary Review* 7, no. 13 (fall–winter 1978): 1–9.

Jacobs, Carol. *The Dissimulating Harmony: The Image of Interpretation in Nietzsche, Rilke, Artaud, and Benjamin*. Baltimore: Johns Hopkins University Press, 1978.

James, Henry. *The Golden Bowl*. New York: Augustus M. Kelley, 1971.

Jameson, Fredric. *The Political Unconscious*. Ithaca, NY, 1981.

Jarrett-Kerr, Martin William R. "Arnold versus the Orient: Some Footnotes to a Disenchantment." *Comparative Literature Studies* 12, no. 2 (June 1975): 129–46.

Jeffares, A. Norman. *A Commentary on the Collected Poems of W. B. Yeats*. Stanford, CA: Stanford University Press, 1968.

Joyce, James. *Finnegans Wake*. New York: Viking, 1947.

———. *Portrait of the Artist as a Young Man*. New York: Viking, 1964.

Kamuf, Peggy. "Counting Madness." *Oxford Literary Review* 28 (2006): 67–77.

Kant, Immanuel. *Critique of Judgment*. Translated by J. C. Meredith. Oxford: Oxford University Press, 1911.

———. *Critique of Practical Reason and Other Writings in Moral Philosophy*. Translated by Lewis White Beck. Chicago: University of Chicago Press, 1949.

Kapoor, Kapil. *Language, Linguistics, and Literature: The Indian Perspective*. Delhi: Academic Foundation, 1994.

Keping, Wan. *Spirit of Chinese Poetics*. Beijing: Foreign Language Press, 2008.

Keyserling, Herman. *From Suffering to Fulfilment*. Translated by Jane Marshall. London: Selwyn and Blount, 1938.

Kim, John Namjun. "Ethnic Irony: The Poetic Parabasis of the Promiscuous Personal Pronoun." *Quarterly* 83, no.3 (summer 2010): 333–52.

Koller, John M. "Dharma: An Expression of Universal Order." *Philosophy East and West* 22 (1972): 131–44.

Lau, D. C. *Lao Tzu Tao Te Ching*. Harmondsworth, UK: Penguin Books, 1963.

Lawn, Christopher. "Gadamer on Poetic and Everyday Language." *Philosophy and Literature* 25, no.1 (April 2001): 113–26.

Lecercle, Jean-Jacques. *Badiou and Deleuze Read Literature*. Edinburgh: Edinburgh University Press, 2010.

Letwin, Shirley Robin. "Matthew Arnold: Enemy of Tradition." *Political Theory* 10, no. 3 (August 1982): 333–51.

Li, Victor. "Elliptical Interruptions." CR: *The New Centennial Review* 7, no. 2 (fall 2007): 141–54.

Liu, James J. Y. *Language-Paradox-Poetics: A Chinese Perspective*. Princeton, NJ: Princeton University Press, 1988.

Loliée, Frédéric. *A Short History of Comparative Literature*. Translated by M. Douglas Power. London: Hodder and Stoughton, 1906.

Longxi, Zhang. *Mighty Opposites: From Dichotomies to Differences in the Comparative Study of China*. Stanford, CA: Stanford University Press, 1998.

———. *Unexpected Affinities: Reading across Cultures*. Toronto: University of Toronto Press, 2007.

Lowry, Howard Foster, ed. *The Letters of Matthew Arnold to Arthur Hugh Clough*. London: Oxford University Press, 1932.

Machosky, Brenda. "Fasting at the Feast of Literature." *Comparative Literature Studies* 42, no. 2 (2005): 288–305.

Mann, Thomas. *The Magic Mountain*. Translated by H. T. Lowe-Porter. New York: Knopf, 1955.

Maritain, Jacques. "Poetic Experience." *Review of Politics* 6, no. 4 (October 1944): 387–402.

Maslow, Abraham H. *Further Reaches of Human Nature*. New York: Viking, 1970.

———. *Religions, Values and Peak Experiences*. New York: Penguin, 1976.

Matchett, William H. "What and Why Is a Poem?" *College English* 27, no. 5 (February 1966): 354–60.

Mayhew, Jonathan. "Jorge Guillén and the Insufficiency of Poetic Language." *PMLA* 106, no. 5 (October 1991): 1146–55.

McCormick, Peter, and Frederick A. Elliston, ed. *Husserl: Shorter Works*. Notre Dame, IN: University of Notre Dame Press, 1981.

Menand, Louis. "Dangers within and without Author(s)." *Profession* (2005): 10–17.

Merrifield, Andy. *Guy Debord*. London: Reaktion Books, 2005.

Miller, J. Hillis. "Anachronistic Reading." *Derrida Today* 3 (2010): 75–91.

———. *Black Holes*. Stanford, CA: Stanford University Press, 1999.

———. "The Critic as Host." In *Deconstruction and Criticism*, edited by Harold Bloom, 217–53. New York: Seabury, 1979.

———. *The Ethics of Reading*. New York: Columbia University Press, 1987.

———. *An Innocent Abroad: Lectures in China*. Evanston, IL: Northwestern University Press, 2015.

———. *The Medium Is the Maker: Browning, Freud, Derrida, and the New Telepathic Ecotechnologies*. Brighton, UK: Sussex Academic Press, 2009.

———. *Others*. Princeton, NJ: Princeton University Press, 2001.

———. "Reading Paul de Man while Falling into Cyberspace." In *In the Twilight of the Anthropocene Idols*, ed. Thomas Cohen, Claire Colebrook, and J. Hillis Miller. London: Open Humanities Press, n.d.

———. *Speech Acts in Literature*. Stanford, CA: Stanford University Press, 2001.

———. "Tales out of (the Yale) School." In *Theoretical Schools and Circles in the Twentieth-Century Humanities: Literary Theory, History, Philosophy*, edited by Marina Grishakova and Silvi Salupere, 115–32. New York: Routledge, 2015.

———. "Temporal Topographies: Tennyson's Tears." *EurAmerica* 21, no. 3 (1991): 29–45.

———. *Topographies*. Stanford, CA: Stanford University Press, 1995.

Mishra, P. K., trans. *Sahityadarpana*. Delhi: Motilal Banarsidass, 1967.

Morton, Timothy. "An Object-Oriented Defense of Poetry." *New Literary History* 43, no. 2 (spring 2012): 205–24.

Myrsiades, Kostas, and Linda S Myrsiades, ed. *Margins in the Classroom: Teaching Literature*. Minneapolis: University of Minnesota Press, 1994.

Nagel, Thomas. *Mortal Questions*. Cambridge: Cambridge University Press, 1979.

Nancy, Jean-Luc. *Being Singular Plural*. Translated by Robert D. Richardson and Anne E. O'Byrne. Stanford, CA: Stanford University Press, 2000.

———. *The Birth to Presence*. Stanford, CA: Stanford University Press, 1993.

———. *The Creation of the World or Globalization*. Translated by François Raffoul and David Pettigrew. Albany: State University of New York Press, 2007.

———. *The Multiple Arts: The Muses II*. Edited by Simon Sparks. Stanford, CA: Stanford University Press, 2006.

———. *The Restlessness of the Negative*. Minneapolis: University of Minnesota Press, 2002.

Narasimhaiah, C. D., ed. *East West Poetics at Work*. New Delhi: Sahitya Academy, 1994.

Neske, Gunter, ed. *Erinnerung an Martin Heidegger*. Pfullingen, Germany: Neske, 1977.

Newfield, Christopher. *Unmaking the Public University: The Forty-Year Assault on the Middle Class*. Cambridge, MA: Harvard University Press, 2008.

Nietzsche, Friedrich. *The Birth of Tragedy and The Case of Wagner*. Translated by Walter Kaufmann. New York: Vintage, 1967.

———. *The Gay Science*. Translated by Walter Kaufmann. New York: Vintage, 1974.

———. *Die Geburt der Tragödie*. In *Sämtliche Werke*. Edited by Giorgio Colli and Mazzino Montinari, 1:9–156. Munich: Walter de Gruyter, 1988.

———. *Jenseits von Gut und Böse*. In *Sämtliche Werke*, 5:9–243. Edited by Giorgio Colli and Mazzino Montinari. Munich: Walter de Gruyter, 1988.

———. "*Nachgelassene Fragmente, 1869–1874.*" In *Sämtliche Werke*. Edited by Giorgio Colli and Mazzino Montinari, 7. Munich: Walter de Gruyter, 1988.

———. "On the Utility and Liability of History for Life." In *The Complete Works*, edited by Richard T. Gray, 2:83–167. Stanford, CA: Stanford University Press, 1995.

Norton, Jody. "Guerrilla Pedagogy: Conflicting Authority and Interpretation in the Classroom." *College Literature* 21, no. 3 (October 1994): 136–56.

Odin, Steve. *Process Metaphysics and Hua-yen Buddhism: A Critical Study of Cumulative Penetration vs. Interpenetration*. Albany: State University of New York Press, 1982.

Oliver, Mary. "For the Man Cutting the Grass." *Georgia Review* 35, no. 4 (winter 1981): 733–43.

Panikkar, Raimundo. "What Is Comparative Philosophy Comparing?" In *Interpreting across Boundaries: New Essays in Comparative Philosophy*, edited by Gerald J. Larson and Eliot Deutsch, 116–36. Princeton, NJ: Princeton University Press, 1988.

Pettersson, Anders. "Transcultural Literary History: Beyond Constricting Notions of World Literature." *New Literary History* 39, no. 3 (2008): 463–79.

Pizer, John. *The Idea of World Literature: History and Pedagogical Practice*. Baton Rouge: Louisiana State University Press, 2006.

———. "Toward a Productive Interdisciplinary Relationship: Between Comparative Literature and World Literature." *Comparatist* 31 (May 2007): 6–28.

Poteat, William H. "What Is a Poem About?" *Philosophy and Phenomenological Research* 17, no. 4 (June 1957): 546–50.

Proust, Marcel. *À la recherche du temps perdu*. Edited by Jean-Yves Tadié. Paris: Gallimard, 1989.

———. *Remembrance of Things Past*. Translated by C. K. Scott Moncrieff, Terence Kilmartin, and Andreas Mayor. New York: Vintage, 1982.

Puglisi, Mario. *Prayer*. Translated by Bernard M. Allen. New York: Macmillan, 1929.

Radhakrishnan, S. *The Hindu View of Life*. New Delhi: Indus, 1993.

———, ed. *The Bhagavad Gita* . New Delhi: HarperCollins, 2011.

———, ed. *The Principal Upanishads*. New Delhi: HarperCollins, 2006.

Radice, William, trans. *Rabindranath Tagore: Selected Poems*. Delhi: Penguin Books, 1985.

Raghavan, V., and Nagendra, eds. *An Introduction to Indian Poetics*. Bombay: Macmillan, 1970.

Rajan, Rajeswari Sunder, ed. *The Lie of the Land*. Delhi: Oxford University Press, 1992.

Rancière, Jacques. "The Politics of Literature." *SubStance* 33, no. 1 (2004): 10–24.

Rapple, Brendan. "Matthew Arnold and Comparative Education." *British Journal of Educational Studies* 37, no. 1 (February 1989): 54–71.

Rigby, H. *Marxism and History: A Critical Introduction*. Manchester, UK: Manchester University Press, 1998.

Rimbaud, Arthur. *Illuminations*. Translated by Louise Varèse. New York: New Directions, 1957.

Robertson, Lisa. *R's Boat*. Berkeley: University of California Press, 2010.

Royle, Nicholas. *The Uncanny*. Manchester, UK: Manchester University Press, 2003.

———. *Veering: A Theory of Literature*. Edinburgh: Edinburgh University Press, 2011.

Rudy, John G. *Wordsworth and the Zen Mind*. Albany: State University of New York Press, 1996.

Ryle, Gilbert. *The Concept of Mind*. London: Hutchinson, 1949.

Sankaracarya. *Brahma Sutra Bhasya*. Translated by Swami Gambhirananda. Mayavati, India: Advaita Ashram, 2000.

Santayana, George. *Interpretations of Poetry and Religion*. New York: Scribner's, 1900.

———. *Little Essays*. London: Constable, 1924.

Sawney, Simona. *The Modernity of Sanskrit*. Minneapolis: University of Minnesota Press, 2008.

Scott, Charles E. *Living with Indifference*. Bloomington: Indiana University Press, 2007.

Selincourt, Ernest de. *The Letters of William and Dorothy Wordsworth*. 2d ed. 8 vols. Oxford: Clarendon Press, 1969.

———, ed. *The Poetical Works of William Wordsworth*. 2d ed. 5 vols. Oxford: Clarendon, 1952–59.

Semah, D. "Muḥammad Mandūr and the 'New Poetry.'" *Journal of Arabic Literature* 2 (1971): 143–53.

Serres, Michel. *Detachment*. Translated by Genevieve James and Raymond Federman. Athens: Ohio University Press, 1989.

———. *The Five Senses: A Philosophy of Mingled Bodies*. Translated by Margaret Sankey and Peter Cowley. London: Continuum, 2008.

————. *Genesis*. Translated by Genevieve James and James Nielson. Ann Arbor: University of Michigan Press, 1995.

————. *The Parasite*. Translated by Lawrence R. Schehr. Baltimore: Johns Hopkins University Press, 1982.

Sethna, K. D. *Talks on Poetry*. Pondicherry: Sri Aurobindo International Centre of Education, 1989.

Seturaman, V. S. "The Scholar Gipsy and Oriental Wisdom." *Review of English Studies* 9, no. 36 (November 1958): 413–18.

Seyed-Gohrab, Ali Asghar, ed. *Metaphor and Imagery in Persian Poetry*. Boston: Brill, 2012.

Sharma, Arvind. *The Philosophy of Religion*. New Delhi: Oxford University Press, 1995.

Sharma, T. R. *Toward an Alternative Critical Discourse*. Shimla: Indian Institute of Advanced Study, 2000.

Sheppard, Darren, Simon Sparks, Colin Thomas, eds. *On Jean-Luc Nancy: The Sense of Philosophy*. London: Routledge, 1997.

Shermer, Michael. "Skeptic: Scientia Humanitatis." *Scientific American*, June 2015, 80.

Silesius, Angelus. *The Cherubic Wanderer*. Translated by Maria Shrady. New York: Paulist Press, 1986.

Simic, Charles. "Notes on Poetry and Philosophy." *New Literary History* 21, no. 1 (autumn 1989): 215–21.

Simon, Roger I. *Teaching against the Grain: Texts for a Pedagogy of Possibility*. New York: Bergin and Garvey, 1992.

Spivak, Gayatri Chakravorty. *Death of a Discipline*. New York: Columbia University Press, 2003.

Staheli, Urs. "The Outside of the Global." CR: *The New Centennial Review* 3, no.2 (summer 2003): 1–22.

Stefans, Brian Kim. "Terrible Engines." *Comparative Literature Studies* 51, no. 1 (2014): 159–83.

Stevens, Holly, ed. *Letters of Wallace Stevens*. New York: Knopf, 1966.

Stevens, Wallace. *The Collected Poems*. New York: Vintage, 1990.

————. *The Necessary Angel: Essays on Reality and the Imagination*. New York: Knopf, 1951.

————. *Opus Posthumous*. Edited by Samuel French Morse. New York: Knopf, 1957.

Steward, Doug. "Taking Liberties: Academic Freedom and the Humanities." *Profession* (2008): 146–71.

Stewart, Ian. *Does God Play Dice?: The Mathematics of Chaos*. Cambridge, MA: Blackwell, 1989.

Stone, Donald D. "Matthew Arnold and the Pragmatics of Hebraism and Hellenism." *Poetics Today* 19, no. 2 (summer 1998): 179–98.

Stovall, Tyler, and Georges van den Abbeele, ed. *French Civilization and Its Discontents: Nationalism, Colonialism, Race*. Lanham, MD: Lexington Books, 2003.

Subramania Iyer, K. A., ed. and trans. *The Vakyapadiya of Bhartrhari*. Delhi: Moti-lal Banarsidass, 1977.

Super, R. H., ed. *The Complete Prose Works of Matthew Arnold*. Ann Arbor: University of Michigan, 1960–1977.

Tagore, Rabindranath. *Gitanjali*. London: Macmillan, 1921.

———. *Letters to a Friend* [1928]. New Delhi: Rupa, 2002.

———. *Personality*. London: Macmillan, 1945.

———. *Rabindra Rachanabali*. Calcutta: Visva Bharati, 1965.

———. *Sadhana*. Madras: Macmillan, 1979.

———. "Visva-Sahitya" [1907]. Translated by Rijula Das and Makarand R. Paranjape. *Journal of Contemporary Thought* 34 (2011): 213–25.

Thévenin, Paule. *Antonin Artaud: Dessins et portraits*. Paris: Gallimard, 1996.

Tillyard, E. M. W. *The Elizabethan World Picture*. London: Chatto and Windus, 1943.

Totosy de Zepetnek, Steven, ed. *Comparative Literature and Comparative Cultural Studies*. West Lafayette, IN: Purdue University Press, 2003.

Trollope, Anthony. *An Autobiography*. Edited by David Skilton. Harmondsworth, UK: Penguin Books, 1996.

———. *Framley Parsonage*. London: Oxford University Press, 1961.

———. *The Last Chronicle of Barset*. Accessed January 4, 2015. www.gutenberg.org.

Ulmer, Gregory. *Applied Grammatology: Post(e)-Pedagogy from Jacques Derrida to Joseph Beuys*. Baltimore: Johns Hopkins University Press, 1985.

Van Buitenen, J. A. B. "Dharma and Moksha." *Philosophy East and West* 7 (1957): 35–36.

Virupakshananda, Swami. *Samkhya-Karika of Isvara Krshna*. Mylapore, India: Sri Ramakrishna Math, 1995.

Vivas, Eliseo. "What Is a Poem?" *Sewanee Review* 62, no. 4 (October–December 1954): 577–87.

Waldrop, Mitchell. *Complexity: The Emerging Science at the Edge of Chaos*. New York: Simon and Schuster, 1993.

Warminski, Andrzej. *Readings in Interpretation: Hölderlin, Hegel, Heidegger*. Minneapolis: University of Minnesota Press, 1987.

———. "Terrible Reading (Preceded by 'Epigraphs')." In *Responses: Paul de Man's Wartime Journalism*, ed. Werner Hamacher, Neil Hertz, and Thomas Keenan, 386–96. Lincoln: University of Nebraska Press, 1989.

Wazzan, Adnan M. "Arabia in Poetry." *Islamic Studies* 29, no. 1 (spring 1990): 221–29.

Williams, Jeffrey J. *How to Be an Intellectual: Essays on Criticism, Culture, and the University*. New York: Fordham University Press, 2014.

Williams, John Phillip. "*Hodos* Infusion and Method." In *Romancing Theory, Riding Interpretation: (In)fusion Approach, Salman Rushdie*, ed. Ranjan Ghosh, 73–88. New York: Peter Lang, 2012.

Wong, Sui-kit, ed. and trans. *Early Chinese Literary Criticism*. Hong Kong: Joint Publishing Company, 1983.

Wordsworth, Dorothy. *Journals of Dorothy Wordsworth*. 2 vols. Edited by Ernest de Selincourt. New York: Macmillan, 1941.

Xie, Ming, ed. *The Agon of Interpretations: Towards a Critical Intercultural Hermeneutics*. Toronto: University of Toronto Press, 2014.

Yao, Steven G. "The Unheimlich Maneuver; or the Gap, the Gradient, and the Spaces of Comparison." *Comparative Literature* 57, no. 3 (summer 2005): 246–55.

Yeats, W. B. *The Variorum Edition of the Poems*. Edited by Peter Allt and Russell K. Alspach. New York: Macmillan, 1977.

Yeh, Michelle. "Metaphor and Bi: Western and Chinese Poetics." *Comparative Literature* 39, no. 3 (summer 1987): 237–54.

Yip, Wai-Lim. *Diffusion of Distances: Dialogues between Chinese and Western Poetics*. Berkeley: University of California Press, 1993.

INDEX

Michelangelo, 214
Middlemarch (Eliot), 51, 54, 191
Mill, J. S., 3
Millais, John Everett, 236; illustrations, 237
Miller, J. Hillis, 116, 118, 130–31, 159; cyberspace, 51–52, 57, 190; not deconstructionist, 9–10, 14, 17; digital media, 23, 32, 46, 186, 194; English Dept. at The Johns Hopkins University, 191; Ghosh, reference to, 9, 21, 45, 48–51, 62, 64, 67, 93–94, 134–36, 139–40, 152, 177–81, 198, 232–35; prestidigitation, 46, 194, 257; Victorians, 47, 54, 211–12, 234, 241, 246. *See also individual works*
Milton, John: *Paradise Lost*, 134, 136; Satan, 136
MIT, 183
Moby-Dick (Melville), 58, 196; characters: Ahab, 66; Ismael, 58, 60; Moby-Dick, 67
Modernity of Sanskrit, The (Sawney), 45
Monolingualism of the Other (Derrida), 219
MOOCs, 186
Morland, Catherine (*Northanger Abbey*), 47
"Motive for Metaphor, The" (Stevens), 21, 84, 94–103
Muir, Edwin, 75. *See also individual works*
Mukherjee, Ramaranjan, 78–79
Must We Mean What We Say? (Cavell), 20

Nagel, Thomas, 168
Nair, Rukmini Bahaya, 157
Nancy, Jean-Luc, 3, 9, 113, 115, 122, 132; Nancyean sounding, 2; Nancyean fragment, 130. *See also individual works*
Napoleon, 144
National Defense Education Act, 192
National Endowment for the Humanities, 192
National Intitutes of Health, 192
National Science Foundation, 192
Nātya Śāstra (Bharata), 78

NBC News, 187; Evening News: "Making a Difference" segment, 54
Necessary Angel, The (Stevens), 96
Newfield, Christopher, 183
New Testament, 48
Newton's laws, 73
New York Times, 188
Nietzsche, Friedrich, 103, 131, 134, 144–51, 209, 218; Nietzschean erotic, 217; professor of classical philology, 135, 143, 151; part of world literature?, 140. *See also individual works*
Niranjana, Tejeswani, 172
Northanger Abbey (Austen), 45
North Sea Jazz Festival, 194
Norton, Jody, 171–72

"Oak Leaves Are Hands" (Stevens), Lady Lowzen, 59
Obama, Barack, president, 188, 203
Oberlin College, 49, 186
O'Connell, Danny, 179–80
"Ode on a Grecian Urn" (Keats), 78–79, 224, 229
Odysseus, 46
Odyssey (Homer), Muse, 67
Oedipus, 46, 117
Oedipus the King (Sophocles), 94; Oedipus complex, 200
Old Testament: Book of Ruth, Moabite Ruth, 247
Oliver, Mary, 75
Oliver Twist (Dickens), 242
"On Sitting Down to Read King Lear Once Again" (Keats), 196
"On the Authority of Literature" (Miller), 235
Opus Posthumous (Stevens), 94, 96
Orientalism (Said), 195
Oxford, University of, 183

Palladio, Palladian architecture, 214
Panikkar, Raimundo, 123
Pantanjali, 162
Paradise Lost (Milton), 57, 67, 134, 136
Parnell, Charles Stuart, 179–80

Paz, Octavio, 90
PBS, 186
Phenomenology (Hegel), 23
Phillips, John W. P., 4
Philosophical Investigations (Wittgenstein), 89
Pierce, Charles, 81
The Pilgrim's Progress (Bunyan), 119
Plath, Sylvia, 77
Plato, 37; Platonic doubt, 34
"Poems of the Imagination" (Wordsworth), 124
Poetics (Aristotle), 84, 94–95
Portrait of a Lady (James), 202; characters: Isabel Archer and Gilbert Osbond, 202
Portrait of the Artist as a Young Man, A (Joyce), character: Stephen Dedalus, 40
Post Card, The (Derrida), 177
Poteat, William, 81
Presidents of the Modern Language Association of America (MLA), 195
Pride and Prejudice (Austen), 57, 203; characters: Elizabeth Bennett, Darcy, 202
Princess, The (Tennyson), 49, 54
"Progress" (Arnold), 212
Protestant Christian, 179
Proust, Marcel, 58, 65–66, 235. *See also individual works*
Putin, Vladimir, 189

The Question of Palestine (Said), 195

Racine, Jean, 195
Radhakrishnan, Savepalli, 3, 161
Raghavan, V., 28
Rajasekhara, 28–29
Ramanujan, A. K., 73
Ramayana, 33
Rancière, Jacques, 37–38, 40
Raphael, 214
Ray, Satvajit, 3
Republicans, 188
Resistance to Theory, The (de Man), 10, 13, 24, 97, 202

Responsibilities (Yeats), 197, 200; epigraph: Khoung-Fou Tseu (Confucius) and Prince of Chang, 200
Rhetoric (Aristotle), 84
Rhetoric of Romanticism, The (de Man), 24
Richards, I. A., 100
Riffaterre, Michael, 23
Rimbaud, Arthur, 128
Romeo and Juliet, 199
Rosa Alchemica (Yeats), 174; characters: Alfārābi and Avicenna, 174
Royle, Nicholas, 120, 244
Rudrata, 86
Ruyyaka, 29

Sadhana (Tagore), 164
Sahitya-darpana (Visvanatha), 29, 85
Sahitya-mimamsa (Mankhuka), 29
Said, Edward, 194. *See also individual works*
Sangallo, 214
Sansovino, 214
Satan, in *Paradise Lost*, 136
Sawney, Simona, 45. *See also individual works*
Schiller, Friedrich, 32
Schoenberg, Arnold, 207
"Scholar Gipsy, The" (Arnold), 7, 210–13, 217, 234
Scholes, Robert: MLA Presidential address (2004), 196
Schopenhauer, Arthur, 145
"Scientia Humanitatis" (Shermer), 10–13, 15
Scientific American, 10
Scott, Sir Walter, 255. *See also individual works*
"Second Coming, The" (Yeats), 174
Semah, 83
Serlio, Sebastiano, 214
Serres, Michel, 6–7, 116–18. *See also individual works*
Sethna, 92
Seturaman, V. S., 210–11, 234
Seven Pillars of Wisdom (Lawrence), 174
Seyed-Gohrab, 85
Shaftesbury, Third Earl of, 27